CRISIS INTERVENTION:
Selected Readings

CRISIS INTERVENTION:
Selected Readings

Howard J. Parad, Editor

FAMILY SERVICE ASSOCIATION OF AMERICA
44 EAST 23RD STREET, NEW YORK, N.Y. 10010

ISBN 0–87304–010–4

Library of Congress Catalog Number: 65-20273

Printed in the U.S.A.

3

To Gerald Caplan

Contributors

Rose Bernstein, Director, Community Shelter Care Project, Boston

Bernard L. Bloom, Consultant in Clinical Psychology, National Institute of Mental Health, Public Health Service

H. Frederick Brown, Executive Director, Protestant Community Services, Detroit

Vera Barad Burditt, Family Work Co-ordinator and Supervisor, United South End Settlements, Boston

Gerald Caplan, Director and Clinical Professor of Psychiatry, Laboratory of Community Psychiatry, Harvard Medical School

Stanley H. Cath, Assistant Clinical Professor, Tufts University School of Medicine

Ruth Chaskel, Director, National Association on Service to Unmarried Parents, affiliated with Child Welfare League of America and Family Service Association of America

Eleanor Clark, Chief of Social Service, Massachusetts General Hospital, Boston

Florence E. Cyr, formerly Assistant in Social Work, Harvard School of Public Health

Everett D. Dyer, Chairman and Professor of Sociology, Department of Sociology and Anthropology, University of Houston

Edith H. Freeman, Research Consultant, Allergy Department, Kaiser Foundation Hospitals, San Francisco

M. Robert Harris, Director of Clinical Services, Langley Porter Neuropsychiatric Institute, San Francisco

Sam M. Heilig, Co-Chief Social Worker, Director of Training, Suicide Prevention Center of Los Angeles

Reuben Hill, Director, Family Study Center and Professor of Sociology, University of Minnesota

Jacob I. Hurwitz, Research Director, Consultation Center for Alcoholism of the New York University Medical Center

Alice Ichikawa, Field Work Assistant Professor, Student Health Service, University of Chicago

Elizabeth E. Irvine, Senior Tutor, Advanced Course in Social Casework, Tavistock Clinic and Institute of Human Relations, London

Mordecai Kaffman, Psychiatrist-in-Chief, Child Clinic of the Kibbutzim, Kibbutz Ramot Menashe, Israel

Elizabeth Kaiser, Director of Social Service, South Shore Mental Health Center, Quincy, Massachusetts

Betty L. Kalis, Clinical Psychology Consultant, Community Mental Health Training Program, Langley Porter Neuropsychiatric Institute, San Francisco

David M. Kaplan, Director, Psychiatric Social Service, University of Colorado Medical Center, Denver

Donald C. Klein, Director, Human Relations Center, and Associate Professor of Psychology, Boston University

David J. Klugman, Co-Chief Social Worker, Suicide Prevention Center of Los Angeles

E. E. LeMasters, Director and Professor, School of Social Work, University of Wisconsin

Charles W. Liddell, Executive Director, United South End Settlements, Boston

Erich Lindemann, Professor of Psychiatry, Harvard Medical School

Edward A. Mason, Assistant Clinical Professor of Psychiatry, Laboratory of Community Psychiatry, Harvard Medical School

Lovick C. Miller, Associate Professor of Clinical Psychology, University of Louisville School of Medicine

James R. Morrissey, Associate Professor of Social Work, Smith College School for Social Work

Howard J. Parad, Director and Professor of Social Work, Smith College School for Social Work

Helen Harris Perlman, Professor of Social Work, University of Chicago School of Social Service Administration

Lydia Rapoport, Associate Professor, School of Social Welfare, University of California

Rhona Rapoport, Director of Family Research Unit and Associate in Sociology, Laboratory of Community Psychiatry, Harvard Medical School

Agnes Ritchie, Chief Social Worker, Division of Child Psychiatry, University of Texas Medical Branch, Galveston

Ann Ross, Research Associate, Department of Psychiatry, Boston University Medical School

Joel Vernick, Group Work Supervisor, Social Work Department, Clinical Center, National Institutes of Health, Bethesda, Maryland

Shirley H. Wattenberg, Caseworker and Student Supervisor, Family Service of Champaign County, Illinois

Foreword

This compilation of readings is especially welcome at this time when innovations in casework treatment and other psychotherapeutic endeavors are receiving widespread attention. The work of the crisis theorists promises to make a number of substantive contributions to intervention efforts undertaken within a psychosocial frame of reference.

The papers selected for the volume will give the reader some idea of the present range of theoretical formulations of crisis theory, the variety of ways it is being applied in practice, and the research studies that are underway. They cannot fail to stimulate him to use short-term treatment contacts more imaginatively and—what may be surprising to many—to reformulate some of the processes of study, diagnosis, and treatment used in traditional long-term treatment approaches. Rooted squarely in psychoanalytic personality theory, crisis theory uses psychoanalytic insights in combination with selected social science concepts to extend and enrich the concept of the person-situation configuration as the unit of attention in psychosocial treatment.

Short-term treatment has been discussed chiefly as a matter of expediency; seldom has it been recommended as the treatment of choice. One can foresee that this attitude toward brief therapy may change under the impact of the crisis formulations, which include new assumptions about the meaning of the "precipitating event" and its significance for focusing the problems to be treated. These formulations describe the dynamics for change that are mobilized under stress and that are more accessible to intervention at the point the client comes for help than they are likely to be at a later point. Obviously, more practice with varieties of cases and more research are needed before practitioners will be able to select and integrate the relevant concepts of crisis theory and assess the results of employing a crisis intervention approach. In the meantime some ideas have emerged that suggest rich insights for experimentation. Even if long-term treatment is the treatment of choice, both its initial and later phases are likely to benefit if some of the crisis concepts are implemented and integrated.

"Precipitating stress," "crisis," and "emotionally hazardous event" are terms that reflect the attempts of the authors of these articles to capture the meaning of stressful life situations that pose "coping" tasks for individuals, families, and groups. Some of these events are related to the normal phases of psychobiological and social development; some are accidental and peculiar to the lives of certain individuals, families, or segments of the population. One of the most valuable contributions of this volume is the specificity with which the authors define the tasks that must be accomplished at transition points in the life cycle and in other stress situations if conflicts are to be avoided or mastered.

The concepts used by several of the authors in analyzing the points at which the "crisis situation" mobilizes the individual's or family's anxiety and disturbs adaptive behavior and interpersonal relationships include social role, family structure, family interaction, and social network. The nature and location of the conflict are elaborated and suggestions are made about the importance of the environment as the source of new satisfactions and supports in the resolution of conflict.

Traditionally, the "precipitating event" has been viewed mainly as a stimulus that reactivates the derivatives of the neurotic conflict, which, in turn, determines the choice of coping responses. Although crisis theory includes this interpretation of the precipitating event, it also takes into account other forces that may be of equal or even greater importance. For example, Erich Lindemann concludes from his study of bereavement that certain factors "seem to be more important in acute grief syndromes than a tendency to react with neurotic symptoms in previous life," if one is to determine the type and severity of grief and the readjustment task. His analysis suggests that although the helping person must be aware of the psychiatric clinical diagnosis and the psychogenetic history, these factors are not always the exclusive—or even the most relevant—determinants for understanding and treating the client's problem.

The article by Donald C. Klein and Ann Ross demonstrates the value of using social perspectives in understanding the stresses of school entry. They view it as a transition period, a turning point in the social experiences not only of the child but of all family members. Their analysis adds new insights to the understanding of "school phobia" which has been treated largely as a problem of mother-child pathology. The concepts of role transition, and of stress induced in the child and his family at this point in their lives, and the authors' suggestions in regard to preventive intervention point to ways in which other kinds of role transition periods can be conceptualized and dealt with more effectively.

Crisis theorists and practitioners also are doing important work on a further refinement of clinical entities. Often the client's symptom picture seems to constitute a psychosocial syndrome rather than a purely clinical syndrome derived largely from intrapsychic disturbances. It is apparent that persons with a variety of clinical diagnoses tend to act in similar ways under the impact of a particular situational provocation. Environmental and psychological helping measures that have many common features can be instituted if the situational determinants of common problems can be identified. For example, Stanley Cath discusses a clinical entity, "ego depletion," which cuts across traditional clinical diagnoses and highlights situational forces as they interact with the defensive structure and restitutional maneuvers of the personality. His suggestion of the "omnicon"—a concept to designate the totality of biopsychosocial forces in operation at any given point in time—merits discussion and further refinement.

Many of the papers point out that the client's "present situation" must be analyzed in dynamic terms. A current rather than a retrospective emphasis in history-taking and the use of "life space" concepts are correctives to the caseworker's lessening but still powerful tendency to view understanding the "presenting problem" as secondary in importance to unearthing the "real problem." The traditional pattern of history-taking that formalizes the procedures and time period for information-getting from the client may sacrifice the worker's vitally important opportunity to relate to the client's felt need. It is in the initial contact that the worker can best view the adaptive and defensive structure of the client's personality; the client's "cry for help," the nature of the disruptive forces in his current life situation, and the range of his successful and unsuccessful coping methods must be given priority.

This volume also offers food for thought about treatment goals within the framework of the concept of the restoration of equilibrium—an ever-shifting balance between the always fluid processes of the ego, the superego, and the id and varied demands of the outside world. The reader will be aware of the application of many familiar concepts from ego psychology. The emphasis on rational action which has goals and means includes Heinz Hartmann's concept of intelligence as an organizing ego apparatus rather than as an ability that takes the place of all other mental functions. His view that the rational plan must include the irrational as a factor is also reckoned with. Moreover, the authors recognize that treatment must always be an experience in which the client's thoughts and feelings are utilized within the context of his emotional and social reality.

These papers on the application of crisis theory in many fields of practice and in a number of commonly encountered stressful situations demonstrate that a great deal of imaginative work is being undertaken to find new ways of reaching a large number of people who need help. Individual and group treatment, as well as the community planning of services, have been given impetus by the social workers, psychiatrists, and other mental health workers who have contributed to this collection.

The editor's introductory notes and suggestions for additional readings will be found most helpful. This volume is worth more than a cursory reading. One fruitful exercise would be for the reader, after serious study of these papers, to examine any five cases with which he is familiar, to see whether he is content with his previous case analysis.

LUCILLE N. AUSTIN
*Columbia University School
of Social Work*
New York, N.Y.

March, 1965

Contents

Page

PART III: Clinical Applications

PART IV: The Measurement of Crisis Phenomena

Introduction

WITHIN THE PAST FEW YEARS formulations of the crisis concept and its various implementations in crisis intervention, preventive intervention, and emergency brief therapy have received increasing attention in the literature of social work and social psychiatry. Social work has, in fact, been defined in terms of its efforts at crisis management: "Generally speaking, social work can be visualized as centering on the management of cases with the object of alleviating a crisis in the life of an individual, family, or group." [1]

The purpose of this collection of readings is to make available, in convenient and readily accessible form, the "practice wisdom" observations, theoretical explorations, and formal investigations of a fairly large and reasonably representative group of practitioners and researchers who have addressed themselves to various aspects of crisis intervention. The papers in this volume are concerned with observing, formulating, defining, and measuring the threats, tasks, and opportunities associated with crisis behavior in individuals and families.

Crisis intervention is in a fair way of becoming a fad or a bandwagon movement in which some concepts are oversimplified and others arouse unrealistic expectations. It therefore seems appropriate to offer serious students and clinicians a collection of readings that reveal the rich complexity and promise of the material, and that may whet their appetite for more knowledge. The readings should discourage the simplistic notion that—as one British critic recently put it—we have in the crisis concept "the means of establishing the future mental health of mankind." [2]

[1] *Action for Mental Health,* Final Report of the Joint Commission on Mental Illness and Health, Basic Books, New York, 1961, p. 151.
[2] M. Harrington, Review of *Prevention of Mental Disorders in Children,* (Gerald Caplan, ed.), in *British Journal of Psychiatric Social Work,* Vol. 6, No. 4 (1962), p. 211.

Crisis intervention means entering into the life situation of an individual, family, or group to alleviate the impact of a crisis-inducing stress in order to help mobilize the resources of those directly affected, as well as those who are in the significant "social orbit," to use Lindemann's term. The interviewer has the dual objective of (1) reducing, whenever possible, the impact of the stressful event, and (2) utilizing the crisis situation to help those affected not only to solve present problems but also to become strengthened in mastering future vicissitudes by the use of more effective adaptive and coping mechanisms. Hence, the now familiar observation that crisis brings both danger and opportunity.

The reader of this volume may wonder what guided the editor in the selection of these papers and their order of presentation. I began with the rather ambitious plan of locating a group of articles that use a common theoretical frame of reference to deal systematically and in depth with a range of normal developmental (or maturational) life crises, as well as with a variety of abnormal and accidental (or situational) crises. I thought that these articles would constitute an excellent section, to be followed by another section on clinical applications, to be arranged logically so that there would be one article on the clinical tasks and techniques for each of the series of common maturational and situational crises. I soon realized, however, that authors write their papers with their own immediate purposes in mind and not those of future anthologists. Thus, it was difficult, if not impossible, to categorize these papers neatly according to a preconceived pattern, except in a somewhat arbitrary manner.

Consequently I have divided this book into four sections: (1) *Theoretical Explorations;* (2) *Common Maturational and Situational Crises;* (3) *Clinical Applications;* and (4) *The Measurement of Crisis Phenomena.* The fact is that virtually all the papers in the collection have theoretical, clinical, and research implications. Like life itself, the book is not altogether neat and tidy. However, the classification to which I have resorted may have the virtue of making the material more easily approached in terms of the reader's predilections and interests.

This is a sourcebook, not a textbook. The reader will not find in these pages an overarching or unifying theory of crisis phenomena, for no such theory as yet exists. Instead he will find many points of view and approaches, reflecting diverse efforts at extending the knowledge and practice base of crisis conceptualizations. Thus, some papers focus on the stressful event, others on the meaning of that event (which serves to remind us that stress does not always result in crisis), and still others on the coping and interventive processes utilized.

In my opinion, the urgent tasks now confronting practitioners and researchers alike are (1) the development of typologies that include all the important elements of the crisis configuration—stress, response, and resolution—thereby promoting the formulation of a general theory of crisis behavior; and, (2) the specification of differential models of intervention, based on increasingly refined definitions of crisis and the use of preventive techniques that are appropriate for individuals, groups, and communities.

If this reader stimulates further endeavors in these directions, its purpose will be achieved.

Additional Readings

I had hoped to prepare a fairly extensive bibliographical appendix. To do this thoroughly would be a mammoth job and would require a separate volume; to do it skimpily would result in a superficial and biased selection. I can, however, refer the interested reader to the following useful guides to the literature:

David Mechanic's study, *Students Under Stress* (Free Press of Glencoe, 1962), includes an interesting bibliography that emphasizes the contributions of social psychology. Mechanic believes that the behavioral disciplines, taken collectively, have neglected the "tools and techniques that are provided by the social environment for dealing with threatening life situations." Richard A. Schermerhorn has edited an excellent *Psychiatric Index for Interdisciplinary Research: A Guide to the Literature, 1950–1961* (U.S. Department of Health, Education, and Welfare, 1964). Designed for the specialist who may be "blind to what he is not up on," this encyclopedic guide includes a listing of papers on stress from a variety of disciplines. A smaller but equally valuable text, citing 1,158 items from 1953 to 1961 is *Community Mental Health and Social Psychiatry: A Reference Guide* (Harvard University Press, 1962) which contains several references to bereavement, disaster, stress, and other aspects of crisis theory. Readers who are particularly interested in disaster studies will find a useful bibliography in Duane P. Schultz's *Panic*

Behavior (Random House, New York, 1964). A comprehensive, up-to-date, specialized "Bibliography on Bereavement" has recently been compiled by Lenin Baler and Peggy Golde in *Working Papers in Community Mental Health* (Harvard School of Public Health, 1964). Gerald Caplan, who, with Erich Lindemann, is one of the major architects of modern crisis theory, refers to the works that have both influenced and resulted from his own studies in this field, in his recent book *Principles of Preventive Psychiatry* (Basic Books, New York, 1964). To all readers, I strongly recommend this lucid presentation of a conceptual framework for community mental health theory and practice in such areas as community planning and consultation, which are only touched upon in this reader.

Acknowledgments

Special thanks are due the authors and publishers who granted permission for the inclusion of the articles in this volume; Lucille N. Austin who warmly supported my interest in doing this reader; my wife, Libbie G. Parad, for her critical advice and editorial help; Lydia Rapoport and Charlotte G. Schwartz for their helpful suggestions; Cora Kasius, who initiated the planning for publication; and Elinor P. Zaki and Shirley M. Martin of the Family Service Association of America who somehow managed to keep me on schedule.

HOWARD J. PARAD

Northampton, Massachusetts
March, 1965

Part I
Theoretical Explorations

To the scientific purists whose conception of theory follows the natural science model I must grant at the outset that the reference to crisis "theory" may be somewhat honorific. Although there is a vast amount of literature that deals with crisis behavior—only a small sample of which is included in this section—this body of writings possesses the spirit of scientific inquiry rather than the formal attributes of systematically validated theory. Despite this lack, however, there is a rich and expanding body of reconnaissance literature that maps out and formulates the diverse problems and processes of crisis. Hence, the use of the word "explorations" in the title of this section.

"Science," according to James Conant, "emerges from the . . . progressive activities of man to the extent that new concepts arise from experiments and observations, and the new concepts in turn lead to further experiments and observations." [1] He goes on to explain that some of these concepts are fruitful, some fruitless—and obviously the fruitful ones are the essence of science because they lead to further testing and observation.

In my view, crisis is a fruitful concept. Erich Lindemann's classic paper, which introduces this section, is, according to general consensus, a prime example of scientific investigation in Conant's sense; that is, inquiry that has encouraged other investigators to test and observe. This seminal paper by an eminent psychoanalyst and social psychiatrist has stimulated a rich succession of studies, not only of the crisis of bereavement but also of many other situational crises. Lindemann's action-research approach, like Freud's, has served as a model; he investigated while he healed.

Lydia Rapoport, who studied under both Lindemann and Gerald

---

[1] James Conant, *On Understanding Science*, Yale University Press, New Haven, 1947, p. 24.

Caplan, weaves together a number of the important strands of theory related to the "state of crisis," including psychoanalytic ego psychology, social system and role concepts, and social work practice propositions. Reuben Hill's paper, reflecting the broad perspective of a social scientist who has done a substantial amount of field research with families under stress, includes a presentation of the equilibrium model which is basic to any understanding of the complex field of forces that metamorphose a "steady state" into a crisis state. The final paper in this introductory section by Parad and Caplan outlines a theoretical framework that emerged from the beginning phase of a study of crisis-ridden families at the Harvard School of Public Health.

1. Symptomatology and Management of Acute Grief *

Erich Lindemann

AT FIRST GLANCE, acute grief would not seem to be a medical or psychiatric disorder in the strict sense of the word but rather a normal reaction to a distressing situation. However, the understanding of reactions to traumatic experiences, whether or not they represent clear-cut neuroses, has become of ever increasing importance to the psychiatrist. Bereavement or the sudden cessation of social interaction seems to be of special interest because it is often cited among the alleged psychogenic factors in psychosomatic disorders. The enormous increase in grief reactions related to war casualties has enhanced the importance of studying bereavement phenomena.

The points to be made in this paper are as follows:

1. Acute grief is a definite syndrome with psychological and somatic symptomatology.

2. This syndrome may appear immediately after a crisis; it may be delayed; it may be exaggerated or apparently absent.

3. In place of the typical syndrome there may appear distorted pictures, each of which represents one special aspect of the grief syndrome.

4. By use of appropriate techniques these distorted pictures can be successfully transformed into a normal grief reaction with resolution.

Our observations comprise 101 patients. Included are (1) psychoneurotic patients who lost a relative during the course of treatment,

* Reprinted from *American Journal of Psychiatry,* Vol. 101 (September 1944).

(2) relatives of patients who died in the hospital, (3) bereaved disaster victims (of the Cocoanut Grove fire in Boston) and their close relatives, (4) relatives of members of the armed forces.

The investigation consisted of a series of psychiatric interviews. Both the timing and the content of the discussions were recorded. These records were subsequently analyzed in terms of the symptoms reported and of the changes in mental status observed progressively through a series of interviews. The psychiatrist avoided all suggestions and interpretations until the picture of symptomatology and spontaneous reaction tendencies of the patients had become clear from the records. The somatic complaints offered important leads for objective study. Careful laboratory work included spirograms and gastrointestinal and metabolic studies. At present we wish to present only our psychological observations.

Symptomatology of Normal Grief

The picture shown by persons in acute grief is remarkably uniform. Common to all is the following syndrome: sensations of somatic distress occurring in waves lasting from twenty minutes to an hour at a time, a feeling of tightness in the throat, choking with shortness of breath, need for sighing, an empty feeling in the abdomen, lack of muscular power, and an intense subjective distress described as tension or mental pain. The patient soon learns that these waves of discomfort can be precipitated by visits, by mentioning the deceased, and by receiving sympathy. There is a tendency to avoid the syndrome at any cost—to refuse visits lest they should precipitate the reaction, and to keep deliberately from thought all references to the deceased.

The striking features are: (1) The marked tendency to sighing respiration; this respiratory disturbance was most conspicuous when the patient was made to discuss his grief. (2) The complaint about lack of strength and exhaustion, which is universal and is described as follows: "It is almost impossible to climb up a stairway." "Everything I lift seems so heavy." "The slightest effort makes me feel exhausted." "I can't walk to the corner without feeling exhausted." (3) Digestive symptoms, described as follows: "The food tastes like sand." "I have no appetite at all." "I stuff the food down because I have to eat." "My saliva won't flow." "My abdomen feels hollow." "Everything seems slowed up in my stomach."

The sensorium is generally somewhat altered. There is commonly a slight sense of unreality, a feeling of increased emotional distance from other people (sometimes they appear shadowy or small), and there is intense preoccupation with the image of the deceased. A patient who lost his daughter in the Cocoanut Grove disaster visualized the girl in a telephone booth calling for him. He was much troubled by the loudness with which she called his name, and was so vividly preoccupied with the scene that he became oblivious of his surroundings. A young navy pilot lost a close friend; the friend remained a vivid part of his imagery, not in terms of a religious survival but in terms of an imaginary companion. The pilot ate with him and talked over problems with him; for instance, he discussed with him his plan of joining the Air Corps. Up to the time of the study, six months later, he denied the fact that his friend was no longer with him. Some patients are much concerned about this aspect of their grief reaction because they feel it indicates approaching insanity.

Another strong preoccupation is with feelings of guilt. The bereaved searches the time before the death for evidence of failure to do right by the lost one. He accuses himself of negligence and exaggerates minor omissions. After the fire disaster the central topic of discussion for a young married woman was the fact that her husband died just after he left her following a quarrel, and a young man whose wife died dwelt on the fact that he fainted too soon to save her.

In addition, there is often a disconcerting loss of warmth in relationship to other people, a tendency to respond with irritability and anger, a wish not to be bothered by others at a time when friends and relatives make a special effort to keep up friendly relationships. These feelings of hostility, surprising and quite inexplicable to the patients, disturb them, and these feelings also are often taken as signs of approaching insanity. The patients make great efforts to handle them, and the result is often a formalized, stiff manner of social interaction.

The activity throughout the day of the severely bereaved person shows remarkable changes. There is no retardation of action and speech; quite to the contrary, there is a push of speech, especially in relation to the deceased. There are restlessness, inability to sit still, an aimless moving about, a continual searching for something to do. At the same time, however, there is a painful lack of capacity

9

to initiate and maintain organized patterns of activity. What is done is done with lack of zest, as though one were simply going through the motions of living. The bereaved clings to the daily routine of prescribed activities, but these activities do not proceed in the automatic, self-sustaining fashion that characterizes normal work; they have to be carried on with effort, as though each fragment of the activity became a special task. The bereaved is surprised to find how large a part of his customary activity had some meaningful relationship in his contacts with the deceased and has now lost its significance. Especially the habits of social interaction—meeting friends, making conversation, sharing enterprises with others—seem to have been lost. This loss leads to a strong dependence on anyone who will stimulate the bereaved to activity and serve as the initiating agent.

These five points—(1) somatic distress, (2) preoccupation with the image of the deceased, (3) guilt, (4) hostile reactions, and (5) loss of patterns of conduct—seem to be pathognomonic for grief. There may be added a sixth characteristic, shown by patients who border on pathological reactions, which is not so conspicuous as the others but nevertheless often striking enough to color the whole picture. This is the appearance of traits of the deceased in the behavior of the bereaved, especially symptoms shown during the last illness, or behavior that may have been shown at the time of the tragedy. A bereaved person is observed—or observes himself—walking in the manner of his deceased father. He looks in the mirror and believes that his face appears just like that of the deceased. He may show a change of interests in the direction of the former activities of the deceased and may start enterprises entirely different from his former pursuits. A wife who lost her husband, an insurance agent, found herself writing to many insurance companies offering her services with somewhat exaggerated schemes. In these patients it was rather regularly observed that the painful preoccupation with the image of the deceased was transformed into preoccupation with symptoms or personality traits of the lost person, and these were now displaced to their own bodies and activities by identification.

Course of Normal Grief Reactions

The duration of a grief reaction seems to depend upon the success with which a person does the "grief work," that is, achieves eman-

10

cipation from the bondage to the deceased, readjustment to the environment in which the deceased is missing, and the formation of new relationships. One of the big obstacles to this work seems to be the fact that many patients try to avoid both the intense distress connected with the grief experience and the necessary expression of emotion. The male victims bereaved by the Cocoanut Grove fire appeared in the early psychiatric interviews to be in a state of tension, with tightened facial musculature, unable to relax for fear they might "break down." They required considerable persuasion to yield to the grief process which would enable them to accept the discomfort of bereavement. One patient assumed a hostile attitude toward the psychiatrist, refusing to allow any references to the deceased and rather rudely asking the psychiatrist to leave. He maintained his attitude throughout his stay on the ward, and the prognosis for his condition is not good in the light of other observations. Hostility of this sort was encountered on only occasional visits with the other patients. They became willing to accept the grief process and to embark on a program of dealing in memory with the deceased person. As soon as this change was accomplished there seemed to be a rapid relief of tension, and the subsequent interviews were rather animated conversations in which the deceased was idealized and in which misgivings about the future adjustment were worked through.

Examples of the psychiatrist's role in assisting patients in their readjustment after bereavement are contained in the following case histories. The first shows a very successful readjustment.

A woman, aged 40, the mother of a 10-year-old child, lost her husband in the fire. She had a history of good adjustment previously. When she heard about her husband's death she became extremely depressed, cried bitterly, did not want to live, and for three days showed a state of utter dejection.

When seen by the psychiatrist, she was glad to have assistance and described her painful preoccupation with memories of her husband and her fear that she might lose her mind. She had a vivid visual image of his presence, picturing him as going to work in the morning and herself as wondering whether he would return in the evening. She would then wonder whether she could stand his not returning, describing to herself his return, playing with the dog, receiving his child. She gradually tried to accept the fact that he was not there any more. It was only after ten days that she succeeded in accepting his loss and then only after she had described in detail the remarkable qualities of her hus-

11

band, the tragedy of his having to stop his activities at the pinnacle of his success, and his deep devotion to her.

In the subsequent interviews she explained with some distress that she had become very much attached to the examiner and that she waited eagerly for his coming. This reaction she considered disloyal to her husband but at the same time she could accept the fact that it was a hopeful sign of her ability to fill the gap his death had left in her life. She then showed a marked drive for activity, making plans for supporting herself and her little girl, mapping out the preliminary steps for resuming her former work as secretary, and making efforts to secure help from the occupational therapy department in reviewing her knowledge of French. Her convalescence, both emotional and somatic, progressed smoothly, and she made a good adjustment on her return home.

A successful businessman of 52 lost his wife, with whom he had lived happily. The announcement of his wife's death confirmed his suspicions of several days. He responded with a severe grief reaction with which he was unable to cope. He did not want to see visitors, was ashamed of breaking down, and asked to be permitted to stay in the hospital psychiatric service because he wanted further assistance, although his physical condition would have permitted his discharge. Any mention of his wife produced a severe wave of depressive reaction, but with psychiatric assistance he gradually became willing to go through this painful process, and after three days on the psychiatric service he seemed well enough to go home. He showed a high rate of verbal activity, was restless, needed to be occupied continually, and felt that the experience had whipped him into a state of restless overactivity.

As soon as he returned home he took an active part in his business, assuming a post in which he had a great many telephone calls. He also took over the role of amateur psychiatrist to another bereaved person, spending time with him and comforting him for his loss. In his eagerness to start anew, he developed a plan to sell all his former holdings, including his house and furniture, and to give away anything that could remind him of his wife. Only after considerable discussion was he able to see that this would mean avoiding immediate grief at the price of an act of poor judgment. Again he had to be encouraged to deal with his grief reactions in a more direct manner. He has made a good adjustment.

With eight to ten interviews in which the psychiatrist shared the grief work, and within a period of from four to six weeks, it was usually found possible to settle an uncomplicated and undistorted grief reaction. This was the case in all but one of the thirteen bereaved Cocoanut Grove fire victims who were interviewed.

Morbid Grief Reactions

Morbid grief reactions represent distortions of normal grief. The conditions mentioned here were transformed into "normal reactions" and then found their resolution.

1. *Delay of Reaction*

The most striking and most frequent reaction of this sort is delay or postponement. If the bereavement occurs at a time when the patient is confronted with important tasks and when there is necessity for maintaining the morale of others, he may show little or no reaction for weeks or even much longer. A brief delay is described in the following example.

A girl of 17 lost both parents and her boy friend in the fire and was herself burned severely, with marked involvement of the lungs. Throughout her stay in the hospital her attitude was that of cheerful acceptance without any sign of adequate distress. When she was discharged at the end of three weeks she appeared cheerful, talked rapidly, with a considerable flow of ideas, seemed eager to return home and to assume the role of parent for her two younger siblings. Except for slight feelings of "lonesomeness" she complained of no distress.

This period of griefless acceptance continued for the next two months, even when the household was dispersed and her younger siblings were placed in other homes. Not until the end of the tenth week did she begin to show a true state of grief with marked feelings of depression, intestinal emptiness, tightness in her throat, frequent crying, and vivid preoccupation with her deceased parents.

That this delay may involve years became obvious first by the fact that patients in acute bereavement about a recent death have been found, upon exploration, to be preoccupied with grief about a person who died many years ago. In this manner a woman of 38, whose mother had died recently and who seemed to have responded to the mother's death with a surprisingly severe reaction, was found to be but mildly concerned with her mother's death but deeply engrossed with unhappy and perplexing fantasies concerning the death of her brother, who died twenty years ago under dramatic circumstances from metastasizing carcinoma after amputation of his arm had been postponed too long. The discovery that a former unresolved grief reaction may be precipitated in the course of the discussion of another recent event was soon demonstrated in psychiatric interviews by patients who showed all the traits of a true grief reaction when the topic of a former loss arose.

The precipitating factor for the delayed reaction may be a deliberate recall of circumstances surrounding the death or may be a spontaneous occurrence in the patient's life. A peculiar form of this is the circumstance that a patient develops the grief reaction at the time when he himself is as old as the person who died. For instance, a railroad worker, aged 42, who appeared in the psychiatric clinic, presented a picture that was undoubtedly one of grief reaction for which he had no explanation. It turned out that when he was 22, his mother, then 42, had committed suicide.

2. *Distorted Reactions*

The delayed reactions may occur after an interval which was not marked by any abnormal behavior or distress, but in which there developed an *alteration* in the patient's conduct, perhaps not conspicuous or serious enough to lead him to a psychiatrist. Such an alteration may be considered as the surface manifestation of an unresolved grief reaction, which may respond to fairly simple and quick psychiatric management if recognized. The manifestations may be classified as follows: (1) *overactivity without a sense of loss,* rather with a sense of well-being and zest, the activities being of an expansive and adventurous nature and bearing semblance to the activities formerly carried out by the deceased, as described above; (2) *the acquisition of symptoms belonging to the last illness of the deceased.* This type of patient appears in medical clinics and the ailment is often labeled hypochondriasis or hysteria. To what extent actual alterations of physiological functions occur under these circumstances will have to be a field of further careful inquiry. I owe to Dr. Chester Jones a report about a patient whose electrocardiogram showed a definite change during a period of three weeks, a change that started two weeks after the time her father died of heart disease.

Although this sort of symptom formation "by identification" may still be considered as a conversion symptom such as we know from hysteria, there is another type of disorder no doubt presenting (3) *a recognized medical disease,* namely, a group of psychosomatic conditions, predominantly ulcerative colitis, rheumatoid arthritis, and

14

asthma. Extensive studies in ulcerative colitis have produced evidence that 33 out of 41 patients with ulcerative colitis developed their disease in close time relationship to the loss of an important person. Indeed, it was this observation which first gave the impetus for the present detailed study of grief. Two of the patients developed bloody diarrhea at funerals. In the others it developed within a few weeks after the loss. The course of the ulcerative colitis was strikingly benefited when this grief reaction was resolved by psychiatric technique.

At the level of social adjustment there often occurs a conspicuous (4) *alteration in relationship to friends and relatives.* The patient feels irritable, does not want to be bothered, avoids former social activities, and is afraid he might antagonize his friends by his lack of interest and his critical attitudes. Progressive social isolation follows, and the patient needs considerable encouragement in re-establishing his social relationships.

While overflowing hostility appears to be spread out over all relationships, it may also occur as (5) *furious hostility against specific persons;* the doctor or the surgeon is accused bitterly of neglect of duty and the patient may assume that foul play has led to the death. It is characteristic that, although patients talk a good deal about their suspicions and their bitter feelings, they are not likely to take any action against the accused, as a truly paranoid person might do.

(6) Many bereaved persons struggle with much effort against these feelings of hostility, which to them seem absurd, representing a vicious change in their characters that must be hidden as much as possible. Some patients succeed in hiding their hostility but become wooden and formal, with affectivity and conduct *resembling schizophrenic symptoms.* A typical report is this, "I go through all the motions of living. I look after my children. I do my errands. I go to social functions, but it is like being in a play; nothing really concerns me. I can't have any warm feelings. If I were to have any feelings at all I would be angry with everybody." This patient's reaction to therapy was characterized by growing hostility toward the therapist, and it required considerable skill to make her continue interviews in spite of the disconcerting hostility which she had been fighting so much. The absence of emotional display in this patient's face and actions was quite striking. Her face had a

15

mask-like appearance, her movements were formal, stilted, robot-like, without the fine play of emotional expression.

(7) Closely related to this picture is a *lasting loss of patterns of social interaction*. The patient cannot initiate any activity, is full of eagerness to be active, is restless and cannot sleep, but throughout the day he will not start any activity unless "primed" by somebody else. He will be grateful at sharing activities with others but will not be able to make up his mind to do anything alone. The picture is one of lack of decision and initiative. Organized activities along social lines occur only if a friend takes the patient along and shares the activity with him. Nothing seems to promise reward; only the ordinary activities of the day are carried on, and these in a routine manner, falling apart into small steps, each of which has to be carried out with much effort and without zest.

(8) There is, in addition, a picture in which a patient is active but in which most of his activities attain a coloring which is *detrimental to his own social and economic existence*. Such patients give away their belongings with uncalled for generosity, are easily lured into foolish economic dealings, lose their friends and professional standing by a series of "stupid acts," and find themselves finally without family, friends, social status, or money. This protracted self-punitive behavior seems to take place without any awareness of excessive feelings of guilt. It is a particularly distressing grief picture because it is likely to hurt other members of the family and drag down friends and business associates.

(9) This leads finally to the picture in which the grief reaction takes the form of a straight *agitated depression* with tension, agitation, insomnia, feelings of worthlessness, bitter self-accusation, and obvious need for punishment. Such patients may be dangerously suicidal.

A young man aged 32 had received only minor burns and left the hospital apparently well on the road of recovery just before the psychiatric survey of the disaster victims took place. Before leaving he learned that his wife had died. He seemed somewhat relieved of his worry about her fate and impressed the surgeon as being unusually well controlled.

Later he was returned to the hospital by his family. Shortly after his return home he had become restless, did not want to stay at home, had taken a trip to relatives trying to find rest, had not succeeded, and had returned home in a state of marked agitation, appearing preoccupied, frightened, and unable to concentrate on any organized activity.

The mental status presented a somewhat unusual picture. The patient was restless, could not sit still or participate in any activity on the ward. If he tried to read, he would drop his book after a few minutes; if he tried to play pingpong, he would give it up after a short time. He would try to start conversations, break them off abruptly, and then fall into repeated murmured utterances: "Nobody can help me. When is it going to happen? I am doomed, am I not?" With great effort it was possible to establish enough rapport to carry on interviews. He complained about his feeling of extreme tension, inability to breathe, generalized weakness and exhaustion, and his frantic fear that something terrible was going to happen. "I'm destined to live in insanity or I must die. I know that it is God's will. I have this awful feeling of guilt." With intense morbid guilt feelings, he reviewed incessantly the events of the fire. His wife had stayed behind. When he tried to pull her out he had fainted and was shoved out by the crowd. She was burned while he was saved. "I should have saved her or I should have died too." He complained about being filled with an incredible violence and did not know what to do about it.

The rapport established with him lasted for only brief periods of time. He then would fall back into his state of intense agitation and muttering. He slept poorly even with large sedation. In the course of four days he became somewhat more composed, had longer periods of contact with the psychiatrist, and seemed to feel that he was being understood and might be able to cope with his morbid feelings of guilt and violent impulses. On the sixth day of his hospital stay, however, after skillfully distracting the attention of his special nurse, he jumped through a closed window to a violent death.

If the patient is not conspicuously suicidal, it may nevertheless be true that he has a strong desire for painful experiences, and such patients are likely to desire shock treatment of some sort, which they picture as a cruel experience, such as electrocution might be.

A 28-year-old woman, whose 20-months-old son was accidentally smothered, developed a state of severe agitated depression with self-accusation, inability to enjoy anything, hopelessness about the future, overflow of hostility against her husband and his parents, and excessive hostility toward the psychiatrist. She insisted upon electric-shock treatment and was finally referred to another physician who treated her. She responded to the shock treatments very well and felt relieved of her sense of guilt.

It is remarkable that agitated depressions of this sort represent only a small fraction of the pictures of grief in our series.

Prognostic Evaluation

Our observations indicate that to a certain extent the type and severity of the grief reaction can be predicted. Patients with obsessive personality make-up and with a history of former depressions are likely to develop an agitated depression. Severe reactions seem to occur in mothers who have lost young children. The intensity of interaction with the deceased before his death seems to be significant. It is important to realize that such interaction does not have to be of the affectionate type; on the contrary, the death of a person who invited much hostility, especially hostility that could not well be expressed because of his status and claim to loyalty, may be followed by a severe grief reaction in which hostile impulses are the most conspicuous feature. Not infrequently the person who died represented a key person in a social system; his death was followed by disintegration of this social system and by a profound alteration of the living and social conditions for the bereaved. In such cases readjustment presents a severe task quite apart from the reaction to the loss incurred. All these factors seem to be more important than a tendency to react with neurotic symptoms in previous life. In our study the most conspicuous forms of morbid identification were found in persons who had no former history of a tendency to psychoneurotic reactions.

Psychiatric Management

Proper psychiatric management of grief reactions may prevent prolonged and serious alterations in the patient's social adjustment, as well as potential medical disease. The essential task facing the psychiatrist is that of sharing the patient's grief work, that is, his efforts at extricating himself from the bondage to the deceased and at finding new patterns of rewarding interaction. It is of the greatest importance to notice that not only over-reaction but under-reaction of the bereaved must be given attention, because delayed responses may occur at unpredictable moments and the dangerous distortions of the grief reaction, not conspicuous at first, may be quite destructive later. These may be prevented.

Religious agencies have led in dealing with the bereaved. They have provided comfort by giving the backing of dogma to the patient's wish for continued interaction with the deceased, have developed rituals that maintain the patient's interaction with others, and have counteracted the morbid guilt feelings of the patient by references to divine grace and by promising him an opportunity for "making up" to the deceased at the time of a later reunion. Although these measures have helped countless mourners, comfort alone does not provide adequate assistance in the patient's grief work. He has to accept the pain of the bereavement. He has to review his relationships with the deceased, and has to become acquainted with the alterations in his own modes of emotional reaction. His fear of insanity, his fear of accepting the surprising changes in his feelings, especially the overflow of hostility, have to be worked through. He will have to express his sorrow and sense of loss. He will have to find an acceptable formulation of his future relationship to the deceased. He will have to verbalize his feelings of guilt, and he will have to find persons around him whom he can use as "primers" for the acquisition of new patterns of conduct. All this can be done in eight to ten interviews.

Special techniques are needed if hostility is the most marked feature of the grief reaction. The hostility may be directed against the psychiatrist, and the patient will have such guilt over his hostility that he will avoid further interviews. The help of a social worker or a minister, or if these are not available, a member of the family, to urge the patient to continue coming to see the psychiatrist may be indispensable. If the tension and the depressive features are too great, some medication may be useful in first reducing emotional distress to a tolerable degree. Severe agitated depressive reactions may defy all efforts of psychotherapy and may respond well to shock treatment.

Since it is obvious that not all bereaved persons, especially those suffering because of war casualties, can have the benefit of expert psychiatric help, much of this knowledge will have to be passed on to auxiliary workers. Social workers and ministers will have to be on the lookout for the ominous signs, referring the more disturbed persons to the psychiatrist while assisting those with more normal reactions themselves.

Anticipatory Grief Reactions

Although the studies described here were limited to reactions to actual death, it must be understood that grief reactions are just one form of separation reaction. Separation by death is characterized by its irreversibility and finality. Separation may, of course, occur for other reasons. We were at first surprised to find genuine grief reactions in patients who had not experienced a bereavement but who had experienced separation, caused, for example, by the departure of a member of the family into the armed forces. Separation in this case is not due to death but the patient feels under the threat of death. A common picture hitherto not appreciated is a syndrome which we have designated *anticipatory grief*. The patient is so concerned with her adjustment after the potential death of father or son that she goes through all the phases of grief—depression, heightened preoccupation with the departed, a review of all the forms of death which might befall him, and anticipation of the modes of readjustment which might be necessitated by it. Although this reaction may well form a safeguard against the impact of a sudden death notice, it can turn out to be of a disadvantage at the occasion of reunion. Several instances came to our attention in which a soldier just returned from the battlefront complained that his wife did not love him any more and demanded immediate divorce. In such situations apparently the grief work had been done so effectively that the patient had emancipated herself and the readjustment must then be directed toward new interaction. It is important to know about this possibility because many family disasters of this sort may be avoided through prophylactic measures.

Bibliography

Many of the observations made here are, of course, not entirely new. Delayed reactions were described by Helene Deutsch.[1] Shock treatment in agitated depressions due to bereavement has recently been advocated by Myerson.[2] Morbid identification has been stressed at many points in the psychoanalytic literature; for example, by H. A. Murray.[3] The relation of mourning and depressive psychoses has been discussed by Freud,[4] Melaine Klein,[5] and Abraham.[6] Bereavement reactions in wartime were discussed by Wilson.[7] The reactions after the Cocoanut Grove fire were described in some detail in a chapter of the monograph on this civilian disaster.[8] The effect of wartime separations was reported by Rosenbaum.[9] The incidence of grief reactions among the psychogenic factors in asthma and rheumatoid arthritis has been mentioned by Cobb, *et al.*,[10, 11] and by Lindemann [12] in relation to ulcerative colitis.

[1] Helene Deutsch, "Absence of Grief," *Psychoanalytic Quarterly*, Vol. 6, No. 12 (1937), pp. 12–22.

[2] Abraham Myerson, "The Use of Shock Therapy in Prolonged Grief Reactions," *New England Journal of Medicine*, Vol. 230, No. 9 (1944), pp. 255–256.

[3] Henry A. Murray, "Visceral Manifestations of Personality," *Journal of Abnormal and Social Psychology*, Vol. 32, No. 2 (1937), pp. 161–184.

[4] Sigmund Freud, "Mourning and Melancholia," *Collected Papers, Vol. IV*, Joan Riviere (ed.), Hogarth Press, London, 1950, pp. 152–170; also in the same volume, "Thoughts for the Times on War and Death," pp. 288–317.

[5] Melanie Klein, "Mourning and Its Relation to Manic-Depressive States," *International Journal of Psychoanalysis*, Vol. 21 (1940), pp. 125–153.

[6] Karl Abraham, "A Short Study of the Development of the Libido Viewed in the Light of Mental Disorders," *Selected Papers*, Basic Books, New York, 1953, pp. 418–479.

[7] A. T. M. Wilson, "Reactive Emotional Disorders," *Practitioner*, Vol. 146 (1941), pp. 254–258.

[8] Stanley Cobb and Erich Lindemann, "Symposium on Management of Cocoanut Grove Burns at Massachusetts General Hospital; Neuropsychiatric Observations," *Annals of Surgery*, Vol. 117 (1943), pp. 814–824.

[9] Milton Rosenbaum, "Emotional Aspects of Wartime Separations," *The Family*, Vol. 24, No. 9 (1944), pp. 337–341.

[10] Stanley Cobb *et al.*, "Environmental Factors in Rheumatoid Arthritis," *Journal of the American Medical Association*, Vol. 113, No. 8 (1939), pp. 668–670.

[11] N. T. McDermott and Stanley Cobb, "Psychiatric Survey of 50 Cases of Bronchial Asthma," *The Journal of Psychosomatic Medicine*, Vol. I (1939), pp. 203–244.

[12] Erich Lindemann, "Psychiatric Problems in Conservative Treatment of Ulcerative Colitis," *A.M.A. Archives of Neurology and Psychiatry*, Vol. 53, No. 4 (1945), pp. 322–324.

2. The State of Crisis: Some Theoretical Considerations*

Lydia Rapoport

SOCIAL WORKERS HAVE ALWAYS been confronted with clients who seek help because of singular or multiple problems and who are suffering from the ill effects of stress. Clients come because they are in "need," have a "problem," are under "stress," or are in a "crisis." All these familiar terms are used interchangeably, or, at best, are used descriptively and not in a sufficiently precise conceptual manner. How we conceptualize the problem and the state of being which propels people to seek help will influence the methods and techniques we develop and the way in which we deploy community and professional resources.

This paper seeks to explore the theoretical underpinnings of the concept of the state of crisis and to examine some of the distinctive ideas that characterize it. It is hoped that such a characterization may help the practitioner to differentiate the theoretical notions about crisis from more familiar but loosely used concepts—such as "problem," "need," and "stress"—found so prominently in social work thought.

Nature of the State of Crisis

The term "crisis," generally used in a rather loose and indeterminate way, covers a variety of meaning. In lay language, a crisis is usually equated with disaster, an environmental event which poses an external threat. Erikson and others talk of developmental crises which are induced by the special tasks required by each new developmental

* Reprinted from *The Social Service Review*, Vol. XXXVI, No. 2 (1962), by permission of The University of Chicago Press. Copyright, 1962, by The University of Chicago.

phase in the sequence of psychosocial maturation.[1] Moreover, the terms "crisis" and "stress" are often used interchangeably. The term "stress" itself is used to denote three different sets of phenomena: (1) stress is equated with the stressful event or situation; (2) it is used to refer to the state of the individual who responds to the stressful event, and thus we talk of the client who responds with feelings or symptoms of stress; (3) more often, stress refers to the relation of the stressful stimulus, the individual's reaction to it, and the events to which it leads.

In addition, it has been noted that the concept of stress tends to carry with it a purely negative connotation: stress is a burden or load under which a person survives or cracks. Thus, stress is assumed to have pathogenic potential. In contrast, a state of crisis is conceived to have a growth-promoting potential. W. I. Thomas, the social theorist, saw crisis as a catalyst that disturbs old habits, evokes new responses, and becomes a major factor in charting new developments.[2] Thus conceived, a crisis is a call to new action; the challenge it provokes may bring forth new coping mechanisms which serve to strengthen the individual's adaptive capacity and thereby, in general, to raise his level of mental health.

The concept of crisis as formulated by its chief theoreticians, Dr. Erich Lindemann and Dr. Gerald Caplan,[3] refers to the state of the reacting individual who finds himself in a hazardous situation. Not all individuals faced by the same hazardous events will be in a state of crisis. On the other hand, there are certain common hazardous events, such as loss by death and its sequel of grief and bereavement, which will induce a state of crisis of lesser or greater intensity, or of lesser or greater duration, in nearly all individuals. This fact, incidentally, has important implications for programs of primary preventions.

A state of crisis is not an illness. Dr. James Tyhurst, a Canadian social psychiatrist, states that what we call illness is also an opportunity for growth, however severe the impasse may appear. He writes: "Too often, with its emphasis upon symptomatic treatment, present-

1 Erik Erikson, "Growth and Crisis of the 'Healthy Personality,'" *Personality in Nature, Society, and Culture*, Clyde Kluckhohn, Henry A. Murray, and David M. Schneider (eds.), second edition, Alfred A. Knopf, New York, 1953, ch. xii.
2 E. Volkhart (ed.), *Social Behavior and Personality Contributions of W. I. Thomas to Theory and Social Research*, Social Science Research Council, New York, 1951, pp. 12–14.
3 Erich Lindemann and Gerald Caplan, "A Conceptual Framework for Preventive Psychiatry" (unpublished paper).

day psychiatry denies the patient this opportunity . . . to benefit from his troubles by dint of personal growth and development in relation to the problem." [4] The person, however, may be suffering from chronic or temporary symptomatology or pathological patterns of behavior when he goes into a state of crisis. These two conditions have to be conceived of and evaluated separately. For example, in response to a hazardous event—the death of a loved person—an individual will react with depression, which is found to be a part of the normal process of mourning.[5] This type of depression has to be differentiated from a clinical syndrome in which a patient presents a pathological degree of depression as the main symptom. In the latter instance it is more nearly correct to speak of a depressive illness, whether it takes the form of melancholia or of an agitated depression. The depressive illness may or may not be the reaction to the hazardous event.

Crisis in its simplest terms is defined as "an upset in a steady state." [6] This definition rests on the postulate that an individual strives to maintain for himself a state of equilibrium through a constant series of adaptive maneuvers and characteristic problem-solving activities through which basic need-fulfillment takes place. Throughout a life span many situations occur which lead to sudden discontinuities by which the homeostatic state is disturbed and which result in a state of disequilibrium. In response to many such situations, the individual may possess adequate adaptive or re-equilibrating mechanisms. However, in a state of crisis, by definition, it is postulated that the habitual problem-solving activities are not adequate and do not lead rapidly to the previously achieved balanced state.

The hazardous event itself requires a solution which is new in relation to the individual's previous life experience. Many individuals are able to develop new solutions by means of the normal range of problem-solving mechanisms stemming from their general life ex-

[4] James S. Tyhurst, "The Role of Transition States—Including Disasters—in Mental Illness," *Symposium on Preventive and Social Psychiatry,* Walter Reed Army Institute of Research, Washington, D.C., 1957, p. 164.

[5] John Bowlby, "Grief and Mourning in Infancy and Early Childhood," *Psychoanalytic Study of the Child,* Vol. XV (1960), pp. 11–12.

[6] Formulated by Gerald Caplan in seminars at the Harvard School of Public Health, 1959–1960.

perience and maturation, and are thereby able to deal adequately with the hazardous event. Others are unable to respond with appropriate solutions, and the hazardous event and its sequelae continue to be a source of stress.

The hazardous event creates for the individual a problem in his current life situation. The problem can be conceived of as a threat, a loss, or a challenge. The threat may be to fundamental, instinctual needs or to the person's sense of integrity. The loss may be actual or may be experienced as a state of acute deprivation. For each of these states there is a major characteristic mode in which the ego tends to respond. A threat to need and integrity is met with anxiety. Loss or deprivation is met with depression. If the problem is viewed as a challenge, it is more likely to be met with a mobilization of energy and purposive problem-solving activities.

Since the hazardous event, although posing a problem in the current life situation, may contain a threat to instinctual needs, it is likely to be linked with old threats to instinctual needs and to trigger off and reactivate unresolved or partially resolved unconscious conflicts. The previous failure may act as an additional burden in the present crisis.[7] It has been observed by various investigators that during a crisis memories of old problems which are linked symbolically to the present are stimulated and may emerge into consciousness spontaneously or can be uncovered and dealt with by relatively brief therapeutic intervention.[8] However, with or without therapeutic intervention, the energy needed to maintain repression of the earlier unsolved problem may now become available to solve the current problem in a more appropriately mature manner. The crisis with its mobilization of energy operates as a "second chance" in correcting earlier faulty problem-solving.

The above discussion indicates that there are three sets of interrelated factors that can produce a state of crisis: (1) a hazardous event which poses some threat; (2) a threat to instinctual need which is symbolically linked to earlier threats that resulted in vulnerability

[7] Lindemann and Caplan, op. cit., pp. 8–9.

[8] Mary A. Sarvis, Sally Dewees, and Ruth Johnson, "A Concept of Ego-oriented Psychotherapy," Psychiatry, Vol. XX (August, 1959), pp. 277–287; and B. L. Kalis et al., "Precipitating Stress as a Focus in Psychotherapy," Archives of General Psychiatry, Vol. V (September, 1961), pp. 219–226.

or conflict; (3) an inability to respond with adequate coping mechanisms.[9]

Characteristics of the State of Crisis

Certain characteristics of the state of crisis may be delineated. The first important characteristic is the view that the crisis is self-limiting in a temporal sense. It does not continue indefinitely. Dr. Caplan maintains that the actual period of the crisis tends to last from one to six weeks. Some solution is sought for the state of upset to restore a sense of equilibrium. The solution itself may lead to the prior level of equilibrium. It may lead to a more adequate or higher level of functioning or to a lower level of functioning and a lower level of mental health.

The second feature of the state of crisis is that there are certain typical phases which characterize the period of upset. One could talk of a beginning, middle, and end.* Dr. Tyhurst, referring to crisis in the nature of more major disasters, identifies the period of impact, period of recoil, and the post-traumatic period.[10] Dr. Caplan describes the phases and the processes of development in the following way: In the initial phase, there is a rise in tension in response to the initial impact of stress. During this period habitual problem-solving mechanisms are called forth. If the first effort fails, there will be an increase in the level of tension with an increase in feeling upset and ineffective. This state may then call forth "emergency problem-solving mechanisms." [11] Three things are likely to happen: (1) the problem may actually be solved; (2) there may be a redefinition of the problem in order to achieve need-satisfaction; (3) the problem may be avoided through need-resignation and the relinquishment of goals. If the problem cannot be solved in any of these ways, a state of major disorganization may ensue.

[9] See Howard J. Parad and Gerald Caplan, ch. 4 of present volume.
* It might be noted that social workers are familiar with individuals and families who live in a chronic state of crisis. Here one might say that being in a crisis state is part of their life style because of a general inadequacy in social functioning. Crises for such individuals do not have a beginning, middle, and end, but flow into each other and are compounded and circular. It is clear that the concepts of crisis and its management discussed above do not apply to individuals and families who are beset by multiple problems, chronic and continual states of heightened tension and disorganization. Here one is dealing with a different order of phenomena, which is not adequately explained by crisis theory as defined in this statement.
[10] Tyhurst, *op. cit.*, p. 150.
[11] See Caplan, n. 6, above.

Various investigators have studied the phases of the state of crisis more systematically in relation to specific hazardous events. For example, Dr. John Bowlby and James Robertson, of the Tavistock Clinic, have studied the separation trauma experienced by young children entering a hospital. Three distinct phases have been isolated—protest, despair, and detachment.[12] In the phase of protest, the young child maintains the hope that the mother will return and protests his condition vigorously and loudly with much crying and overt distress. In the phase of despair, there is increasing hopelessness. The predominant effect is depression, as part of grief and mourning. There is increasingly withdrawn behavior and inactivity. The third stage is detachment, which Bowlby formerly called "denial." It is a quiet period in which the young child seems to be making an "adaptation"; indeed, it is often mistaken for contentment, rather than seen as the result of resignation. In this phase defenses are developed, such as denial of the longing for the mother and detachment in relation to nurturing adults. The child at best forms shallow attachments, becomes increasingly self-centered, and becomes attached to material objects.

Dr. Erich Lindemann has observed another example of the phases of the state of crisis and of coping mechanisms linked with it in acute grief following bereavement.[13] In studies made after the disaster of the Cocoanut Grove fire in Boston, Dr. Lindemann noted that the duration of the grief reaction seemed to be dependent on the success with which a person did his "grief work." A normal course of grief reaction begins when the bereaved (1) starts to emancipate himself from the bondage to the deceased, (2) makes a readjustment in the environment in which the deceased is missing, (3) forms new relationships or patterns of interaction that bring rewards and satisfactions.

A third example of phases of crisis that have been identified comes from studies of families in crisis as a result of the event of the birth of a premature infant. These studies, still in progress, are being made by Dr. Caplan and his team of research workers at the Family Guidance Center in Boston. From the work of one of the team members, David Kaplan, four phases have been isolated which are

---

[12] John Bowlby, "Separation Anxiety," *International Journal of Psychoanalysis,* Vol. XLI (1960), pp. 89–113.
[13] See ch. 1 of present volume.

linked with the psychological tasks that need to be achieved in order for the crisis to be resolved in a healthy way.[14] First, the mother must prepare herself psychologically for a possible loss—stillbirth or postnatal loss—through the process of anticipatory grief work. Second, the mother needs to acknowledge to herself some feelings of maternal failure and guilt in her inability to deliver a normal, full-term baby. Third, when it is clear that the baby will survive, there needs to be a resumption of the process of relating to the baby. Fourth, the mother must be able to recognize the special needs and requirements of a premature infant.

In addition to isolating temporal and phasic aspects of the state of crisis, various investigators have described other characteristics of the upset state. As previously mentioned, there is a rise in tension which may push toward a peak. There is also a general feeling of helplessness. In part, this may be a state of cognitive confusion wherein the individual literally does not know how to think of his problem, how to evaluate reality, and how to formulate and evaluate the outcome of the crisis and possibilities for problem-solving. In extreme states, there may also be perceptual confusion such as in the temporal or spatial sense.

Some disorganization and lack of effective functioning may ensue. Disorganized behavior may take the form of activity which is related to attempts to discharge inner tension, rather than to solving the problem in the external situation. It should be noted that the feelings of tension that arise are in themselves a problem with which the individual seeks to deal. The rise in tension may be experienced as anxiety; it may be converted into somatic symptoms; or it may be denied by means of repression.

Various characteristic coping patterns have also been described. Certain patterns of coping while in crisis are essentially maladaptive. For example, an individual may deal with the hazardous event and his feelings about it with magical thinking or with excessive fantasy; he may respond with regressive forms of behavior, with somatization, or, in extreme situations, with withdrawal from reality.

Other types of coping patterns are essentially adaptive in nature. For example, the activity of the individual or family may be task-oriented. The problem may be broken down into component parts and efforts made to solve each aspect of it. The "mental work"

[14] See ch. 9 of present volume.

28

may be directed to correct the cognitive perception, which means predicting and anticipating outcome through cognitive restructuring. The mental work may also entail "rehearsal for reality"— preparation for the anticipated activity or affect. The individual or family may actively seek out new models for identification and for the development of new interpersonal skills as part of problem-solving, particularly in crises of role transition. In general, the patterns of responses for an individual or family necessary for healthy crisis resolution may be described as follows: (1) correct cognitive perception of the situation, which is furthered by seeking new knowledge and by keeping the problem in consciousness; (2) management of affect through awareness of feelings and appropriate verbalization leading toward tension discharge and mastery; (3) development of patterns of seeking and using help with actual tasks and feelings by using interpersonal and institutional resources.[15]

Implications for Practice

Problem-solving during a state of crisis is facilitated by various conditions. The above formulation of patterns of response necessary for healthy crisis resolution also contains guides for intervention. For example, if need for cognitive grasp and restructuring is crucial as a first step in problem-solving, then the first task of the professional caretaker or social worker is to clarify the problem that leads to the call for help. Factors leading to the disruption of functioning are often preconscious and unintegrated. Identifying and isolating these factors to arrive at a formulation of the problem and hence to facilitate cognitive restructuring and integration, in and of itself, may be enough, in many instances, to promote a return to the previously achieved balanced state. In the precipitating stress studies of Dr. Kalis, previously referred to, the conclusion has emerged that the individual is not fully aware of the precipitating stress and its consequences and that prompt therapeutic focusing on the precipitating stress, with clarification of relevant circumstances and conflicts, facilitates restoration of emotional equilibrium.

Second, for the expression and management of feelings, there needs to be an explicit acceptance by the helping person of the dis-

[15] Gerald Caplan, "Patterns of Parental Response to the Crisis of Premature Birth," *Psychiatry*, Vol. 23 (1960) pp. 365–374.

ordered affect, irrational attitudes, or negative responses, but this needs to be placed in a rational context by understanding and clarifying the natural history of such reactions.

The third point is the availability and use of interpersonal and institutional resources. It has been noted that a major upset in a system—be this in an individual, family, or community group—tends to arouse supporting features and to mobilize energy for reaching out by others in the social network. This is dramatically demonstrated in times of actual disaster. Thus, the individual or group can draw comfort, support, and need-satisfaction from the network of human relationships. Formal institutions and agencies, caretakers in the community, and social processes developed in the culture—such as rites of passage—all serve to offer support, to restore equilibrium, and to ease role transition. In this connection, Dr. Tyhurst offers a provocative opinion. He states that some people in turmoil come to the attention of the social institution called "psychiatry," where they are usually defined as "ill," largely as a matter of social convention. He states further that "turning to the psychiatrist may represent an impoverishment of resources in the relevant social environment as much as an indication of the type of severity of disorder." [16]

The major observation, worthy of note because of its implications for social work practice, is the fact that the person or family in crisis becomes more susceptible to the influence of "significant others" in the environment. Moreover, the degree of activity of the helping person does not have to be high.[17] A little help, rationally directed and purposefully focused at a strategic time is more effective than more extensive help given at a period of less emotional accessibility. In addition, the helping person needs to view himself as intervening in a social system—as part of a network of relationships—and not as a single resource. These considerations raise important issues for the activities of all helping professions, not only for social work. There is a need to develop programs and skills that are geared to making help rapidly available at times and places where a state of crisis may develop. Only then can preventive or corrective intervention be maximally effective.

[16] Tyhurst, *op. cit.*, p. 164.
[17] *Ibid.*

Conclusion

Crisis theory, as conceptualized by Lindemann, Caplan, and other mental health workers, is particularly compatible with general social work theory. The crisis-theory framework is applicable to the individual, to the family, and to the group. It makes use of ego psychology as well as newer social science concepts now being incorporated into social work theory, such as role, role-transition states, and social network. It offers the additional advantage of more sharply defining and characterizing a state which occurs frequently in the life cycle of the individual or family and during which the helping professions and caretakers are likely to have access to people and are likely to be active. The theoretical formulations give greater precision and clarity to the nature of the operative conditions, processes, and hence possible techniques which might be developed for intervention.

3. Generic Features of Families Under Stress*

Reuben Hill

Two STREAMS OF RESEARCH concerned about social stresses and the family have been running parallel for some time. This conference should stimulate their early convergence. I refer to the research on crisis-proneness in families carried out by family sociologists and the cumulating work of latter-day social work researchers on the properties of the "multi-problem family." To facilitate further the merger of these two professional groups, I shall undertake in this paper to summarize the major issues and findings in family crisis research as seen by family sociologists. I shall first attempt to provide the broad outlines of the conceptual framework most used by family sociologists in the study of family crises. Second, I shall attempt to catalog the stressful events that have been studied and those that remain unstudied, using classifications developed to differentiate crises into types. Third, our chief findings to date will be listed, indicating types of families which thrive and which wilt under stress. Fourth, the generic phases and modes of adjustment to stress will be demonstrated. Fifth, the short-run and long-run effects of stress on families will be assessed. I shall conclude with speculations about the implications of these findings for agency policies and practices.

A Conceptual Framework for Viewing Families in Crisis

The conceptual scaffolding on which the research to be summarized in this paper has been built makes frequent use of three variables: family, crisis-provoking event, and meaning attached to the event. Let us begin by identifying the major conceptual properties of the family.

The Family as an Interacting and Transacting Organization. Family sociologists have come to view the family as a small group,

* Reprinted from *Social Casework*, Vol. XXXIX, Nos. 2–3 (1958). This paper was presented in October 1957, in Chicago, at the Conference on Family Casework in the Interest of Children, sponsored by the Family Service Association of America and the Elizabeth McCormick Memorial Fund.

intricately organized internally into paired positions of husband-father, wife-mother, son-brother, and daughter-sister. Norms prescribing the appropriate role behavior for each of these positions specify how reciprocal relations are to be maintained as well as how role behavior may change with changing ages of the occupants of these positions.

Viewed externally, the family often appears to be a "closed corporation," particularly in urban areas where the nuclear group of father, mother, and their children is clearly differentiated from the kinship extensions of maternal and paternal grandparents and collateral relatives. Such a family performs like a closed corporation in presenting a common front of solidarity to the world, handling internal differences in private, protecting the reputation of members by keeping family secrets, and standing together under attack. Nevertheless, the closed nature of the family is selectively opened for transacting business with other agencies, including kin and professionals. These agencies can be ranked on their accessibility to the interior of the family: immediate kin highest, family friends and neighbors next, the family physician, the family pastor, the family lawyer, and so on. Other agencies enter the family with greater difficulty and often through the intermediation of individual family members who act as liaisons for the family: the school, the employer, the health clinic, the casework agency, and other such formal agencies. Recent research has suggested that the more open the community (as in the modern city), the more likely the family is closed in form; and the more closed the community (as in the isolated mountain village), the more open are the doors and windows of the family to non-family members.*

Compared with other associations in the society, the average family is badly handicapped organizationally. Its age composition is heavily weighted with dependents, and it cannot freely reject its weak members and recruit more competent team mates. Its members receive an unearned acceptance; there is no price for belonging. Because of its unusual age composition and its uncertain sex composition, it is intrinsically a puny work group and an awkward decision-making group. This group is not ideally manned to withstand stress, yet society has assigned to it the heaviest of responsibilities:

* In this connection, see the reports of European research by C. D. Saal of Holland and Elizabeth Bott of England, in *Recherches Sur La Famille,* published by UNESCO Institute of Social Science, Cologne, 1956, pp. 29–69, 229–247.

the socialization and orientation of the young, and the meeting of the major emotional needs of all citizens, young and old.

When the family is viewed historically, we can see that it is more dependent today than it was formerly on other agencies in society for fulfilling its purposes. Once a self-contained economic and social unit buttressed by kinship supports, the family now has interdependent relations with many other associations in working out its problems. I have elsewhere described the ways in which the family functions in equilibrating troubles of its members:

> The modern family lives in a greater state of tension precisely because it is the great burden carrier of the social order. In a society of rapid social change, problems outnumber solutions, and the resulting uncertainties are absorbed by the members of society, who are for the most part also members of families. Because the family is the bottleneck through which all troubles pass, no other association so reflects the strains and stresses of life. With few exceptions persons in work-a-day America return to rehearse their daily frustrations within the family, and hope to get the necessary understanding and resilience to return the morrow to the fray.
>
> Thus, the good family today is not only the focal point of frustrations and tensions but also the source for resolving frustrations and releasing tensions. . . . Through its capacity for sympathy, understanding, and unlimited support, the family rehabilitates personalities bruised in the course of competitive daily living. In that capacity the family is literally love in action.[1]

In sum, the concept of the family which we have identified above is that of an arena of interacting personalities, intricately organized internally into positions, norms, and roles. When viewed externally it can be seen as an organized group engaged in transactions with other associations. It is not new to trouble. Indeed, problems and exigencies beset American families from wedding day to dissolution day. Most families have had a long history of troubles and have worked out procedures and a division of responsibility for meeting problematic situations as they arise. These can be viewed broadly as the family's repertory of resources for dealing with crises which we shall have occasion to return to later.

The Crisis-Precipitating Event. The second major concept in our scaffolding is the *stressor,* or crisis-provoking event. A stressor in this context is a situation for which the family has had little or no prior preparation and must therefore be viewed as problematic. It is often difficult empirically to disentangle the problematics and

[1] Reuben Hill, *Families Under Stress,* Harper & Bros., New York, 1949, pp. 50–97.

the hardships of the stressful event from the definitions the family makes—the meaning aspect of the event. To make the distinction conceptually is one step in the direction of doing so empirically. Actually the hardships of the event lie outside the family and are an attribute of the event itself, constituting a distinct variable requiring separate attention.

No crisis-precipitating event is the same for any given family; its impact ranges according to the several hardships that may accompany it. We might take, as an illustration, the dismemberment of a family through conscription of the husband-father into the armed services in wartime—an event that appeared to be uniform, striking, as it did, hundreds of thousands of families in America in World War II. Hill and Boulding,[2] studying this phenomenon, found the number of hardships accompanying the event ranging from none to six, including sharp changes in income, housing inadequacies, enforced living with in-laws or other relatives, illness of wife or children, wife's having to work and be both mother and father, child-discipline problems stemming from the father's absence. There were, on the other hand, families where the war separation event produced father-substitutes who were an improvement on the absentee, improved housing, increased income, and a more relaxed family life. Similarly the catastrophic event of a tornado strikes unevenly as a crisis-precipitating event. Some families lose not only property but life and limb too; many experience reduced income only; still others suffer fright and anxiety, but in the short run make net gains financially because of the moratorium on debts and the grants from relief agencies which often accompany severe catastrophes. Clearly, the stressor event must be seen as a variable rather than as a constant in family crisis research.

Since no stressor event is uniformly the same for all families, but varies in striking power by the hardships that accompany it, the concept of hardship itself requires some additional attention. Hardships may be defined as those complications in a crisis-precipitating event which demand competencies from the family which the event itself may have temporarily paralyzed or made unavailable.

Definition of the Event as Stressful. It has always puzzled observers that some families ride out the vicissitudes of floods and disasters without apparent disorganization, whereas most families are at least

2 Reuben Hill, *op. cit.*

temporarily paralyzed by such catastrophes. The key appears to be at the "meaning" dimension. Stressors become crises in line with the definition the family makes of the event.

A boy caught stealing in one neighborhood may be ostracized and bring his family shame and disgrace, while a boy in a different social grouping may well achieve standing within his family and in his neighborhood through an identical act. To transform a stressor event into a crisis requires an intervening variable that has been variously termed, "meaning of the event" or "definition of the event."

Placing this final variable in an equation with the other elements in our conceptual framework, we get a formula as follows: A (the event) → *interacting* with B (the family's crisis-meeting resources) → *interacting* with C (the definition the family makes of the event) → *produces* X (the crisis). The second and third determinants—family resources and definition of the event—lie within the family itself and must be seen in terms of the family's structures and values. The hardships of the event, which go to make up the first determinant, lie outside the family and are an attribute of the event itself.

This threefold framework enables us to ask the proper questions to account for crisis-proneness in families, identifying as it does the interplay of the most important explanatory variables. We turn now to our findings about the stresses studied to date, the properties of the crisis-prone, and the phases of adjustment characteristic of families under stress.

A Classification of Stressor Events

Three systems of classification of family troubles have been used by investigators in cataloging crises: (1) by source, whether extra-family or intra-family, (2) by effects upon the family configuration, which combine dismemberment, accession, and demoralization, and (3) by type of event impinging on the family.

Source of Trouble. If the blame for the stressor can be placed outside the family, the stress may solidify rather than disorganize the family. Crises differ in their sources—some originate within, others outside the family. Crises that arise as a result of economic depression or of war, both of which are beyond the individual family's control, present quite different problems from the crises arising out of the interpersonal relations within the family such as infidelity, nonsupport, or alcoholism. The loss of life's savings due to bank failure during a depression will induce a crisis for most families, but consider the impact created by the loss of life's savings through the improvidence of an alcoholic father, which event was in turn precipitated by a serious rift in the affectional relations within the family. It is not the loss of life's savings in this instance so much as it is the interpersonal relations which constitute the matrix of trouble.

Classified by source of trouble, stressor events divide into three categories: (1) extra-family events which in the long run tend to solidify the family, such as war bombings, political persecutions, religious persecutions, floods, tornadoes, hurricanes, and other "acts of God," defined as stressful but solidifying because external to the family; (2) intra-family events such as illegitimacy, non-support, mental breakdown, infidelity, suicide, and alcoholism, which are defined as stressful but usually are more disorganizing to the family because they arise from troubles that reflect poorly on the family's internal adequacy; and (3) some extra-family events that are often not defined as critically stressful and are assimilable because other persons are in the same situation or worse, or events similar to others the family has previously undergone, such as some war separations, some war reunions, loss of home in a disaster, forced migration, sudden decrease in income during a depression, and premature births.

Combinations of Dismemberment—Accession and Demoralization. A second type of classification first suggested by Eliot [3] and expanded by Hill [4] involves the combination of loss of family member (dismemberment) or addition of an unprepared-for member (accession) and loss of morale and family unity (demoralization), or all three. (See chart on the next page.)

Closely allied with this classification are stressor events that do not result in dismemberment in the sense of a change in the plurality pattern of the family, but do bring marked changes in the family configuration. Those family situations where roles are involuntarily vacated through illness, or are not fulfilled at all as in families with mentally retarded children, might be cited as examples. Families experience significant strains when members become diabetics

[3] Thomas D. Eliot, "Handling Family Strains and Shocks," *Family, Marriage, and Parenthood,* Howard Becker and Reuben Hill (eds.) Heath and Co., Boston, 1955.

[4] Willard W. Waller, *The Family: A Dynamic Interpretation,* rev. by Reuben Hill, Dryden Press, New York, 1951, ch. 21.

or experience congestive heart failure, and require special consideration. Such illnesses require a reallocation of the patient's roles to others within the family.

Most crises of dismemberment, accession, and crippling illness sooner or later involve *de-morale-ization,* since the family's role patterns are always sharply disturbed. Dismemberment creates a situation in which the departed one's roles must be reallocated, and a period of confusion-delay ensues while the members of the family cast learn their new lines. The addition of a new member resulting

---

A CLASSIFICATION OF FAMILY CRISES OF DISMEMBERMENT— ACCESSION AND DEMORALIZATION

Dismemberment Only

Death of child, spouse, or parent
Hospitalization of spouse
War separation

Accession Only

Unwanted pregnancy
Deserter returns
Stepfather, stepmother additions
Some war reunions
Some adoptions, aged grandparents, orphaned kin

Demoralization Only

Nonsupport
Infidelity
Alcoholism
Drug addiction
Delinquency and events bringing disgrace

Demoralization Plus Dismemberment or Accession

Illegitimacy
Runaways
Desertion
Divorce
Imprisonment
Suicide or homicide
Institutionalization for mental illness

from the marriage of a divorced or widowed person strains the resources of a family that "closed ranks" too well.

Types of Impact of Stressor Events. Ernest W. Burgess [5] has added two categories for further classifying family crises: (1) sudden change in family status, and (2) conflict among family members in the conception of their roles.

A sudden upturn in economic and social status may constitute a crisis quite as disruptive as that of economic loss or social disgrace. The price of upward mobility for some families may be family breakdown. We are only beginning to learn something of the conditions under which the family survives or goes to pieces when there is a swift change from poverty to riches or from obscurity to fame. More usually we think of stressor events bringing sudden changes downward in status. The variety of crises of this type is well known.

TYPES OF STRESSES INVOLVING STATUS SHIFTS

Sudden improverishment
Prolonged unemployment
Sudden wealth and fame
Refugee migrations, political and religious
Disasters, tornadoes, floods, explosions
War bombings, deprivations
Political declassing, denazification

Many of the difficulties that build up into crises involve differences in conception of their respective roles by family members. Conflicts between parents and children should be understood and studied in terms of their differences in role expectations. Koos [6] finds the adolescent-parent relationships to be a focal point of crisis in the middle-class family. In upward-mobile families, the appropriate roles for wife and mother differ by socioeconomic groups, and the work-a-day housekeeper roles of one's original class may have to be unlearned and the hostess roles of the next class may have to be learned to fit the changed expectations of husband and children.

The current crisis of desegregation in the South is a stressful event for both white and Negro families, largely because of the great differences in role expectations held by parents and children. As

[5] "The Family and Sociological Research," *Social Forces*, Vol. XXVI, No. 1 (1947), pp. 1–6.

[6] Earl L. Koos, "Class Differences in Family Reactions to Crisis," *Marriage and Family Living*, Vol. XII, No. 3 (1950), pp. 77–78.

the schools are integrated, children of both groups tend to forget color as the individual personality shines through. They make friends on the basis of congeniality rather than color alone. Parents and some teachers lag behind the children in this respect. Parents try to limit friendships and home associations, thus producing conflict with their volatile adolescents. Dating, dancing, and contact games become focal points of disagreement, since these activities violate the Southern mores which parents feel obliged to perpetuate. The children may only partially accept these mores and resent their parents' restrictions. Conflicts develop between families whose restrictions differ, since styles for adolescents are often set by the freedoms that the most permissive parents allow their children. Thus the full-blown dimensions of a family crisis are experienced until a new set of norms accepted by both generations develops.

With this background of the range of types of stressful events spelled out, we turn to a consideration of the factors making for crisis-proneness and freedom from crisis among families. It has been suggested that crisis-proneness runs in families as does accident-proneness. What support can be adduced for such a proposition? We know that some families can handle stress better than other families. In what ways do they differ from the crisis prone?

Factors Making for Crisis-Proneness in Families

We can profitably take advantage now of an equation that summarizes the conceptual framework of most of the family crisis research I am reporting: A (the event) → interacting with B (the family's crisis-meeting resources) → interacting with C (the definition the family makes of the event) → produces X (the crisis). Crisis-proneness is in effect the phenomenon of experiencing stressor events (A) with greater frequency and greater severity and defining these (C) more frequently as crisis. In other words, crisis-prone families appear to be more vulnerable to stressor events of the types we have just cataloged, and more likely because of meager crisis-meeting resources (B) and failure to have learned, from past experience with crisis, to define these events as crisis-provoking. The explanation for crisis-proneness therefore lies primarily in the B and C factors in our equation.

Note the differences in vulnerability when families are assessed on a class basis alone. To the lower-class family, living up to and even beyond its income, there may be a quality of desperation in a financial crisis that is lacking for the middle-class family with reserves upon which it can draw. The lower-class family not only is restricted in income, but in health, energy, space, and ideas for coping with crisis—owing to its hand-to-mouth existence, it lacks defense in depth. Conversely, the lower-class family with little to lose in the way of prestige or status and little opportunity to climb upward may be able to react more favorably to endangered reputation than can the respectability-focused, middle-class family.

Crisis-Meeting Resources, the B Factor. The vulnerability of the lower-class family, however, is no greater to certain stressor events than that of the middle-class family. Each has its characteristic Achilles heel. Robert C. Angell [7] was the first among family sociologists to seek for the B factor in our equation, a set of resources in family organization which, by their presence or absence, kept the family from crisis or urged it into crisis. His findings go beyond the points of vulnerability identified above by class. He employed two concepts—family integration and family adaptability. By the first he meant the "bonds of coherence and unity running through family life, of which common interests, affection, and a sense of economic interdependence are perhaps the most prominent." By the second he referred to the family's capacity to meet obstacles and shift courses as a family. He was trying to get at the family's latent predisposition to action in the face of challenges to its usual mode of existence. These latent action patterns, which are most clearly observable at times of crisis, are integrated, in turn, by the values held by the family. Angell found it possible to explain the different reactions of crisis-proof and crisis-prone families to sharp decreases in income during the depression by these twin factors of integration and adaptability, with a restudy of the cases suggesting the greater importance of family adaptability.

Cavan and Ranck [8] and Koos [9] used somewhat different concepts but were in essential agreement. To these researchers a crisis-proof

[7] *The Family Encounters the Depression,* Chas. Scribner's Sons, New York, 1936.
[8] R. S. Cavan and K. H. Ranck, *The Family and the Depression,* University of Chicago Press, Chicago, 1938.
[9] Earl L. Koos, *Families in Trouble,* King's Crown Press, New York, 1946.

41

family must have agreement in its role structure, subordination of personal ambitions to family goals, satisfactions within the family obtained because it is successfully meeting the physical and emotional needs of its members, and goals toward which the family is moving collectively. Having all of these, the family is adequately organized. Lacking them, the family is inadequately organized and likely to prove vulnerable to crisis-precipitating events. In both the Cavan-Ranck and Koos studies, the B factor is, in effect, adequacy-inadequacy of family organization.

Social workers have long employed the term "problem family" to designate the crisis-prone family. Early social work viewed problem families primarily as reactors to the conditions of poverty, and saw a shoring up of the economic resources as all-important. Subsequently the shift to a more psychological emphasis established that parents and children in problem families were maladjusted individuals in need of individual treatment. Problem families became not so much victims of a poor distributive order as aggregates of neurotic or psychopathic individuals. More recently the work of Community Research Associates with problem families emphasizes the importance of the distortions of the marital axis, the incompatible combinations of personalities which make for divided and incompetent family headship.[10] Such families are "disorganized" social failures when judged against generally accepted family objectives, and tend to be *multi-problem* families collecting attention and services from public and private agencies all out of proportion to their number in the community.

English researchers have written considerably on problem families, labeling them as deviant, antisocial, and lower class. Irvine [11] stated that "Problem families can be most usefully defined as socially defective families characterized by child neglect and squalor, which defeat current efforts at rehabilitation." Stephens [12] observed that the most obvious common feature of these families is the disorder of their lives. Baldamus and Timms [13] see them as having

[10] *Classification of Disorganized Families for Use in Family Oriented Diagnosis and Treatment,* Community Research Associates, New York, 1954.
[11] Elizabeth E. Irvine, "Research into Problem Families," *British Journal of Psychiatric Social Work,* No. 9 (1954), p. 32.
[12] Tom Stephens, *Problem Families,* William S. Heinman, New York, 1947.
[13] W. Baldamus and Noel Timms, "The Problem Family: A Sociological Approach," *British Journal of Sociology.* Vol. VI, No. 2 (1955), pp. 318–327.

defective standards of behavior: "The more extreme cases of disorganization and inefficiency in problem families approach a situation of retreatism, as defined by Robert Merton. Conformity to established values is virtually relinquished, especially in respect to standards of behavior."

Max Siporin,[14] in summarizing the work on the problem family, has made the cogent observation that present-day American social workers and sociologists, in contrast to our English colleagues, have preferred to concentrate on the process of family maladjustment rather than to focus on the stereotyping of families with the use of such epithets as hard-core, inadequate, and disordered. Behind the use by these Americans of terms like "disorganized" is a theory of disorganization and recovery which they seek to study further. This is evident in the attempt we shall make below to link together crisis-meeting resources of family organization and the definitions the family makes of a stressor event in accounting for it crisis-proneness.

Family Definitions, the C Factor. The C factor in our equation has received attention only recently from students of the family. Hill and Boulding,[15] studying war separation and reunion crises, perceived three possible definitions of the crisis-precipitating event: (1) an *objective* definition, formulated by an impartial observer, (2) a *cultural* definition, formulated by the community, and (3) a *subjective* definition, provided by the family. The most relevant definition in determining a family's crisis-proneness is the third, that provided by the family. The researcher and the community stand outside the situation looking in, but the family members are on the inside, and the family's attitudes toward the event are all-important in this connection.

A family's definition of the event reflects partly the value system held by the family, partly its previous experience in meeting crises, and partly the mechanisms employed in previous definitions of events. This is the *meaning* aspect of the crisis, the interpretation made of it.

Not infrequently families with objective resources adequate to meet the hardships of sickness or job loss crack under the stress be-

14 Max Siporin, "The Concept of the Problem Family," Baylor University College of Medicine, Texas Medical Center, 1956, p. 8 (unpublished).
15 Reuben Hill, *op. cit.*

cause they define such hardship situations as insurmountable. Accident-proneness is disproportionately high among individuals who lack self-confidence and are characterized by anxiety. Crisis-proneness in families also proves related to outlook—to whether or not the event is defined as challenging or crisis-provoking.

Crisis-Proneness, a Function of Both B and C Factors. If we combine deficiency in family organization resources (the B factor) and the tendency to define hardships as crisis-producing (the C factor) into one concept of family inadequacy, we may analyze its major features in a polygon wheel of interacting forces which we reproduce below from the work of Koos and Fulcomer.[16] As they explain it, there is sometimes an initial cause that tends to create tensions in other areas of family life, which, in turn, become conflicts themselves. For example, cultural disparity may cause a lack of sexual satisfaction because of the differing ideas and standards of sex behavior, which in turn may lead to suspicion of the mate and lack of co-operation as breadwinner or homemaker, which in turn may create

[16] Earl L. Koos and David Fulcomer, "Families in Crisis," *Dynamics of Family Interaction*, E. M. Duvall and Reuben Hill (eds.), Women's Foundation, New York, 1948, ch. 8.

A SCHEMA FOR DEPICTING THE INTERPLAY OF STRESSOR EVENT, CONTRIBUTING HARDSHIPS, AND FAMILY RESOURCES IN PRODUCING A FAMILY CRISIS

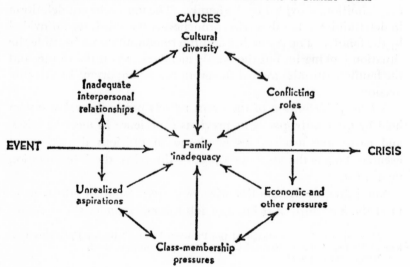

conflicting roles in the family and draw individual members into new positions of responsibility in the family at the expense of other members. The accumulation of these tensions so weakens the affectional relationships and integration of the family as to render it unable to meet even a simple departure from its ordinary life patterns. The result, when an out-of-ordinary event occurs, is a crisis.

Adjustment to Crisis

Koos and Fulcomer's ingenious diagram, if carried another step into the adjustment of the family to the crisis, would reveal again an interplay of many of the same factors reflecting family adequacy-inadequacy which made families prone to crisis originally. Causation is just as complex in adjustment as it is in the definition of, or sensitivity to, crisis.

Adjustment to a crisis that threatens the family depends upon the adequacy of role performance of family members. As we have already shown in our discussion of the conceptual framework, the family consists of a number of members interacting with one another, and each member is ascribed roles to play within the family. The individual functions as a member of the family largely in terms of the expectations that other members place upon him; the family succeeds as a family largely in terms of the adequacy of role performance of its members. One major effect of crisis is to cause changes in these role patterns. Expectations shift, and the family finds it necessary to work out different patterns. In the process the family is slowed up in its affectional and emotion-satisfying performances until the new patterns are worked out and avenues for expressing affection are opened once more.

The Course of Adjustment. What can we say about the course of adjustment to crisis? We know that it varies from family to family and from crisis to crisis, but the common denominator may be charted in the truncated form of a roller-coaster. As a result of meeting a crisis, the family members are collectively numbed by the blow. They may meet friends, at first, as if the blow had not fallen. Then, as the facts are assimilated, there follows a downward slump in organization, roles are played with less enthusiasm, resentments are smothered or expressed, conflicts are expressed or converted into tensions that make for strained relations. As the nadir of disorganization is reached, things begin improving, new routines arrived at by trial-and-error or by thoughtful planning and sacrificing are put into effect, and some minimum agreements about the future are reached. The component parts to the roller-coster profile of adjustment are: crisis→disorganization→recovery→reorganization.

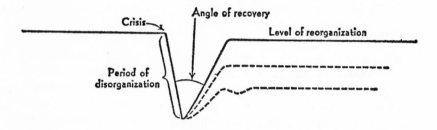

Refinements of this basic pattern have been worked out by Hill [17] on adjustment to war separation and by Jackson [18] on adjustments to alcoholism. Jackson identifies seven stages of adjustment: (1) attempts to deny the problem, (2) attempts to eliminate the problem, (3) disorganization, (4) attempts to reorganize in spite of the problem, (5) efforts to escape the problem: the decision to separate from the alcoholic spouse, (6) reorganization of the family without spouse, (7) reorganization of the entire family. These stages parallel closely the stages of adjustment and recovery to bereavement. An analysis of what happens as the family breaks old habits and organizes new routines during the downhill and uphill part of the roller-coaster figure above shows some interesting changes in family organization.

Generic Effects of Crisis on Family Behavior. In one of the most sensitive areas of family life, the sexual area, sharp changes are noted. The frequency and pattern of sexual relations change, ceasing altogether for some couples. In crises involving interpersonal recriminations, where the crisis is regarded as the fault of any one member, the position of that member is greatly devaluated. Personality changes in members reflect the anxiety and feelings of insecurity engendered by the crisis, and in a sense each responsible member experiences a roller-coaster pattern of personal shock, disorganization, recovery, readjustment. Particularly is this evident in be-

[17] Reuben Hill, *op. cit.*
[18] Joan K. Jackson, "The Adjustment of the Family to Alcoholism," *Marriage and Family Living*, Vol. XVIII, No. 4 (1956) pp. 361–369.

reavement, where the adjustments of family members follow a course of disbelief → numbness → mourning → trial-and-error adjustments → renewal of routines → recovery.

Changes in parent-child relations are frequently reported in adjustment to crisis. In well-integrated families, Angell [19] found few changes in relative position of parents and children as a result of the impoverishment but did find changes in less well-integrated families.

In summarizing the impressions of disaster workers and making inferences from the relatively scanty firsthand information from families experiencing such catastrophes as tornado, hurricane, or flood, we find a confirmation of the roller-coaster pattern at the beginning of the crisis experience. In the immediate recovery period, however, there is an almost euphoric increase in family solidarity (with high solidarity also in the network of neighbors and friends) in the first weeks after the disaster.

Inter-family activities vary as a result of crisis. Some families withdraw from all activities until the "shame"is over and become more than ever closed systems. Others become quite outgoing in their open-window policy during the troubled period.

These are all *short-time* effects of crisis. The evidence concerning the long-time effects of crisis on families is conflicting. Cavan [20] found that, if the families were well organized before the crisis of impoverishment, they tended to remain well organized; moreover, it seemed that previous successful experiences with crisis were predictive of recovery in a new crisis. Angell found well-integrated and adaptable families invulnerable to crisis; that is, they took it in stride without marked changes in their organization or role structure. Helmut Shelsky,[21] studying post-World-War II German families who had experienced severe bombing and the post-war deprivations of denazification and underemployment, found families in general more solid as a consequence. He explains the phenomenon of higher family solidarity as a reaction to the unstable larger society in which home and family are made into a haven from the uncertainty and insecurity of the post-war world. Kent Geiger,[22] studying refugee

[19] Robert C. Angell, *op. cit.*
[20] Cavan and Ranck, *op. cit.*
[21] *Wandlunger in der Deutschen Familien in der Gegenwart*, Enke-Verlag, Stuttgart, 1954.
[22] "Deprivation and Solidarity in the Soviet Urban Family," *American Sociological Review*, Vol. XX, No. 1 (1955), pp. 57–68.

families from the U.S.S.R. in Europe and the U.S., found families that had been terrorized politically by the regime to be more frequently solidified than disorganized by the experience. The impact of economic deprivation on these families, however, was seen to be detrimental to interpersonal solidarity within the family. Thus, from Geiger's study, political persecution appears to be positively, and deterioration of material living conditions to be negatively, related to family unity. Koos, focusing on the troubles of low-income families in New York City over a two-year period, found among those initially disorganized by crisis evidence of permanent demoralization, a blunting of the family's sensitivity, and a tendency to be more vulnerable in future exposures. "Once having been defeated by a crisis, the family appears not to be able to marshal its forces sufficiently to face the next event; there is, in other words, a permanent defeat each time." [23]

If conflicting evidence were reconciled, this synthesis might follow: Successful experience with crisis tests and strengthens a family, but defeat in crisis is punitive on family structure and morale.

Types of Families Best Equipped to Meet Troubles

In this brief discussion of family adjustment to stress, there may be some merit in listing the attributes of family organization, modes of adjustment, and factors making for adjustment which have grown out of the studies of families in crisis and which have been confirmed in an entirely new context by Hill in an analysis of family adjustments to war separation and reunion. In it the findings of earlier studies were treated as hypotheses to be tested in the as-yet-unstudied crises of war separation and reunion. The findings of this analysis divide between factors making for adjustment to crisis and a confirmation of generalizations about modes of adjustment that work out best in the face of crisis (see especially Table 28 in Hill [24]).

Factors Conducive to Good Adjustment to Crisis. Family adaptability, family integration, affectional relations among family members, good marital adjustment of husband and wife, companionable parent-child relationships, family council type of control in decision-making, social participation of wife, and previous successful experi-

---

[23] *Families in Trouble,* King's Crown Press, New York, 1946.
[24] Reuben Hill, *op. cit.*

48

ence with crisis were all confirmed as important factors in enabling families to adjust to crisis.

Rather fully corroborated within the new contexts of war separation and reunion were these generalizations from previous studies:

1. Crisis-proneness, the tendency to define troubles as crises, is distributed disproportionately among families of low family adequacy.
2. The course of adjustment is a roller-coaster pattern of disorganization—recovery—readjustment (corroborated as modal pattern for separation but not for reunion).
3. Family reactions to crisis divide between short-time immediate reactions and secondary long-time adjustments.
4. Demoralization following a crisis usually stems from incipient demoralization before the crisis.
5. The length of time a family continues to be disorganized as a result of crisis is inversely related to its adequacy of organization.
6. Unadaptable and unintegrated families are most likely of all to be unpredictable deviants in adjusting to crisis.
7. Foreknowledge and preparation for a critical event mitigates the hardships and improves the chances for recovery.
8. The effects of crisis on families may be punitive or strengthening depending on the margin of health, wealth, and adequacy possessed by the family.

Implications for Agency Policies and Practice

My statement of implication for agency policies and practices is offered most tentatively. It attempts to answer two questions: (1) How does research on families under stress change our views of family organizational needs? (2) How might practices be changed in line with these needs?

Family Organizational Needs

We find families increasingly vulnerable as they are shorn of kin, neighbors, and friends. Centered as they are about the husband and wife and their one or two children, modern American families are highly mobile, precariously small, and poorly structured units to survive life's stresses—death, unemployment, war separations, infidelity, desertion, and so on.

The goal of self-sufficiency, of families' being capable of surviving by themselves, may have had some merit in pioneer days when the family groups were large and included several relatives besides the children. Today the myth of family self-sufficiency requires dis-

49

crediting. To replace it we bring the concept of interdependence of families within communities. This concept will need to be implemented in our communities with appropriate organization, to be sure, if it is to have any meaning to people.

In my war-separation study the families who adjusted least well and most slowly were frequently solitary families characterized by past mobility and transiency, or they were families whose relationships with relatives and neighbors had become tenuous. In either case, these families lacked the nests of supporting families with which to share their troubles and were, therefore, forced to live *alone* in an enforced anonymity. Left to their own devices, crisis-stricken families in a new neighborhood withdraw into their narrow family circles and fester inwardly rather than risk being rebuffed.

Several studies have offered evidence that families whose economic well-being is marginal are more vulnerable to crisis. Koos [25] eloquently portrays the marginality of living in such families:

As the investigator strips off the outer layers of low-income urban existence he becomes increasingly aware of its hand-to-mouth quality. Only the things that must be done managed to get done. There are no sheltered reservoirs within which man can store up his surplus thoughts, energies and products— and not surprisingly, because for people living under these conditions there are no surplus thoughts and energies and products. They need all of their energies and every cent they can earn in order to meet the day-by-day demands, and they know that their environment will make endless demands upon them whichever way they turn. Life under such conditions takes on a nip-and-tuck urgency that belies our culture's middle-class *ethos* of a reasoned calculation of one's future.

Individuals and whole families of individuals suffer from these pressures. Housewives lament that they can buy only for the next meal because there is no place in which to store additional foods. Wage earners know that every cent they make is mortgaged in advance simply to keep up with basic expenditures, and they curse and worry because they cannot save for a rainy day. Adolescent girls have no place in which to entertain the "boy friend" because home offers no opportunity for privacy. Only the youngest members of the family can dawdle and dream beyond life's immediacies, and they, too, suffer indirectly.

Implications for Family Services Needed

The high mobility of young families results in feelings of "aloneness" as they move into new communities or join the stream moving out of the central city into the suburbs. Separated from kin and home-town neighbors, to whom do they turn for counsel and help when

[25] Earl L. Koos, *op. cit.*

they want to spill their troubles? How do they become integrated into a new neighborhood or community? The challenge for social work is to develop institutions less commercial than the "welcome wagon" and more neighborhood oriented. We need community organization and neighborhood development activities in this direction, such as Milwaukee supported in its department of health for a time. We need to institutionalize the status of "newcomers" and utilize it to provide orientation and welcoming activities into neighborhood and community.

It is noteworthy that those families that best succeeded in meeting the crisis of war-time separation made frequent mention of the accessibility of relatives, neighbors, and friends. They rarely mentioned, we are sad to report, the churches, the family agencies, or other welfare groups that claim in their annual bid for contributions from the community that they provide services of this kind to families in trouble.

In shaping a community program that is more family-centered, we need to face the fact that many families that once received help and comfort from kin and neighbors have now lost contact with them and live in anonymity. We must recognize that their problems are often such that they do not know which, if any, social agency could or would help if asked. We need to reorganize our agency offerings to meet families at their own level of need. As we have seen the need among the families in the studies reviewed here, help might often have consisted simply of providing an opportunity to ventilate their anxieties, share their woes, and ask for reassuring, simple advice about problems occasioned by the absence of the husband and father, or the changed regulations for children attending schools in double shifts. There are, at the present time, few agencies to which families willingly turn for help on the more superficial levels of life.

Even if social workers were willing to extend such superficial services broadly, there are only a few hundred family service agencies in the entire United States, and marriage counseling services are limited to the metropolitan centers and to a few college campuses. The professional services for nonindigent families in trouble must be drawn mainly from the family physician, the teacher, the minister, the family lawyer, and the occasional child welfare worker with the public welfare department. To these professionals, the following suggestions from the researches I have summarized appear justified:

1. Professional services will make their greatest contribution if

they are made with the total family context in mind. Particularly is this true in crises of dismemberment and demoralization.

2. Families, like combat teams and other collectivities, have a morale and *esprit de corps* to maintain if they are to be effective. Physicians have found that illnesses that yesterday were called psychosomatic are today regarded as products of family aggravations.

The helping professionals will need to approximate family group workers, serving the child's family *as a family* rather than serving the child solely as a personality. This involves becoming an artist in relationship therapy, keeping all the family relationships healthy.

3. Families need to be kept intact and relatively self-sustaining.

Both war separations and peacetime separations render a net disservice to most families, although many ride them out successfully. Voluntary separations should not be undertaken without serious thought as to the consequences. Employers should know that transferring an employee to a position in a distant community where tight housing prevents his taking the family along is doing the employee a serious disservice. However, if separation is forced upon the family, our research shows that it is much more easily assimilated if prepared for well in advance. Making this fact known widely may greatly mitigate the untoward effects of separation because of employment, hospitalization, institutionalization, and so on.

4. Counseling and casework become patchwork remedies unless a strong program of preventive social work and education is undertaken by agencies.

We know that families of various types are capable of meeting crises, that we do not have to stamp out uniform models. Successful families, however, share the resources of good marital adjustment, family adaptability, and, to a lesser degree, family integration. Their communicative lines must be kept open through frank discussions and the use of the consultative process in arriving at family decisions. Caseworkers will see the challenge to train young people, and they will seize the opportunity through parent education to reach young parents, to encourage the development of patterns of family organization which make for survival in the face of trouble. To date, few programs have attempted, even experimentally, to produce students competent to exercise family leadership in flexible family organizations of this sort. Here lies the challenge of preventive social work and family life education of tomorrow.

4. A Framework for Studying Families in Crisis*

Howard J. Parad
and *Gerald Caplan*

WHAT IS FAMILY diagnosis? If we agree that it is more than a listing of individual-centered clinical observations, we immediately encounter many technical problems, for we find ourselves dealing
with a complicated field of forces requiring a three-dimensional
perspective that involves not only *intra*personal but also *inter*personal and *supra*personal (or "transactional") processes. Recognizing the family's strategic importance in human life, investigators
in social work and social psychiatry have shown increasing interest
in grappling with these problems. Consequently the development
of a multifaceted formulation for describing and classifying the
dynamics of family behavior has attracted a good deal of attention
in recent professional literature.[1] The purpose of this paper is

* Reprinted from *Social Work*, Vol. 5, No. 3 (1960). This article is based on the
pilot phase of a research project financed by the Commonwealth Fund and conducted by the Harvard School of Public Health Family Guidance Center at the
Whittier Street Health Center of the City of Boston Health Department. The
authors are pleased to acknowledge the help they have received from the other
members of the multidisciplinary research team of the Family Guidance Center
at the Harvard School of Public Health: Barbara Ayres, Ph.D., anthropologist;
Paul A. Hare, Ph.D., sociologist; Edward A. Mason, M.D., psychiatrist; Mary Foster, A.M., R.N., public health nurse; Thomas Plaut, Ph.D., M.P.H., psychologist;
and Harold Stalvey, M.D., psychiatrist.

[1] See, for example, "Family Casework in the Interest of Children," report of
an interdisciplinary conference, *Social Casework*, Vol. XXXIX, Nos. 2–3 (1958);
Viola W. Weiss and Russell R. Monroe, "A Framework for Understanding Fam-
ily Dynamics," *Social Casework*, Vol. XL, Nos. 1 and 2 (1959), pp. 3–9, 80–87;
Gerald Caplan, ed., *Emotional Disorders of Early Childhood*, Basic Books, New
York, 1955, pp. 155–156; Nathan W. Ackerman, *Psychodynamics of the Family*,
Basic Books, New York, 1958; John P. Spiegel and Florence R. Kluckhohn,
Integration and Conflict in Family Behavior, Group for the Advancement of
Psychiatry, Topeka, Kansas, 1954. Especially pertinent is a critique of recent
literature on this subject by John P. Spiegel and Norman W. Bell, "The Family
of the Psychiatric Patient," *American Handbook of Psychiatry*, Basic Books, New
York, 1959, pp. 114–149.

to outline a theoretical framework found useful in a study of family functioning in its relationship to mental health. Our report will focus on the mental health implications of the mechanisms that families characteristically use to solve the problems of a crisis situation. Part I will introduce our broad conceptual framework; Part II will demonstrate the use of this framework through a case analysis of a family experiencing a serious crisis situation.

The project from which our observations are taken has served the twin goals of (1) investigating how best to integrate a mental health program within an operating public health unit,[2] and (2) studying how families cope with selected stress situations (prematurity, congenital abnormality, and tuberculosis) commonly encountered and routinely reported in public health programs. The reconnaissance phase has included exploratory investigations in fifty cases involving these stress categories.

A word should be said about the setting in which this interdisciplinary research operation took place. We were routinely introduced to our study families by the public health nurse with whom we had the dual role of mental health consultant and research collaborator.[3] The nurse continued in her ordinary role with the family while we carried on our investigation of the family's perception of and response to the crisis situation.

By design, we used what Bowlby calls a "current" rather than a "retrospective" study approach.[4] We found that useful information about the crisis could be obtained only by interviewing the family while it was actively engaged in its coping efforts. Retrospective accounts of crisis events were typically colored by tremendous distortions. Family members were interviewed individually and in groups, often at mealtime or while engaged in household or child care tasks. From time to time, with the family's permission, interviews were tape-recorded for detailed subsequent analysis. Although the interviewing style was informal and unstructured, data were systematically accumulated in terms of the following major categories:

---

[2] For a detailed exposition of this phase of the program, see M. B. Hamovitch *et al.*, "Establishment and Maintenance of a Mental Health Unit," *Mental Hygiene*, Vol. 43, No. 3 (1959), pp. 412–421.

[3] *Ibid.*, p. 420.

[4] John Bowlby, *Maternal Care and Mental Health*, World Health Organization, Geneva, 1952, p. 15.

1. Identifying information
2. Dynamic description of individual family members
3. Primary medical stress
4. Attendant and secondary stresses
5. Relationships among family members
6. Relationships with persons outside the family
7. Family activities
8. Relationships between the family and the Family Guidance Center
9. Solution to the problem

The last category, intended as an analysis of the family's adaptive and maladaptive responses to the problem, is based on summary data contained in the other eight categories.

In all but a few experimental cases, every effort was made to keep our therapeutic intervention to a minimum during the crisis period. However, since it was obviously impossible to be the proverbial "fly on the wall," interviews inevitably provided a certain amount of nonspecific emotional support. In a few instances some degree of therapeutic contact was necessary in order to maintain a meaningful research relationship.

I. CONCEPTUAL FRAMEWORK

From time immemorial novelists and dramatists have stressed the significance of crisis periods in determining the fate of individuals and groups. The element that makes for dramatic excitement is the fact that crises have a peak or sudden turning point, and as this peak approaches, tension rises and stimulates the mobilization of previously hidden strengths and capacities. Similarly, in our day-to-day clinical work we have long been impressed by the significance of periods of life crisis, which in the early stages of illness seem to determine its direction.[5] However, our present knowledge of the extremely intricate relationship between family functioning and mental health bristles with methodological and conceptual difficulties. We are therefore still at a reconnaissance stage, where the most we can expect is to isolate useful questions and promising avenues of exploration rather than to aim for definitive answers.

[5] Gerald Caplan, "An Approach to the Study of Family Mental Health," *U.S. Public Health Reports*, Vol. 71, No. 10 (1956), p. 1027.

When we evaluate mental health or ill health, we are implicitly or explicitly making a rating of an individual's equilibrium in adapting to his environment. Among the important criteria for this rating we include such factors as the individual's ability to (1) initiate and maintain satisfying emotional relationships with others, (2) work productively and fulfill inner resources, (3) perceive reality undistorted by fantasies, and (4) adapt to his environment if this is conducive to his welfare, or (5) change the environment, when not conducive to his welfare, in a way that impinges minimally upon the rights of others.

This equilibrium is kept stable by a complicated series of re-equilibrating or homeostatic mechanisms operating on both the intrapsychic and interpersonal levels.[6] A crisis is a period of disequilibrium overpowering the individual's homeostatic mechanisms. During a crisis a person is faced by a problem which, on the one hand, is of basic importance to him because it is linked with his fundamental instinctual needs, and on the other, cannot be solved quickly by means of his normal range of problem-solving mechanisms.[7] In this connection it is important to stress that conflict and unhappiness are not synonymous with mental ill health; [8] in fact, at the appropriate time and place the presence of conflict and unhappiness is a criterion of mental health. For example, the misery of mourning and the anxiety and tension of dealing with role transition or any demanding learning experience would be accepted by most of us as unpleasant emotions that inevitably accompany healthy ego adaptation. We must also beware of cultural and countertransference biases in evaluating patterns of family functioning as "healthy" or "unhealthy" without very clear reference to their effects on individual family members.

Hazardous life events likely to induce crisis reactions as defined by these two broad criteria—basic importance combined with difficulty of solution by familiar methods—include such commonly encountered stresses as pregnancy, birth, death, important role transitions (for example, entering school, acquiring a new job, or getting married), incapacitating illness, and a wide variety of

6 John P. Spiegel, "The Resolution of Role Conflict Within the Family," *Psychiatry*, Vol. 20, No. 1 (1957), p. 9.
7 Caplan, "An Approach to the Study of Family Mental Health," *op. cit.*, p. 1027.
8 For an interesting elaboration of this principle, see Marie Jahoda, *Current Concepts in Positive Mental Health*, Basic Books, New York, 1958, pp. 18–21.

other happenings. Such problems demand solutions that are often novel in the light of the individual's previous life experience. [9] During the period of disorganization normally associated with crisis, old conflicts, symbolically linked with the present problem, are revived. As we know from clinical experience, the way in which the "old" conflict was resolved influences the ego's method of adaptation to the current stress. By the same token, however, adaptive responses to the new stress often produce mentally healthy solutions to hitherto unresolved problems. Thus, clinical experience abounds with examples of individuals and families who "rise to the occasion" when confronted with crisis, thereby not only successfully mastering the exigencies of the current stressful situation, but also dealing more adequately with long-standing conflicts that had been suppressed or repressed.

In our framework for the study of the family in crisis, we find it useful to assemble and analyze data under the following basic classifications: (1) *family life-style,* which refers to the reasonably stable patterning of family organization, subdivided into three interdependent elements of value system, communication network, and role system; (2) *intermediate problem-solving mechanisms,* which represent the family life-style in action in a situational crisis context that calls forth the family's effort for coping with stress; and (3) *need-response pattern,* which describes the ways in which the family as a group perceives, respects, and satisfies the basic needs of its individual members.

Family Life-Style

When the family faces a stressful event, its life-style places at its disposal a range of problem-solving possibilities from which the family members individually and collectively may choose according to their perception of the demands of the situation. As we have said, the essence of a crisis is that the situation cannot be easily handled by the family's commonly used problem-solving mechanisms, but forces the employment of novel patterns. These are necessarily within the range of the family's capacities, but may be patterns never called into operation in the past. Our analysis is complicated by the fact that the new solution, after a period of consolidation, may be-

[9] See Spiegel, "The Resolution of Role Conflict Within the Family," *op. cit.,* p. 15.

come a stable part of everyday functioning, thereby altering the family's future life-style.[10]

For our purposes, *values* refer to the system of ideas, attitudes, and beliefs which consciously and unconsciously bind together the members of a family in a common culture. This configuration automatically defines the meaning of certain critical situations and at the same time suggests ways of reacting to them. It provides definitions of the time dimension, contains concepts concerning the responsibility and worth of individual members of the family, points to certain commonly held life goals, imposes a framework within which the pursuit of—and risks connected with—the pleasure impulse takes place, and involves a system of sanctions.

Our second major grouping in characterizing the life-style of a family is the patterning of *roles*. This patterning provides for a definition of what is to be done in a family (obviously influenced by the system of values), who is to do it, and who is to decide on allocation of tasks (leadership). Role-patterning make provision for carrying out family tasks on the basis of age, sex, and personality traits; it also provides sanctions for dealing with the neglect or poor performance of agreed-upon tasks, thus including the authority functions of the family.

The third dimension, *communication,* is a network for carrying messages and transmitting information, feelings, ideas, among the various family members of the nuclear family (internal communication) as well as between the family and the outside community (external communication). It includes definitions as to which messages are perceived as worth transmitting (again very much influenced by the value system) and provision of channels for transmission (word symbols, body behavior, gestures).

Intermediate Problem-Solving Mechanisms

When we refer to the intermediate problem-solving mechanisms triggered by the actual impact of crisis, the word "intermediate" emphasizes the temporary, dynamic nature of processes in flux as compared with the more stable equilibrium of the life-style. Although

[10] Hence the familiar observation that some families emerge from crises as stronger and more effective units, while others become weaker and still others become dismembered. See Earl Koos, *Families in Trouble,* King's Crown Press, New York, 1946, and Reuben Hill, *Families Under Stress,* Harper & Brothers, New York, 1949, which has differential examples of stress profiles.

certain family life-styles may be clearly seen as conductive to mental ill health, in that the group may actively overburden or inadequately satisfy the emotional needs of some of its members, in many cases what happens is that the life-style merely affords greater or lesser opportunities for such a state to develop. Whether it develops or not will be determined by the choices made during crisis periods. The current factors influencing maladaptive choices are, therefore, of crucial concern.

During the period when new solutions are being worked out, certain patterns can be recognized in which tension is reduced for the family as a group, but at the emotional expense of one or more individual members. This can happen in two main ways: *passively,* by *emotional neglect* through concentrating family energies in such a way that the needs of an individual are not attended to, though the details of his own role may not be important in reducing tension; and *actively,* by the *emotional exploitation* of a family member through investing him with a role which does violence to his needs as an individual.

In such cases we have observed that the emotional problem facing the family was not handled in terms of group action—whether because of poor leadership, disorders of internal communication, or other organizational inefficiencies. Thus the group could not augment the sum of the capacities of its individual members, or, still worse, even reduced its combined strengths by dissipation of effort. The exploitation mechanism, serving an important purpose in each family member's psychic economy, reduced group tension by allowing displacement of individual anxieties or ventilation of guilt in relation to an object acceptable to the value system of the family. We are beginning to tease out the factors which cause one or more family members to be singled out by the rest of the group for exploitation in this manner. The Adams case, presented on page 61, is a vivid example of the use of emotional exploitation as an intermediate problem-solving mechanism.

To sum up, the intermediate mechanisms refer to the family's problem-solving efforts through various transactional, interactional, and intrapersonal methods for adapting to and dealing with the emotional difficulties associated with stress situations—in this case Mrs. A's tuberculosis and absence from the home. At some point in time, the use of these mechanisms produces certain re-equilibrating forces, which in turn may bring about (to use Spiegel's term) a "novel solution" to the problem. It is at this point on the time continuum that we say that one significant phase of the crisis is ended, and introduce our third area of inquiry, namely, the mental health of the individual member of the family as measured by the need-response pattern.

Need-Response Pattern

The *need-response pattern* provides a dynamic assessment of the mental health of an individual family member within the context of family interaction processes, thus furnishing a conceptual link between family functioning and the health of the individual. Certain types of basic needs may be considered relevant to mental health—such as (1) love for one's own sake, (2) a balance between support and independence with respect to tasks, (3) a balance between freedom and control with respect to instinctual expression, and (4) the availability of suitable role models. In analyzing the response to these categories of need expression, we are impressed by the importance of three separate and interlocking phases: the *perception* of the needs of the individual by other family members and by the culture of the family, the *respect* accorded to these needs as being worthy of attention, and the *satisfaction* of such needs to the extent possible in the light of family resources.

We are aware that evaluation of this triad of perception, respect, and satisfaction is very much influenced by sociocultural factors, since it is based upon our own views of the individual as a separate person in his own right, worthy of a measure of recognition and respect as well as an equitable share in the family's resources. Clearly, these criteria have to be judged differently in a different culture; modifications are also necessary from one socioeconomic class to another.

Assessment of need-response. The need-response pattern, which may be altered during a period of crisis, is an instrument for assessing the family's solution of the problem in terms of the mental health of its members. In elaborating its use we have explored a number of different methods of assessment in order to use it as a definable consequent factor in evaluating the mental health outcome of the family's intermediate problem-solving efforts. For example, we tried various types of systematic time-sample observations. Records were bracketed into interaction units, coded into need categories, and rated by independent judges. Using an adaptation of the Bales method,[11] reliability reached 0.80 to 0.90 after a short training period. However, this and similar methods proved uneconomical and unwieldly, and we still doubted whether we could place any more confidence in the validity of these ratings than those derived from our usual processes of clinical inference.

After a good deal of experimentation, we decided upon a short-cut approach based on over-all clinical impressions. After each interview, the interviewer recorded his clinical judgment of the need-response pattern of each family member, based on inferences from verbal content and behavior of interpersonal significance. Frequent checks on these ratings were made on interview records and summaries by other staff members. These procedures enabled us to make satisfactory judgments about significant changes in need-response patterns.

During the crisis period there are often temporary shifts in the need-response pattern. We do not believe that temporary periods of low need-response are necessarily harmful to mental health. However, persistent need frustration is likely to endanger the future mental health of a given family member, and even "temporary" low need-response is likely to have an important effect on an individual's future mental health if it takes place because the individual is peculiarly vulnerable at a critical phase of development. One further caveat should be mentioned. Need-response material must always be evaluated very critically because of the possibility that signs of frustration are being covered up by adaptive reactions with the passage of time, so that at the stage where they would be most significant to judgments on the danger to future mental health, they may be absent. We must also realize that signs of emotional upset may be coincidental and due to causes other than need-frustration within the family under study.

For reasons of simplicity, the need-response pattern will be discussed for only one member of our illustrative family.

II. CASE ANALYSIS

Our case example in demonstrating this conceptual framework involves the Adams family, who were studied intensively for over a

[11] See Robert F. Bales, *Interaction Process Analysis,* Addison-Wesley Press, Cambridge, Mass., 1950.

year. Our summary, extracted from a wealth of data, unavoidably excludes diagnostically rich life history material, neighborhood and extended kinship group affiliations, projective test data, and a great deal of medical and psychiatric information. Because of space limitations our analysis is focused on the interpersonal and transactional levels, although this is in no way intended to minimize the importance of individual psychological determinants.

Mr. A, a white 39-year-old factory worker, has a wife, age 37, suffering from tuberculosis, and three children: Alice, 14, Susan, 11, Jackie, 8. They were a fairly happy, stable family until Mrs. A's illness. A year prior to our introduction to the family by the public health nurse, Mrs. A had been admitted to a sanatorium with a diagnosis of pulmonary tuberculosis, but had discharged herself against medical advice after a few months' treatment. During the following months she remained at home and resisted the nurse's attempts to induce her to attend the health center for X-rays or treatment. Her physical condition proceeded—at first gradually and later rapidly—to deteriorate, the home became disorganized, and Mr. A and the children became quite miserable. Finally the nurse made direct contact with Mr. A and stimulated him to take effective action. He brought his wife to the clinic for a diagnostic work-up, despite her protests, and saw to it that she returned to the sanatorium, as was urgently recommended by the physician. She was admitted in July, in a state of physical and mental exhaustion. Two weeks later she developed epileptiform seizures, and a tuberculoma of the brain was suspected. In late September she developed tubercular meningitis and nearly died. She was given a new type of drug therapy and by mid-October began to show an almost miraculous recovery. Her subsequent improvement has been steady and uneventful.

We shall now discuss the life-style of the A family in the light of three interrelated factors—values, roles, and communication—which will be separated for purposes of convenient analysis.

Life-Style of the Adams Family

Value System. The value system of the A family involves a mixture of prevailing American lower- and middle-class attitudes. The time orientation of the family emphasizes the present: "Let the future take care of itself—especially in time of trouble." This aspect of family structure favors the use of group denial mechanisms in dealing with future events likely to imply present pain, thus controlling the leakage of anxiety in the family social system. In accordance with this orientation, the family's consumption pattern encourages impulsive purchases producing long-term indebtedness.

Humor is an important part of the family's culture. Teasing, joking, and good-natured ridicule are regularly used in a predictable manner for masking certain kinds of direct emotional expression which the family would find threatening and therefore shuns. Feelings calling forth these defensive maneuvers for which free emotional outlets are unavailable include: (1) anxiety, (2) dependence, and (3) deeper levels of aggression. Attempts at emotional expression in these threatening areas are likely to elicit from the family as a whole responses such as, "You're a character," "cry-baby" (for crying or admitting fear), "jerk" (for directly asking for emotional support not connected with a specific task—for example, feeling lonely, missing mother, being unsure of one's identity). Jackie, the 8-year-old boy, whose behavior became quite threatening to the family during the crisis period, was often the target of much of this name-calling. With respect to the expression of dependency needs, positive value is attached to *not* asking for help with basic life goals outside the day-to-day routine of the family—such as help from the outside community involving advice, financial assistance, comfort and consolation.

The family's general life-style places a premium on the worth and value of children. Despite the emphasis on gratification of their own pleasure needs, both Mr. and Mrs. A have indicated their willingness to make sacrifices. The children, especially the girls, know they are loved and appreciated as persons in their own right and do not appear to have any major doubts about their importance in the family scheme. During previous periods of trouble the affectional ties between parents and children had been strengthened, thus underscoring the family's importance as a nest to protect its members against an outside world often regarded as harsh and unyielding.

Fair play is an important part of the family code. Although the children are free to express superficial resentments and criticisms, the parents place high value on "not squealing." Most everyday sins of omission and commission are easily forgiven and forgotten. However, feelings about underlying instinctual needs—for example, fears of desertion—are expressed in symbolic terms only, thus producing defensive formations which encapsulate underlying emotional problems, simultaneously holding the family in stable equilibrium.

Role Pattern. This system of values permeates the family definition of roles. In general, in the pre-crisis picture, the pattern of defining tasks, assigning them, and carrying them out had been rather loose and fluid but still functioned as part of a stable and workable system. A high degree of complementarity is manifested in the willingness to work together on the spur of the moment when a member of the family needs help with a specific task. Despite the over-all flexibility of the role pattern we can delineate broadly the typical role performance of the members of the family. For reasons of space, however, we shall concentrate on Mr. A's role position.

As the source of authority in the family, Mr. A is expected to take over in matters of discipline, which usually involves tongue-lashings and impulsive physical punishment. He is also clearly cast in the role of breadwinner, since Mrs. A has not worked since their marriage. There is no doubt in the minds of the family members that when they violate the fair play code they will be lectured or punished by their father. It is equally clear that after the punishment the matter will be forgotten. During periods of trouble it is taken for granted that Mr. A will assume responsibility for meeting the expressive needs of the children. This role flexibility—an important structural feature for survival in crisis—provides an automatic temporary method for filling the vacuum created by the mother's absence. It permits the family to retain its equilibrium and keep tensions reasonably under control. Because of Mr. A's willingness to take up the slack, he has earned, both from his wife and children, considerable respect for his role as father and for his own needs when he, too, is temporarily thrown off balance.

The most important expectation in the role performance of the children is that they supply gratification to the parents. This is linked with the parents' personal dependency needs. The parents gain support from their relationships with the children in erasing some of the hurt, loneliness, and bitterness that are residual feelings from their own childhood experiences. Role-patterning, then, is highly influenced by psychodynamic factors. For example, both Mr. and Mrs. A have "guilty feelings" about expecting too much of the children—"They are only kids, what can you expect?" This aspect of role determination makes it difficult for Mr. A, during the crisis, to distribute appropriately and effectively the physical and emotional burdens resulting from the mother's absence from the home, thus demonstrating how one aspect of family life-style obviously influences intermediate problem-solving behavior during the crisis period.

A final aspect of role distribution is especially important in the light of what later happens to Jackie. Since the family's expectation is that a small boy cannot do much to help, he is not given any regular chores. Even during the pre-crisis period, Jackie was stereotyped by his mother as a "character" or "bandit"; these epithets were used to mask her feeling that the child was not getting enough attention or love. Because of this feeling, it was considered unfair to expect much of him. He was therefore deprived of a good deal of training in instinctual control and was given too much freedom to roam recklessly about the neighborhood.

Communication Network. The internal communication network of the family provides open channels for free interchange of all pleasant and gratifying news. All members of the family are normally talkative, particularly about happy tidings: for example, gifts, vacations, celebrations, good grades in school, special delicacies, information about mother's progress, jokes, and humorous neighborhood episodes. On the other hand, the communication network is much more restrictive in relation to unpleasant or anxiety-laden situations. The communication between Mr. and Mrs. A, for example, at the time of her initial discharge against advice, is a clear example of the kind of nonverbal contact associated with unpleasant occurrences. At that time Mr. and Mrs. A had been longing for each other but had concealed their feelings of loneliness through an unspoken agreement to displace painful emotions on external events.

The same attitude about communication of painful experiences pervades the family's perception of other separation phenomena. For example, feelings about a couch used by Mrs. A during periods of illness were expressed symbolically rather than through direct statements. During the initial period of Mrs. A's second hospitalization no member of the family would sit on her "spot" on the couch, because to do so would acknowledge the mother's separation from the home, which in turn would trigger feelings of anxiety. When the couch was finally moved, we observed a new kind of communication in motion, thus indicating a beginning state of readiness to be confronted with the reality of the mother's separation and its meaning for the family.

According to the family's democratic ethic, any member is free to originate a message or transmit information—subject to certain ground rules. The message to be conveyed must obviously be harmonious with the family's value and role patterns. This is, of course, true of any social system which is a going concern, the parts of which must be well integrated. We see dramatic examples during the crisis period when Jackie repeatedly shouts, "I want my mother! I miss my mother!" When he openly expresses feelings tabooed by the family system, communication barriers are erected, immediately obstructing further discussion. On several occasions Jackie was attacked by other members of the family who told him quite forcefully, "Shut up!" Consequently, a good deal of aggressive affect is discharged somatically, that is, through body gestures, transitory functional symptoms, and guttural noises.

The Impact of Crisis

Using the life-style of the family as a backdrop against which the crisis drama takes place, it is now appropriate to consider our definition of the meaning and signs of crisis as applied to the A family. We shall mention briefly five related aspects of the perceptual meaning of crisis to the family.

1. *The stressful event poses a problem which is by definition insoluble in the immediate future.* The stress of tuberculosis and hospitalization is obviously beyond the control of the family as a group. The family has no knowledge of the probable duration and outcome of Mrs. A's illness.

2. *The problem overtaxes the psychological resources of the family, since it is beyond their traditional problem-solving methods.* Despite their previous experiences with the same stress, at the crisis peak they verbalize feelings of helplessness because they cannot do anything about the mother's illness. They can only wait, hope, pray for a change—and trust the doctors! The problem is so massive that it overtaxes traditional problem-solving mechanisms such as avoidance, denial, suppression, and masking of feelings. Because of its very enormity it cannot be pushed out of awareness.

3. *The situation is perceived as a threat or danger to the life goals of the family members.* Mrs. A obviously perceives herself in danger

of dying when she urges her husband to promise to look out for the children. Mr. A is threatened by the realization that his much-cherished goal of family integrity is endangered when, near panic, he blurts out, "Everything is going down the drain!"

4. *The crisis period is characterized by tension which mounts to a peak, then falls.* Tension reaches a peak in October, when a guarded prognosis is offered concerning Mrs. A's condition. Falling as the family begins to cope with the problem, it rises again in response to attendant stresses (such as Jackie's runaway episode in November), but does not again reach such a high level during the period under study.

5. Perhaps of the greatest importance, *the crisis situation awakens unresolved key problems from both near and distant past.* Mr. A's response to stress indicates, for example, a frightening reawakening of feelings of object loss associated with the death of his mother. Mrs. A's illness also evokes in him hitherto suppressed guilt feelings: "I messed up my life—didn't plan things properly." At the peak of stress, referring to ancient problems connected with earlier experiences, he groans in a tormented way, "I worked all my life and what have I got? Nothing!" Grinding hostility toward Mrs. A, previously held in check, finally emerges in full force: "I could shove my fist right down her throat!"

For the family as a whole, too, Mrs. A's illness and absence reactivate group problems of unfulfilled dependency needs and unexpressed aggression.

Intermediate Problem-Solving Mechanisms Used by the A Family

Having established that the stress of tuberculosis is in fact a crisis-producing event, we now come to a brief discussion of the family life-style in action during the actual crisis period. The following is a highly compressed summary of how Mr. A and his children reacted to the impact of crisis, with particular reference to Jackie. The family's reactions are divided into three stages, overlapping along a time continuum. The first stage begins in July and continues until early September when Mrs. A's condition worsened. The second stage continues through early November and covers the period when Mrs. A nearly died and then began to recover; and the third stage coincides with her subsequent progressive improvement.

67

First Stage. July to early September. The initial response of Mr. A and his daughters to the hospitalization of Mrs. A is to defend themselves against the emotional implications of the problem. They deny feelings of anxiety for her welfare or pain at her absence, and in fact pretend to be relieved of the burden of caring for her. Their expressed attitude is a rather affected one of "good riddance to bad rubbish." They do not speak much to one another about her, and for the first two weeks Mr. A does not even visit her in the sanatorium. Mrs. A is, then, superficially extruded from the family group.

The housework is managed rather ineffectively by Mr. A and the girls. The home is even more untidy than it had been during the last few months when the mother had been seriously ill and had refused to visit the public health clinic.

On the day of the mother's admission to the sanatorium Jackie is sent for a few weeks to Mrs. A's parents, where he is not visited by other members of the family. Later he is brought home. He is quite miserable, cries profusely, freely proclaims his longing for his mother and his fears that "the doctors will kill her." The rest of the family, reacting with complete lack of sympathy to these outbursts, begin to show extreme hostility. They shout at him and beat him at the least provocation. They let him wander around the neighborhood without supervision and treat him as an outcast and a pest. At the beginning of this period Mr. A and his younger daughter, Susan, show some consideration for Jackie, but by the middle of it nobody has a kind word for him. In Mr. A's words, "The girls help me a bit in the house but Jackie's only job is to worry me."

Jackie in turn responds to being made the scapegoat with increasing misery and rebellion. He runs away from home on two occasions, overeats in a disgustingly gluttonous way calculated to provoke more hostility from the family, and begins to steal pennies from Susan's bank, no doubt to compensate for inner feelings of emptiness, but at the same time engendering more hostility from the group.

In this stage we see the family defending itself against its emotional problem by various denial mechanisms and relieving its unexpressed tension through focusing hostility and anxiety on Jackie, whose age and sex prevent him from taking over any of the absent mother's roles and whose uninhibited expression of feelings threatens the defenses of the other family members. Jackie's needs are being intensively frustrated, and he reacts in a characteristic rebellious way which aggravates the situation in a vicious spiral.

Second Stage. Early September to early November. During this stage the members of the family, individually and as a group, show signs of confronting their feelings about the mother's illness. They begin to talk to each other about the danger to her life and about how much they miss her in the home. They begin to show overt signs of anxiety, to weep, to suffer from sleeplessness and poor concentration. And they begin to support and comfort each other. These reactions reach a peak at the end of September, when it seems that Mrs. A is at death's door. At the crisis peak Mr. A, suddenly challenged to mobilize his latent strengths, becomes more effective as a leader in directing the activities of the household. He allots housekeeping tasks to the two girls; they carry out his instructions willingly, and the home becomes much tidier.

Simultaneously, Mr. A and the girls diminish their harassing behavior toward Jackie. They scold and beat him less and occasionally comfort him when he cries for his mother. He runs away from home during this period, and though he is soundly whipped upon his return, his father and sisters verbalize a good deal of anxiety for his welfare while he is lost.

It appears that the increasing danger to Mrs. A's life during this period overpowers the family's defensive denial of their complex of emotional problems. Their tension is then released through abreaction of anxiety and mutual support and reassurance. They no longer need to relieve tension by resorting to a scapegoat mechanism, and Jackie's direct expression of feeling no longer threatens them. Also, the strengths of the family are mobilized by the increasing threat of Mrs. A's deteriorating condition.

Third Stage. After the end of October. Toward the end of October Mrs. A begins to improve, so that her life no longer appears in danger. At the same time a relative visits the home for a few weeks, acting as a mother substitute. Tension is relaxed in the family's day-to-day functioning, and the intensity of its emotional burdens is reduced. Their previous effectual handling of their problems is gradually consolidated, though not without some strain. They continue to express feelings of anxiety and longing quite openly and to gain much comfort from mutual support. During this stage, Jackie is received back into the family fold as a member in good standing.

69

Formerly regarded as a pest with no useful job to perform, he is now assigned a role consistent with his age and capacities—is allowed to help with minor household chores. He changes dramatically from the role of a wretched rebel to that of a responsive small boy, and although he continues to steal pennies occasionally, Mr. A speaks compassionately about this behavior, saying, "When he gets home from school and feels the need for his mother, I suppose the next best thing is to go and take something from his sister." Thus we see, during the later stages of this problem-solving period, that the A family is able to forge a novel solution to its problems by learning, under the impact of stress, to cope directly with reality difficulties through open acknowledgment of sources of tension and anxiety.

Need-Response Patterns of Jackie

In reviewing briefly the resultant need-response pattern with respect to Jackie, we notice increased perception, respect, and satisfaction of his basic mental health needs. Specifically, our analysis reveals a heightened response to his need for affection, dependency gratification, and support in regard to physical tasks. As a result, he presents a considerably brighter appearance, discontinues runaway episodes and stealing, improves in school performance, and in general is a much happier youngster. These improvements in Jackie's level of need satisfaction are also reflected in certain changes in the family's role and communication patterns. Emancipated from the unhappy role of "pest" or "worrier," Jackie now begins to carry out the simple tasks assigned to him. When, in his eagerness to help, he attempts tasks beyond his capacity, his father firmly yet gently prevents him from doing them. Another interesting sign of the resultant changes in Jackie's mental health picture is apparent during a school vacation when he is again sent for a visit to his grandmother's house. Whereas during previous separations the family avoided seeing him, this time Mr. A not only telephones but also visits, and reports that Jackie perceives the visit to grandmother's as a "vacation" rather than another depriving experience in his life.

A number of follow-up interviews indicate that Jackie's emotional health continued to improve after the harrowing experience of the crisis period. His morale received a tremendous boost when his mother, because of her improved condition, was given permission for a brief visit to the home. Jackie minced no words about his desire to "sit right next to Mother at the table," nor did the family in any way disapprove of this direct expression of feelings.

A few significant changes in various phases of the family's transactional behavior, having important implications for the future mental health of the family members, are also worth mentioning. The family's value system is characterized by greater tolerance of painful events, and concomitantly there is a shift from present toward future time orientation (advanced financial planning for purchase of furniture, increased willingness to ask for help from social service and other care-taking agencies). In allocating roles, Mr. A is able to maintain a position of reasonably effective leadership. The children take initiative in doing things "to surprise Dad" when he comes home from work. As a result of the crisis experience, channels of communication are less constricted for the discussion of anxiety-laden topics. For example, Mrs. A's vacillation in returning to the hospital following a home visit was discussed very directly in the family, resulting in a healthy type of quarrel and open expression of anger toward Mrs. A, eventuating in resolution of the problem by Mrs. A's request that Alice, the older daughter, call the husband at work and inform him of Mrs. A's decision to return to the hospital.

Because of limitations of space, this survey has focused upon the resultant need-response pattern of only one member of the family following a sequence of crisis events. A more extensive analysis would appropriately be concerned with a systematic review of the functioning of the family in relation to resultant factors influencing the future mental health of each member.

CONCLUSION

Using the concepts of family life-style, intermediate problem-solving mechanisms, and need-response pattern, we have presented an approach to the observation and study of the family in crisis. We have briefly demonstrated this conceptual framework by tracing the need-response pattern of one member of a family through a series of crisis events to which the family reacted with a range of mechanisms, described in the general context of its value, role, and communication patterns. It is hoped that in subsequent investigations this approach

71

will be useful for developing additional formulations concerning a typology of family structures, crisis-problem classification, and the dynamics of crisis behavior in relation to family mental health.

Finally, our study of families in crisis—including a range of selected cases in which methods of preventive intervention were deliberately used—suggests a number of implications for the development of a rationale and technique for preventive programs in public health and other settings.[12] We are impressed with the need for precise articulation of focused casework techniques of anticipatory guidance, support, and clarification.* Of particular importance is the need for reliable predictive guides for precision in timing efforts at intervention *while* the family is in the throes of crisis, so that a minimal therapeutic force will produce maximal benefit.

[12] Caplan, *Emotional Disorders of Early Childhood, op. cit.,* pp. 153–163. For a thoughtful appraisal of some technical problems, see Bertram M. Beck's statement on "Prevention and Treatment," based on the work of the Subcommittee on Trends, Issues, and Priorities of the NASW Commission on Social Work Practice, National Association of Social Workers, New York, 1959. (Mimeographed).

* See ch. 24 of the present volume.

Part II
Common Maturational
and Situational Crises

MATURATIONAL OR developmental crises are often regarded as "normal" crises because all human beings experience them in the process of growing up. They are generally viewed as periods of marked physical, psychological, and social change that are characterized by common "disturbances" in thought and feeling. At such times— for example, at puberty—a complex of biopsychosocial stimuli poses certain tasks that must be faced and mastered with a reasonable degree of effectiveness if the next maturational stage is to yield its full potential for further growth and development.

Fundamental to the understanding of these maturational crises are Freud's theory of psychosexual development and Erikson's formulation of the eight stages in the human life cycle, from infancy to senescence. It is important to remember that Erikson's familiar and perhaps somewhat overpopularized eight developmental tasks (trust, autonomy, initiative, industry, identity, intimacy, generativity, and integrity) are, in his own words, "inextricably entwined in and derived from the various stages of psychosexual development that were described by Freud, as well as from the child's stages of physical, motor, and cognitive development." [1]

It is also well to keep in mind that the concepts of psychoanalytic ego psychology formulated by Erikson, Hartmann, and other theoreticians, which illuminate our understanding of coping behavior during various maturational crises, deal with unconscious instinctual behavior, as well as with preconscious phenomena and conscious adaptive mechanisms. In addition to those of dynamic psychology, the contributions of all the behavioral and social sciences are, of course, constantly augmenting our storehouse of knowledge about the average expectable characteristics of each phase of psychosocial maturation.

[1] "Youth and the Life Cycle: An Interview with Erik H. Erikson," *Children,* Vol. 7, No. 2 (1960), p. 45.

As Erikson, Bowlby, and other clinical investigators have frequently pointed out, when a situational or accidental crisis—a stressful external event—is superimposed on a normal-phase-of-development crisis, the combined impact of these simultaneous events can often lead to a crisis of major proportions.* Among the papers in this section there are several examples of this twin-crisis phenomenon: for example, Joel Vernick's discussion of the impact of hospitalization on a youth who is struggling with the normal turmoil of adolescence; Alice Ichikawa's example of a college student who, while struggling with the tasks of emancipation from possessive parental ties, has also to cope with the adjustive stresses of the college environment; and Stanley H. Cath's poignant example of Mr. A, who is flooded by an onrush of situational and developmental crises related to the death of his son, the loss of his job, physical illness, a marital upheaval, and a premature climacteric.

The selection of papers in this section makes no pretense of thoroughness in covering all phases of the life cycle or all types of situational, transitional, or accidental stress. There has been an effort, however, to bring a variety of perspectives to bear on a series of common life crises related to marriage, pregnancy (in and out of marriage), parenthood, the birth of a premature baby, the child's entry into school, the impact of hospitalization on a child, puberty, the adjustment to college life, young adulthood, the climacteric, retirement, bereavement, and senescence.

The reader may be surprised that this section begins with the normal crisis of getting married rather than, as is customary, with the birth of the child. The purpose for choosing this sequence is to foster an orientation to the normal stages of the family life cycle. Thus, this section begins with Rhona Rapoport's paper on the establishment of a new family unit and ends with Cath's discussion of the crisis of the three-generation family unit.**

* The difficulty in making consistently precise differentiations between maturational and situational crises reflects an important gap in our current state of knowledge, as well as the current variations in the use of these terms. While most observers would agree that adolescence constitutes a maturational crisis (in Erikson's sense) and bereavement a situational crisis (in Lindemann's sense), many life experiences (for example, becoming a parent or the child's first entry into school) have both maturational and situational components. John and Elaine Cumming (*Ego and Milieu*, Atherton Press, New York, 1962, pp. 47–48.) suggest a preliminary conceptual framework for dealing with this classification dilemma. Further and more detailed classification efforts are needed.

** E. E. LeMasters' paper on parenthood is included here in order to emphasize the normal stresses associated with accessions to the family. This paper, however, as well as others in this section, might just as well have been relocated in Part IV where the focus is on the use of research methodology to measure crisis phenomena.

5. Normal Crises, Family Structure, and Mental Health*

Rhona Rapoport **

THERE IS A GROWING body of work in the social-psychiatric field known as "crisis" studies. Although these studies have been conducted by people with different approaches and different topics, with no single set of theroetical and clinical interests, there is a common factor among them in that the crises being considered are viewed as *turning points*—as points of no return.[1] If the crisis is handled advantageously, it is assumed the result for the individual is some kind of maturation or development. If the stresses engendered by the crises are not well coped with, it is assumed that old psychological conflicts may be evoked or new conflicts may arise and a state of poorer mental health may be the result. Further, it is suggested that persons undergoing the crisis are amenable to influence when skilled intervention techniques of relatively brief duration are applied.

* Reprinted from *Family Process*, Vol. 2, No. 1 (1963).

** Many colleagues have contributed to the work reported on in this paper, which was done under the auspices of the Community Mental Health Program of the Harvard School of Public Health under the direction of Dr. Gerald Caplan. I wish particularly to thank Robert Rapoport for his help at all stages of this work. In addition, thanks are due to the following for help at different stages of the research: Thomas Brigante, Ivor Browne, Peggy Golde, Beatrice Horvitz, David Kaplan, Thomas Plaut, and Rae Sherwood. This work was supported by funds from the National Institute of Mental Health, Developmental Grant #6710.

1 See Gerald Caplan, "Patterns of Parental Response to the Crisis of Premature Birth: A Preliminary Approach to Modifying the Mental Health Outcome," *Psychiatry*, Vol. 23 (1960), pp. 365–374; Erich Lindemann, "Symptomatology and Management of Acute Grief," chapter 1 of the present volume; James S. Tyhurst, "Individual Reactions to Community Disaster," *American Journal of Psychiatry*, Vol. 107 (1951) pp. 764–769; Erik Erikson, "Identity and the Life Cycle: Selected Papers," *Psychological Issues*, Vol. 1 (1959), pp. 1–171; Greta Bibring, *et al.*, "A Study of the Psychological Processes in Pregnancy and of the Earliest Mother-Child Relationship," *Psychoanalytic Study of the Child*, Vol. 16, International Universities Press, New York, 1961, pp. 9–27; and Irving Janis, *Psychological Stress*, Wiley, New York, 1958.

In a program of family research recently initiated in the Community Mental Health Program at the Harvard School of Public Health, there is an attempt to focus on the application of some of these ideas to a more prevalent type of crisis than in the studies referred to above. Our concern is with the critical transition points in the *normal, expectable* development of the family life cycle: getting married, birth of the first child, children going to school, death of a spouse, or children leaving home. These, too, are seen as points of no return. Although both normal and expectable, these standard status transition points in the life cycle of the family always have elements attached to them that are novel for the individuals experiencing them. This is perhaps especially true in our society where *rites de passage* are limited, where anticipatory socialization for new familial roles tends to be minimal, and where the prescriptions for behavior expected in the new roles may be highly variable. Thus these critical turning points often provoke disequilibria both in the individuals concerned and in the family system. It is postulated that the way these normal crises or status transitions are handled or coped with, will affect outcome—both in terms of the mental health of the individuals and in terms of the ensuing family relationships. It is also assumed, in line with Lindemann's and Caplan's assumptions that, to the extent that these critical periods have a limited time of "acute" disequilibria, it may be possible to do preventive intervention in a limited time so as to improve outcome levels.

The Initial Exploratory Study

For this program of family research the initial exploration lasted nine months and was aimed at collecting data that would improve and alter our early conceptualizations about engagement, honeymoon, and early marriage. It was undertaken, too, to map the field of our interest and to order it in such a way that it would be possible to make intelligent strategy decisions for future research.

Although we are interested in various developmental phases of the family, the study has so far focused systematically on the first phase, *getting married*. Some data have been obtained on the next phase —the first pregnancy and the critical point of having a first child— as some of the young couples we have worked with enter this phase quickly. In the "getting married" phase we have delinated three subphases: the engagement period which ends with the *rite de pass-*

age of the wedding, the honeymoon period, and the early marriage period up to three months after the wedding. For each of these subphases we postulate a series of tasks inherent in it, and we shall attempt to see how people have performed these tasks and how their performance is related to outcome a year after marriage. The types of variables we are concerned with in outcome are: (a) individual health status, including physical and psychological symptoms, feelings of satisfaction with the marital relationship and other spheres of life, and happiness; (b) the state of interpersonal relationship—an evaluation of the "fit" between the couple and the degree of harmony in their relationship; and (c) the state of functioning of the couple as a social system, which includes the degree to which the functions of the family group are performed and the readiness of the couple for the next phase, that of having a child.

Gaining access to engaged couples presented a number of difficulties. For various reasons it was not feasible to obtain lists of couples from the local marriage registries, newspaper marriage announcements, or public health nurses, all of which sources were explored. Finally, we obtained our initial subjects from the clergy, who were most co-operative. We worked with various denominations, making it a point to go from the top level of the clerical hierarchy down. This procedure was particularly helpful in our Catholic contacts. The Catholic Church runs a large pre-Cana (premarital) counseling program which seemed to be a potential pool for later research subjects.

In our first efforts, we were not very selective about the characteristics of the couples we obtained. We tried to obtain young married couples, allowing them to vary in social class, religion, and occupation. In the initial period we ended up with six couples, three having been referred by the Catholic clergy (one engaged, one just married, one just pregnant and in second month of marriage); one Unitarian couple, and two Episcopalian couples. Both Catholic and Protestant clergy referred couples to us randomly from among those on their lists awaiting marriage. Among the Catholics, the sanction of the clergy was usually more effective in assuring participation in the research, with only one couple so referred (a mixed marriage) declining co-operation. Among the Protestant couples, the clerical referral was a much less decisive factor in determining individuals' responses to our approach, with about half the couples refusing to participate.

77

The initial sample of six couples was investigated in a relatively intense way. One problem in the search for complex, intimate data is how to get meaningful material from contacts with a limited number of subjects. Unless this problem is solved, we cannot obtain a sufficient volume of data to test our hypotheses and we can draw only very tentative formulations. In addition, repeated intensive research contact with the same people increases the chances of affecting our subjects and altering the very phenomena we are studying.

Our interviews were relatively unstructured for this exploratory phase because we were experimenting with methods to obtain data about extremely complicated social and psychological phenomena of whose specific crucial dimensions we are uncertain. Many aspects of these complex phenomena are preconscious or unconscious and these areas are differentially sensitive for the respondents. Also the data collected are obtained through an interpersonal relationship of interviewer and interviewee, the nature of which affects the data. Furthermore, since we were dealing with concurrent processual material obtained by repeated contacts (approximately twelve interviews over a period of five months) there was the probability that we might actually change some aspects of the phenomena under study. In such a situation it was felt that the continued contact might set up expectations (countertransference) in the interviewer which might affect his eliciting subsequent data. One attempt to minimize the effect of the latter was to supervise each interview and deal both with countertransference problems and with data gaps from the research point of view.

Although we still place high value on obtaining current data, we also feel there is a definite place for retrospective data. In some instances we found retrospective data to be more accessible and accurate. This was especially true of certain events that were emotionally loaded at the time of the interview but which could be talked about with less anxiety later. For example, it seemed that most couples could discuss details of honeymoon only some time after the event.

The Conceptual Framework Developed

The six couples of the original samples were followed for varying periods after marriage. Some wives became pregnant, and we continued work with them in a relatively unstructured way up to six months after marriage. We then attempted to examine the data and organize them in more manageable form. The conceptual framework diagramatically represented in the chart indicates our over-all orientation to the data on the "getting married" phase. From this field of concern, we have selected a portion in which to do more systematic research in a later phase of the research.

The chart presents a schematic organization of concepts that have been found useful in organizing the data on the process of "getting married" as a role-transitional crisis. At present, problems of carrying out research on these concepts and testing out our ideas about the ways in which they are interrelated are less fully worked out than the framework itself. (See chart on p. 80.)

Research Strategy

It can be seen from the diagram that we are concerned with the personal and social resources that couples bring to a marriage, the way they cope with the tasks presented by the first phase of family life, how much their personal resources alter between engagement and the first few months of marriage, and how coping techniques and task accomplishment relate to outcome, say a year after marriage. These concerns imply at least five substudies. They are:

A study of the relation of a couple's task accomplishment to outcome; a study of the relation of coping processes (individual and couple) to outcome; a study of the fit between the salient intrapsychic levels of each of the two persons and the relation of the various types of "fit" to outcome; a study of the relation of intrapsychic level development of the individual to coping processes, to task accomplishment in each subphase, and to total outcome; and a study of change in the level of intrapsychic development along salient dimensions, after one year of marriage.

We decided to begin with a study of the *relation of a couple's accomplishment of the postulated phase-specific tasks to outcome, measured independently one year later.* (See III, 2.[b][ii] in diagram.) In the present paper only the tasks specified for the engagement period are presented as illustrative of our methods in this exploratory study.

The tasks that confront engaged persons have been divided into two major groups—intrapersonal and interpersonal. It should be noted that different people accomplish the tasks at different times; some only begin working on them during the engagement period,

FRAMEWORK FOR CONCEPTUALIZING "GETTING MARRIED" DATA

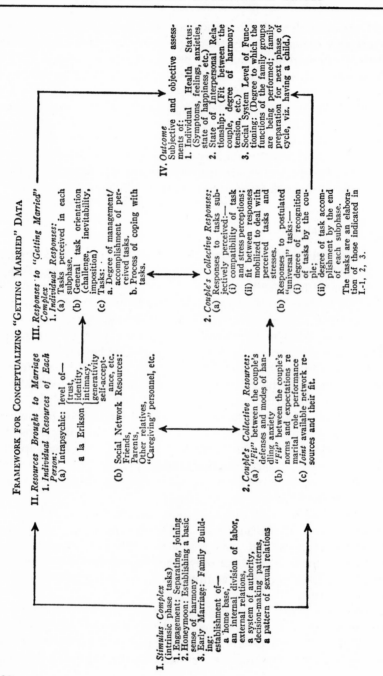

II. Resources Brought to Marriage

1. *Individual Resources of Each Person:*

(a) Intrapsychic: level of —
a la Erikson { trust, identity, intimacy, generativity self-acceptance, etc.

(b) Social Network Resources: Friends, Parents, Other relatives, "Caregiving" personnel, etc.

2. *Couple's Collective Resources:*

(a) "*Fit*" between the couple's defenses and modes of handling anxiety

(b) "*Fit*" between the couple's norms and expectations re marital role performance

(c) *Joint* available network resources and their fit.

III. Responses to "Getting Married" Complex

1. *Individual Responses:*

(a) Tasks perceived in each subphase.

(b) General task orientation (challenge, inevitability, imposition)

(c) Tasks: ·
a. Degree of management/accomplishment of perceived tasks.
b. Process of coping with tasks.

2. *Couple's Collective Responses:*

(a) Responses to tasks subjectively perceived:—
(i) compatibility of task and stress perceptions;
(ii) fit between responses mobilized to deal with perceived tasks and stresses.

(b) Responses to postulated "universal" tasks:—
(i) degree of recognition of tasks by the couple;
(ii) degree of task accomplishment by the end of each subphase.

The tasks are an elaboration of those indicated in I.-1, 2, 3.

IV. *Outcome*

Subjective and objective assessments of:

1. Individual Health Status: (Symptoms, feelings, anxieties, state of happiness, etc.)

2. State of Interpersonal Relationship: (Fit between the couple, degree of harmony, tension, etc.)

3. Social System Level of Functioning: (Degree to which the functions of the family groups are being performed; family preparation for next phase of cycle, viz. having a child.)

I. *Stimulus· Complex*

(intrinsic phase tasks)

1. Engagement: Separating, joining
2. Honeymoon: Establishing a basic sense of harmony
3. Early Marriage: Family Building: establishment of —
a home base;
an internal division of labor,
external relations,
a system of authority,
decision-making patterns,
a pattern of sexual relations

while others have accomplished many of them by the time they get engaged. Our concern is with where individuals and couples stand with regard to task accomplishment by the *end* of the engagement period, that is, by the time they actually get married, irrespective of when they began working on them.

The Intrapersonal Tasks

With regard to the intrapersonal tasks, we are concerned with the way people become *personally prepared* for marriage and how far they get by the time they actually do get married. This set of tasks is the most "individual," relating primarily to each person's intra-psychic factors as they interplay with the requirements of the inter-personal and sociological requirements of "getting married." This set of tasks implies some review on a conscious, preconscious, or un-conscious level of psychological maturity or readiness for marriage. The standards used for "readiness" will be affected both by the individual needs of a person and by his perceived subcultural norms.

The three tasks considered by us to be salient in this area of intra-personal preparation for marriage are: (1) making oneself ready to take over the role of husband or wife; (2) disengaging (or altering the form of engagement of) oneself from especially close relationships that *compete* or interfere with commitment to the new marital re-lationship; (3) accommodating patterns of gratifications of premari-tal life to patterns of the newly formed couple (marital) relationship.

For the first task concern is to assess each person's degree of *readiness to take over the new role of husband/wife* by the time of marriage. How ready is each, *as an individual,* to enter into the new status of married person and to perform adequately in the marital role? In speaking of personal readiness we refer to a general "set" of expectations for oneself and the other person which cross-cuts subcultures. The detailed aspects of what we mean can be sub-sumed under the two large categories, emphasized by Freud and others, as the individual's capacity to love and to work, whether it be "woman's" or "man's" work.

For both man and woman, the love relationship involves the whole prospect of living in close physical relationship with another person. Although it is extremely difficult to gauge a person's readiness for entering into this new dimension of intimacy, it seems essential to make some assessment of it—based on the person's own expressed

81

feeling of readiness and the interviewer's assessment of whether or not the individual has a realistic notion of what this will involve. We can already indicate some of the signs of readiness among individuals of the lower middle-class range, from which most of our exploratory research couples come. It is expected that the male will be prepared to take on the breadwinner role in the family. Signs that he is ready to do this are found in his work plans, his assessment of the financial requirements of the marriage, his activities toward fulfilling these requirements, and his readiness to accept the idea that others will be dependent on his stability and productivity.

Whatever the work situation, we are concerned with whether the particular individuals feel ready to enter into a situation in which they know what the potentialities and limitations are from an economic point of view, and in which they are able to work out an arrangement that deals both with keeping the household financially viable and with their own self-images—as worker, breadwinner, and supporter on the one hand, and as homemaker, helper, and enhancer on the other—so that the individual's sense of readiness is realistic in the context of the relationship that he is entering.

For the second task, we are concerned with assessing *how far people have disengaged themselves from relationships that interfere with commitment to the marital relationship.* Some people have dealt with this issue before they become engaged to marry; others deal with it focally during the engagement period. From our exploratory material, it seems that avoiding the issue altogether leads to difficulties later. These close relationships may be with a parent, a sibling, some other relative, a friend, a workmate, a peer group, and so on. In order to assess the degree of accomplishment on this task, we shall want to know whether each person had such relationships and with whom, and how he, or she, perceives that such ties relate to the proposed marital relationship. We are concerned with the fiancé(e)'s perceptions, what each person does with these relationships, and how conflicts are handled. We wish to know how much actual work of reconciliation has been done and how much still remains. Where the relationships have been gratifying, the work may be the loosening of a positive dependency tie. This process then becomes involved in the third subtask of this area—giving up premarital gratifications. When the negative aspect is uppermost, the work of the subtask involves revising one's ideas about familial roles and attempting to make one's behavior fit this revision.

Accommodating the competing gratifications of premarital life to the new couple (marital) relationship is the third task in making oneself personally prepared for marriage. We are concerned here with whether individuals feel that getting married does involve relinquishing gratifications. Some can tell us the answer to this, others cannot, and we shall have to infer from what they say what the psychological reality is for them. For instance, if someone thinks that such premarital activities as going to frequent dances will continue during marriage, and we find that the prospective spouse has no interest in this activity and does not intend to pursue it, we probably have a situation in which relinquishing this premarital gratification is not being dealt with. We want to know what individuals find particularly gratifying in their premarital life, whether these gratifications are likely to be possible in married life and, if not, to what extent individuals have given them up by the time they get married. It may be extremely difficult, for instance, for a woman to give up the gratifications of romantic courtship behavior. Outcome may be greatly affected, however, by how much recognition is given to this task and how far she is able to accomplish it. In our exploratory couples this task seems to center more, for a man, on the question of whether or not his "freedom" will be drastically curtailed. What is involved is no longer being able to think only of oneself in decisions and actions.

What we are primarily concerned with here, then, is estimating how far the *shift from self-orientation to mutuality* has been made by the end of the engagement period, by both the man and the woman. It is necessary to obtain data from the couple on how far they already have gone in the development of a couple identity. Again, the actual form of the couple identity will vary by subculture and should be rated accordingly. Agreeing to segregate activities may involve as much idea of such couple identity as agreeing to do things jointly.

The Interpersonal Tasks

The second major group of engagement tasks consists of those involved in the couple's *interpersonal* preparation for marriage. We are concerned with the work the couple has to do to develop an interpersonal adjustment or accommodation that will be satisfactory in the marital relationship. We are interested in relating how far

83

the couple get in their interpersonal tasks by the time of marriage to various outcome measures a year after marriage.

The set of *interpersonal tasks* that we are concerned with here relates to and draws on intrapersonal phenomena and extra familial (or couple) relationships, but focuses on the phenomena in the pre-marital (engaged) couple's relationship. The concern throughout is on the work necessary to make this relationship a satisfactory and harmonious one. Our key organizing concept is that of *fit*.[2] We wish to assess the couple's *fit* on a number of salient variables. A good fit may be arrived at in various ways. Partners need not be identical in the way they do things or in their personality configurations. Two partners may have a similar orientation to some aspect of life and the result may be conflict or unhappy competition in their new relationship. Conversely, discrepant orientations do not necessarily indicate a poor fit; they may complement one another. The essential point is the effect of the "fitting together" efforts. A good fit is one that has the effect of harmonizing needs and values whether these are similar or dissimilar at the outset of the relationship. Conversely, a bad fit is one in which there is disabling discord or conflict regardless of *a priori* resemblances or dissimilarities.

We are interested in knowing how far the couple has accomplished the work involved for each of the tasks detailed below. We need to understand where each person is on the dimension in order to make a rating about the degree of accomplishment for the couple on the task. Thus, in considering a task such as "developing a mutually satisfactory friendship pattern for the couple," we need to know about each person's norms about friendship patterns, what each considers the pattern ought to be for an engaged couple, and what each feels he needs in his or her friendships. The rating, however, relates primarily to the accommodation made by the two persons to achieve a mutually satisfactory pattern, during the engagement phase.

The tasks we have specified in this area are:

1. Establishing a couple identity

2. Developing a mutually satisfactory sexual adjustment for the engagement period

3. Developing a mutually satisfactory agreement regarding family planning

[2] Rhona Rapoport, "The Family and Psychiatric Treatment," *Psychiatry,* Vol. 23 (1960), pp. 53–62.

4. Establishing a mutually satisfactory system of communication between the pair

5. Establishing a mutually satisfactory pattern with regard to relatives

6. Developing a mutually satisfactory pattern with regard to friends

7. Developing a mutually satisfactory pattern with regard to work

8. Developing mutually satisfactory patterns of decision-making

9. Planning specifically for the wedding, honeymoon, and the early months of marriage that lie ahead.

Assessing Task Accomplishment

Each task has been broken down into a battery of items which are rated on a 7-point scale both for the individual and for the couple at the completion of our interviewing program. For example, the intrapersonal task of "making oneself ready to take over the new role of husband or wife" has a battery of ten items: degree to which the individual shows signs of readiness to be an exclusive sexual partner; shows signs of being able to enter freely into an intimate sexual relation with his or her fiancé(e); shows signs of tenderness, affection, for the other; shows signs of interest in the other's emotional life and development; shows signs of sharing intimacies with the other; shows signs of merging his own plans with those of the other; has a realistic appraisal of the personal characteristics of the prospective spouse; has formed a realistic conception of the economic problems entailed in forming a marital pair; has formulated a realistic picture of his own capacities to contribute to the economic needs of the new family unit; and is ready to become a husband or wife (global rating).

We have now started to work with a second exploratory series of six young couples. Our major aim with this group is to work out more clearly what items seem useful to retain, to define them as operationally as possible, and to work out coding procedures so that we shall cease to be dependent on the ratings of expert clinical judges for our assessments.

In order to serve all these aims, we adopted the following procedures: A pair of interviewers, one male and one female, interview each couple; four interviews are conducted during the engagement period, spaced so as to allow for one immediately before the wedding; a further interview is conducted as soon as possible after the honeymoon, one three months later, and one a year later; the partners are interviewed jointly and separately. All interviews are taped. Each couple is then rated for all the items three separate times—once by the interviewers together with the supervisor of all the interviews, while second and third ratings are made by other interviewers who do not know the subject couple but have only listened to the recorded interviewing sessions. In these ratings by interviewers and supervisor—all of whom are trained clinicians and sociologically oriented—rationales for choosing one point in the scale rather than another have been elicited.

One further procedure we are attempting with this group of couples is to use an adaptation of what has been called a self-anchoring scale by Kilpatrick and Cantril.[3] This enables each subject to indicate the content of the scale on the item in which we are interested. We have used this scale for two main areas—to get at individuals' own ideas of the characteristics of a man and a woman who are most ready for marriage, and their own ideas about what constitutes a happy marriage one year after the wedding. After giving these notions, the interviewees are asked to rate themselves and each other on a scale anchored by the content they have given. We thus hope to get at their psychological realities about these factors and to relate them to outcome. This in itself might turn out to be a significant predictive device for types of outcome.

Summary

This paper has emphasized some aspects of the conceptualizations and formulation of a research design to investigate a complex series of problems in the field of community psychiatry. The phenomena that have been discussed operate on many different levels, and it can be seen that personality dynamics are only one set of contributing forces in explaining them. It will be a long time before we are able to understand the weight and combinations of different kinds of factors in explaining the total variance of the phenomena with which we are concerned. However, we do know that it is important in understanding how people cope with various critical situations to take systematic account of significant elements of the

[3] F. P. Kilpatrick and H. Cantril, "Self-Anchoring Scaling, A Measure of Individuals' Unique Reality Worlds," *Journal of Individual Psychology,* Vol. 16 (1960), pp. 158–173.

family structures from which they come; the network of family and other relationships that is available to them when they enter the "newly married" state, and their own expectations of the way familial roles should be performed. Both the personal and social resources a couple bring to their marriage will affect its outcome, as will new aspects that later develop autonomously from their daily living together.

This paper has not concentrated on results, since these are not yet systematically available. It has, rather, elaborated on the development of ideas and methods in an intensive exploratory study which may well form the basis for a more decisive formulation and testing of hypotheses.

6. Social Work in a Preventive Program of Maternal and Child Health*

Florence E. Cyr
and *Shirley H. Wattenberg*

A MATERNAL AND child health program, which is primarily concerned with the development of healthy mothers and babies, offers a rich opportunity for social casework directed not only toward physical health, but also toward emotional and social well-being. Promotion of good mental health in the mother, the key figure in the life of her baby, can do much in creating a healthy social and emotional climate for the development of her child's personality.

It is well established that many emotional disorders and social maladjustments originate in this early period of life, in the mother-child relationship in particular, and in family life in general. It is a potentially critical period for the mother, especially during the pregnancy and immediate postpartum period when there are biological and emotional changes going on within her that are peculiarly related to her role as a woman and mother. Preventive or interventive measures during this period may enable her to resolve stress in such a way that she does not involve her child in her own problems and will be free to recognize and meet his needs. Hopefully, a woman can emerge from her first experience of pregnancy with a healthy realistic attitude toward child-bearing which will act as a positive force in future pregnancies.

An ideal maternal and child health program can offer a mother guidance through her child's infancy which will foster healthy relationships and prepare her to meet emotional and physical hazards commonly experienced during this period. Total family interrelationships and the father's role should be recognized and his partic-

* Reprinted from *Social Work*, Vol. 2, No. 3 (1957).

ipation in the program encouraged.[1] These goals have been a primary consideration in the maternal and child health program discussed in this paper.

The Family Health Clinic

In 1950, under the auspices of the Harvard School of Public Health, affiliated for this purpose with the Boston Lying-In Hospital and the Children's Medical Center in Boston, the Family Health Clinic was established to provide a service-study program for health supervision of mothers and infants.[2] This clinic, supported by a special grant from the Association for the Aid of Crippled Children of New York and the Charles P. Hood Dairy Foundation, has offered complete service in prenatal, postnatal, and well-child care to 116 families having first babies. The mothers came from the regular outpatient department at Boston Lying-In Hospital and elected to participate in the program, knowing that it embodied both service and study aspects. The criteria for their participation, other than being primiparae, were that they have no medical or physical complications requiring attendance at other special clinics, and that they live nearby for convenience in continuing with the clinic for at least one year after the birth of the child.*

The Family Health Clinic has a multi-discipline staff consisting of obstetricians, pediatricians, nutritionists, public health nurse, social workers, and consultant psychiatrist, all of whom were available to serve the patient or family during the pregnancy and, with the relationship established, after the birth of the child. There has been a well-formulated and close, co-operative, working arrangement with the Visiting Nurse Association. Other community agencies have also been called upon when needed for specialized services.

The project has allowed for carrying out the dual responsibilities of service and study. Because the clinic has devoted a great deal of staff and time to a small number of patients, its program is not in

[1] O. Spurgeon English, "Psychological Role of the Father in the Family," *Social Casework*, Vol. XXXV, No. 8 (1954), pp. 323–329. See also Rose Bernstein and Florence E. Cyr, "A Study of Interviews with Husbands in a Prenatal and Child Health Program," *Social Casework*, Vol. XXXVIII, No. 9 (1957).

[2] Gerald Caplan, "Preparation for the Healthy Parenthood," *Children*, Vol. 1, No. 5 (1954), pp. 171–175.

* The clinic discontinued active service to patients in 1956. Its staff is now engaged in disciplinary and interdisciplinary studies based on the accumulated data.

all respects adaptable to general use. But it was not designed to serve this purpose. Rather, it has been a clinic where service could be examined and evaluated, and where increased understanding of pregnancy and infancy could be gained. Some of the techniques and knowledge described may be helpful to others involved in planning programs and giving similar services to mothers and children.

The atmosphere of the Family Health Clinic was specifically planned to implement preventive mental health services for the pregnant woman. Although her relationships with the clinic staff were only a small part of her total social experience, these relationships were occurring at a potentially vulnerable time in her life, and the way in which her physical and emotional needs were met was important. The clinic was designed to represent the warm, accepting atmosphere that is an attribute of the good mother—the very kind of relationship it was hoped she could foster for her child. In pregnancy, passive-dependent feelings are normal, often even accentuated. These feelings were encouraged to a degree that might not be considered appropriate except during this special period of her life, and were based on the psychiatric assumption that this would enable her later on to fulfill the same kinds of needs in her infant. In the words of the consultant psychiatrist, "It is similar to filling a reservoir for later use." Not only did the clinic as a whole often represent the mother figure, but individual staff members, especially the social workers, were given this attribute by the patient. The kind of relationships the patient made with each member of the staff gave valuable insights into future parent-child relationships.

Since there were many persons serving one patient, a unified treatment plan was imperative. This was accomplished by preclinic and postclinic conferences during which each staff member shared his knowledge of the patient and family seen on a given day, and during which a treatment plan and goal were formulated, evaluated, or revised. There were also special conferences with the psychiatrist during which staff members could initiate full discussion of a particular family if additional consultation seemed necessary. Detailed information was exchanged freely by members of the team as the need arose, both through formal records and informal conversations. These experiences also highlighted a well-known fact— that individuals working together on a team need to understand each other's techniques, frames of reference, and goals so that the patient will receive service free of professional misunderstandings or confusions.

Role of the Social Worker

The role of the social worker in this clinic was comparable to her role in any multi-disciplinary setting where she offers direct service to clients with problems and shares knowledge of social factors with the staff. As the specialist in social relationships, she was responsible for evaluating those key figures in the patient's environment who were important in a given situation.[3] In addition, because of the nature of the clinic's goals and its study purpose, all patients were seen routinely by the social worker, thus providing opportunities for preventive work as well as for gathering data.

The patient was usually seen by the social worker eight to ten times in the prenatal clinic and monthly at the well-child clinic; other visits, to the home or in the office, were arranged if necessary. There was, also, at least one ward visit made during the eight-day period of hospitalization, although more frequent contacts might have been helpful.

Casework interviews were primarily unstructured in an effort to find out what the patient herself wanted to discuss. However, the content of the interviews was influenced by the casework plan and by the introduction at particular periods by the social worker of certain subjects based on her knowledge of pregnancy and infancy. Thus, for study and preventive purposes, there was a flexible semistructured interview aimed toward particular goals that the worker wanted to achieve.

The husband, often an unknown entity in such a program, was encouraged to attend the prenatal clinic with his wife and to come with her when she brought the baby for medical supervision. Occasionally, other close relatives were included to facilitate a treatment plan. In the majority of cases the husband was seen at least once. (Initially, this was interpreted as one of the requirements for the patient's participation in the clinic, but daytime employment was a practical obstacle in some cases. It was not possible to hold evening clinics even though it would probably have encouraged greater husband participation.) Because the individual interview

[3] Gerald Caplan, "The Role of the Social Worker in Preventive Psychiatry," *Medical Social Work*, Vol. 4, No. 4 (1955), p. 147.

and joint interview each had distinct advantages, it was found that a combination of both types produced the greatest understanding of the total family. When husbands did attend, either alone or with their wives, it was clear that the knowledge gained added greatly to the staff understanding, broadened the effectiveness of service, and offered an opportunity for help to both parents during this crucial period of family change and development.

In addition to the several visits by the visiting nurse, the social worker usually made a home visit during the period between hospital discharge and the first clinic appointment with the baby.[4] During this visit problems could be discussed, family interaction and home atmosphere could be observed, significant behavior patterns noted, and general understanding increased, to aid the staff in giving future health supervision. The values derived from the home visit suggest that a visit during pregnancy and evening visits to include the husband would have added advantages.

Each mother used the home visit according to her own needs, but often the social worker had to focus the interview in a helpful way. Problems that had loomed large in pregnancy were submerged, but the social worker's awareness of them as part of the personality structure guided her in treatment. During this period of readjustment, it was often necessary for the worker to make clear her continuing interest in the mother since the mother frequently felt that the baby had become the center of attention.

Until the baby was four or five months old, the relationship between the mother and worker was somewhat different than before —now the patient was closer to the pediatrician, nurse, and nutritionist because of the focus on the physical care of the baby. Primarily, the social worker maintained a supportive relationship, and not until several months had passed were patients able to talk about many intrapersonal problems that were apparent in other ways to the worker. In retrospect, mothers described overwhelming feelings of inadequacy, annoyance, and distress about motherhood and themselves. Some had resolved these feelings in a healthy way, but others had not. However, the past supportive relationship with the caseworker enabled them to enter into a treatment situation more readily, which indicated that the social worker should not

4 Sibylle Escalona, "The Psychological Situation of Mother and Child upon Return from the Hospital," *Problems of Infancy and Childhood*, Josiah Macy, Jr., Foundation, New York, 1949, pp. 30–96.

withdraw during the early infancy period. This experience also demonstrated the fact that need for casework help might be present but not evident at this time, and that workers need to develop skill in identifying these needs and formulating techniques to deal with them.

Treatment Focused on Prevention

All families attending the Family Health Clinic were seen by the social workers for preventive purposes. The usual methods employed in any casework situation were used, but the difference was that treatment was focused on and related to good mental health in mother-child relationships, and the formation of a stable, healthy family equilibrium. This focus was achieved by giving particular consideration to the attitudes of the wife and husband toward pregnancy and parenthood; to their relationships with their own parents; and to the family potential for fostering healthy experiences for the child.[5] Past and present personality difficulties of the parents were evaluated; then a decision was made as to whether these might invade parent-child relationships, and if so, whether intervention could prevent this happening. Certain casework techniques were considered applicable to work with all women undergoing this common experience, but at any time the caseworker could be flexible and discriminating according to the needs of the individual patient.

Ego support. Ego-supportive treatment was used with the patients of the Family Health Clinic to reinforce and strengthen the capacities of these essentially healthy women to deal specifically with the experiences of pregnancy and early motherhood. Particular attention was given to such matters as attitudes and feelings about the pregnancy; the patient's image of herself; the way pregnancy and parenthood affected personal and family goals and husband-wife relationships; stresses created by physical and emotional changes of this period; anxieties about labor and delivery; and doubts about capacity for mothering and assuming a new role. The value of this treatment method can readily be seen in a prenatal and well-child service, and it was utilized not only in social work treatment but permeated the entire atmosphere of the clinic. Ego-strengthening measures were often sufficient to enable patients to function with a

[5] Herschel Alt, "Mental Health Planning for Children," *Social Casework*, Vol. XXXI, No. 2 (1950), p. 50.

minimum of disorder and to approach parenthood with healthy attitudes.

Clarification. At times the technique of clarification for specific problems that might affect the mother-child relationship was used. This meant treatment of a more intensive nature and involved help to the patient in understanding her conscious attitudes and behavior, which required broader knowledge of the individual personality and social situation. The social worker did not attempt insight development. Clarification was indicated with the patient who seemed unable to resolve feelings about the experiences of pregnancy and parenthood noted above, or who had such problems as unusual doubts and anxieties, traumatic experiences connected with the pregnancy, disordered relationships indicating possible transference of inappropriate feelings into the mother-child relationship, or confusions about femininity and motherhood. If the problem was so acute that it could not be resolved without some change in the personality structure, treatment was directed toward recognizing this and getting psychiatric help. In most of the cases in this clinic, however, this was not necessary.

Modification of the environment. To illustrate some of the realistic social aspects of family living, all families received help in planning for a healthy social environment; *e.g.,* living arrangements that would foster optimum physical and mental health during the pregnancy and later on; economic, educational, or vocational adjustments; management during the period when the mother returned from the hospital with the baby. In some cases more specific treatment was necessary to enable the patient to have a less critical experience emotionally. This was done not only by having the clinic staff meet the woman's needs in a specialized way, but also by encouraging those in her family to do this as well.

Anticipatory guidance. Another method, sometimes designated as educational, was anticipatory guidance, which is particularly applicable in a preventive service. In the clinic, anticipatory guidance was twofold. It was used to encourage better understanding on the part of both parents of the normal changes in growth and development common to pregnancy and early childhood. It was also used as advance preparation for meeting the stress situations of this period with less anxiety, and in a way that favored a healthy outcome for the mother as well as for her relationship with her child.

Anticipatory guidance included giving information, but also

94

necessitated participation on the part of the wife and husband and expression of their feelings. Such participation, or even lack of it, gave the social worker clues about possible sensitive areas where interventive work was needed. The use of anticipatory guidance assumed that the social worker had a sound background of knowledge of the normal physical and psychosocial factors of this period, and the skill to give information without producing anxiety.

Since the crises and stresses of pregnancy vary from woman to woman, only those that were most common and identifiable were discussed. For example, the emotional lability and irritability of the pregnant woman; the changes that often occur in sexual feeling; the probable increase in passive-dependent needs as the pregnancy progresses; variations in development of full maternal feeling; attitudes about breast feeding; and the worries about a healthy outcome for mother and child.

Some preparation was also given during pregnancy about the physical and emotional reorientation of the mother after the birth of the baby, and for the time it takes after delivery for her biological and emotional system to readjust. Most prospective mothers are unprepared for feelings of annoyance and timidity toward their babies. Discussion about such matters was found to have most value late in pregnancy, or in early infancy, when the baby was better established as a reality. Even in pregnancy, thought was given to the impending shift in the husband-wife relationship, the changes in family life resulting from the birth of the baby, and the growth and satisfactions that would emerge in the family unit. In considering the early postpartum period beforehand, the idea was expressed that husbands could be helpful and enjoy participation in infant care, and that this could enrich their own experience in parenthood as well as be a source of support to the wife at this time and enable her to give the baby the mothering that is required.

Anticipatory guidance after the birth of the child was predicated on the worker's having considerable knowledge of the growth and development of the normal child as well as patterns of family development and interaction. This guidance (given by other members of the team also) quite naturally differed in content during the various periods of the baby's development, and was related to such matters as weaning, nursing, socialization, curiosity, exploration, beginning independence, negativism, toilet training, and changes in food and sleep patterns. In the interviews, staff members attempted to avoid generalities, and, indeed, anticipatory guidance was a means of clarifying misinterpretations gleaned from outside sources.[6] The ultimate goal was to help the mother see the child as an individual from whom she could take her clues as to his needs and readiness for change. Many of the women expressed a positive response to this kind of treatment and felt that they had been much better "prepared" for their experience than their friends who had not had a chance to discuss such matters.

Illustration of Methods

The following cases illustrate some of the methods used by the social worker in the Family Health Clinic, and show some of the ways the staff worked together, picking up clues and sharing a unified treatment plan:

A twenty-eight-year-old woman who had been enthusiastic about joining the Family Health Clinic had a pleasant but reserved manner at her first visit. On her second visit she was quite diffident with the obstetrician and nutritionist, and left before the social worker could see her. In case conference the first visit was reviewed. The doctor recalled that the patient's reserve had impelled him to resort to numerous questions to indicate an interest in her. The nutritionist had asked many specific questions about the patient's food intake as part of the routine method of collecting dietary data. The social worker had kept the patient waiting while she had other interviews. The consultant psychiatrist pointed out that this woman's reactions indicated she had probably been unable to give of herself in response to questions, and felt hurt and deprived by what she misinterpreted as the social worker's lack of interest. It was felt that she might see pregnancy as a depriving experience and might involve her feelings in attitudes toward her baby. The larger question was whether she could tolerate giving to the demands of an infant.

At subsequent appointments all the staff made efforts to give to her, rather than take from her by questioning. The obstetrician gave her information about pregnancy, and used questions only when necessary to ascertain her physical condition. The nutritionist put dietary recommendations in terms of a good diet rather than stressing necessary omissions of food. As might be expected, this woman resented restrictions in her diet. Therefore, the technique of helping her to see diet as a medical prescription, for her good, was used. This discouraged stresses around food as

[6] M. Robert Gomberg, "The Responsibilities and Contributions of Social Work in Strengthening Family Life," *Social Casework*, Vol. XXXIV, No. 8 (1953), p. 331.

such, which might have been paralleling old difficulties with her mother and be carried on later in child feeding.

The social worker handled directly the feelings which had arisen because of the delay in arranging an interview, and pointed out her constant interest and availability. This woman responded by discussing herself quite freely, which seemed an encouraging sign of her ability to meet her child's needs if she had sufficient satisfactions herself.

The pediatrician, who became acquainted with the prospective mothers in pregnancy, was able to outline a régime for the baby in line with the woman's needs, and one that emphasized the satisfactions the baby could give to her.

The social worker, in a joint interview with the parents, was able to encourage the husband toward active participation in meeting his wife's dependency needs. These were masked by her aggressive independence which had frightened him away from giving the help and solicitous attention she wanted. Through a routine discussion of passive-dependent needs of pregnancy, he became more comfortable in doing things for her, and she was more accepting of them as appropriate. Again, since she accepted this change without undue anxiety and could see dependent feelings as permissible, it was felt she might be able to tolerate her infant's dependency.

The parents were seen together after the birth of the baby and the husband was encouraged to continue giving his wife attention in the postpartum period, and to carry out his desire to take part in baby care. He had been reluctant to consider this, thinking his wife would object and that it was not a manly activity. He was surprised and pleased when she welcomed the plan, and a few months later she told the worker that this had been an important factor in uniting them as a family.

Another Illustration

A young woman who seemed to have a good personal and social adjustment in marriage, work, and general relationships became upset when her mother began to make financial and emotional demands upon her during pregnancy. This pressure came at a time when she was experiencing normal, passive-dependent feelings herself, and reactivated the experiences of her adolescence when her mother was overly dependent upon her after her father's death. She became so anxious she could not tolerate her own dependency feelings and engaged in compulsive activity which was threatening her health in pregnancy. She openly expressed fear that if she allowed herself to become dependent, her child's relationship with her might follow the pattern of her relationship with her mother.

It was the opinion of the staff that this woman had many positive potentials for a healthy relationship with her child, but that intervention was indicated for the sake of her health and to prevent her involving the baby in her problem with her mother.

The woman was encouraged by the social worker to discuss her own usual adequate functioning, to see her present dependency feelings in true perspective as appropriate and different from the kind of behavior her mother had shown, and in general to clarify her feelings. She was given some help with her current guilt feelings about inability to meet her mother's demands, but this was done around the current situation, without any attempt to deal with the old problem. She responded by becoming less tense and less impelled to hyperactivity, and although doubts occasionally plagued her because of the proximity of her mother, there was no evidence during the period in which she was known to the clinic that the problem affected her relationship with her child.

Offering Preventive Service

In a health program such as the Family Health Clinic, the social worker was offering service to many individuals who had no established pathology and who were not seeking help with social or emotional problems. Not only the patient, but also the worker, had to make some adjustments in thinking in order to enter effectively into a helping relationship. The social worker was in reality obliged to take a more active role than was her custom—she was incorporating educational techniques with which she was not entirely comfortable at first, and had to develop skill in offering preventive services in a meaningful way. There was some evidence of patient resistance, even more unconscious than conscious, because of the common association of social workers with pathology. It was rewarding, however, to see how quickly most of the patients and families in this clinic oriented themselves to this type of service from the social worker.

Conclusions

The Family Health Clinic has demonstrated the value of having several professions join together for the guidance of families on the threshold of parenthood. Special emphasis was placed on the promotion of good mental and physical health through incorporation of preventive measures. The social workers employed casework methods common to general practice, but adapted them to the particular goal of prevention. Also, the treatment was focused on the reinforcement of capacities to handle crises or stress situations and the development of healthy relationships during the period of pregnancy and infancy. The usual techniques of ego support, clarification, and modification of the environment were used. In addition, educational methods were applied to advantage and included anticipatory guidance.

It is recognized that the concept of prevention need not be confined to programs established exclusively for this purpose. However, in order to do preventive work, the social worker needs to have special understanding and knowledge about the normal or usual experiences of life. It has been relatively easy to identify pathology, but less easy to make a differential diagnosis as to when a normal life experience may become pathological. The social workers in the Family Health Clinic are making a detailed study of the social and emotional problems occurring in pregnancy and the immediate postpartum period, although the number of cases studied will not be statistically significant for conclusive results. However, through identifying these problems and the periods when they occur, it is hoped that more dynamic and timely service may be given.

7. Are We Still Stereotyping the Unmarried Mother?*

Rose Bernstein

THE THEORY OF out-of-wedlock pregnancy currently accepted among social workers and members of other helping disciplines is that it is symptomatic and purposeful, an attempt by the personality to ease an unresolved conflict. The extent to which we are committed to this point of view can be seen in some typical excerpts from the literature:

> The caseworker should recognize that pregnancy for the unmarried woman is a symptom of underlying emotional difficulty. [She] is a person who solves her emotional problems through acting out, as exemplified by the pregnancy.[1]

> We recognize unmarried motherhood as a symptom of a more pervading personality difficulty.[2]

> Her illegitimate pregnancy is the result of an attempt to solve certain emotional conflict. . . .[3]

> [The unmarried mother] . . . has failed to attain a mature pattern of adaptation to the demands of her social reality.[4]

> . . . everything points to the purposeful nature of the act. Although a girl would . . . not plan consciously . . . to bear an out-of-wedlock child, she does act in such a way that this becomes the almost inevitable result.[5]

---

* Reprinted from *Social Work*, Vol. 5, No. 3 (1960).
[1] Margaret W. Millar, "Casework Services for the Unmarried Mother," *Casework Papers 1955*, Family Service Association of America, New York, 1955, p. 93.
[2] Louise K. Trout, "Services to Unmarried Mothers," *Child Welfare*, Vol. 35, No. 2 (1956), p. 21.
[3] Jane K. Goldsmith, "The Unmarried Mother's Search for Standards," *Social Casework*, Vol. XXXVIII, No. 2 (1957), p. 69.
[4] Irene M. Josselyn, M.D., "What We Know About the Unmarried Mother." Paper read at National Conference of Social Work, June 1953.
[5] Leontine Young, *Out of Wedlock*, McGraw-Hill Book Co., New York, 1954, p. 22.

The popular magazine articles have been echoing this point of view. In many situations it may be a useful approach. The results of treatment are often dramatic and gratifying when a girl is able to make use of help in understanding and dealing with some of the underlying problems related to her out-of-wedlock pregnancy. However, in contacts with residents in a maternity home, one becomes concerned about the limited applicability of this theory in a number of cases. One has the impression that in some situations factors other than, or in addition to, underlying emotional pathology have been of greater significance; that emphasis on a single point of view has prevented us from seeing other essential aspects of the experience and, correspondingly, has resulted in a limited treatment offering. This has seemed a good time, therefore, to re-examine the theory and look at other hypotheses which might be applicable in our work with unmarried mothers.

Social Mores

By and large, unmarried motherhood in our society is looked on as the violation of a cultural norm. It should therefore be possible to isolate and identify the norm in question. But this is not easy. For one thing, it is not clear whether the offended norm is the taboo against extramarital relations or against bearing a child out of wedlock. We point to the symptomatic nature of the pregnancy ("there are no accidental conceptions"), but in speaking of prevention we are unable to clarify what we are trying to prevent—unsanctioned sex experience or out-of-wedlock pregnancy.

Some communities are more or less resigned to widespread sexual experimentation (among teen-agers), yet indignantly aroused and condemning when such experimentations result in out-of-wedlock pregnancy.[6]

If one observes public reactions today, one can hardly escape the conclusion that it is not so much the sexual relationship to which we object as the fact of the baby.[7]

Actually we are not dealing with a single norm, but with a multiplicity of norms which will vary according to cultural and ethnic groups, social or educational sophistication, peer practices, and so forth. These norms will vary not only from one girl to another but

[6] Lola A. Bowman, "The Unmarried Mother Who Is a Minor," *Child Welfare*, Vol. 37, No. 8 (1958), p. 13.
[7] Leontine Young, *op. cit.*, p. p.6.

101

also for the same girl, according to the group she is most strongly related to at a given period in her life. The girl whose group or family loyalties at the age of seventeen preclude sexual experience may be safer from out-of-wedlock pregnancy at that time than she is at the age of twenty-two, when her major satisfactions may reside in a group whose climate sanctions or invites such activity.

Our society has been undergoing a change in its sexual behavior. The relaxation of taboos which usually accompanies the upheavals of war has been accelerated in the last two generations by the development of a widely publicized psychology. Permissiveness, self-expression, sexual adjustment, and freedom from inhibition have become in some quarters the marks of the well-adjusted American. The idea of extramarital sex experience is accepted among many college students; among some groups its practice is almost a social *sine qua non*.

However, the professed code of behavior has not kept pace with the changing practices, and the ideal of chastity and marriage continues to be cherished along with other cultural fictions.[8] As long as the violation of the professed value is conducted with a decent regard for secrecy or is not otherwise detected, society is content to accept the implied and overt contradictions resulting from the gap between our professed and operational codes.

Most adults sooner or later arrive at some sort of equilibrium in this cultural tightrope-walking act within which their satisfactions and their consciences manage a reasonably peaceful coexistence. For the young person searching for standards such a balance is not so easily achieved. When those from whom her standards are to be derived—the guardians of our social mores—are operating on more than one set of values, it is not surprising that she herself should question the validity of the professed code. The realism in the seemingly cynical "It's just that I was unlucky enough to get caught" cannot be lightly dismissed.

The uncertainty in our point of view as professional people may well be a reflection of the confusion in the society in which we participate and the role to which the community assigns us as social workers. As members of contemporary society we tolerate the original sexual activity. In deriving our social attitudes from the society that fosters the agencies we represent, we are expected to de-

[8] For an extended discussion of this problem see Max Lerner, *America As a Civilization*, Simon & Schuster, New York 1957, pp. 657–688.

plore the activity when confronted with its outcome. Identified with the unmarried pregnant girl who must hide from a censuring community, we reach out to comfort and counsel her. In addition we have our own private views to deal with. To say that a girl is in some respects an inevitable casualty of social change would almost make it appear that we approved of her sexual activity. We are uncertain as to what stand we should take toward extramarital sex experience, or whether we wish to take a stand at all. Yet a noticeable increase in the incidence of illegitimate births compels our attention. We are indeed on the horns of a dilemma.

The extension of unmarried motherhood into our upper and educated classes in sizable numbers further confounds us by rendering our former stereotypes less tenable. Immigration, low mentality, and hypersexuality can no longer be comfortably applied when the phenomenon has invaded our own social class—when the unwed mother must be classified to include the nice girl next door, the college graduate, the physician's or pastor's daughter. In casting about for an appropriate explanation for her predicament we find it more comfortable to see the out-of-wedlock mother as a girl whose difficulty stems from underlying, pre-existing personality problems. We are forced into the position of interpreting the situation primarily in terms of individual pathology, failing to recognize the full extent to which the symptom may be culture-bound. We do, when pressed, acknowledge the possible influence of cultural factors, but in the main we do not tend to incorporate these elements significantly into our thinking.

There are no ready answers to this perplexing question, but as social workers we cannot deal adequately with the problem of the unmarried mother unless we see it within the framework of our conflicting mores. We must make room in our thinking for factors in the social scene—not only as they contribute to unwed motherhood, but also as they color the girl's reaction to her out-of-wedlock status in pregnancy.

It is understandable that we should incline toward a theory of underlying pathology as the cause of unmarried motherhood. Frequently, when we see the illegitimately pregnant girl, she presents a picture of severe disturbance. Guilt, panic, suspicion, and denial are not uncommon reactions. More often than not she will give a history of deprivation in primary relationships. However, if we are to assess correctly the sources and appropriateness of these reactions, we must take into consideration the circumstances under which we are seeing them. Two compelling factors in these circumstances are the crisis itself and the specifics of pregnancy and maternity. They are important not only for their diagnostic meaning but also because of their implications for practice in our work with unmarried mothers.

Crisis

We know that in a crisis situation current functioning may be disrupted, past vulnerabilities exposed, and hitherto manageable conflicts stirred up. Earlier feelings of guilt, deprivation, and the like may be reactivated. The unmarried pregnant woman, seen at a point of crisis, may exhibit a whole range of disturbed reactions. To be sure, each girl will experience her unwed motherhood in accordance with her basic personality make-up and will integrate it into her own patterns of reaction and behavior. However, crisis can produce distortions of one's customary patterns, and we cannot assume that her reactions in a crisis situation represent her characteristic mode of adaptation to reality any more than we can say that an acute pneumonia is characteristic of a person's physiological endowment, even though he may have some pulmonary susceptibility. A girl may become an unmarried mother because she has had pre-existing problems, or she may be having problems because she is an unmarried mother. Her behavior may be a true reflection of underlying emotional pathology, or it may be an appropriate response in an anxiety-producing situation. She may be manifesting primarily a resurgence of the latent guilt and unresolved conflicts which are ingredients in all human adjustment and which have been stirred up under acute stress.

Unmarried mothers as seen in a maternity home appear to experience these crises in stages, with periods of relative calm between, rather than in an unbroken line. Each girl seems to have her own pattern of stress alternating with well-being. For each the crisis-precipitating factor seems to be different at different times. It may be related to elements in the pregnancy. ("The emotional crises of pregnancy are produced mainly through stimulation by biological processes within the mother. . . ." [9]) or it may result from news of

[9] Gerald Caplan, *An Approach to Community Mental Health,* Grune and Stratton, New York, 1961, p. 165.

the baby's father, her own parents, or some other external source. Our knowledge and experience are rather limited in this area. Perhaps we should be directing some of our efforts toward learning to recognize the signs of these crises, in order to anticipate and prepare for them if possible—to know when intervention is indicated and when the potentials for self-healing inherent in crisis situations had best be left to do their own work; to try to understand so that we may learn to deal with the rhythms of crisis in the unmarried mother.

A recognition of the crisis factor in unmarried motherhood should give us pause in our routine use of psychological testing of the resident in a maternity home, and in the requirement for prescribed casework interviews. One may hope that it will prompt us to interpret with great caution the results of projective tests and questionnaires, devices which appear to be taking on increasing importance in the diagnosis of unmarried mothers. Personality traits registered at a time of crisis, though applicable to the time and circumstances under which the tests are administered, can be interpreted in only a limited way as ongoing characteristics of the unmarried mother, individually or as a group. (The provocative nature of some of the test questions might also be considered.) Otherwise we are likely to emerge with a personality picture that does not fit the observations of many of us who are seeing unmarried mothers in their day-to-day living.

Note some conclusions from a recent study:

. . . acting out anti-socially is a primary characteristic of the unwed mother. . . . There does not appear to be much difference between the unwed mother and other delinquent females.

The unmarried mother is bitterly hostile . . . more so than all patient groups.

They are unfitted for psychotherapy because they deny problems and in their defensiveness appear aloof and independent, thus rejecting help and their basic dependency needs.[10]

Pregnancy and Motherhood

It is generally accepted that the experience of pregnancy can contain elements of crisis even for the married woman. "So-called 'normal

10 Edmund Pollock, "An Investigation into Certain Personality Characteristics of Unmarried Mothers." Unpublished doctoral dissertation, New York University, 1957, pp. 103, 110, 141.

pregnant women' might be highly abnormal, and even if they are not, they are anxious to a degree beyond that of the so-called 'normal non-pregnant female.' " [11] "Particularly during the first pregnancy women are apt to suffer terrifying dreams and phantasies of giving birth to a dead or misshapen child." [12] With the additional pressures to which the unmarried pregnant woman is subjected, we should not be surprised to see an intensification of the reactions which in her married counterpart we are prone to accept with tolerant indulgence. In themselves they are not necessarily signs of severe pathology. By the same token, the "normal deviations" of adolescence should figure prominently in our assessment of the meaning of out-of-wedlock pregnancy in the teen-ager.

Pregnancy and parturition constitute a continuing experience in physiological and emotional change. Each period seems to have its biological characteristics and typical emotional concomitants. There is still much uncharted territory in our knowledge of this psychobiological phenomenon, but obstetricians, psychiatrists, and others working with married pregnant women are becoming increasingly interested in the importance of these factors. As members of a helping discipline we have an obligation to incorporate into our work with the unmarried mother whatever relevant information is available. We may not be able to apply it very specifically as yet, but recognition of the significance of such factors can influence the ways in which we respond to a girl's reactions, the areas in which we offer help, and the manner in which we offer it.

It can affect our decision whether to reassure or to explore for deeper meaning at a given point. It may influence our interpretation of a girl's dependent leaning toward her mother or a mother-person. It will have a bearing on our reaction to her apprehensiveness about her growing attachment to a baby which she must relinquish—the ease with which we can help her to accept herself as a prospective mother and experience pregnancy and motherhood in as constructive a way as possible. It will have much to do with the strength we can lend her in the face of a separation from her baby, so that she can liberate and experience her feelings of mother-

[11] J. C. Hirst and F. Strousse, "The Origin of Emotional Factors in Normal Pregnant Women," *American Journal of the Medical Sciences,* Vol. 196, No. 1 (1938), p. 98.

[12] Florence Clothier, M.D., "Psychological Implications of Unmarried Parenthood," *American Journal of Orthopsychiatry,* Vol. 13, No. 3 (1943), p. 541.

liness toward her child. The "some day if I marry and have a baby *of my own . . . ,*" inadvertently voiced by many girls who will be surrendering their babies, should give us pause as to its implications regarding their efforts to prepare for the interruption of a biological process which does not readily lend itself to alteration by social stricture.

For most unmarried mothers this is a first experience in motherhood and as such it may be an important influence in the image a girl establishes of herself as a mother-person. Part of our goal should be to help her emerge from it with as positive an image of herself as a mother as her personality and circumstances will permit. To do this we need to be ready, at appropriate points, to de-emphasize the unmarried, socially deviant aspect of her experience and accentuate its normal motherhood components. In fact we may well ask ourselves whether, in failing to exploit the full possibilities of motherhood for the unmarried mother, we may not be encouraging the blocking out of large areas of affect in her experience in maternity, whether she is surrendering her baby or keeping it.

In general, it might be well to examine our uncritical assumption that for the mother who must relinquish her child early separation is invariably indicated. Perhaps we need to consider the possibility that there are differences in the rates at which biological ties between mothers and babies are loosened, just as there are differences in the strength of these ties; that variations in the timing of the separation may therefore be indicated; that a premature separation may be as injurious as indefinite temporizing; and that perhaps the community has a responsibility to furnish the resources whereby such individual differences can be provided for.

If we see illegitimate pregnancy primarily as a symptom of underlying emotional pathology, we are likely to interpret much of an unmarried mother's behavior in similar terms. We shall be on the alert for signs of pathology and shall undoubtedly find them; one wonders whether we may not sometimes even be guilty of promoting the "self-fulfilling prophecy." [13] In trying to assess the nature and degree of disturbance, no matter how skillfully we proceed we may turn valid exploration into inappropriate probing, and find ourselves contributing to the very disturbance we are trying to diagnose.

13 Robert K. Merton, *Social Theory and Social Structure,* Free Press of Glencoe, 1957, pp. 421–426.

107

The extent to which pathology orientation can skew our thinking can be illustrated in two fairly typical experiences we are likely to meet in our work with unmarried mothers—"denial" and planning for the baby.

Denial

The unmarried mother's use of "denial" is a source of some concern to social workers. We tend to see it in her efforts to delay her admission to the maternity home, in her remaining in ordinary clothing beyond the appropriate time, in her reluctance to discuss plans for the baby just yet, in her unwillingness to talk. This may well be a denial of sorts, but is it bad?

Unless a girl is seriously disturbed, it is a fairly safe guess that she is not denying to herself the *fact* of her pregnancy. The question then is, what is she denying and to whom? Is she expressing the feeble hope that there may have been an error in diagnosis after all (a not uncommon reaction in married women), or could she be trying to minimize the implications of her abandonment by the baby's father? She may be struggling with the problem of maternal affect, seeking to protect herself psychologically from a growing interest in a baby she may have to give up.

In assessing the meaning of denial, we may do well to take cognizance of our own role in fostering it. As agents of the community, we offer the unmarried pregnant girl anonymity in a protected shelter; we provide out-of-town mailing addresses; we encourage her to deny her maternity by plans for the early placement of her baby, so that she can resume her place in the community as though nothing had happened. What we interpret as pathology may be the girl's valid use of a healthy mechanism to protect herself in crisis from a threatening reality. She is behaving the way society requires, in order to avoid permanent impairment of her social functioning. There are times when the girl who does not deny should perhaps be of greater concern to us than the one who does.

Planning for the Baby

Our assumption that illegitimate pregnancy is invariably rooted in personality pathology has led us to accept uncritically certain further assumptions deriving from the basic ones:

1. That the same neurotic conflict which resulted in the out-of-wedlock pregnancy will motivate the girl in planning for her baby.

Her decision about the baby is based not upon her feeling for him as a separate individual but upon the purpose for which she bore him.[14]

2. That adoption is the preferred plan for the babies of unmarried mothers.

It is not an unwarranted interference with the unmarried mother to presume that in most cases it will be in the child's best interests for her to release her child for adoption. . . . The concept that the unmarried mother and her child constitute a family is to me unsupportable.[15]

3. That the girl who relinquishes her baby is healthier than the one who keeps hers.

No doubt many girls who should be relinquishing their babies are keeping them. Conversely, it may well be that some girls who are relinquishing their babies should keep them. One mother may be giving up her baby for reasons as neurotic as another's who keeps hers. However, if we are committed uncritically to the assumptions outlined here, we are less likely to give the adoption plan the thorough-going exploration that we devote to the plan to keep the baby, nor are we likely to examine the extent to which factors in the girl *and* in society are responsible for making one plan more desirable than another.

Actually we do not have enough verified data regarding the long-range outcomes of either plan to substantiate one assumption over the other. In the meantime we are subscribing to a point of view that states in effect that the presence of neurotic conflict automatically cancels out the validity of an impulse which is biologically determined. A mother, married or unmarried, may be severely neurotic in her motivation toward motherhood and still be substantially maternal. If we fail to take cognizance of this, we are taking only a partial view of the problem and are likely to give the unwed mother an incomplete or distorted service in the various aspects of her problem.

Technically we may claim that our underlying point of view does not influence us and that each girl is allowed to make her own decision regarding her baby. And technically this is probably cor-

---

[14] Leontine Young, *op. cit.*, p. 199.
[15] Joseph H. Reid, "Principles, Values, and Assumptions Underlying Adoption Practice," *Social Work*, Vol. 2, No. 1 (1957), p. 27.

rect in most cases. But the subtle communication of our essential attitude cannot be denied—as observed by one girl who felt she was being pressured into surrendering her baby: "It's not what Mrs. K says exactly, it's just that her face lights up when I talk about adoption the way it doesn't when I talk about keeping Beth."

Summary

In our emphasis on a single theory of causation with regard to unmarried motherhood we are overlooking other important aspects of this phenomenon. As a result we may be depriving ourselves of meaningful diagnostic perceptions and failing to make full use of the rich treatment possibilities inherent in the experience for the girl. The additional factors of social mores, crisis, and the specifics of pregnancy and motherhood are offered for consideration here. They are presented not as substitutes for the currently accepted theory of underlying emotional conflict as causative in out-of-wedlock pregnancy, but rather as added dimensions which can extend our horizons and increase the effectiveness of our work in this area. Nor are these factors thought of as relevant for all unmarried mothers. It is hoped that they may be evaluated and applied with the same diagnostic discrimination, and on as individual a basis, as any theory.

If we are to help the unmarried pregnant woman to weather her experience with a minimum of damage, and if possible exploit it as a point of departure for her maturing as a woman, we must help her understand what is happening to her in terms of her personal psychological make-up, her biological experience, and the social world of which she is a part. To do this we must be ready to accept multiple theories of causation; we need to explore without bias as many of the relevant ingredients as we can identify, and bring them all to bear in our effort to understand and help her. We must be ready to divest ourselves of some of the stereotyped images of the unmarried mother to which we have uncritically committed ourselves, and to recognize the conflicts in our own roles as social workers in relation to this problem.

We need to search for ways of broadening our knowledge and applying it more meaningfully in diagnosis and treatment of the unmarried mother. We need to think in terms of hypotheses to be truly tested rather than closed systems of explanation for which we are impelled to find substantiating evidence.

8. Parenthood as Crisis*

E. E. LeMasters

IN RECENT DECADES the impact of various crises on the American family has been subjected to intensive analysis. Eliot, Waller, Angell, Komarovsky, Cavan and Ranck, Koos, Hill, and Goode have published what is perhaps the most solid block of empirical research in the field of family sociology.[1]

In all of these studies of how the modern family reacts to crisis, it appears that the shock is related to the fact that the crisis event forces a reorganization of the family as a social system. Roles have to be reassigned, status positions shifted, values reoriented, and needs met through new channels.

These studies have shown that crises may originate either from within the family itself or from the outside. It has also been demonstrated that the total impact of the crisis will depend upon a number of variables: (1) the nature of the crisis event; (2) the state of organization or disorganization of the family at the point of impact; (3) the resources of the family; and (4) its previous experience with crisis.[2]

These studies report a sequence of events somewhat as follows:

* Reprinted from *Marriage and Family Living*, Vol. XIX, No. 4 (1957).

[1] See Thomas D. Eliot, "Bereavement: Inevitable but Not Unsurmountable," *Family, Marriage, and Parenthood*, Howard Becker and Reuben Hill (eds.), Heath and Co., Boston, 1955; Willard W. Waller, *The Old Love and the New*, Liveright, New York, 1930; Robert C. Angell, *The Family Encounters the Depression*, Charles Scribner's Sons, New York, 1936; Mirra Komarovsky, *The Unemployed Man and His Family*, Dryden Press, New York, 1940; Ruth Cavan and Katherine Ranck, *The Family and the Depression*, University of Chicago Press, Chicago, 1938; Earl L. Koos, *Families in Trouble*, King's Crown Press, New York, 1946; Reuben Hill, *Families Under Stress*, Harper and Bros., New York, 1949; William J. Goode, *After Divorce*, Free Press of Glencoe, 1956.

[2] See Hill, *op. cit.*, for an excellent review of this research.

111

level of organization before the crisis, point of impact, period of disorganization, recovery, and subsequent level of reorganization.

This study was conceived and designed within the conceptual framework of the above research.

The Present Study

In the study described in this report the main hypothesis was derived through the following line of analysis:

A. If the family is conceptualized as a small social system, would it not follow that the *adding* of a new member to the system could force a reorganization of the system as drastic (or nearly so) as does the *removal* of a member?

B. If the above were correct, would it not follow that the arrival of the *first* child could be construed as a "crisis" or critical event? [3]

To test this hypothesis, a group of young parents were interviewed, using a relatively unstructured interviewing technique. In order to control socioeconomic variables, couples had to possess the following characteristics to be included in the study: (1) unbroken marriage; (2) urban or surburban residence; (3) between twenty-five and thirty-five years of age at the time of the study; (4) husband college graduate; (5) husband's occupation middle class; (6) wife not employed after birth of first child; and (7) must have had their first child within five years of the date interviewed. Race and religion were not controlled.

Using these criteria, forty-eight couples were located by the device of asking various persons in the community for names. As a precaution, the exact nature of the study was not stated in soliciting names for the sample—the project was described as a study of "modern young parents."

Once a name was obtained that met the specifications, every effort was made to secure an interview. No refusals were encountered, but two couples left the community before they could participate, leaving forty-six couples for the final study group. The couples, then, were not volunteers. All of the interviewing was done by the writer during the years 1953–1956. Both the husband and wife were interviewed.

Typical occupations represented include minister, social worker,

[3] To some extent, the original idea for this study was derived from Hill's discussion. See *op. cit.*, ch. 2.

high school teacher, college professor, bank teller, accountant, athletic coach, and small business owner.

Various definitions of "crisis" are available to the worker in this area. Webster, for example, states that the term means a "decisive" or "crucial" period, a "turning point." [4] Koos specifies that crises are situations "which block the usual patterns of action and call for new ones." [5] Hill defines as a crisis "any sharp or decisive change for which old patterns are inadequate." [6] This is the definition used in this analysis.

A five-point scale was used in coding the interview data: (1) no crisis; (2) slight crisis; (3) moderate crisis; (4) extensive crisis; (5) severe crisis.

The Findings

The essential findings of this exploratory study are as follows:

1. Thirty-eight of the forty-six couples (83 per cent) reported "extensive" or "severe" crisis in adjusting to the first child. This rating was arrived at jointly by the interviewer and the parents.

In several cases there was some difference of opinion between the husband and wife as to what their response should be. In all but two cases, however, the difference was reconciled by further discussion between the interviewer and the couple. In the two cases, the wife's rating was recorded, on the theory that the mother makes the major adjustment to children in our culture.

For this sample, therefore, the evidence is quite strong in support of the hypothesis. The eight couples (17 per cent) who reported relatively mild crisis (values 1–2–3 in the above scale) must be considered the deviants in this sample.

Stated theoretically, this study supports the idea that adding the first child to the urban middle-class married couple constitutes a crisis event.

2. In this study there was strong evidence that this crisis reaction was *not* the result of not wanting children. On the contrary, thirty-five of the thirty-eight pregnancies in the crisis group were either "planned" or "desired."

3. The data support the belief that the crisis pattern occurs

[4] *Webster's Collegiate Dictionary*, G. and C. Merriam Co., Springfield, Second Edition, 1944, p. 240.
[5] Koos, *op. cit.*, p. 9.
[6] Hill, *op. cit.*, p. 51. See also his review of definitions in ch. 2.

whether the marriage is "good" or "poor"—for example: thirty-four of the thirty-eight in the crisis group (89 per cent) rated their marriages as "good" or better. With only three exceptions, these ratings were confirmed by close friends. By any reasonable standards, these marriages must be considered adequate.

4. There is considerable evidence that the crisis pattern in the thirty-eight cases was not the result of "neurosis" or other psychiatric disability on the part of these parents. Judging by their personal histories, their marriages, and the ratings of friends, it seemed clear that the vast bulk of the husbands and wives in the crisis group were average or above in personality adjustment.

5. The thirty-eight couples in the crisis group appear to have almost completely romanticized parenthood. They felt that they had had very little, if any, effective preparation for parental roles. As one mother said: "We knew where babies came from, but we didn't know *what they were like."*

The mothers reported the following feelings or experiences in adjusting to the first child: loss of sleep (especially during the early months); chronic "tiredness" or exhaustion; extensive confinement to the home and the resulting curtailment of their social contacts; giving up the satisfactions and the income of outside employment; additional washing and ironing; guilt at not being a "better" mother; the long hours and seven day (and night) week necessary in caring for an infant; decline in their housekeeping standards; worry over their appearance (increased weight after pregnancy, et cetera).

The fathers echoed most of the above adjustments but also added a few of their own: decline in sexual response of wife; economic pressure resulting from wife's retirement plus additional expenditures necessary for child; interference with social life; worry about a second pregnancy in the near future; and a general disenchantment with the parental role.

6. The mothers with professional training and extensive professional work experience (eight cases) suffered "extensive" or "severe" crisis in every case.

In the analysis of these cases, it was apparent that these women were really involved in two major adjustments simultaneously: (1) they were giving up an occupation which had deep significance for them; and (2) they were assuming the role of mother for the first time.

Interpretation of the Findings

There are, of course, various ways of interpreting the findings in this study. It may be, for example, that the couples obtained for the sample are not typical of urban middle-class parents. It might also be true that the interviewing, the design of the study, or both, may have been inadequate. If we assume, for the present, that the findings are reliable and valid for this social group, how are we to interpret such reactions to parenthood? It is suggested that the following conceptual tools may be helpful.

1. That parenthood (and not marriage) is the real "romantic complex" in our culture. This view, as a matter of fact, was expressed by many of the couples in the study.

In a brilliant article some years ago, Arnold Green [7] suggested as much—that urban middle-class couples often find their parental roles in conflict with their other socioeconomic commitments. If this is true, one would expect to find the reconciliation of these conflicts most acute at the point of entering parenthood, with the first child. Our findings support this expectation.

2. Ruth Benedict has pointed out that young people in our society are often the victims of "discontinuity in cultural conditioning." [8] By this she means that we often have to "unlearn" previous training before we can move on to the next set of roles. Sex conditioning is perhaps the clearest illustration of this.

Using this concept, one can see that these couples were not trained for parenthood, that practically nothing in school, or out of school, got them ready to be fathers and mothers—*husbands* and *wives*, yes, but not *parents*. This helps explain why some of the mothers interviewed were actually "bitter" about their high school and college training.

3. One can also interpret these findings by resorting to what is known about small groups. Wilson and Ryland, for example, in their standard text on group work make this comment about the two-person group: "This combination seems to be the most satisfactory of human relationships." [9] They then proceed to pass this judgment

[7] Arnold W. Green, "The Middle-Class Male Child and Neurosis," *American Sociological Review*, Vol. 11 (1946), pp. 31–41.

[8] Ruth Benedict, "Continuities and Discontinuities in Cultural Conditioning," *Psychiatry*, Vol. 1 (1939), pp. 161–167.

[9] Gertrude Wilson and Gladys Ryland, *Social Group Work Practice*, Houghton Mifflin Co., Boston, 1949, p. 49.

on the three-person group: "Upon analysis this pattern falls into a combination of a pair and an isolate. . . . This plurality pattern is the most volatile of all human relationships." [10] This, of course, supports an earlier analysis by von Wiese and Becker.[11]

Viewed in this conceptual system, married couples find the transition to parenthood painful because the arrival of the first child destroys the two-person or pair pattern of group interaction and forces a rapid reorganization of their life into a three-person or triangle group system. Owing to the fact that their courtship and pre-parenthood pair relationship has persisted over a period of years, they find it difficult to give it up as a way of life.

In addition, however, they find that living as a trio is more complicated than living as a pair. The husband, for example, no longer ranks first in claims upon his wife but must accept the child's right to priority. In some cases, the husband may feel that he is the semi-isolate, the third party in the trio. In other cases, the wife may feel that her husband is more interested in the baby than in her. If they preserve their pair relationship and continue their previous way of life, relatives and friends may regard them as poor parents. In any event, their pattern of living has to be radically altered.

Since babies do not usually appear to married couples completely by surprise, it might be argued that this event is not really a crisis— "well-adjusted" couples should be "prepared for it." The answer seems to be that children and parenthood have been so romanticized in our society that most middle-class couples are caught unprepared, even though they have planned and waited for this event for years. The fact that parenthood is "normal" does not eliminate crisis. Death is also "normal" but continues to be a crisis event for most families.

4. One can also interpret the findings of this study by postulating that parenthood (not marriage) marks the final transition to maturity and adult responsibility in our culture.[12] Thus the arrival of the first child forces young married couples to take the last painful step into the adult world. This point, as a matter of fact, was stated or implied by most of the couples in the crisis group.

5. Finally, the cases in this sample confirm what the previous stud-

[10] *Ibid.*
[11] Leopold von Wiese, *Systematic Sociology,* adapted and amplified by Howard Becker, Wiley, New York, 1932.
[12] This is essentially the point of view in Robert J. Havighurst's analysis, *Human Development and Education,* Longmans, Green, New York, 1953.

ies in this area have shown—that the event itself is only one factor determining the extent and severity of the crisis in any given family. Their resources, their previous experience with crisis, the pattern of role organization before the crisis—these factors are equally important in determining the total reaction to the event.

Conclusion

In the study described, it was hypothesized that the addition of the first child constitutes a crisis event, forcing the married couple to move from an adult-centered pair type of organization into a child-centered, triad group system. Of the forty-six middle-class couples studied, thirty-eight (83 per cent) confirmed the hypothesis.

In all fairness to this group of parents, it should be reported that all but a few of them eventually made what seems to be a successful adjustment to parenthood. This finding does not alter the fact, however, that most of them found the transition difficult. Listening to them describe their experiences, one felt that these young parents could be compared to veterans of military service; they had been through a rough experience, but it was worth it. As one father said: "I wouldn't have missed it for the world."

It is unfortunate that the number of parents in this sample who did not report crisis is so small (eight couples) that no general statements can be made about them. Somehow, however, they seem to have been better prepared for parenthood than was the crisis group. It is felt that future work on this problem might well include a more extensive analysis of couples who have made the transition to parenthood with relative ease.

If the basic findings of this study are confirmed by other workers, it would appear that family life educators could make a significant contribution by helping young people prepare more adequately for parenthood.

9. Maternal Reactions to Premature Birth Viewed as an Acute Emotional Disorder*

David M. Kaplan
and Edward A. Mason

TRADITIONALLY, psychiatric theory, in referring to acute problems, conceives them as primarily stemming from previously existing chronic conditions. Thus a combat fatigue reaction is viewed as an exacerbation of an existing neurosis and an acute psychotic episode is seen as arising out of a previously quiescent schizophrenia. "Stress" may be defined as a state of psychological upset or disequilibrium in an individual. This disequilibrium is of relatively brief duration and is generally self-limiting. It is a reaction to a specific event which is commonly perceived by those who experience it as an unexpected threat or loss. Examples of such events are death, retirement, serious illness, birth, loss of job, loss of income, or a surgical operation. In this paper, we propose to focus on a specific stress situation—the one occasioned by a premature birth—and to show that the maternal reactions to this event can usefully be described as acute emotional disorders. There are many parallels between these reactions and those in an acute infectious process. For example, the range of severity of reaction to a psychologically stressful event is a broad one ranging from the mild and generally self-correcting type to the severe, in which the likelihood of adverse sequelae is high.

The expanded idea of acute emotional disorder has been developed from the theory of traumatic neurosis [1] from "crisis" theory,[2]

* Reprinted, by permission, from *The American Journal of Orthopsychiatry*, Vol. XXX, No. 3 (1960). Copyright, American Orthopsychiatric Association.

[1] See Otto Fenichel, *The Psychoanalytic Theory of Neurosis*, Norton, New York, 1945; Sigmund Freud, *Beyond the Pleasure Principle*, Hogarth Press, London, 1920, and "Mourning and Melancholia," *Collected Papers, IV*, Hogarth Press, London, 1925, pp. 152–170; Abram Kardiner, *The Traumatic Neuroses of War*, National Research Council, Washington, 1941.

[2] Gerald Caplan, *Concepts of Mental Health and Consultation*, Children's Bureau, Washington, 1959.

118

from such studies as the one of bereavement by Lindemann,[3] and from the model of the acute infectious diseases.[4] We believe the occurrence of an acute disorder does not depend upon the prior existence of an established chronic process; rather it results from the individual's attempt to cope with a threatening event for which he is not sufficiently psychologically prepared.

This concept of illness does not preclude the fact that the reactions to a stressful event will be heavily conditioned by previously existing personality factors. However, even where such chronic conditions exist, they alone do not necessarily determine outcome. There are current situational forces which have an important bearing on outcome, such as hospital practices, the behavior of the father, and the role of health agencies.

The most important advantage of this concept of acute emotional disorders is that it helps direct attention to the significant mental health problems of the more "normal" group in the population. It also makes possible the clinical treatment of this relatively healthy group which is affected, as all human beings unavoidably are affected, by a variety of stressful events. We believe the successful resolution of stress can avert chronic conditions which might otherwise result. This approach illustrates the preventive orientation in the field of community mental health.

Study Data

The present study * of the maternal reaction to premature birth is one of several approaches to the analysis of our data on the responses of family members to stress. These studies are being carried out in the Harvard School of Public Health Family Guidance Center.[5] To date, 60 families have been interviewed during the period following the premature birth and continuing until the baby has been home for two months. Examination of the clinical material from these interviews indicates that there is a typical psychological experience for the mother of the premature baby which can be distinguished from the experience following full-term delivery.

[3] Erich Lindemann, ch. 1 of this volume.

[4] J. L. Halliday, "Principles of Aetology," *British Journal of Medical Psychology*, Vol. 19 (1943), pp. 367–380.

* This project was supported by a grant from the Commonwealth Fund and was under the direction of Dr. Gerald Caplan and Dr. Edward A. Mason.

[5] Gerald Caplan, *An Approach to the Study of Family Mental Health*, Public Health Report 71, 1956, pp. 1027–1030.

119

The maternal stress accompanying premature birth begins with the onset of labor, and the experience she must face should be seen in contrast to what most women expect in a normal delivery.[6] At term the woman is impatient both to see the baby and to discharge her burden. Whether she comes to delivery anxious or calm, the atmosphere encourages her to feel that she will produce a normal child. The setting is geared to her needs and she manages the discomforts of labor because they are seen as temporary. When the events follow the expected pattern, the mother more readily feels a pride in her achievement and she receives rewards and recognition on the part of the doctor, hospital staff, husband, family, and friends. She is encouraged to feel happy and proud, and after a brief period of rest begins to share this with her baby as she holds and feeds it. This closeness and the feeling of success serve to encourage the continuation and heightening of the relationship to the child. The baby's presence can be openly acknowledged and plans and expectations can continue on the basis of its established normality. Having accomplished her first major maternal task successfully, the mother moves from one step to the next on the basis of success, and she is carried along in spite of any anxiety she may feel by the immediacy of the needs of the infant.

Premature Labor and Delivery. In contrast to the normal pregnancy there are distinct differences in the experience of the mother of a premature. In spite of her anxieties about possible pregnancy failure, the average pregnant woman does not seem to be concerned about premature delivery. Rather, she has the notion that a baby born before term is nonviable or deformed. Even during pregnancies where there has been bleeding, amniotic fluid loss, or pain, the expectant mother's primary concern is to "hold on" until term, believing the alternative is miscarriage. As a result, premature labor comes as a shock and the woman, even though intellectually aware of the possibility, is emotionally unprepared when it happens to her. The import of earlier signs of difficulty is frequently ignored, denied, or minimized. These women often misinterpret the onset of labor and describe the experience later as "unreal," as though clinging to the wish that delivery would not be early.

The hospital atmosphere is more characteristic of an emergency than of a normal labor; there is more than usual listening for the

6 Helene Deutsch, *The Psychology of Women: Motherhood,* Grune & Stratton, New York, 1945.

fetal heart, there is general apprehensiveness, and the woman is informed that for the protection of the baby there will be no anesthesia. These experiences confirm the woman's feeling that this is a dangerous situation for the baby, but there is often, even at this late point, a disbelief that delivery will follow.

Mrs. A said she was admitted for a "virus infection" and she considered delivery "impossible." She had bleeding during her first four and a half months and was "wet continually" in her sixth month. Many times she had thought that miscarriage or delivery was imminent and the child would be abnormal if it lived. Her doctor had warned her not to expect a live birth and she was admitted for observation at six months. An attempt to induce labor was unsuccessful, and several hours later she had a "shaking chill" which she believed was "appendicitis." There followed a period when first the students and then "a procession of doctors" tried to find the fetal heart and could not. When labor finally began three doctors tried to start intravenous feeding. She was told she would have no anesthesia whereas she had wished for a deep anesthesia; she remembered no "real labor."

A mother of a premature as opposed to a full-term baby has a *heightened* concern after delivery about whether the baby is alive and will live, and later whether there is any abnormality. She sees the baby briefly before it is hurried into an incubator and taken off to a separate nursery or even a different hospital. Her most vivid recollections are about the baby's small size; its unusual color and unattractive appearance add further to the shock.

The mother frequently returns to a ward with other women who have lost their babies, and typically feels "lonely" and "lost." Mrs. T wandered about the ward, eating and sleeping poorly, missed her baby and her husband, and only went to look at her baby once in the four days she was there. Many a mother expects at any moment to hear news of her baby's death. Mrs. K described herself as upset and feeling like crying, but unable to *do* anything; it was the "worst time" in her life because of the lonesomeness and separation. She felt the ward was full of "worthless souls" and "no one" talked to her until the baby was better.

Usually the physician talks to the mother in guarded words, or else avoids contact with her for a few days. In general, there seems to be no prompt and frank discussion about the prognosis or cause of prematurity, and a state of suspense is encouraged. The hospital staff finds it difficult to know how to respond; the mother needs sup-

121

port, but it is hard to give without confirming her feeling of failure or futilely raising her hopes. A mother expecting to hear at any moment that her baby has died is apprehensive and prone to pick up the anxieties of other mothers or of the staff.

> Mrs. K was unable to get in touch with the pediatrician, who deliberately talked instead with Mr. K and encouraged him not to "worry" his wife. The nurse told Mrs. K, "We don't want you to feel the baby is better or worse so that you won't pin too much hope on what we say." She therefore didn't know how serious the situation was until three days after the birth when she went to have her first look at the baby.

The nursery for the prematures frustrates most mothers in their desire to see the baby. Often it is on a different floor. The incubator obscures a good view, and often must remain on the other side of the room from the window in order to have oxygen immediately available. When mothers do visit, their babies' appearance is frightening. Mrs. A commented that she felt as if she were visiting a "zoo" with many "strange creatures" behind the glass. Mrs. K said her baby "looked awful" and "his terrible color was more of a shock than his size." Mrs. T said her baby reminded her of a "turtle without a shell," a "frog," or a "chicken." Most frequent is the comment that it is so tiny and weak. It is hardly a baby to inspire pride, and if anyone visits at all there is no cause for the normal congratulations. Visitors usually speak with sympathy and caution, and generally cards, cigars, and christenings are delayed at least several weeks. Mothers feel helpless and useless, separated from the baby, and frequently remark that they don't even deserve to be in the hospital. They may avoid visiting the nursery altogether or else be drawn to look at the baby in spite of the baby's reminding them of their failure.

There are some notable exceptions * to the pattern as generally described above, and comment should be made here on the group of women who experience minimal shock, failure, and grief. These are a portion of those women who have already experienced premature delivery or who have had previous pregnancy failure. They are often pleased to have any baby, no matter how small, and they feel a sense of achievement as long as it is a baby that may live.

* Very few of the mothers in our study had private obstetrical and pediatric care. Probably such care alters the experience but it does not eliminate the stress.

Mrs. G had several miscarriages and previous premature deliveries, and although she was anxious and upset she showed no preoccupation with failure. She wanted the baby and was happy that it might live—she was ready to accept it because she had managed her feelings about the failure to deliver a normal baby in earlier pregnancies.

The Mother's Homecoming Without her Baby. When the mother leaves the baby in the premature nursery and returns home empty-handed she experiences a reinforcement in her feelings of disappointment, failure, and deprivation.[7] There is wide variation in the amount of contact she maintains. Some mothers go daily to see their baby even though hospital regulations allow them only a few minutes' look through the nursery window. There is little noticeable change from day to day in the beginning. Others never visit, feeling it is a "waste of time." There is also variation in the use of telephone contact to learn about the baby's weight. The universal concern focused on weight change results from the mother's using weight gain as evidence of progress and the hospital's using a weight criterion for determining readiness for discharge. Some hospitals do not give out weight reports on the telephone; some insist that the mother visit the nursery or ask the private physician for information. A rare mother maintains a more personal contact by the considerable effort of pumping her breasts and sending the milk to the hospital.

After the Baby is Home. Although mothers anticipate the time when the baby can be brought home, they are frequently anxious when the moment comes. Their worry focuses on the smallness of the baby. They feel that it is fragile and they worry about their competence in adequately handling a child who has needed such expert care and who has been so inaccessible to them. Typically, the mother finds herself more anxious at first. In others there is often a persistent eagerness for weight gain and a focus of concern on food intake.[8] Some mothers begin to give the baby cereal before it is recommended by the physician. There are continuing concerns in some about congenital abnormalities which might show up later, and there is a variable amount of anxiety or curiosity about when the baby will "catch up" with the full-term infant.

[7] Dane Prugh, "Emotional Problems of the Premature Infant's Parents," *Nursing Outlook,* Vol. I (1953), pp. 461–464.

[8] Benjamin Spock, "Avoiding Behavior Problems," *Journal of Pediatrics,* Vol. 27 (1945), pp. 363–382.

The Psychological Tasks Posed by Prematurity

Having thus far described the typical experience of the mother of a premature baby, we now turn to a discussion of the special ways in which such a mother copes with the stress. We have found that she has four psychological tasks that appear to be essential both to successful mastery of the situation and to a sound basis for a future healthy mother-child relationship.

The *first* of these tasks should take place at the time of delivery. It is the preparation for a possible loss of the child whose life is in jeopardy. This "anticipatory grief" [9] involves a withdrawal from the relationship already established to the coming child so that she still hopes the baby will survive but simultaneously prepares for its death. In a *second* task she must face and acknowledge her maternal failure to deliver a normal full-term baby. The anticipatory grief and depression which can be observed are signs of the fact that she is struggling with these tasks. These reactions are healthy responses and usually last until the baby's chances for survival seem secure.

The baby may remain in the hospital from two to ten weeks. During this period the third and fourth tasks need to be performed. The *third* is the resumption of the process of relating to the baby which had been previously interrupted. The mother has lost the opportunity that full-term delivery would have provided for the development of readiness for the mothering role. She has previously prepared herself for a loss, but as the baby improves she must now respond with hope and anticipation to this change. The baby's improvement symbolizes to the mother the possibility of retrieving, from what had been a total disappointment, a good measure of her hopes during the pregnancy.

Characteristically, there is a point at which the mother really begins to believe that the baby will survive. The event which serves to stir her may be the baby's regular gain in weight, a change in feeding pattern or method, a change in the nurses' manner, the baby's "filling out," or its becoming more active. She then begins to prepare herself, gathers the layette, watches closely and seeks information on the baby's care. After a period of increased anticipation she knows the baby will be coming home, and is ready, though anxious.

[9] Lindemann, *op. cit.*, p. 19.

124

Mrs. A went almost daily with her husband and began gradually to respond with expectation as the baby filled out, became more active, and his eyes opened. They read Spock and pamphlets they obtained about prematurity, hesitantly at first, and more openly after they felt more hope by his change to bottle feedings, his "amazing strength" in turning around, banging his head, and crying lustily. The A's saw the baby fed once (against the usual rules) and at this time felt it was fun to visit, became certain the baby would come home, and longed for him. Mrs. A was making preparations at home, and gathering information about care—it was as though she used the time to catch up and finish the preparation for maternity interrupted by premature delivery.

In the *fourth* task the mother must come to understand how a premature baby differs from a normal baby in terms of its special needs and growth patterns. This is in preparation for her imminent job of caring for the infant, and takes place while she is visiting the nursery, talking with nurse or doctor, reading baby care books, or discussing baby care with other mothers of prematures. In order to provide the extra amount of care and protection, the mother must see the baby as a premature with special needs and characteristics. But it is equally important for her to see that these needs are temporary and will yield in time to more normal patterns. Generally she is advised to be careful about infections, and given special feeding advice. Her task is to take satisfactory precautions without depriving herself and the child of enjoyable interactions.

Mrs. B had a "sinking feeling" before she brought her twins home, was nervous and developed a gastrointestinal upset, but within a few days the schedule seemed to be more settled. The B's became more confident and realized "the babies won't break"; they were concerned about such things as overfeeding and temperature regulations of the room, but not so much about infection. They thought of the babies less as prematures than as twins and foresaw a normal development.

In those cases which appear to have a good outcome, the mother has accomplished the four tasks: anticipatory grief; acknowledgment of failure; resumption of active relating to the baby; seeing its special needs as a premature and prematurity as a temporary state yielding to normality. Thus far in the evaluation of outcome, we have used clinical impressions of the early mother-child relationship. A good outcome has been considered one in which the

125

mother sees the baby as potentially normal, gives it realistic care, and takes pride and satisfaction in that care.

Pathological Deviations

On the other hand, deviations from the typical pattern appear to be associated with poor outcome of the stress situation. Some mothers handle the real threat to the baby and their own maternal failure to carry to term by denying either the threat or the failure, or both. When denial is used as a defense there are certain observable changes in the mother. Although an early depression may be evident following delivery, this may too rapidly give way to a more cheerful appearance. Such mothers eat and sleep well and do not appear to have difficulty in talking with other mothers about their babies or in seeing mothers with normal babies in the same room or ward in the hospital.

> Mrs. V was subject to acute depersonalization episodes after her baby came home. In discussing these attacks, which are referred to as "headaches," she said that she did not cry in the beginning, but felt that she let her feelings build up. She thought this was the reason for her "headaches." In the hospital she slept and ate well. She remembers missing the baby, but she was not aware of a feeling of sadness. She recalled that when the baby was moved to another hospital (for special premature care) she pretended that she visited the baby and imagined what he was like. The other mothers, particularly the one she roomed with, were quite free to tell about their babies because Mrs. V did not seem to be upset about not having hers with her. She thought she had not been upset by the baby's difficulties because she had had a lot of experience with illness, which she had learned to take calmly. She didn't become weepy until she came home.

When the mother fails to respond with hope to the indications of survival and development of the infant, we have another pathological deviation. A number of factors may underlie this failure to respond to the infant's progress. For example, the infant may continue to symbolize her failure despite its progress and thereby impede the task of relating to the baby. This feeling may be reflected in her inability to discuss the experience retrospectively with the interviewer.

> In one family, although the interviewer made a number of attempts to discuss the baby, the parents avoided discussion except for brief perfunctory comments. Instead they talked at

126

length about themselves and their extended families. At the end of the interview the father smiled and commented that "Every time we get together to talk about the baby it seems that we don't do this, but switch to talk about other things in the family!" In this family the adjustment to the baby was unusually difficult, with poor outcome for mother-child relationship.

If the mother sees the baby as continuing to represent the threat of death or abnormality, or of unusual difficulties and care, such perceptions can seriously impede the tasks of relating to and caring for the infant.

Mrs. Q's mother is a patient in a state mental hospital. In a number of interviews Mrs. Q talked at length about mental health and her concern about transmitting illness hereditarily. Although the medical evaluation of her premature was quite good, she remained preoccupied with his "mental development." She began to refer to him as a "nervous baby," expressing concern about the noise her older children made, which she thought contributed to the baby's nervousness.

Mrs. B expressed concern soon after the birth of her premature baby that he might have heart trouble. She has a functional heart murmur. Although he progressed well, gaining weight and developing normally, she continued to express concern about the baby's heart, asking the doctor at each examination if he could detect heart trouble, although each time she was assured that no signs of it showed in these examinations.

The following case also illustrates the unsuccessful resolution of the necessary psychological tasks we have described:

In discussing their immediate reactions to having such a small baby, a father described himself as "shocked." He "almost keeled over" when she lost weight, dropping from 4 pounds, 6 ounces, to 3 pounds, 12 ounces. The mother, in contrast, said she "wasn't worried about it" and expected a loss of weight. Her first reaction to seeing the baby was that the baby was so tiny. "The pediatrician said she was beautiful. I couldn't see anything beautiful about her. I was worried in the beginning but the doctor and nurse reassured me." The mother had no previous experience with prematures.

During the period when the baby was in the hospital nursery, there was little visiting by the mother. She said there was not too much advantage in going to see the baby, "You can't tell much by looking at her."

In anticipation of the baby's homecoming the mother compared the premature to her previous full-term baby and "didn't think any extra care would be needed," since it would only weigh

127

a half pound less than the previous normal baby at homecoming. When the premature came home, the early adjustment was good; the mother seemed loving and able to handle the baby. The situation quickly deteriorated when the full impact of the difference between the babies became apparent. The baby's cry was weak, the parents said she did not have a good pair of lungs, and they were afraid they would not hear her.

They became increasingly fearful of handling her, of bathing her; they began to treat her as if she were very fragile. The mother later commented that one pound certainly made a lot of difference. She became progressively negative to the baby and was overwhelmed by the need to care for the children and keep up housecleaning at the same time.

We believe the mother must accomplish each task in the appropriate period in order to deal successfully with the stress of premature birth. For example, the inability to face and accept the failure connoted by premature birth makes it difficult for the mother to use the opportunity to visit with the baby in a psychologically productive way. In turn, the failure to visit and observe the baby in the nursery makes the adjustment to the baby at home a more difficult one. In the case just cited, the mother so quickly and completely denied her concern about danger to the child that she found herself grossly unprepared for meeting its needs and became burdened and resentful. Although such a woman may appear to the hospital staff to have adjusted promptly to the stress, the signs of potential difficulty are present. When these signs can be used by all health workers to screen women who deliver prematurely, it will be possible to direct preventive intervention to those more likely to have a poor outcome.

Future plans for this study include the testing of the ideas concerning reactions to premature birth by objective measurement and an exploration of intervention techniques appropriate to this stress.

10. Working with Families in Crisis: An Exploration in Preventive Intervention*

Lydia Rapoport

THIS PAPER DESCRIBES preventive intervention work done with families considered to be in a state of crisis because of the birth of a premature infant. The work was an exploratory phase of a larger project conducted at the Harvard School of Public Health Family Guidance Center,** which studied the reaction patterns and coping mechanisms of families in crisis. Identifications of patterns, both adaptive and maladaptive, could serve as indices for prediction of outcome and also as a guide to caretakers and helping professions for the deployment of resources and for focused intervention.

Two related frames of reference guided this work: that of prevention as formulated and utilized in the public health field, and that of crisis theory as formulated by mental health investigators and social psychiatrists.

Prevention, in the public health field, is conceived of as a continuum of activities to protect the health of the community. These activities are classified as (1) health promotion, (2) specific protection, (3) early diagnosis and treatment, including case-finding, (4) disability limitation, and (5) rehabilitation.[1] The first two categories are in the nature of primary prevention, that is to say, intervention before a problem is manifest. Early diagnosis and treatment are considered to be secondary prevention, while the last two categories are classified as tertiary prevention. In general, most public health activities are directed at designated groups in the

---

* Reprinted in abridged form from *Social Work*, Vol. 7, No. 3 (1962).
** Editor's Note: See chapters 4, 9, and 24 of this volume.
1 Hugh R. Leavell and E. G. Clark, *Preventive Medicine for the Doctor in His Community*, McGraw-Hill Book Co., New York, 1958, pp. 21–29.

community which are considered, on the basis of epidemiological study, to be populations at risk. In this study, prematurity was considered to be a hazardous circumstance which poses a threat to family equilibrium and is likely to precipitate a family into a state of crisis. Therefore these families were designated as a "population at risk" and became a target for efforts of preventive intervention. The aim was to prevent mentally unhealthy consequences of the crisis which could interfere with the development of a sound mother-child relationship.

Description of the Study

The following observations of the impact of the birth of a premature baby are based on work with 11 families comprising a total of sixty interviews, all held in the home.* In addition, there were contacts with health and welfare agencies in behalf of some of the families.

The case-finding aspects of the project were handled as follows: A psychiatrist staff member developed liaison with the city hospital and was notified of all premature births.** During the period of case-finding for this study, he interviewed mothers on the ward soon after delivery. These interviews were brief and were not traditional psychiatric interviews with intent of probing. Instead the aim was twofold. First, to make a rapid assessment of the mother's (and when available, the family's) reaction to the current stressful event; to note coping mechanisms with which the stress was being handled; and to make predictions at this early stage regarding the outcome, to be verified later. Second, to obtain sanction for a social worker to visit the family in the home in order to follow developments and offer any help that might be needed. It should be noted that because of hospital regulations the social worker, coming from an outside agency, was not permitted to visit and work with the mothers in the hospital. Therefore no work could be done with the mothers during the first important phase of the crisis.***

The families were then visited, whenever possible, during the

* Five families of the 11 were visited by a graduate student from the Smith College School for Social Work, supervised by the author.
** Dr. Edward Mason, who also served as consultant to this study.
*** It may very well be that the inaccessibility of the mothers to the social worker during the stress impact period brought into focus some emotional tasks and needs during the second phase which might better have been resolved earlier.

first week following the mother's discharge from the hospital. The frequency, spacing, and duration of contacts were determined flexibly on the basis of assessment of the families' needs and were sustained wherever possible only until the crisis appeared resolved. The following three case examples are cited to illustrate the range of problems encountered and the kinds of intervention offered.

Case One

The Brown family consisted of a young working-class Negro couple and their premature first-born baby. The mother was 17, the father 24. The baby was born during the seventh month, weighing 4 pounds and 4 ounces. The mother was seen twice by the project psychiatrist, on the second and fifth days after delivery. She was being treated for a kidney infection, which explains her longer hospitalization. She was in a markedly sullen mood on both occasions, but did warm up to the doctor. She indicated to the worker later that this contact meant a great deal to her because she had an opportunity to talk to someone. She was quite worried about the baby's welfare, exasperated at not getting news, but unable to be insistent in making inquiries. She became more anxious on hearing of the death of a smaller premature infant. She tended to blame overwork, not taking vitamins, and the kidney infection as possible causes for the premature delivery. On the basis of her concern, her ability to express normal anxiety, and her wish to have the baby home soon, it was predicted that she would make a good relationship with the baby and would be a competent mother, although somewhat anxious.

There were six home visits, numerous phone calls, and contacts with health agencies regarding the Brown family. The first visit occurred one week after the mother's discharge from the hospital, at the paternal grandparents' home. The mother was able to express disappointment that the baby was not yet home. Despite a characteristic guardedness, abruptness, and sullen, hostile defense displayed at each contact, she soon warmed up and was eager to discuss the baby, and asked very specific questions. The father was acutely uncomfortable, taciturn, and soon fled from the interview. He was not seen again, and the next visits were focused on the mother's needs.

In the first interview the mother was still troubled with feelings of guilt and responsibility for the baby's early arrival, which had caught her unprepared, especially psychologically. She did not get

131

a chance to wear her new maternity suit, which meant she really did not have a long enough period as a young wife without motherhood. Nevertheless, she was eager to get the baby home, was defensive about not having visited, and took pride in the layette she was readying. She and her husband visited subsequently until the baby's discharge. She was appropriately anxious, in view of her inexperience, about the care of the baby. It was the worker's initial impression that she would have ample help from extended family and public health nurses. This was an erroneous impression. The female family members were not helpful and no public health nurse or well-baby clinic was available in this town. The worker's role therefore became primarily an educational one. The mother was extremely eager to learn and was found to be very responsive and educable. The emphasis was on helping her find ways of getting information she needed as well as on supplying basic knowledge of infant care and development.

The second visit, a long one, was scheduled the day after the baby came home at the age of 4 weeks. Gradually the mother's uncertainties unfolded. She was alone with the newborn, had never made a formula, was worried about room temperature and about his weight. She was upset by his diaper rash, blamed the hospital for negligence, and changed his diapers every fifteen minutes, washing them by hand. She gave the baby orange juice and vitamins, and had little idea of quantity; a month later it was learned that she was giving the baby concentrated undiluted orange juice, which explained his diarrhea. This happened despite carefully detailed discussions regarding routines. Her attitude toward the baby was one of great concern and wanting to do right. She did not appear overly warm or maternal, yet was attentive to the baby's communications and needs.

On subsequent visits more concerns were expressed, despite the fact that the baby was progressing well. The hospital discharged the mother with some printed instructions she had not read: they were in small print and hard to understand. The worker presented her with a copy of Spock's baby book. Some of the language was found to be geared to middle-class education and sophistication. Worker and mother studied the book together; the latter was charmed with the pictures, and learned to use the index. She was eager to make use of health facilities but needed precise information as to how to initiate things. When told exactly, she always followed through. With the worker's active intervention and enlistment of the help of medical social workers at a private pediatric hospital, the baby was taken on for care. The mother followed through, although it required a long trip to a strange community. Despite careful preparation, as with the orange juice, communication failed. The mother went to the hospital without the baby to inquire about eligibility. This was misinterpreted by the medical personnel as an expression of her suspiciousness and resistance. The worker's active and rapid clarification once again smoothed the pathway for this family to develop good patterns of health care.

Case Two

The Kellys, an Irish Catholic working-class family, are an example of prediction of a healthy outcome, confirmed by three follow-up visits. The mother delivered a 4-pound premature boy and a stillborn male twin of 12 ounces. Her water bag had broken two months previously and she was carefully followed prenatally. A premature birth had been anticipated, but not a stillborn twin. When interviewed briefly by the project psychiatrist three days after delivery, she had already seen the baby three times through the glass of the nursery. She had three children under 6 years at home. She was able to express concern about the needs of the newborn and was eager to get some idea of when he might come home. She was active in "pestering" doctors and nurses to seek out information about the baby, who was jaundiced and edematous. On the basis of the mother's ability to mourn for the dead twin, to express open concern for the surviving infant, to seek medical information aggressively, and to use warmth and support of the extended family and religious institutions, it was predicted that the outcome of the crisis would be excellent and the mother-child relationship satisfactory. There was no need for preventive intervention, but follow-up was initiated for research purposes and to verify the prediction.

The first visit was made five weeks after delivery. An earlier visit failed to locate the family, who had no telephone. The parents were pleased to see the worker, despite the fact that the visit was unscheduled and the mother in bed with flu. Noteworthy were the parents' ease in communication with each other and the worker and their spontaneous ability to recount in detail, with appropriate affect, the painful events of pregnancy, precipitous birth, the death of the twin, and the prolonged hospitalization of the baby. Before

133

her current illness the mother had visited the baby three times. The father visited daily. More remarkable was their active communication with the medical staff. It was against hospital policy to give telephone information even to parents. Nevertheless the pediatrician frequently telephoned the parents at a neighbor's. The baby was in the hospital longer than anticipated because of anemia, necessitating blood transfusions. During the second visit, five weeks later, the mother was seen alone. The baby was still not at home because of the blood level and need for surgery for umbilical hernia. The striking feature was the mother's active seeking and using medical knowledge as a way of mastering the crisis. She was appropriately concerned, but also optimistic. There was a definite reduction in her level of tension, despite the disappointment of the long hospitalization.

The third visit, one month later, found the family at home, elated and happy. The baby had been home a fortnight. Prior to his actual homecoming they had suffered a needless trauma due to communication failure; they were told to get the baby and went with great anticipation, only to learn it was an error. They came home, again empty-handed, and were disappointed and depressed. This reactivated the original disappointment and loss, but gave them a second chance to work out the mourning process. Now they were relieved and less anxious, even coping comfortably with the baby's colic. It may be noted that from the beginning the infant had an identity and place in the family. He was "little Joey" and was talked about easily and freely. In this last contact with the worker the opportunity was created for the family to relive once again the whole experience from beginning to end. The fortuitous outcome in this case, despite long hospitalization and medical complications, was related to the family's close ties, shared goals, communication patterns, and capacity for conscious problem-solving. The mother had a high degree of interpersonal skills and was able to handle medical personnel in order to get needed information. She did this aggressively but with kidding and lightness of touch, managing her own anxiety and thus avoiding stimulating the feelings of guilt of professional personnel, which so often result in their withdrawal and withholding. Despite the mother's experience in raising babies, she welcomed the possibility of visits by the public health nurse and used the social worker constructively for abreaction and mastery.

Case Three

The Minellis, an Italian Catholic working-class family, illustrate the need for long-term intervention dictated by the fact that the current crisis was superimposed on chronic family problems and repeated crises which were the characteristic family life style. On the basis of two brief contacts in the hospital, the first with the husband present, the project psychiatrist in his prediction expressed uneasiness about the family's adjustment to the new baby. There were indications that the family needed to be visited, for there was danger of neglect for the baby. These ominous predictions were based on the following observations: The baby was born at seven months weighing 3 pounds. The parents insisted that everything was fine and expected the baby to be home in a month. Two important facts stood out: This was the sixth premature child in the family, all of whom had survived. However, this infant had the smallest birth weight.

It might be expected that with this family history confidence and hope might be high.* On the other hand, the expectation of the baby's homecoming in a month showed evidence of unrealistic thinking and denial in view of the extensive prior experience with prematurity. There were other indications of denial. The husband, particularly, did not permit his wife or himself to express any feelings of anxiety. He insisted that once the baby began to eat everything would be all right. When the wife was seen alone without the repressive presence of her husband, she was indeed visibly more anxious but still clung to her denial defenses. For example, at the time of delivery she had been ill with a strep throat, but denied its significance. There was indication that the mother had some real conflict about this baby. Prediction therefore was of a dubious outcome and guarded prognosis.

All the early cues of a very troubled family situation and problematic mother-child relationship were unfortunately confirmed. The family was visited five days after delivery, when the mother had been at home two days. During this visit the family presented a solid, united, euphoric front. The father handled his anxiety regarding the newborn by boasting of the good health and strong development of the other children. Later it was found that all the

* A finding of the research project revealed that prior experience with prematurity was not a significant factor in the outcome of the crisis. Birth weight as a factor showed surprisingly that the outcome of the family crisis was better with smaller premature infants than larger ones.

135

children had numerous health problems, some severe, all of which were being neglected. The mother was taking expensive medicine (antibiotics)—her "Christmas present"—not knowing what it was for. Her husband's fantasy was that it would "heal up her insides." The parents hardly discussed the baby. The nurse in the premature nursery reported that the mother had shown no interest in the baby and had not come down to visit while she was in the hospital.

This family was visited twenty times, with numerous phone contacts and collaborative contacts with health agencies. Every area of their social functioning was problematic and chaotic. They were in severe and chronic financial difficulties despite the husband's fairly steady and well-paid employment. The children were malnourished and chronically hungry. They were periodically threatened with loss of utilities and eviction by the housing project. There were periodic altercations with neighbors and recriminations in court. Two of the school-aged children were slow learners and were threatened with being left back in school. All the children had uncared-for health problems; they were in need of eye surgery, tonsillectomies, orthopedic attention, and polio shots.

There were severe problems also in the mother's inability to manage and control the children. The older ones were defiant and attacking. The mother handled discipline by explosive outbursts, ineffectual threats, bribery, and virtual encouragement of the children to lie and steal. There were severe marital problems. The mother was terrified of another pregnancy but could not handle the sexual relationship because of internal conflicts and external religious prohibitions regarding birth control. The husband was depressed and disgruntled with his job and plagued by physical symptoms for which he refused medical attention. The extended family was in proximity but could offer no help.

The baby was very slow in his development both at the hospital and at home, despite the absence of any abnormalities. For example, at 6 weeks he weighed only 3 pounds and 11 ounces. At 8 weeks he came home weighing 5 pounds and 2 ounces. The relief about this was noted by the mother only in terms of the children having quieted down. The mother had visited the baby in hospital only once, and only at the worker's urging. She did not visit at the time of her postnatal check-up. The baby's subsequent slow development was of concern. He was extremely lethargic, apathetic, and unresponsive, making few demands of any kind. He was given very

136

cursory and minimal handling. His bottle rolled around in the crib and whoever passed by might pop it in his mouth. In contrast to many mothers of premature babies who are overly concerned with diet and push feeding, this mother seemed unconcerned and unable to request help with change of formula even after months had elapsed, although her other children's diet at a comparable age had been enriched. The baby received very little handling and stimulation and was picked up and held, briefly at best, only with the worker's encouragement. He did not have a real place in the family, and began to be identified by name only at the age of 6 months. The mother found very little pleasure in him. She saw him in a positive way only insofar as he provided something for her—that is, he helped her "keep her mind off her worries." There was evidence that her greater attentiveness at night enabled her to use the baby as a way of avoiding sexual contact with her husband. She admitted that she had tried to abort him.

The contacts with this family had a multiple purpose. The primary task, in keeping with the research, was to focus on getting a relationship going between mother and infant—a relationship in this instance ruptured by the baby's prolonged separation while in hospital and further weakened by the fact of his being unwanted. Active intervention via encouragement and demonstration consisted of stimulating visiting, physical contact, and more adequate nurturing. The mother made fleeting efforts, but her responses were not sustained. Active intervention was also offered regarding health needs for the baby and other children, by opening contacts with public health nurses who had become hostile to this family. Rules were modified, fees were waived, and punitive or negative attitudes on the part of other caretaking personnel were modified by consultation and collaboration methods.

The secondary task (but of prime importance in this chronically disordered family) was to break through denial and inactivity and to involve them in beginning problem-solving and coping with urgent demands. Active intervention in this respect consisted of securing free school lunches, concrete help with budgeting, meal-planning, and management of debts; some demonstration of child management, since efforts at modifying attitudes and handling failed; pushing the mother out of her fruitless obsessional worrying by activating some beginning of coping with small pieces of problems and tasks; getting her out of the house, where she was characteristically immobilized over coffee and cigarettes and aimless fretting. It was recognized that this family would need long-term intervention for any sustained results. As is true of many chronically needy and dependent families, this one made no demands and did not make use of resources even when the family was eligible and the resources available to them. Most needs were handled by means of magical thinking and wish fulfillment, or frantic worrying leading to rumination and inactivity rather than direct action. The mother enjoyed the "friendly visiting," made no demands, held herself aloof and detached except for rare occasions when some genuine affect broke through and she turned to the worker to unburden.

The husband was seen less frequently. He managed to remove himself physically or refused to participate, encouraged by his wife, who tried to shield him from worries. Among the children, all but the oldest formed strong attachments to the worker, displayed their great hunger for affection and contact, and at times saw the worker as the embodiment of standards and benign controls for which they still yearned despite the prevailing influences of corruption and chaos that ruled their lives.

Summary and Conclusion

These three cases illustrate a range of responses to the crisis of prematurity. In the first case the family's coping mechanisms were not adequate to the task essentially because of lack of knowledge. Intervention therefore was largely educational in purpose. The second case illustrates adequate coping with the crisis. The third case illustrates great inadequacy during the crisis—a cumulative product of chronic inadequacy which even extended preventive intervention failed to modify.

Preventive intervention with the families studied consisted of a range of activities. They can be classified into three broad categories:

1. Keeping an explicit focus on the crisis. Four specific goals may be subsumed in this category.

a. Help with cognitive mastery: not all families consciously perceive a hazardous event and their reactions to it as a time of family crisis. A major task of preventive intervention is to help the family gain a conscious grasp of the crisis, in order to enhance purposeful problem-solving, leading toward mastery. It has been noted by various investigators that clarification of the precipitating stress, or connection of subjective distress with stressful event, is in itself of therapeutic significance.[2]

b. Help with doubts of feminine adequacy, guilt, and self-blame stimulated by the failure to carry the pregnancy to term.

c. Help with grief work and mourning in relation to feelings of loss and emptiness stimulated by separation from the infant.

d. Help with anticipatory worry work and anticipatory guidance. These activities are carried on in the context of supportive and clarifying techniques with which social workers are familiar. Sometimes it is sufficient to work out the crisis on the level of the "here and now." At other times it may be necessary to make more explicit the symbolic link of the present crisis to earlier unresolved conflicts. These links may be difficult to establish within the context of a brief relationship which is not geared to conflict resolution, or clarification leading toward insight. Nevertheless, because of the pressure of the crisis, such conflicts or derivatives may surge nearer to consciousness and may be accessible to direct interpretation.

2. Offering basic information and education regarding child development and child care through a variety of devices, including use of relationship for demonstration and identification.

3. Creating a bridge to community resources, opening pathways of referral, and intervening in communication failures and in problems of stereotyping and misinterpretation of motivation and need.

2 Betty L. Kalis, M. Robert Harris, A. R. Prestwood, and Edith H. Freeman, "Precipitating Stress as a Focus in Psychotherapy," *Archives of General Psychiatry*, Vol. V, No. 3 (1961), pp. 219–226.

11. Kindergarten Entry: A Study of Role Transition*

Donald C. Klein
and *Ann Ross*

WHILE EDUCATORS HAVE BEEN concerned with the child's adjustment to school, little attention has been given to the impact of school entry on the family. Kindergarten teachers, first-grade teachers, and school administrators have palpable evidence of the child's disturbance at school entry in his crying, vomiting, incontinence, anxieties, refusal to permit the mother to leave the classroom, and refusal to attend school at all. This article reports on a systematic study of the impact of school entry on the family.

The research was based in the Human Relations Service of Wellesley, a community agency founded in 1948 to develop theory and methods in community mental health.** It is one of a series of cross-sectional studies, relating to a preventive or public health orientation and aimed at making contact with "emotionally hazardous situations," which individuals have continually to meet, and which in the normal course of development pose problems for many or most people. Stemming from Lindemann's work on the grief reactions of bereaved individuals,[1] the assumption is made that certain life events that involve rapid role change or redistribution of role relationships among groups of people represent potential hazards for those experiencing them.

The transition of the young child from his family into school is one of the first important role changes in the growing-up process. Furthermore, it is seen as requiring some reorientation of the total

---

*Reprinted from *Orthopsychiatry and the School*, Morris Krugman (ed.), American Orthopsychiatric Association, New York, 1958.
** The cost of the study was partially covered by the C. H. Hood Foundation.
1 See ch. 1 of the present volume.

family in terms of intrafamilial role relationships and in terms of home-school relationships. The present study is concerned primarily with the impact of entry into kindergarten upon child and family as observed and reported by parents themselves. It is related to a long-range program of research into early school adjustment, begun in 1950, previous phases of which have been reported by Gruber [2] and by Ross and Lindemann.[3]

Research Objectives and Method

The primary purpose of the present study was to determine the extent to which school entry was accompanied by strains or tensions among family members. A second major objective was the identification of regularities in the process of adaptation—of phases or trends in reactions of family members during the transition period. A third objective was the determination of characteristic ways families have of meeting and adapting to the new status and life situation of the kindergartener. A fourth and subsidiary purpose was determination of the usefulness of the group interview method itself for investigation of family strains during the period under study.

Although this report will present some observations bearing on the last two purposes, it will primarily concern itself with the first two hypotheses: (1) that kindergarten entry is an emotionally hazardous circumstance (that is, a period of quick transition marked by denotable tensions within the family group); (2) that the transition period is marked by regularly occurring phases over a limited time-period.

Recruitment of Subjects

Research subjects were recruited at general meetings of parents of prekindergarteners, held under sponsorship of parent-teacher groups in two middle-class suburban communities. The research was presented as a study of the "normal responses" of children at a time of transition. Parents were invited to participate as volunteer observers and reporters. A further selective factor is that the pro-

2 Sigmund Gruber, "The Concept of Task Orientation in the Anaylsis of Play Behavior of Children Entering Kindergarten," *American Journal of Orthopsychiatry*, Vol. 24 (1954), pp. 316–343.

3 Ann Ross and Elizabeth B. Lindemann, "A Follow-up Study of a Predictive Test of Social Adaptation in Pre-School Children," *Emotional Problems of Early Childhood*, Gerald Caplan (ed.), Basic Books, 1956, pp. 79–93.

portion of parents volunteering ranged from 50 to 90 per cent of those who attended parent-teacher meetings; all parents do not attend such meetings. Therefore, further investigation will be needed to determine the extent to which the sample is unrepresentative of normal reactions to the kindergarten experience.

The present report is based upon experience with six groups of parents, including 45 mothers and 9 fathers, representing a total of 46 families.

Procedure

A group interview technique was used, involving weekly meetings of from one and one-half to two hours' duration with from 6 to 10 parents each. The series of meetings began just prior to the first day of school and continued for five to six weeks. Participants were encouraged to pool information and observations regarding the behavior and reactions of the kindergarteners, other siblings, and the parents themselves.

Group leaders included two clinical psychologists, two psychiatrists, and a psychiatric social worker.* The aim of the leader was to facilitate discussion, to keep it as goal-directed as possible, and to take into account personal needs and anxieties of participants. Although the leader was sensitive to personal and group tensions, he responded only to those that appeared to interfere seriously with individual or group productivity.

In each group there was a staff observer who noted sequence of topics as well as the initiators and participants for each topic area. In addition, ratings of group climate in terms of tension levels and degree of group involvement were made at five to ten minute intervals. Observers did not participate in the group discussions.

Settings varied, depending on convenience. Groups met in members' homes, the public school, and at the Human Relations Service. Meetings were informal.

Analysis of Data

The data included: (1) verbatim records of group discussions for each meeting; (2) observer notes on sequence of topics, as well as initiators

* The authors gratefully acknowledge the material contributions to this study made by the following people, who participated in data collection and analysis: Helen Herzan, M.D.; Marie McNabola, M.S.W.; Pearl Rosenberg, Ph.D.; Arnold Schwartz, M.D.; John M. von Felsinger, Ph.D.

and participants for each topic area; (3) observer ratings of group tension level and degree of involvement at intervals of approximately five to ten minutes throughout each meeting. Further data were provided by recorded postmeeting discussions of the observer and the leader.

Following the final meeting of each group, each leader-observer team prepared a meeting-by-meeting summary of major themes, in which an attempt was made to pick out possible sequences in the content and affect areas. This analysis was based on the observational records and the recorded postmeeting discussions. The analysis for each group by the leader-observer team was carried out independently of analyses of every other group.

The next step entailed a comparative analysis of content and affect areas for the six groups in the attempt to determine the degree to which sequences of content and affect were similar from group to group. A separate analysis was carried out of the verbatim records and tabulations made in the following areas: (1) reports of child behavior reflecting tension or regression; (2) reports of child behavior reflecting increased independence, responsibility, sociability, and other indications of maturity; (3) parental concerns about school entry; (4) factors facilitating or hindering initial adjustment to school, as judged by parents.

Findings

Subject to limitations of sampling both as to size and possible bias, the data give support to the two major hypotheses. It would appear that kindergarten entry is an emotionally hazardous circumstance, in that it represents a time-limited transition period marked by increased tension within the family group. It further appears that the transition period is marked by a regular sequence of phases in the adaptation process as reflected by the emotional reactions of the parents.

The following discussion will concern itself, first, with the extent to which school entry was accompanied by strains or tensions as these were reflected in parental reports of shifts in child behavior, and the anxieties of the parents themselves as these were reported in or inferred from group discussion. It will then take up trends in family reactions as these were reflected in the week-by-week discussions.

143

Hypothesis One

With respect to *altered patterns of behavior,* it is probably no surprise to anyone that parental reports were far more complete about items of child behavior than they were about parent-to-child or parent-to-parent interaction. All parents reported alterations in one or more items of child behavior during the first weeks of school.

All parents noted signs of increased stress or tension during the first few weeks, and some children reported directly to parents that they were or had been apprehensive during this time. There was a wide range of individual differences in ways in which tension was expressed. The following categories were noted: (1) physical reactions, such as loss of appetite, fatigue, stomach upsets; (2) intensification or resumption of previous behaviors, such as a return to bedwetting, increase in thumb-sucking, dawdling, and so on; (3) increased irritability, expressed in hitting out at siblings or other children, uncooperativeness, freshness with parents; (4) increased dependence on mother; (5) generalized signs of tension, expressed in such things as "keyed up" behavior, a "worried" expression, increased talkativeness or reticence, reluctance to go to school.

Signs of increased tension and of growth went hand in hand during these early weeks. While concerned about the reactions noted above, parents were often surprised—and sometimes even disconcerted—at the rapidity with which children were learning new skills and developing new attitudes and ways of relating to parents. A variety of behaviors indicating growth and increased maturity were noted by all parents. These were mainly in three areas: (1) increase in independence from family, including such items as increased assertiveness, acting like a "big shot," not wanting to be watched or to have a baby sitter, playing farther from home, and visiting neighbors' homes more often; (2) more grown-up behavior, such as assumption of more responsibility for self-help, increased cooperativeness, imitation of older children, rejection of babyish pursuits, and taking more responsible role with younger siblings; (3) development of new attitudes and interests, including, for example, more interest in other children, decrease in shyness, interest not shown before (for example, singing, painting), wanting to do work rather than play, more awareness of mother as a person, and heightened consciousness of own clothing and appearance.

Parental concerns regarding school entry can be grouped under

144

four major headings: anticipatory tensions, reactions to separation, value conflicts, and shifts in parental role.

Anticipatory Tensions

A major content area during the meetings prior to school concerned factors in the child's history or current situation which might help or hinder him in making the change to the school milieu. Among the areas discussed were the following: (1) expectations and attitudes fostered by older siblings or children in the neighborhood; (2) nature and extent of group play experience with other children; (3) presence or absence of organized play experiences, including nursery school training; (4) availability of neighborhood friends in the kindergarten itself; (5) degree to which families have fostered independence and self-help, acceptance of discipline and the like; (6) degree to which child is geared to educational goals, for example, knowing the alphabet and wishing to learn to read; (7) degree to which families have anticipated the nature of school adjustment in discussions with the child, through appropriate books, and so on; (8) specific ways of relating child to the school environment, such as trips to the grounds, getting acquainted with teacher, and visiting a kindergarten class.

The discussions naturally did not uncover any single set of factors presumed to relate to competence in school. Quite the contrary! The research team was impressed with the extreme heterogeneity of experiences and attitudes in the areas mentioned above. For example, with regard to play groups, the sample ranged from an only child, who had no contacts with other children, to another four-year-old who ranged freely around his extensive neighborhood in a large, heterogeneous, and loosely organized play group of some thirty to forty children.

With the first day of school imminent, there was some focus of the parents' concern on real or imagined physical dangers, which seemed to represent at least partial canalization of more diffuse anxieties. There were images of older children bullying the tiny kindergartener. The all too real threat of heavy traffic and speeding automobiles also was emphasized. However, the more general and probably more fundamental concern about rejection, criticism, and attack was expressed in all groups, at first by those who were more communicative about such matters. Those who said, in effect, "I've been spending five years doing my job. Now everyone will soon see

145

whether I'm a success or not!" struck a responsive chord in all groups.

Reactions to Separation

A feeling even less acceptable to most parents was the profound sense of loss experienced, especially by mothers, during the first days of school. Characteristically, it was revealed indirectly at first through the behavior of most group members, expressing a feeling of letdown and vague dissatisfaction. It was later expressed directly by someone in the group. One mother asked her group why she should have felt so sad and so near to tears when she had expected to feel relieved and happy that her child was growing up.

Value Conflicts

Each group focused on the same three areas of value conflict or confusion: (1) a desire to have the child learn how to conform to the group vs. equally strong emphasis on the importance of maintaining individuality; (2) restraint of aggression vs. the importance of self-assertiveness and fighting back when attacked; (3) the importance of learning how to get along with the opposite sex vs. discomfort over possible premature development of cross-sex interests. These conflict areas are so well embedded in our culture it was not altogether surprising to have them expressed so universally in the groups. What was striking, however, was the extent to which the advent of school into the social space of the family served to upset the uneasy equilibrium of these conflicting values. The result appeared to be a readiness to project one or another of the polarities onto the school, to perceive school values as being in striking contrast to the values of the home. As a result, members expressed irritation with the school for "creating" a problem, which, in essence, already existed within themselves.

Change in Parental Role

Although parents expressed recognition of the importance of a satisfactory relationship between teacher and child, for most it presented a troubling problem of divided loyalties. Negative feelings regarding intervention of the school into the life of the child were displayed primarily in four ways: (1) direct annoyance with the child for hold-

146

ing up teacher as an authority; (2) expression of feelings of inadequacy in the face of teacher competence as a disciplinarian and motivator of the child, coupled with excessive eulogizing of the teacher as a model of perfection; (3) annoyance with the child and/or school as a result of feeling in the dark about schoolroom events, parental responsibilities with regard to materials needed by the child, and the teacher's appraisal of the child; (4) direct criticism of teacher for some alleged mishandling of a classroom crisis, usually regarding someone else's child.

Hypothesis Two

There was a high degree of congruence both of topic areas and related tensions for the several groups at similar time points. Sequence analysis led to identification of three affect areas which fell into unique patterns related to different times in the transition period. The affect areas included tension, depression, and hostility.

Four general phases were noted in the sequence of group discussion. The first phase reflected anticipatory concerns prior to school entry. These concerns were reflected in the first meeting of each group by a high tension level, high degree of involvement in discussion, and focus of content on ways of preparing a child for kindergarten, fear of physical attack, or criticism aimed against child or parent because of the child's inadequate preparation for the "acid test." The second phase reflected relief that the waiting was over and that the child had successfully started off to school. The relief was coupled with lethargy or apathy in group discussion, little focus of content during most of the second meeting in each group, with increasing awareness that pleasure over successful school entry was in part outweighed by mild depression and a sense of loss. The third phase was marked by attempts at role redefinition and reconstitution of meaningful parent-child ties. It was reflected during the third and fourth meetings in each group by criticisms of school and teacher, at first veiled, general, and highly intellectualized, later more open and related to specific classroom incidents. The final phase included a restoration of equilibrium in the fifth and sixth meetings of the groups. It was marked by a sense of comfort and relaxation, and within some groups return of a mild depressive flavor, which is presumed to have been related to the termination of the research group itself.

147

Discussion

Having established the probability that school entry, for certain levels of the population at least, is accompanied by specific tension areas and strains related to redistribution of family roles vis-à-vis the outside world, further research is needed to determine what, if any, relationships exist between degree or type or sequence of concerns and the nature of a child's attempts at integration in the kindergarten and succeeding years of school. Invoking the principle of primacy, it may not be farfetched to consider that inadequately resolved intra-familial and parental role tensions generated by school entry may not only hamper a child's school adjustment, but may also tend to block needed school-home collaboration should educational problems arise in succeeding years.

Further research also is needed to determine the potential value of small group discussions with parents at the time of school entry, for the parents themselves and, indirectly, as an aid in the child's development of a suitable school-related role. Parents themselves universally report that the discussions have helped them understand and accept their own feelings and concerns and have provided a sense of fellowship with others going through the same experience. The nature and extent of data regarding parental feelings tend to confirm a basic premise upon which the crisis group approach is based: that so-called normal individuals are more accessible to the mental health worker at a time of personal challenge involving a need to re-examine old patterns of behavior and to meet new environmental expectations. At such points of rapid transition, there is reason to believe, a relatively few hours of group meetings may help participants identify and cope with deep areas of feeling and important points of personal and family conflict and concern.

We can hardly say that school entry is a major crisis with a high casualty rate. Nonetheless, as we have seen, it appears to involve important feeling areas and to engage families in significant role shifts. Moreover, intervention at this time provides potential access to a large segment of the child population in a way which, it is hoped, will ultimately lead to important developments in case-finding, early diagnosis, and reduction of vulnerability to later emotional hazards.

12. The Use of the Life Space Interview on a Medical Ward*

Joel Vernick

DURING THE past three years the Metabolic Nursing Service of the National Institute of Arthritis and Metabolic Diseases and the Social Service Department of the Clinical Center, National Institutes of Health, have engaged in a joint project to develop techniques for coping with the problems of hospitalized children. The purposes were, first, to give staff members an opportunity to increase their skill in working with hospitalized children, and, second, to provide the the children with services that would help them to cope with the many varied, strange, and often frightening experiences they encounter during hospitalization. This article is concerned with one part of the project—adapting the life space interview for use with children who were hospitalized in the Clinical Center for treatment of arthritis, cystic fibrosis, various types of anemia, and other metabolic diseases. The term *child* is used to refer to any patient in the hospital approximately 6 to 20 years of age. Any patient in this age group was automatically included in the program. The length of stay of the patients ranged from several days to several years.

An underlying assumption of the project was that hospitalization always represents a period of disruption in a child's life, no matter how well he is prepared for it or how old he may be. The energies he needs for coping with the psychosocial developmental problems or tasks usual for his age become absorbed in his struggle to meet a new set of demands imposed by the new environment. He has to seek ways of integrating these strange, new experiences, and his constructive coping patterns or mechanisms must be reinforced if he is to master both his normal developmental problems and the superimposed tasks.

* Reprinted from *Social Casework,* Vol. XLIV, No. 8 (1963).

The Life Space Interview

The life space interview was identified and primarily developed by Fritz Redl and David Wineman in their work with disturbed children in camp and residential treatment settings.* It is based on the theory that problem situations in the child's day-to-day life have strategic therapeutic importance when they can be dealt with immediately before or immediately after they occur, and even more when the person who deals with them has witnessed the incident. The goals of the life space interview are the "clinical exploitation of life events" and the provision of "emotional first aid on the spot." [1] In working toward the first goal, the therapist (who may be anyone who is part of the child's environment) exploits an appropriate experience of the day to help the child work on specific problems of adjustment; in working toward the second goal, he offers the child immediate help in coping with situations that provoke an overload of hostility, anxiety, guilt, or frustration.

To promote the use of this technique in the Clinical Center, provision was made for (1) an activity program to facilitate interaction among the children and (2) staff conferences to help the hospital personnel develop therapeutic techniques and attitudes toward the children.

The Activity Program

The activity program that provided the framework for the life-space-interview technique was planned to accommodate all the children whose physicians had granted them permission to participate. It could be carried out wherever the children were. Because the program had to be highly flexible, many adaptations had to be made in the usual play activities. The medical programs of individual children often led to a rapid change in the composition of the group or to the necessity of moving the group, for example, from one child's bedside to the playroom. Moreover, of course, many games had to be modified because of various children's physical limitations.

* The writer participated in these projects at Camp Chief Noonday and Pioneer House in Detroit, Michigan, and at the Child Research Branch, National Institute of Mental Health, Bethesda, Maryland.

[1] Fritz Redl, "The Life Space Interview. Workshop, 1957. 1. Strategy and Techniques of the Life Space Interview," *American Journal of Orthopsychiatry*, Vol. XXIX, No. 1 (1959), p. 6.

In addition to ward activities, there was at least one trip planned each week to an interesting place in the community. The purpose was to provide the children with the normal experiences they would have had at home. Some of the places visited were a zoo, a museum, a hot-dog factory, a circus, a potato-chip factory, an ice-cream plant, a dairy, and a nature center. In the summertime there were picnics and cookouts. On many trips a visit to a store was included, for shopping or browsing. Sometimes trips were planned for particular age groups. Nine children could be accommodated in each trip of the station wagon unless space was needed for a wheel chair.

Decisions about the place, the form, and the content of each interview took into account the special characteristics of the individual children, the group as a whole, the immediate problem, and the location. The variety in the interview settings provided a natural opportunity for each child to express feelings and behavior with considerable spontaneity.

Examples of Life Space Interviewing

In providing first aid on the spot, the following life space interview was focused on alleviating a young child's anxiety about a seemingly routine medical procedure.

> The social worker was in the room when a physician was telling Nancy, aged 8, about the biopsy she would soon undergo. When the physician left, the social worker discussed the matter further with her, and remarked that she must be scared. In as much detail as seemed feasible, he described the entire series of events that would take place: her being given a pill to make her sleep, her trip to the operating room, the preparation of her underarm, her return to her room, her awaking and seeing a nurse she knew. He told her she might feel "punky" when she awaked and her arm would be sore—but she would soon feel as she did just then. Nancy said nothing but nodded from time to time, indicating she understood. Later, in the playroom, the entire procedure was acted out, with other children playing various roles. Nancy refused to play the role she would soon enact but wished to stand aside and watch the play-acting; so the social worker enacted her role.
>
> When he visited her the day after the biopsy, she immediately shouted, cheerfully, "N'yah, things weren't like you said they'd be." She explained that, although everything else he had said was true, he had been wrong about her being taken to the operating room on a table with wheels. "A nurse carried me up," she reported.

151

From her cheerful statement about the one "error," and her general emotional tone, it was obvious that she had been helped to bring this experience to the level of ego-manageability.

Almost without exception, the subject of injections produces an immediate response in a child. He is likely to say, "They don't bother me," "I don't mind them," or even "I like needles." Defenses of denial and reaction formation, however, crumble rapidly at the time of the injection.

Timmy, aged 5, had been chronically ill for several years. Because of his obesity he was openly rejected by his parents, and he was extremely anxious about being abandoned by them. His surface behavior was that of an extremely bright, polite, cheerful, friendly, and co-operative child. He emphatically denied that any medical procedure bothered him, and said he "liked needles." When he was scheduled to receive an injection, however, he was visibly apprehensive, though he almost always succeeded in controlling any verbal expression of his feelings.

At first Timmy could not participate in any individual or group interviews about injections, but he gradually came to be able to discuss the problem. A milestone was passed when he said, "Some needles hurt and some don't." Afterward, little by little, he grew more comfortable in expressing hostility toward the social worker, other members of the staff, and his peers. First, while the social worker was on vacation, Timmy expressed his hostility toward him by saying repeatedly that he was going to poke him in the nose. Later he was able to say this directly to the worker, indicating his increasing feeling of acceptance. He recognized that the world would not crumble if he expressed his true feelings, and that the worker would still be his friend and like him even if he showed anger, or if he cried.

Timmy's original adjustment to the ward had been almost entirely oriented to pleasing the adults, leaving him little energy for gratifying his own needs. It was important to help him express his real feelings about his chronic illness, his separation from home, and his stay in the hospital. His need to expend his emotional energy in placating the adult world left him with a minimal supply for attaining a more normal adjustment to the "strange world" of the ward. Though it was not possible to make the injections less painful, it was possible to lessen his fear of not being accepted and liked if he expressed his true feelings. Thus some of his emotional energy would be freed for coping with more important tasks. After his fears were reduced, he was able to function less often as "Timmy the adult-pleaser," and more often as "Timmy the child," a role more appropriate to his age and experience.

Working with the Hospital Staff

Weekly team meetings were initiated with members of the nursing personnel to help them learn about the effects of illness and hospitalization upon the normal emotional and physical growth and development of children. Current problems with individuals and groups were reviewed and specific techniques for handling them were agreed on. As a result of these meetings the staff moved toward the establishment of an environment characterized by a consistent, individual approach to the problems of each child.

It was also necessary to work with members of the staff individually in order to teach them about the purpose and use of the life space interview. From the actual experience of working with the children and with the knowledge gained from their participation in team meetings, many staff members became skillful in coping with situations that aroused an overload of hostility, anxiety, and guilt, in the children and in themselves.

Like all new programs begun on a ward with a time-honored structure, this one was tested by the staff. After the testing period was over, however, the staff members were able to accept the social worker as a member of a team working to create a more tolerable hospital experience for the children and staff; they realized that this goal could be attained by diminishing the number of crises that arose out of the children's adjustment problems. Then they were better able to participate in the discussions at the team meetings. Their greater participation, in turn, led them to achieve greater freedom in utilizing the techniques discussed. As they learned that their successes with the new techniques outnumbered their failures, their incentive to master them increased, and they participated even more freely in the meetings. The process of program integration on the wards was greatly facilitated by the social worker's availability to the staff and the children during the working day.

Nancy's biopsy, for example, was discussed. Because of the frequent use of the biopsy, some staff members tend to relegate it to the position of a "minor medical procedure." Often an adult's "preparation" of the child is an effort to minimize or reduce the significance of the procedure. However, the amount of anxiety aroused in

153

the child by such a "minor" procedure is often overwhelming. The social worker helped the staff to consider the possible meanings of this experience to the child and to realize that it is not possible to assist the child through it by minimizing it. Before Nancy's operation took place, the staff discussed her possible responses to the biopsy and its possible effects on her emotional adjustment. They agreed on the general approach to be used by those who were to care for her. Afterward they discussed the results of their planning and handling.

Another problem that was dealt with was staff members' support of extreme dependence or independence in the children. Once having realized that maintaining a balance between dependence and independence is crucial for the success of a child's hospital adjustment, the staff succeeded in creating a climate that was favorable to it. The handling of 3-year-old Lucy is an illustration.

> Lucy had been hospitalized for most of her life and was the pet not only of the staff of her ward but also of numerous other wards throughout the hospital. A nurse who had a particularly parent-like relationship with the child was helped, however, by the learning she acquired as a member of the project, to relinquish this role and replace it by a more appropriate one—that of the warm, accepting adult. This shift in role enabled the child to make a successful transition from the hospital ward to a foster home.

In the case of Charles, the staff found the life space interview a useful tool, not only in alleviating the child's internal conflict but also in helping him to deal with his external problems.

> Charles was an 18-year-old boy with a metabolic disorder that was accompanied by difficulty in muscular co-ordination. Immediately after his admission to the hospital the staff grew concerned about his frequent sexual overtures to the nurses. In addition, he abused other members of the staff verbally. Most of them were uncomfortable with Charles, and they dreaded their assignments to care for him. The information the social worker gained from his work with Charles, together with that obtained by the staff, enabled the team to arrive quickly at a "plan of attack."
>
> The plan called for the social worker to have a number of interviews with Charles. Sometimes these occurred after his verbal assaults on the staff; at other times he was interviewed when no episode had occurred, and then he could look beyond any immediate problem and view his general situation. The interviews might take place in his room while he played cards or during a trip.

154

At first he vehemently denied that he was worried about such problems as his medical condition, his acceptance by adults or peers, or his sexual adequacy. After a number of interviews, however, he was able to say that he did care what people thought of him and that he felt bad when he was considered "crazy" because of his unsteady gait and the cast of his eyes. He told how much he worried while he was dancing because he was not sure which way his feet would move.

Besides conducting these interviews with Charles, the social worker worked with the staff in the weekly team meeting to help them understand his behavior. One nurse reported she had become extremely upset when Charles had verbally assaulted her; he had responded by increasing his aggressive behavior. Gradually, however, she and the other staff members learned to view his behavior as symptomatic of his unhappiness, and they came to realize that they were not the true objects of his abuse. Furthermore, as they came to understand that he had no intention of carrying out any of his threats to the nurses, their attitudes toward Charles became more perceptive. Despite the fact that his behavior continued to be a problem on the ward, their reaction to it was more appropriate. All were gratified by their increasing adequacy in coping with Charles's hostility, and after the tension had lessened, they were able to focus their attention on some of Charles's other adjustment problems.

After the life-space-interview approach had been added to the ward program, the nursing staff handled day-to-day problems more therapeutically than under the usual hospital regimen, whereby conformity would have been obtained from the patients by "bribery" or coercion rather than by attempts to enable the patients to utilize their coping mechanisms.

Summary and Conclusions

The life-space-interview technique can be applied in other medical settings so long as the necessary adaptations are made. Someone might argue that "there just isn't enough time to get into all this business—there are too many patients in the hospital." For precisely this reason, it is of particular importance that the staff learn to handle problems therapeutically, for doing so will prevent minor problems from developing into major crises. In addition, though it may not be possible to obtain a full-time social worker skilled in the use of the life space interview, it is possible to increase the skill of the ward staff so they can cope with the adjustment problems of patients more adequately and therapeutically.

Establishing such a program in any form requires the involvement of the ward staff. In some settings staff resistance may exist initially, but after the nurses and physicians are helped in their attempt to handle the patients' problems, and if they are allowed to proceed at their own pace, the eventual success of the program is assured. The result will be better service to patients.

Modifications of the program should depend upon the setting, the staffing structure, the physical plant, and the kinds of illness being treated. A number of aspects of such a program that have not been discussed should be considered: activity planning on a medical ward; the use of equipment and supplies in program planning; the co-ordination of group work and casework programs in patient care; the modification of traditional goals and techniques of group work and casework in a specific setting; the role of the social worker in the staff development program of a medical ward; and life space interviewing with adult patients.

The rapid flow of events in the hospital evokes much anxiety and fantasy in the patient, which he needs to verbalize and discuss. His thoughts and feelings need to be redirected and clarified as soon as possible. Through the life-space-interview technique the hospitalized person can work through a number of difficult emotional experiences. He can thus become free to cope more adequately with succeeding events. Just as the staff on a psychiatric service carefully considers all aspects of the patient's behavior as he reacts to the daily events of the ward, so also on a medical service the staff should give close attention to the patient's day-to-day behavior so that they can understand him. Such careful attention can enable the staff to help the patient attain the maximum adjustment possible during his stay.

Finally, the life-space-interview technique should be applied to other areas of social work practice and should continue to be developed and refined in those areas in which it has already been successfully tested.

13. Short-Term Therapy with Adolescents*

Lovick C. Miller

THIS PAPER BRINGS together some observations on short-term individual therapy made over the past eight years with a middle- and upper-class group of adolescent boys of above average intelligence and interest in intellectual achievement. It is a clinical supplement to a previous report.[1]

Despite much variation on specific points there appear to be a number of generally accepted therapeutic principles among writers who hold to a psychodynamic theory of personality. Briefly, the therapist's role consists of listening intelligently to the patient's communications, encouraging the production of relevant historical and current life data by asking pertinent questions, offering reassurance at times, encouraging and accepting emotional discharge and insight, interpreting associations at the proper time, and waiting for and guiding the patient in his assimilation of recovered unconscious memories and the emotional experiences that occurred during treatment.

These principles are essential concepts for any age group, and the theoretical framework guiding their application is derived from psychoanalytic theory and psychoanalysis as a therapeutic technique. Since most therapists working with adolescents are not analysts there is a need for a frame of reference incorporating dynamic principles applicable to short-term therapy. This paper will attempt to derive the broad outlines of a theoretical orientation for short-term therapy with the adolescent age group.

Erikson describes the central process of adolescence as the establishment of an "ego identity." He points out that this is more than

* Reprinted, by permission, from the *American Journal of Orthopsychiatry*, Vol. XXIX, No. 4 (1959). Copyright, American Orthopsychiatric Association.

[1] James T. Heyl, Richmond Holder, and Lovick C. Miller, "A Psychiatric Program in a Boys' School," *Orthopsychiatry and the School*, Morris Krugman (ed.), American Orthopsychiatric Association, New York, 1958, pp. 257–265.

the sum of childhood identifications. It is the "accrued experience of the ego's ability to integrate these identifications with the vicissitudes of the libido, with the aptitudes developed out of the endowment, and with the opportunities offered in social roles. The danger during this stage is role diffusion." [2]

Most adolescent problems can be viewed as a crisis in the maintenance or establishment of an ego identity. The primary goal of short-term psychotherapy with the adolescent should be to abet and support his efforts to achieve an integration. By short-term we refer to therapeutic contacts ranging from three to thirty hours. The early phases of therapy should be directed toward determining the factors that block integrative efforts; later phases should be given to working through anxiety associated with overcoming these inhibiting factors and to developing new coping mechanisms. Conditions that hinder the development of an identity are considered under four categories: failures in coping with previous developmental problems; accidental or motivated exposure to overwhelming tension-producing situations; failures in the value area; and withdrawal from societal channels which facilitate identity formation.

Failures in Coping with Previous Developmental Problems

Here we refer to boys whose histories reveal severe adjustment problems. Adolescence has simply put additional strain upon inappropriate adjustment mechanisms. In general, but not always, short-term therapy has little to offer this group.

An exception to this general rule was John, 18, seen for sixteen interviews during the last six months of his senior year. He came because of a mild anxiety attack, but his real worry was homosexuality. Until the age of 8 he had been "more girl than boy." Between 12 and 15 he was actively homosexual; during these years he had a five-month affair with an adult. To reverse this pattern, he had become fanatically religious, but this defense was beginning to break down shortly before he sought therapy.

The first problem was to get through the glib façade by which John maintained emotional distance and narcissistic control of the interview and other interpersonal situations. The therapist accomplished this directly and rather bluntly. Mainly by his attitude, he got across the fact that John's manner was neither funny nor cute, but reflected considerable anxiety. In the third interview the patient-therapist relationship was openly clarified,

[2] Erik H. Erikson, *Childhood and Society*, Norton, New York, 1950, p. 228.

which prepared the way for John to work more directly on his problem.

John was principally concerned with his unsatisfactory relations with others and his disgusted and self-deprecatory feelings about himself. He controlled, manipulated, mothered, and seduced his male friends. With girls he discussed politics, religion, and sex. He seemed compelled to become involved in highly elaborate seductive controlling situations. These he gradually became aware of and slowly tried to change. This change came hard and was associated with much anxiety and many setbacks, but by the end of therapy he had disengaged himself from much of this activity and formed some new nonerotic relationships.

Occasionally during the sixteen hours John discussed his past life, but this seemed to have little meaning to him. As he put it, he had told this story many times before. One thing that proved meaningful was his having to tell his father that he was in therapy. This brought out much hatred against the father, not so much because of events of the past but because of John's current fear of his father and his inability either to stand up to him or to separate from him. Telling his father that he needed treatment became a living experience in facing up to these fears. Much symbolic material suggested that his father was an unconscious love object and that John identified with his mother, who died when he was 3, but this material was never discussed in the interviews.

In these three months the object aim was not reversed, for he was still much more aroused by the male body than by the female. However, he surrendered—at least in therapy—much of his façade; he made real efforts to change his way of relating to others; he vented much hatred that he held for himself and others and he faced his father directly for once. He kept overt homosexual activity under control; and, most important, he made a close and trusting relationship with an adult male.

This case has been presented to illustrate the fact that chronic characterological problems can sometimes be helped in a short contact if the therapeutic goals are limited. The main therapeutic progress seemed to occur with the patient's exploration of his feelings about himself and others and his failures to gain satisfaction because of his inadequate coping mechanisms. Interpretations were used to help the patient to clarify what he did that led to dissatisfaction both in relationship to the therapist and to others. John was further supported in his attempts to change lifelong patterns which arose out of deep loss and a gross sense of inadequacy. No attempts were made to connect current behavior with past events. Life history data served as a frame of reference for the therapist, but seemed unimportant to the patient. At no time were interpretations of deep unconscious conflicts given. For an adolescent in search of an identity, overcoming present fears and failures is more important than knowing the events that led to them.

Accidental or Motivated Exposure to Overwhelming Tension-producing Situations

This section is concerned with boys who have been exposed to a traumatic episode which they could not master. Two cases will be discussed.

Joe, an 18-year-old senior seen for fifteen interviews, revealed that his younger brother had died suddenly the previous year. He had been found dead, hanging from a tree with his bicycle below. Joe assured the therapist a number of times that it was not suicide. He had experienced no grief following the death, and therapy consisted primarily of grief work. Joe began by recounting his brother's admirable characteristics; then he revealed his own guilt because of mean things he had done to him in the course of growing up. Only later was Joe able to discuss a few of his brother's irritating characteristics, interspersed with a discussion of his parents and particularly of his mother's domination. Toward the end of the sessions he related a recent series of dreams in which his brother appeared back in the family as he used to be. At the same time Joe had the conscious feeling that a big hole had been closed within him and once again he was complete. This grief work, however, occurred along with much discussion of his life philosophy, his trip to the Far West, and his friends. At times he would drift back to the incident and then drift away again. He never discussed his obvious fear that the death was suicide or his concern about why such a thing had to happen.

The second case was Frank, a senior who showed a dramatic change of character from a conscientious, hard-working, well-mannered boy to a surly, undependable person who refused to study or to participate with others and dropped from a B average to failures in several courses. Frank's parents were divorced during his freshman year and his mother remarried in his junior year. All this he accepted with equanimity. In the summer before his senior year his mother became pregnant. When this happened he became morose, irritable, and disgusted with his mother and his stepfather. Back at school he found little to interest him, and the academic pressure and rules were very aggravating.

Frank was seen for twenty interviews. The first efforts were directed at getting him to discuss his feelings surrounding the divorce, remarriage, recent pregnancy, and his parents. The pregnancy apparently reawakened old oedipal attachments. This approach resulted in an increase of anxiety coupled with further

160

withdrawal and disinterest in life. The emphasis was then shifted away from these areas entirely toward his own interests and everyday concerns. Several hours, for example, were spent in discussion of aeronautics, an interest of his held in common with the therapist. Diminution of anxiety accompanied this shift. As he became more comfortable he discussed at considerable length his own social-sexual inhibitions and his failure to find ways of gaining satisfaction in these areas. Frank recovered remarkably well and graduated close to his original position. Despite many unresolved problems and much guilt and self-denial, he looked forward to the next phase of his life with much more zest than one would have thought possible a few months earlier.

These two cases of identity confusion resulting from overwhelming tension states are cited to illustrate one principle, that the primary therapeutic goal in such cases is supporting the integration process by facilitating the development of new coping mechanisms. In general, focusing upon the traumatic episode itself and the motivations and events leading up to the crisis increases anxiety and identity confusion. What appears more effective is (1) interest in the adolescent himself, which has the primary effect of diminishing the intensity of his reaction to the trauma; (2) exploration of current life events with which he copes successfully and those with which he copes unsuccessfully; (3) recognition of the "working through" process that always has to accompany trauma; and (4) when necessary, careful exploration of earlier life events which may be blocking current adaptation.

Failures in the Value Area

Ego identity hinges upon the establishment of an economical, workable, and stable set of values. Much identity confusion in adolescence concerns the need to reformulate a personal value system which can reconcile values learned in childhood with the new internal pressures and the more complex society of adolescence.

In general, when a child reaches adolescence with a grossly inconsistent set of values or when his values are contrary to those of society, as in the case of the recidivist delinquent, short-term therapy has little to offer, for the problem is too profound. On the other hand, short-term therapy can often facilitate the resolution of a value crisis whose origin may be temporary or even of long standing. The next case involves the conflict of a boy seeking an individual identity within an integrated family value system.

Bill, a senior, was referred three months before graduation because he was failing two subjects and was in danger of not graduating. He came from a family of wealth and social position. Over several generations, family members had attended the same college and then gone on to assume responsible professional or public careers. As a senior he became disillusioned, losing interest in studies and in graduation as he became acutely aware of his future rolling dully before him. He felt that he was going to be no different from all those who had gone before.

In the course of twelve interviews he brought out his identity disillusionment and his wish to be something in his own right. Two things preoccupied him: He always did what he thought he should do rather than what he wanted and he always did what he thought would please his father. He said that his older brother had always been favored by the father, and that he felt he had to try to please his father in order to receive the affection and approval afforded his brother. He never revealed the hostility underlying his compliance but he did come to recognize his disinterest in school as a form of rebellion.

The opportunity to vent some of his jealousy and feelings concerning the futility of his efforts to satisfy his father and the recognition that his academic performance was a disguised form of rebellion enabled him to reconsider for himself what he wanted in life. Time was too short for anything more than a recognition that graduation and college could be a means of liberation as well as conformity, and hence not something that must be avoided at all cost. He mobilized himself sufficiently to graduate from prep school and enroll in the family college. In effect he postponed his individual identity solution and, although much more contented, recognized that the main conflict was still to be faced.

This case was selected because it poses one of the more difficult technical problems facing the therapist working with the adolescent —how to facilitate an adolescent's quest for an identity without imposing one's own values. In this case there was a problem of how to refrain from encouraging either rebellion or conformity. We hear often that rebellion is a means to an identity solution, and one wonders how often this value concept comes into our work with adolescents. What appears most important is to support adolescents in making their own decisions so long as the decisions do not involve action that would seriously hinder the achievement of an identity solution, such as passive submission to authority, leaving school, committing a crime, withdrawing from interpersonal contact, and other behavior extremes.

162

Withdrawal from Societal Channels that Facilitate Identity Formation

Since many authors [3] have described the numerous sources of tension in adolescence we shall turn from intrapsychic events to consider some of the societal processes involved in the development of new coping mechanisms.

We recognize as important the integrating and channeling effects of education and formal group activities, but we are perhaps less aware of the value of informal discussions among groups of peers of the same or opposite sex. These "bull sessions" appear to be much more than a forum for the release of pent-up energy and frustrations. Among other things, they provide a means for communicating that vast store of unwritten knowledge which is so essential to life. Such things are discussed as the intimate details of sex behavior as participated in by both sexes; the breaking of social taboos, such as stealing and truancy; the personal characteristics of adults; the identification of subtle nuances of behavior patterns for adaptation in the more complex society of adolescence; and the more personal views on the great problems of mankind such as religion, politics, and morals. The mutual interchange of actual and fantasy experiences provides a forum for the acquisition of new ways of looking at and experiencing the inner and outer world which in turn leads to new values, new identifications, new and more subtle behavioral patterns and emotional nuances, and hence to a new ego identity.

It is at times important for the therapist to recognize normal social mechanisms used by the adolescent in his search for an identity. In short-term therapy, the main identity effort will not be made within the therapy hour but rather in the social milieu. Therefore, the therapist's efforts should be directed toward aiding the adolescent to take full advantage of normal societal processes. This truth was most strikingly revealed by many instances of isolated boys who found friends during the course of therapy, and discussed with these friends things that came to their attention during therapy as well as other things that they were reluctant to bring out in therapy. They often hinted tantalizingly about the discus-

[3] For example, Irene Josselyn, "The Ego in Adolescence," *American Journal of Orthopsychiatry*, Vol. 24, (1954), pp. 223–237; also Leo A. Spiegel, "A Review of Contributions to a Psychoanalytic Theory of Adolescence: Individual Aspects," *Psychoanalytic Study of the Child, Vol. VI*, International Universities Press, New York, 1951, pp. 375–395.

sions they had, generally adding parenthetically that it was of little use to discuss the subject further. They appeared to be "acting out" tensions and conflicts arising in therapy, and hence this practice was discouraged. Subsequently, there was always increased resistance. Only gradually did it become clear that "talking with a buddy" is a vital process for the adolescent and that therapy was enabling the patient to do what previously he had been unable to do. Now, far from discouraging these discussions, we take them as a sign that the patient is beginning to make use of the normal social channels for identity formation. It also became apparent that adolescents can often discuss much more intimate and anxiety-producing material with contemporaries than they can with an adult, even one who creates a permissive and understanding atmosphere.

The therapist can also use normal social processes as a strong adjunct to therapy itself. When strong inhibitions and repression exist within a patient, this person will generally avoid discussing with his peer group topics reflecting the repressed feelings. Leading the adolescent to discover how he avoids these topics and encouraging him to participate in group discussions often facilitates release of the prohibitions. However, helping a boy to take advantage of societal processes must be done with the same skill as bringing unacceptable impulses to consciousness.

An example of this occurred when a boy was discussing his unawareness of sexual feelings and denied masturbatory activity. He was asked if he ever discussed this topic with friends, and he said of course he had not. He then was informed that most boys his age masturbated and that they also discussed sex quite freely among themselves. Later he told how upsetting this information had been since it only served to prove again how different he was from others. This is not to say that the information should not have been given, but rather that such information should be considered as an interpretation, and the effects it generates in the patient should be worked through in the same way as any other interpretation. In this particular instance, once the boy's anxiety had been worked through, the information enabled him to participate in numerous all-night "bull sessions" involving sex among other things. These discussions served as an entrée into group relationships from which he had been excluded.

Termination

One difficulty the short-term therapist faces is the lack of a personality theory that provides a frame of reference for termination.

Psychoanalysis sets its ideal as the recovery of the major inhibiting unconscious repressions and obtainment of genital object love. Client-centered therapy permits the patient to set his own termination as part of the self-determining principle. Obviously object love for the adolescent is not possible, and it has been the thesis of this paper that uncovering unconscious memories within the time span of short-term therapy is generally disruptive to the integration of an identity. On the other hand, permitting complete self-determination has often proved in this writer's experience to be equally threatening. The adolescent needs to feel that the therapist has a clear-cut tangible goal in mind and often demands that it be stated.

A theoretical framework that visualizes life, from birth to old age, as a continuous, but at the same time a discrete process with disruptions likely to occur all along the line, partly due to events of the past, but also due to the limitations of the organism to meet stresses of the present, should prove helpful. This would mean that each life crisis is, to some degree, independent of other crises and that the goal of short-term therapy in adolescence should be the formation of an identity sufficient to cope with current life crises. In many cases there will be unresolved problems—some conscious, some unconscious—some of which will be conpensated for while others will be resolved in the course of normal life events. In other cases a deep working-through of unconscious conflicts may be necessary when the patient becomes an adult. The practical solution appears to be one of terminating when there is satisfactory adaptation to the present, letting the future take care of itself.

Summary

It has been emphasized that the primary objective in working with adolescents is to facilitate the formation of an ego identity. People at this age are vitally concerned with their new bodies, new impulses, and new social roles. They feel strange, awkward, and often panic-stricken at their inability to integrate these new experiences into an organic unity. This panic we referred to as "identity confusion." The first concern is for the adolescent himself: his interests, his philosophy, his experiences, his skills, and finally his worries. The therapist with this age group must always provide an interested ear, and time for discussion of the adolescent's new sense of awareness and his intense interest in the inner and outer world.

The next considerations are ego defects that prevent satisfaction and the establishment of adequate identifications; specific impulses that are being blocked, current and past experiences that inhibit impulse expression, and social mechanisms that are avoided and could be made use of.

Once a relationship of trust has been established and the principal conflicts and ego defects are known, the emphasis should be upon the development of new coping devices. At times it is helpful to clarify the source of tension, whether it arises from blocked impulses or from the person's own inadequate coping mechanisms. In cases involving identity confusion due to traumatic events it was suggested that one should minimize the events, thereby decreasing the adolescent's reaction and self-awareness. Seldom, in this writer's experience, has it proved helpful to connect trauma with unconscious motivations or historical events. Sometimes confession of current or earlier thoughts or experiences offers considerable relief and leads to better coping efforts, but seldom in short-term therapy does the adolescent achieve insight into unconscious conflicts or motivations.

When an adolescent begins to change he should be supported in his efforts through encouragement, through acceptance of failures, through recognition of anxiety that accompanies change, and through help in recognizing and making use of typical societal adjustment processes. At times it is necessary to explore historical events that may be blocking current adaptation. However, we have tended to de-emphasize the use of historical exploration, focusing instead upon successes and failures in coping with the present. Uncovering unconscious conflicts and motivations generally proves disruptive, for they add strain to an already overtaxed ego.

The value for the therapist in knowing the normal social processes through which most adolescents achieve a considerable part of their identity was touched upon. There is benefit in knowing how to make use of these processes. It has been particularly emphasized that providing information in the attempt to relieve inhibitions should be done with the same skill as making interpretations. Finally, a plea was made to forego a termination model based upon either an ideal concept of maturity or a completely laissez-faire self-determinism in favor of a model that describes termination as the point at which there is sufficient identity to make a satisfactory adaptation to the current stage of development.

166

14. Observations of College Students in Acute Distress*

Alice Ichikawa

MANY STUDENTS COME to a university mental health clinic because of difficulties arising from an acute situational stress. The young college student is in a new setting away from home and close parental ties, with greater opportunities for new experiences and keener competition. Some students respond to these changes in their lives by becoming acutely upset. We shall report which of these problems are handled by the social worker in the initial application process, and what factors may contribute toward their early resolution.

The interest over the years in brief or goal-limited therapy has special relevance for the kinds of situations dealt with in a college setting. Franz Alexander, Thomas M. French, and the staff of the Chicago Institute for Psychoanalysis first introduced efforts to define the basic principles that make possible a short but nonetheless efficient means of psychotherapy.[1]

Mary Sarvis, Sally Dewees, and Ruth Johnson state that relatively time-limited ego-directed psychotherapy is a method of choice for a wide range of patients. They believe that many patients if seen promptly can be helped to achieve adaptive integration out of the disruptive experience with this kind of psychotherapy, and they describe how timing and spacing of therapeutic transactions can be done usefully and economically.[2]

Peter Blos has written several articles pertaining directly to the

* Reprinted from *Student Medicine*, Vol. 10, No. 2 (1961), by permission of *The Journal of the American College Health Association* (formerly *Student Medicine*).

[1] *Psychoanalytic Therapy*, Ronald Press, New York, 1946.

[2] "A Concept of Ego-Oriented Psychotherapy," *Psychiatry*, Vol. 20, (1959), pp. 277–287.

college student. In his article on psychological counseling he states that young people in college tend to maintain adolescent modes of adaptation that reactivate and precipitate personality disturbances that interfere seriously with successful life, academically and socially. He feels that psychological counseling services that are intramural, with a simple but effective referral system, can detect maturational disturbances at an early stage and facilitate resolution of the acute conflict.[3]

The help of the Student Mental Hygiene Clinic at the University of Chicago is readily available to all students, and many use the service who would not ordinarily go to a psychiatric clinic or to a psychiatrist in private practice.

Each year about 450 students are seen at the university clinic. Of this group about 25 per cent seek help because of acute distress related to current life situations. We find these students can usually be helped to resolve their difficulties in a few interviews.

All new applicants are seen by the social worker. There is virtually no waiting period, and students are seen either in the order in which they apply or immediately, if the distress is acute. The primary focus of the intake interview is on presenting difficulties and evaluation of the problem with the student to determine what he is seeking and whether the services of the clinic are suited to his needs. Assessment of the severity and the urgency of the situation is made, and a decision is promptly made as to the next step.

Problems Presented

Students often come in to discuss their problems prior to an important decision or in anticipation of some experience that may seem frightening to them. This accounts for the high number of applications soon after arrival on campus or before Christmas vacation, comprehensive examinations, and graduation. Students who have not dealt adequately with feelings of separation from home will often become acutely upset when they meet with frustrations such as low marks, termination of a relationship with a girl friend or boy friend, or a family emergency. Many students come in when dating imposes demands that are in conflict with values learned at home.

[3] "Psychological Counseling of College Students," *American Journal of OrthoPsychiatry*, Vol. 16 (1946), pp. 571–580.

Some students who have severe personality problems are able to compartmentalize their problems and to be effective in their academic efforts until they are exposed to an unusual stress. These students sometimes can be helped in a relatively short time to integrate the insight gained about the current experience and return to their previous functioning.

Case Illustrations

1. A 20-year-old third-year student came to the clinic before the end of the quarter. She was anticipating marriage and complained of anxiety following a dream. Her mother had agreed to the marriage, and plans for the future sounded reasonable. She described a good relationship with her fiancé, who was practicing medicine in another part of the country where she expected to resume her education.

The setting for the dream was a party where she was being prevented from joining an older man who was both attractive and frightening to her. She was with her mother and seemed unable to leave her, so she returned home with her. The sophisticated girl interpreted her dream to mean that she must not want to get married. She began to doubt her decision and wondered whether she really loved her fiancé.

Exploration indicated that the patient's father had died when she was 5 years old, and she and her mother had been quite close. She still lived with her mother, and her marriage would mean separation from her for the first time. The therapist did not talk about her infantile conflicts but discussed what seemed obvious— her feelings about separation from her mother and about living with someone else. Expression of her doubts and of her mixed feelings seemed to relieve her even during the first interview. In the second interview she stated that she felt more comfortable and was going ahead with her plans.

2. Another student was referred by the head of her dormitory because she had lost her bubbly, enthusiastic manner and had become depressed, despondent, and tearful when she received notice of her low marks on return from Christmas vacation. The first year she had done well academically and had lived in a dormitory with other entering students. She was caught up in the excitement of new experiences and participated in many social activities. She returned for her second year with expectations that things would go in the same light vein. She had moved to another dormitory to cut down on expenses and was no longer with the same group of girls. The demands of her courses were greater and dates were not as frequent. With a drop in grades,

169

the student became very anxious, assuming blame for all her difficulties. She had done very well in high school and achieved recognition in her community for her musical ability. She blamed her inability to study on the noise in the dormitory and had moved only to find the new one noisier. She was asking to move again. Dissatisfied with her classes, she began to change instructors. She stayed up all night, talking to matrons about her parents—how good they were to her and how she had failed them.

Her response seemed to be a delayed separation reaction from home. Because of her past performance she had an exaggerated expectation of herself. That her parents had not reprimanded her but had accepted the low grades further increased her guilt and her need to project her own frustrations onto external reasons. Changing rooms, changing class instructors, talking to night matrons seemed to be her effort to re-establish a familiar situation. It was clear even in the first interview that she wanted to use the social worker as a substitute for her mother. Seen for three sessions, the student quickly gained insight about her reaction to leaving the protective relationship offered by her parents and her fears of having to assume some responsibility for herself. Rather than transplant the dependent relationship to herself by continuing regular contact, the therapist encouraged the student to reach out into the community for those experiences that would help her in the maturation process. A follow-up interview indicated that she was trying out new types of relationships and appeared to be making considerable progress in coping more adequately with her total situation.

3. A 26-year-old married student had recently enrolled as an undergraduate. His self-referral to the clinic followed an episode late at night when he had suddenly come upon a man being slugged by another. The incident precipitated acute anxiety in which he began to fear violence to himself and to his wife and to fear the loss of his sanity. The resultant anxiety totally immobilized him and he was no longer able to cope with his school work. When separated from his wife he was constantly preoccupied with thoughts of violence—such as his wife being kidnapped.

His wife had employment that entailed late working hours and made it necessary for him to accompany her home. Her job not only interrupted his studying, but also limited the hours he could be with her. The student's only conscious thoughts, however, were of utter gratitude to her for enabling him to continue his education.

Exploration of his past revealed a tremendously deprived background; his parents had separated shortly before his birth and he was brought up by elderly relatives. When he was 6, his mother remarried and took him to live with her. His stepfather assumed responsibility but was never close to him. His mother had become involved in a fundamentalist religion, and much of her time was occupied in working for the church. Many times he recalled coming home from school, finding her gone, and being frightened that Christ had come and taken his mother away. Finally, at the age of 15, he could no longer tolerate the pressures of the religion and his mother's involvement in it. He left home and became essentially self-supporting. He worked at menial jobs and through persistence in attending night school had earned enough credits to enroll at the university. He had been married a year when he came to the clinic.

In spite of the marked deprivation he had experienced, he had tremendous drive for helping himself. He revealed many ego resources, as demonstrated by what he was accomplishing in his life. The problem seemed directly related to his dependence on his wife and the demands her odd working hours made upon him. Rather directly, the social worker clarified the connection between his anxiety reaction and his current situation. He began to be able to admit his irritation toward the work arrangement and toward his wife. As he did so, the physical feeling of helplessness disappeared and he was able to cope better with the situation by not fearing the loss of control, although he felt badly because his wife was doing so much for him.

The student described his feelings as similar to those he had had when his mother was not at home. The worker pointed out that he was reacting in his relationship to his wife with the same feelings he had felt as a child in relation to his mother. Recognition of his overreaction in much of his feeling toward his wife made the current stress more understandable. Although not sophisticated, the patient seemed responsive and could integrate the experience of freer expression of feelings. In four interviews he showed ability to cope with the situation. He wanted to try to manage on his own, and contact was terminated with the mutual understanding that he could return at some future time should he so desire.

Discussion

Just as it is necessary to give support to young adults when support is needed, it is equally important to encourage them to rely on themselves when they feel adequate. When asked whether they want regular interviews to discuss their problems, they frequently respond, "Oh, I don't want to come in every week, but I'd like to come in when I run into another problem." It is important to encourage them to try out their own ideas and not to interfere in their efforts toward maturity.

The opportunity to talk about their problems at the moment of distress, with an interviewer who helps them to see the situation in an orderly and reality-oriented framework, makes the problem less overwhelming. For most students, the contact with the clinic social worker is the first opportunity to talk to someone who listens and believes that what they say is of utmost importance. The communication of the worker's firm conviction that the students are seen as individuals who have achieved considerable growth and are capable of further maturity is particularly significant to the college-age group. The interviewer understands the regressive, more infantile reactions to stress but also recognizes that a part of the student is striving for more adult behavior. One student commented, "The most helpful thing is that you seem to feel I'm not entirely in the wrong and that I have some ability to handle my problem." Assistance given when needed provides an opportunity for them to reassemble their defenses in such a way as to obtain more gratification from their environment and to encourage their efforts in the maturation process.

What the clinic has to offer is explained to the student, but an attempt is made to leave the responsibility for seeking help to him. Pressuring the student to get help is interpreted by him as a continuance of parental authority, which he is trying hard to renounce. The fact that the student is given the responsibility for making a choice is in itself of great importance. One student was told that continuing contact was up to him and, should he decide that he wanted another appointment, he could call. He telephoned, leaving the message that after thinking the situation over he wished to try to get along on his own; he emphasized that he had been given the choice and this was his decision.

In handling situations at the intake level, we have found it more effective to plan that one worker will see the patient throughout the entire process. When one person is responsible, there has not been a single failure by a student to keep a second appointment with the same person. It would seem that, after having opened up to one person at the moment of stress, the student who is shifted to another therapist loses a sense of continuity and is less motivated to begin over again.

We recognize and utilize the inherent growth potentialities in the student. Rather than to encourage reliance upon a therapeutic relationship, we attempt to allow and encourage the student to find gratification in the university environment. The door is left open so that contacts can be easily renewed. Of students who were seen in the last academic year, 26 per cent were known to us previously. Most of these former patients were those who came in for limited service on some specific issue; others, with vaguer difficulties, nonetheless seemed to get support at the time. A significant number who failed to accept the initial recommendation for treatment returned after a lapse of time when they themselves were ready to use the services of the clinic.

Summary

In a college setting, service is given students who often have no definite symptom pattern but temporarily have become overwhelmed by an acute life situation. Offering service at the point of stress when they seek help is important. Selection of students who can be helped at this supportive and remedial level is done on the basis of sound diagnostic understanding of the total situation, including an assessment of ego resources. The therapist intervenes in the student's life to foster his ego-adaptive capacity within the context of his present situation. The focus on his current reactions enhances his ability to assume responsibility for his problem and assists him in coping with his acute situational stress, thus enabling him to continue in the maturational process.

15. Some Dynamics of the Middle and Later Years*

Stanley H. Cath

ALL PEOPLE GROW OLD—normals, neurotics, psychotics, defectives, and delinquents, the single and the married—and throughout life they share certain basic anchorages: (1) an *intact body* and *body image*; (2) an *acceptable home*; (3) a *socioeconomic anchorage*; and lastly (4) a *meaningful identity and purpose in life.*

From a combination of very early experiences centering on physical care and psychological well-being, and the personal history of accidental trauma or injury, an anchorage of basic personal and physical security is or is not established which is related to the capacity to bear anxiety and stress. All recent studies point to the significance of these very earliest experiences in later object relationships. From the security of the intact home one learns or derives those facets of personality related to trust, tenderness, self-control, autonomy (in contrast to their opposites, mistrust, exploitation, shame, and doubt) as delineated by Erikson.[1] The social anchorage is based upon these early phases and includes friendships or object relationships in which trust, faith, constancy, and the like are tested and experienced in school and away from home. Finally, by achievement of an inner identity through the adolescent years, one may achieve the "meaningful purpose," which may be one's family, science, art, literature, religion, or other sublimated activities that give life its purpose and flavor.

* Adapted, with permission, from *Smith College Studies in Social Work,* Vol. XXXIII, No. 2 (1963).
[1] Erik H. Erikson, "Identity and the Life Cycle," *Psychological Issues,* Vol. I, No. 1 (1959).

Stress, Anxiety, and "Fate" Neuroses

Each person's life is a continuous process, with one normal or abnormal crisis following another. At each critical point of growth
and stress, there are several paths that a person can take. He may
cope relatively easily, mastering and integrating the stress and in
this way maturing; he may engage in serious conflict and regress;
or he may perpetuate the conflict as a "fate neurosis" that is manifested by themes of constant anxiety and repetitive tragedies that
are never resolved. We are familiar with those masochistic characters who live out their need for punishment. Other persons dread
closeness or responsibility. Still others, constantly helpless and im-
potent in the face of life's demands or their own inner drives,
remain perpetually indecisive, unable to find themselves or to integrate a satisfying self-image with the actuality of their life. Ethical
or characterological defects not only become significant to them in
their own pattern of living but are transmitted from generation to
generation.

Yet, what may be stress for one person is merely a challenge to
another. It is generally acknowledged that at any point of crisis
the ability to adapt or integrate is related to the maturity of certain
ego functions, that is, the capacity to tolerate tension, endure anxiety,[2] postpone pleasures for reality demands, and synthesize the
past and present within the current situation. Clinical experience
suggests the error of assuming that a person in the middle or later
years is unable to demonstrate tremendous and variable capacities
for integration and development or for enduring loss. The human
ego can tolerate tremendous shock and loss and still expand, grow,
and create.

Perhaps the greatest stress on the adult human organism is in the
last third of life. What better place, then, is there to study ego
functioning as the individual prepares "to be through having been"
and "to face not being at all" [3] and confronts the ultimate in loss
of self and objects? Granted a relatively intact psychic structure
with capacity for insight, foresight, and judgment, it is a unique
situation in which one may study grief and abandonment reactions
to inevitable internal physiological depletion, as well as to a shifting
and often decreasing external cosmos.

[2] Elizabeth Rosenberg Zetzel, "Anxiety and the Capacity to Bear It, "*International Journal of Psychoanalysis,* Vol. 30 (1949).
[3] Erikson, *op. cit.*

175

"Omniconvergence"—A New Construct

It is not quite sufficient or accurate to describe these losses and events either as ego changes or as attrition in life-space. For ease of communication and conceptualization, a new topographical and dynamic psychological construct is useful—"omniconvergence" (or "omnicon"). This term includes not only phenomena in the personality structure (ego, superego, and id) but also in the physical structure of the organism (the body and the body ego) and the socioeconomic, ethical, and purposeful environment. Omnicon thus signifies that the total human being and his personal cosmos are involved in the various epigenetic phases of loss of self and others that result, first, in depression and, second, in depletion. The ego's attempts at restorative processes will best be understood when seen in this total perspective of multiple converging epigenetic variables, and we are thus spared from taking sides in what appears to be a re-creation of the conflict between theorists on the significant external and internal factors.

At any age the balance of forces, as they impinge upon the capacity to adapt, depends on what has gone before. Since the term "dynamic" refers to the science of forces, let us try to break "omniconvergence" reactions down into their component parts, remaining aware that several factors may be operating simultaneously.

Id Reactions: As people grow older instinctual life appears to be less intense. One may indeed speculate that with the attrition of the biological substrata, such forces may well be in the process of decline. Simultaneously, a reduction in the tyrannical demands of the superego and ego ideal may facilitate the ego's task of mediation, especially since demand from the outside for achievement may also be lessened. This apparently ideal state of relative peace may, however, indicate a renunciation of object searching, and it is difficult to determine at this stage of knowledge how much is a biological (organic) decline and how much an adaptive protective maneuver.

Ego Reactions: It is important to recognize gross ego incapacity or excessive neurotic anxiety. Some symptom complexes, including distorted perceptions or poor contact with reality are often inappropriate life-long residuals of early deprivation and insecurity. Inferiority feelings, perhaps due to unresolved pre-oedipal crises or derivatives of the oedipal conflict, make one constantly unsure of sufficient strength to cope with inner dangers. These feelings, usually the result of excessive early frustration of aggression or sexuality, are often aggravated by external changes in long-established anchorages. These stresses now threaten mechanisms of defense that were previously erected to cope with inner anxieties. For example, in the male, we are continuously aware of a basic struggle centering on activity and passivity. This struggle is paralleled in the female by a conflict over anatomic differences and feelings of inequality.

The External World: Reality Feedback

By middle life a storehouse of experience with significant others and the world-at-large has resulted in a substantial body of reality feedback which has had a significant role in determining one's image of the self as significantly helpful or detrimental in the life of others—as "good" or "bad." A positive self-image obviously enhances the ego's capacity to cope with loss and depletion. One woman's regression, for example, stopped abruptly after she began to work as a volunteer in a hospital. Her daily reality feedback had changed, resulting in a dramatic improvement in her self-image. Instead of constant reproach from a daughter she had really neglected, she experienced gratitude from a diffuse mass of patients for whom she had no real responsibility. This observation is consistent with Hartmann's views of the mutual influence and interaction between the ego and the id.[4] This concept of mutuality, it should be stressed, includes external events and losses, increasingly significant in later years, as they are reflected from the anchorages established.

On the physical level, the maintenance of a healthy body, reasonably good co-ordination, and orgastic potency, with the ability to create children—all related to the basic anchorage of body image —are a source of continuous input. With loss or depletion of outlets of discharge and functioning capacity, a devastating blow to the narcissistic sense of invulnerability is struck, faith is shattered, and the ego is confronted with overwhelming depletion anxiety.[5]

[4] Heinz Hartmann, "The Mutual Influences in the Development of Ego and Id," *Psychoanalytic Study of the Child, Vol. VII,* International Universities Press, New York, 1952, pp. 9–30.

[5] Stanley H. Cath and others, "Role of the Body Image in the Psychotherapy of the Physically Handicapped," *Psychoanalytic Review,* Vol. 44, No. 1 (1957), pp. 34–40.

Other returns for the investment in living include a home, the remnants of relationships with families of orientation, interaction with offspring, and social affiliations in the community. But these relationships continually change. This change, while inherent in life, is also due to the balance of forces related to internal and external circumstances, between progression and regression, between loss and restitution. The whole process brings about—often at surprisingly early ages—conscious subjective feelings of aging, often expressed in terms of depression, emptiness, despair, or futility. These states, perceived by an enteroceptive structure, the sensor, demand restitutive action or substitute object relationships. The result may be influenced by the degree of ego strength available in shifting libido to other objects or by the ability to erect compensating defenses if the shift is not possible either because of internal danger or external prohibition.

Timing, as a dimension, is significant because, during the depressive phase that usually follows a call for shift in psychic investment based on apparent or real loss, circumstances sometimes conspire so that nothing of value for substitution is available or acceptable. Occasionally, suicide or less fatal but equally pathological solutions become permanent ways out. A mother's involution may occur at the time of her daughter's engagement or wedding, a time when the daughter is least able to give and wishes primarily to turn away. The satisfaction of one's needs is related, then, not only to individual relationships but also to the time and history of crucial events in the lives of significant loved ones; and together all these factors are operative in determining what is available in the individual's small cosmos that may permit re-contact and a chance to begin again. One may need to re-anchor or re-secure the self repeatedly in order to restore a sense of self-esteem and worth in the course of a lifetime.

The Middle Years

In the face of continuous internal and external demands for performance that include providing or taking care of a home, managing finances, and giving emotional security to children, one is often inwardly concerned about gradual psychological and physiological changes that are sensed, if not consciously perceived, in the self, or mirrored in others. Yet there are continuous demands, from the

178

ego ideal for achievement and simultaneously from the ego for approval from without. By this time, compelling images of goals and models upon which to achieve have been established. Depending upon the degree to which these goals have been reached, the ego ideal will or will not have been partially pacified, and at this phase a searching self-assessment is likely to be made. There is also an increasing insistence on a sense of permanence, with considerable anxiety if this is not possible. One often hears, "I realized I was committed to this way of life. I couldn't change it or run away any more."

Should relative physical well-being continue, there is, nevertheless, an inevitable gradual transition and decline on the physiological level. It may go unnoticed or little anxiety may be felt until a threat suddenly appears on the horizon—one of those daily incidents that prove one is vulnerable and older. The incident may bring about a recrudescence of genital or pregenital concerns, and old neurotic conflicts may be reactivated. These may be precipitated by a major or minor external event, for example, an insignificant illness, a coronary, or an automobile accident, all threatening a change in established anchorages or relationships.

Castration anxiety over sexual performance or bodily intactness, usually associated with climacteric change, may be reflected in specific derivatives of earlier conflicts related to problems of control, or "holding on." The inevitable struggle for power between generations is often accentuated at this time. Later derivatives of oral needs, such as anxiety about one's own dependency, may be camouflaged by concern about separation and loss, either of substance from the self (hypochondriasis) or of children from the home. There are changes in sexual potency as well as in the secondary sexual characteristics that determine attractiveness and actualize the transition from a youthful parental phase through the menopause. For some persons, the loss of narcissistic gratification through changes in attractiveness constitutes the greatest threat of this period, if not of their entire life. Accordingly, a phase of preparation and final integration of an altered body and self-image is one of the maturational challenges in the middle years. This transition includes changes from creator and doer to progenitor and observer, from guiding parent-with-authority to a role of either limited influence or intruding in-law. Once regarded as an overflowing fountain of knowledge with significant skills, one may now be tolerated

179

only if one is accepting and acceptable. All this change must be synthesized and integrated within the self and family image.

One sorrowfully begins to acknowledge or realize the possibility that tomorrow may not be the same and for some it may not come at all, as disease and death begin to afflict one's friends and relations. It is usually in these years that one's parents are lost, after which loss significant changes in ego and superego structure frequently occur.

In women, the change of life is keenly marked. With the advent of non-functioning gonads and associated bodily changes, an inner awareness of aging is associated with a sense of loss and disillusionment that finds its most extreme expression in the depressions of the involution. Here we see an example of one of those continuously reverberating circuits, so characteristic of the complex structure, the "omnicon." As the body attempts a new equilibrium, the external world and the psychic apparatus are in a position to oversee the ongoing physiologic process; that is, they may accelerate and/or inhibit it. Events that enhance or destroy self-esteem interdigitate with the the physiological changes to tip the scales toward higher adaptive levels or toward regressive breakdown.

Some older persons emerge with an inner calmness, appearing to accept the inevitable changes and even to be enriched by them. Others seem released so that they meet head on the challenge to live, love, and think more effectively. They increasingly feel the need to leave something of themselves in other individuals, or something of worth to society as a whole as a result of their creative activity and thought. This period may witness the activation of forces directed toward the outside which had been previously directed toward the self or family.

As one becomes aware of sexual decline in the self, one's children may be emerging as vibrantly alive and extremely sexual. In the face of this contrast, mothers and fathers may be upset by either sons or daughters who, in seeking completion and closeness in the opposite sex, turn outward and away. Hence, the conflict between generations: the child moves toward the genital act and parents move away; great anxiety is generated and the family interaction suffers. In men, we sometimes see homosexual panic or paranoid or depressive reactions, as their daughters develop and become more seductive. Women, on the other hand, are more likely to cling to their sons, devalue their prospective daughters-in-law, and become either psychosomatically ill or overtly depressed. On occasion they become extremely hostile to their husbands, blaming them for the loss; they lack sexual interest and encourage infidelity by frigidity and the repression of tenderness.

At this point, timing, ego strength, and mutual interaction play important roles. If there is a continuity of sharing and a preservation of basic anchorages, if the need to give as well as to receive can be met, and if the family can be helped to realize it is in a crisis shared by many families at this stage, a pathological reaction is not likely. Even if an adolescent is just turning away from the home at the time of the mother's involution and depression, fate may determine an accentuation of the depleting process, but not necessarily a serious one because new relationships and restitutive efforts are still possible. The relative preservation of various sublimations results in the maintenance of sufficient free, neutralized energy with which to cope with each crisis. Yet, both the capacity and opportunity to regress in the service of the ego, in terms of periodic restorative withdrawals or just a time to be alone and away from daily energy-draining emotional interactions, seem important. Some persons are aided by a day of sleep, a vacation, or other periodic changes in the feedback situation, thus reducing the energetic expenditure of either family interaction or occupational drudgery.

Depletion Phenomena

When age and time begin their demand for self-assessment and reappraisal, there may well be a denial of failure and limitations, with a resultant sense of bitterness. Some individuals are caught in a series of traumatic events that precipitate the ego into a state of depletion. Libidinal energy is so consumed in maintaining countercathexis that it must be replenished by drawing from other essential ego functions.

Mr. A, for example, lost his job while he and his wife were still grieving over the death of their only son. The crisis of bereavement had rekindled guilt over not having had more children. Feelings about the emptiness in their relationship, previously held in check, engulfed them. Now forty-five years old and suffering from hemorrhoids, Mr. A faced a hostile world which in effect said: "We don't hire men your age. You're a 'has-been' and have nothing to offer compared to younger men. *They* have a future." At the same time, he became more conscious of reproachful feel-

181

ings in his wife. Mrs. A struggled to counteract her own depression through renewed sexual activity but could not be satisfied. Confirmation of unpleasant but previously denied aspects of themselves and their limited generativity, resulted in an inner restless dissatisfaction and an unreasonable hostility toward each other. As in her adolescent years, Mrs. A's anxiety over incestuous longings and flirtatiousness erupted in a psychosomatic skin condition.

Unable to appease his anger or contain his anxiety, Mr. A's self-contempt increased. His agitation so overwhelmed him that even the restorative functions of sleep or food were no longer effective, and hospitalization was required. He felt utterly empty, depleted by the loss of his son and his job, and the abandonment by his wife.

It may have been within Mr. A's capacity to tolerate any *one* of these losses without severe regression, but together they resulted in a state of depletion. Every crisis in marriage has a potentiality for increased closeness or distance. Each marital partner has the possibility of rewarding generativity or denying self-respect and esteem. The need for feedback of positive aspects of the self from others, especially from one's spouse and children, to replenish depleting biological processes or accidents of fate (as seen in the case of the A family) never ceases.

Marital crises in the early years are more likely to be a result of disappointment felt in the other person, or, more accurately, in the image of the object on whom idealized values (often of the self) were projected. Marital crises in the later years are more reflective of the depletion and disappointment felt within the self as extreme anxiety related to unrealized self images. They are often expressed as a search for rebirth (perhaps through younger lovers) or a magical elixir of youth (sometimes alcohol) to escape reality and superego pressures. At first, failure is projected and therefore due to the partner's failings, but later in life this defense may not be operable. Thus, awareness of one's own incapacity may be neutralized or coped with by paranoid feelings of being attacked. Anxiety is lessened by feeling hated by someone else other than the self. Some of the marriages that do not terminate can be described as bat-like; the participants pass in the night without touching, seeing, or feeling the other's presence. With the breakdown of sublimated defenses, deneutralized aggression is released, and anxiety breaks through. A retreat to pregenital levels follows and, depending on the individual ego, a search in other areas for new lines of defense and attempts at restitution may supervene.

With the loss of a sexual partner through death or divorce, one faces the problems of dealing with loneliness and sexual impulses. The surviving partner may attempt to relieve loneliness by a quick excursion into renewed heterosexual activity. It is surprisingly difficult for significant others, especially children, to accept the fact that an older person still has sexual feelings and a continuing desire for companionship and completeness.

For symbiotic couples, one of the most serious threats may be the loss of the crucial person on whom one has so depended for existence itself. But on rare occasions we are surprised to find, instead of a helplessly depressed and self-castigating patient, an individual emancipated for the first time who is able to live independently, even if still in a seriously disturbed and neurotic way. More often a prolonged period of mourning follows. One woman of 74 wore black for eight years and did not leave her house after the death of her husband, with whom she had both lived and worked.

Restitution Phenomena

In an effort to compensate for increasing insecurity, identification with more perfectly idealized objects may occur; for example, many become active in the political area for the first time. In this outward turning a comparison with adolescence is possible, where the search and desire to appropriate another person's way of life or to perfect the world is equally urgent and may be "identity-saving." Association with others who are creating in the sciences or arts, or, if finances permit, support of philanthropic institutions, are common. Shifts within the psychic structure of the more fortunate may permit the acquisition or emergence of new skills, indicating the possibility that there was an over-all restraining or inhibiting force that has been released when sexual processes are no longer in ascendancy and new creative forces emerge.[6]

In some individuals, the loss of self-esteem caused by shifts in body image is counterbalanced by a gradual acquisition of the feeling of dignity and respect that comes with middle age. Comfort with age-

6 Irving Kaufman, "Psychodynamic Considerations in Normal Aging," *Normal Psychology of the Aging Process*, Norman E. Zinberg and Irving Kaufman (eds.), International Universities Press, New York, 1963, pp. 118–124.

mates and the maintenance of contact are the rule here. One notes adaptibility to the demands of and changes in more youthful persons and less inclination to ridicule their efforts. This group contrasts markedly with those who are continuously indignant at any alteration within the culture or within other people and who imply that all faults in society are due to the deficiencies of the younger generation. This latter group is a counterpart of the angry young men who feel past generations have failed them. The failure to achieve permanent independence, integrity, and security can be projected forward or backward in time. Thus each generation scapegoats the other to a greater or less extent.

Another comparison of adolescence and the middle years is in order. The identity crisis often manifests itself as a search for a structured life. Day-to-day regimentation may be desired, and a fusion of one's role with that of a larger group may be extremely valuable. A renewed interest may be awakened in religion, which in the middle years is even more appealing than before because it promises future reward to those who deserve it and another future, with punishment, to those who do not; for all it structures a future.

We are well acquainted with the defensive value that activity has for thousands of people who work long hours either to avoid family contact or to counteract deep feelings of passivity. This activity provides a safe distance between inner feelings, the images of the self, and external performance. It is not limited to men, but includes many women who are involved in work, a social whirl, or community activities. Should physical or psychological illness limit this defensive activity, intensified feedback from the warded-off instinctual derivatives or from the family may result in a breakthrough of intolerable anxiety.

Proper perception and cognition are based on the hold on reality, and, in turn, on reality feedback, both of which determine that which is "actual" in life. Under stress or change in feedback, preexisting pathology may be activated, and extreme anxiety that paralyzes thought or action may appear. Former signals of distress may reappear. These, however, are now anachronistic and unacceptable to the self or others; an older individual demonstrating signs of confusion, weakness, or crying may cause the opposite reaction to that originally experienced as a child. Instead of finding comfort, one may be regarded with repugnance and become increasingly isolated.

Turning to offspring rather than to parents for help is doubly difficult because the latter had been habitually conceived of as more energetic and strong, and the former as the opposite. With this transposition of role and reversal of generations, loss of face is likely.

Toleration for rejection may have decreased, and many people solve this problem by becoming non-offensive background shadows rather than expose themselves as lost souls or the beggars that they feel themselves to be. So it is for many that the search for peace and relaxation through the use of anachronistic mechanisms yields only lonely isolation, without meaningful human bonds to sustain them.

Dynamics of the Later Years

"What kind of a person have I become? How self-sustaining? How much of a burden? How crippled and restricting of others? How healthy or capable? What respect is due me? What has happened to my plans? What next?"

These are some of the questions that plague the elderly person. At roughly the age of sixty, generational bonds and horizontal ties with age-mates often show signs of weakening. It may be that few friends remain.

In the sixties and seventies, when one can no longer realistically look forward to new starts, more positive identifications, or readily changing one's ways, the number of depressive mood swings tends to increase, and there is a shift in frequency along the mood spectrum, from days of heightened well-being to those of mildly depressive preoccupation, during which one searches for tokens of past affection and responses from memories. But to live in the company of one's memories may serve little purpose if it awakens regrets as well as pleasures. This condition, of course, may not be accepted lightly, and rebellion may be manifested by temper outbursts.

It is not difficult to understand why strong reaction-formation defenses are likely to become increasingly necessary and, accordingly, more noticeable. As there is less energy to cope with change, deceased tolerance for deviations and newness is commonly observed. If a reversal of roles has taken place, with the parent now in the role of child, tremendous fear of being treated like a child arises. Still, anxiety about losing dependency gratifications so colors the relationship that there is an increased tendency to suppress feelings of disappointment or anger.

185

Approval or rejection by other persons, essentials of the feedback process, are often based on superficial judgments. Certain elders are particularly likely to evoke avoidance reactions rather than absolute rejection and are acknowledged as less desirable sources of identification and information than others. First-generation immigrants are often in this unenviable position with their children. On the other hand, respect for certain desirable traits may permit an anchorage of positive self-esteem.

Retirement

In these later years another rung of the ladder is reached. An intense crisis may develop around the problem of retirement. Not everyone objects to this change, and some older persons accept a passive life quite easily. Many retain some meaningful activity or become secondarily interested in another person's activities; for example, some men take over housework, much to their wives' chagrin. Yet the loss of identity as a productive worker or as member of a particular group may precipitate or accelerate a person's natural physiological or social depletion. Either the ache of emotional separation from family members or too intensive daily contact with them may result in his partial retreat from the reality world and sometimes, a recathexis of fantasy. "Achievers" may suffer a loss of anticipatory joy in daily activity as each succeeding experience brings greater anxiety, frustration, and pain. Always they had held the blind faith that the future was ahead, but now it is here—and what next? As a consequence, they are repeatedly confronted with the question of their intrinsic value in this world.

Some lonely retired elders turn to community agencies in various stages of aggressive but confused searching. At times they become migratory, for, despite their advanced age, they travel from agency to agency or community to community, seeking someone who will care for them in the way that will re-establish their past and substitute for a lost object relationship or occupation. The ebb and flow between loss and restitution, between aggression and regression, continues, depending on the circumstances in which they are involved. Disappointed in a particular agency, they go on to another. After each crisis and its ensuing frustration, the older person may experience a period of paranoid depression. In order to restore a partial sense of basic trust, memory traces of earlier successful situations are revived—often providing great comfort, like old shoes that are worn with deep pleasure. And images of earlier, more satisfying love objects may be evoked, even from the grave.

Three-Generation Home

To provide care for the elder in the family three-generation homes are often established. Almost every relatively intact aged person I have interviewed felt he had to mute discordant feelings and decrease inner demands lest he lose whatever residual love and affection remained for him within the new family setting. This adaptation may indeed give the impression of decreased instinctual pressure, but I believe a greater demand for countercathexis is operative, and so an illusion is gained. The ego, in a relatively weakened state, is taken up even more in a desperate countercathectic move, leaving less energy to cope with the new external situation.[7] Temporarily, during this particular phase of readjustment (either to a three-generation home or to solitary living in a small apartment) the elder finds himself tense and anxious, unable to give, testing those around him as to his "place" and what the future may hold. At this time, withdrawal and depression, as well as rigid clinging to the more successful modes of coping, may well be observed. Such a psychological state, instead of reducing family tension, is a source of irritation, and the ordeal fosters regressive behavior in all participants. The older person is most vulnerable because he is the one with the greatest investment in already established techniques and has the least number of resources.

Many possible outcomes have been clinically observed. When the illusive support of memories and fantasies suffice and passivity is tolerable, life goes on at a subdued pace within the family setting, with small decrements of aging destined to continue to play their part. The therapist can provide reassurance and clarification of this state and, if the regressive process is still reversible, intelligent manipulation can be most helpful. Many people succeed in overcoming the initial crisis, depression, and test period when a three-generation home is established, and a higher level of adaptation can be reached. The search for meaningful relationships may be gratified and serious pathological consequences averted.

[7] Stanley H. Cath, "Psychodynamics of the Three-Generation Home," *Tufts Folia Medica, Bulletin of Tufts—New England Medical Center,* Vol. VIII (1962), pp. 43–53.

Neurotic Traits as Defensive Maneuvers

Although it may be true that some of the strength of instinctual forces is diminished in later years, neurotic conflict does not seem lessened. In fact, it has been said that in old age neurotic characteristics are accentuated and pathological disturbing traits become worse under stress, as efforts to repress call forth the more readily available defenses. These defenses may well protect the individual against further anxiety about depletion. It has often been clinically shown that psychotherapeutic intervention for the affective state of depression-depletion aids more healthy restitutive efforts of the ego, and the neurotic accentuation frequently diminishes. Functioning can thus be restored to the predisturbance level.

I prefer to think of this phenomenon not as "depression," but rather as a continuous process of depletion and restitution. Psychoanalysis, aimed at replenishment of all basic anchorages, is rarely possible.[8] One does not treat the neurotic character trait or defense in exacerbation per se but rather the reaction to the stress or precipitating factor causing the depletion, while offering the patient a significant reality relationship to assist his natural restorative potential.

Sensory Isolation

My thesis, then, is that isolated living without the stimulating input of meaningful and repeated human interaction results in psychologically regressive and physiologically degenerative processes. Failure to restore meaningful object relationships is often followed by ego disorganization, with loosening of the chain of retrospective thought and fantasy. Connections to the present seem lost. In the face of reality abandonment, every effort is made to avoid severe anxiety and depression. Humiliation and anger are introjected and self-castigation expressed. As an abortive attempt to restore contact, outbursts of rage may occur, but I believe the main motives are to gain attention, respect, and some restitution of self-esteem. In protected settings, particularly in group living situations, such outbursts tend to be less frequent. Should intact ego and embers of ambition and desire still be present, an outburst of hate may be turned on the self, particularly the ailing body for its failure in free-

---

[8] See Hannah Segal, "Fear of Death—Notes on the Analysis of an Old Man," *International Journal of Psychoanalysis,* Vol. XXXIX (1958), pp. 178–181.

ing the self from this prison of unrewarded dependency or isolation. The effects of isolation and decreased object cathexis upon the aged ego are yet to be fully studied.[9]

Without protective intervention the following chain of events may ensue:

1. The world of make-believe and the illusion of memories conspire with the effects of sensory deprivation to accelerate a process in which sight, sounds, and words may begin to lose meanings. Disturbances in language and muscular movement appear.

2. The innate tendency to hold on to people and objects may then give away to an abandonment of the external world. With prolonged isolation and weakening of both physical and mental facilities, there may be an irreversible state, analogous to the anaclytic depression in children that has been described by Spitz.[10] Thinking may be gradually decathected both because of its painful content and because of deficits in the ego's perceptive apparatus.

3. Positive images of the past and the body self may be the only available sources for protective intervention. One often finds recathexis or redistribution of libido into certain organs or parts of the body that are still intact and, therefore, should work. They are particularly expected to salvage the whole. We know that with younger people the loss of one part results in a recathexis of an adjacent part. In the aged it is the intact part—the mind if the body fails—that is so cathected.

4. A split between the offending, weakened body and a relatively intact mind may accentuate certain mechanisms of despersonalization. Fugue states, recently linked to oral aggression by Easton [11] are often not recognized in the elderly and may be taken for cerebral episodes.

5. A wish to destroy weakness wherever it is encountered is a defense against the strong passive wishes that might complete frustration and loneliness if revealed in their nakedness. A serious withdrawal or psychiatric break with reality, if not suicide, may occur at this time.

[9] For examples of studies in this field, see Philip Solomon and others, *Sensory Deprivation*, Harvard University Press, Cambridge, 1961.

[10] Rene A. Spitz, "Anaclytic Depression," *Psychoanalytic Study of the Child*, *Vol. II*, International Universities Press, New York, 1946, pp. 313–342.

[11] Karl Easton, "Further Remarks on Fugue and Orality," *Psychoanalytic Quarterly*, Vol. XXIX, No. 4 (1960), pp. 555–558.

Conclusion

Living sufficiently long, in itself, brings inevitable personal loss, psychic and bodily depletion, and disease. Specific defensive maneuvers have been studied by which one copes with the overwhelming vicissitudes of loss and depletion that each individual encounters. Anxiety has been viewed as qualitatively and quantitatively different in the aged, related to the threat of total emotional exile and eventual annihilation, calling forth more primitive defenses, facilitating regression to the earliest modes of gratification and adaptation to the lowest levels of bodily and psychic need.

It is our task not only to determine every possible means to develop each person's greatest potential, but also to preserve the intactness of his defenses as long as possible. Some special techniques of therapy, related to the severity of object loss and depletion, have been suggested. The problems of restitution and maintaining the hold on reality are considered in detail, for human stature and destiny are ultimately to be measured by the finest development and preservation of the human mind.

Part III
Clinical Applications

ALTHOUGH THEY PRESENT many different programs and points of view, the papers in this section all illustrate important practice implications of the crisis intervention concepts set forth in the previous two sections of this book. A brief listing of these concepts might well include the following: (1) the importance of immediate diagnostic assessment; (2) selective emphasis on history-taking procedures which, if used in routine fashion, may leave the worker with all the information and the client or patient with all the problems; (3) the need to focus on specific interventive tasks and achievable treatment goals; (4) the avoidance of overspecialized or overcentralized intake assignments that often require an inordinate number of case transfers, and which may add a new stress dimension—the disruption of a meaningful therapeutic relationship at a critical moment; (5) an open-door policy that invites people to return for help with recurrent crisis situations; and (6) planned follow-up safeguards to ensure that families who have received short-term services know that the agency's interest continues, should further service be needed, even though the formal period of help has terminated.

Helen H. Perlman's paper points up the connection between an important aspect of crisis theory—the client's subjectively apprehended "sense of crisis"—and the almost ubiquitous "phenomenon of the waiting list" that frustrates his search for help.

Oriented to the "effective alleviation or removal of a disorganizing stress situation," Mordecai Kaffman's methodology for short-term family therapy seems to offer promise for intervening not only in acutely stressful problems in parent-child relationships but also in the acute eruptions of chronic personality disorders which initially seemed unsuitable for a time-limited treatment approach.

Elizabeth E. Irvine and Agnes Ritchie describe programs for children and youth that explicitly draw on crisis propositions.

191

Irvine emphasizes the need to make preventive services promptly available to children who are "at risk" because their parents have been hospitalized for mental illness, and Ritchie outlines the use of "multiple impact" techniques to assist families of adolescents.

Two types of relocation crises are illustrated in this section. Ruth Chaskel deals with the impact of voluntary relocation, as the newcomer on-the-move encounters a variety of emotional and environmental problems, while H. Frederick Brown, Vera B. Burditt, and Charles W. Liddell portray the plight of the family caught in a relocation crisis that is forced upon them by the urban renewal juggernaut. Both papers emphasize the hazards as well as the opportunities that inhere in the crisis situation.

The movement for the establishment of around-the-clock emergency psychiatric clinics is now gaining momentum. Eleanor Clark describes the initiation of such a program in a large urban general hospital. This experimental program makes help easily accessible to patients in their "moment of crisis." At the same time it affords continuity of care; the drop-out rate is thus much lower than that of emergency programs which typically refer their cases, after an initial screening interview, to what has been described as the "referral merry-go-round."

Another type of crisis-oriented emergency service, with literally life and death implications, is that of the Suicide Prevention Center, which in the last few years has elaborated a series of specific clinical techniques for intervening in the life crises of suicide-prone individuals. As with a number of the other programs depicted in this section, the emphasis in this program is on the immediate and constant availability of the therapist in response to the cry for help, the flexible use of environmental as well as clinical resources, and an innovative approach to the mobilization of significant others in the patient's family and social network.

The final paper in this section advances the threefold thesis (1) that brief interventive services for families in crisis should be planfully incorporated in the community's total spectrum of social services; (2) that such services may be properly characterized as "early secondary prevention"; and (3) that our present pattern for the distribution of family-oriented social services should be reorganized so that certain "dysfunctional agency rituals," now hindering proper delivery of services to the community, may be eliminated.

16. Some Notes on the Waiting List*

Helen Harris Perlman

THE PHENOMENON of the waiting list poses a dilemma for the social agency and raises a host of provocative questions. Apparently there is an ever-widening gap between the number of applications for help and the staff time available for casework service. Apparently, too, the use of a waiting list is on the increase. Many applicants are given a first interview and then, if judged to need and to be able to use the agency's services, are placed on the waiting list until time is available in a staff member's caseload. The phenomenon of the waiting list stands in interesting juxtaposition to recent propositions about crisis and prevention and about class culture and the use of social services. It deserves examination.

The Family Service Association of America recently published a report on a census of family agency applicants, their problems, and their use of agency service.[1] One fact that stands out in bold relief in the FSAA study is the high incidence of dropout among applicants who waited for service nine weeks or more: half did not return. Presumably they had been given full-fledged intake interviews, had been judged to need and to be able to use the agencies' services, had been promised help, and had agreed to wait. But when they were called back, they did not return.

What happened to these applicants, one wonders. What happened to the problems with which they sought help? A problem that pushes a person to apply to a social agency can rarely be "put on ice." Some sort of adaptation (or maladaptation), some kind of problem-solving efforts, must be made even while one waits. What are these efforts? Do they lead to a constructive solution or do they mainly produce further complications? It would be interesting and

---

* Reprinted from *Social Casework*, Vol. XLIV, No. 4 (1963).
[1] Dorothy Fahs Beck, *Patterns in Use of Family Agency Service*, Family Service Association of America, New York, 1962.

useful to know, through a follow-up study of these applicants, what they did about their problem and what factors, including their single experience with the agency, affected their decision not to return.

The Non-Returners and the Returners

Probably many non-returners use other sources of help. Some, if the original application was more impulsive than thought out, perhaps resign themselves to the inevitability of the problem they momentarily found intolerable. Others, who ended the first interview with unresolved ambivalence about the agency's usefulness in relation to their problem, may retreat to their original trench of resistance. For a few, perhaps, some lucky circumstance erases the problem or eases its stresses.

The fact that half the applicants who are interviewed, accepted, and put on a two-months-or-more waiting list do not return is of concern not only because of what happens to the applicants themselves, but also because intake is an expensive operation. The usual intake interview absorbs at least an hour of a caseworker's time. Another hour is spent in recording the interview, particularly when the case is to be held until a later date when details may have been forgotten. In addition, time must be expended by the person who transcribes the interview, by the supervisor who reads it and decides to whom the case is to be assigned, and by the continuing worker who must both read it and think about it. When all these expenditures of professional and clerical time and effort yield no client, there is reason to be troubled about the waste of scarce and costly manpower—if such manpower were in ample supply, a waiting list would not be necessary. A follow-up study of the waiting-list dropouts might provide useful information about the ingredients necessary to an intake interview if the applicant must wait. It might also enlighten us on the substitutes people find and use when they cannot get casework help.

Of equal interest are the waiting-list applicants who tolerate the postponement period and return to the agency to pick up where they left off. The first question that comes to mind is: Do they actually pick up where they left off? Is the problem the same as it was when they brought it two months before? Are they the same in their relation to and interaction with it? In what ways, by what means, and with whose involvements was balance kept? Have the means used or the persons involved—the dynamics of adaptation—changed both

194

the nature of the problem and the applicant's relation to it? Have his symptoms multiplied and his circumstances worsened? Or has the stress lessened, by virtue of the capacities and resources of the persons involved or by virtue of a happy accident? Have the promise and hope of the agency's help or the release of tensions experienced in the one interview with the caseworker served as a "holding" device?

When a client begins to receive casework help after many weeks of waiting, the answers to all these questions must be ascertained. Because problems do not remain unchanged and because the problem-carrier and his interactors must be continuously at work, with or without help, trying to erect defenses against or cope with the difficulty, it is inevitable that the person-problem configuration is not the same as it was weeks ago. Even when the problem has been present for a long time and the client avers wearily that "It's the same old thing as before," there remains the fact that his feelings about it and about his unsuccessful coping with it have become more deeply entrenched.

What must happen, then, is that, when considerable time elapses between the original intake interview and the assignment of a case, the worker must hold what is virtually a "re-intake" interview. If he does not, he starts working with the client not where he *is* but where he *was*. Again one is faced with the problem of the time and effort expended in the first application interview when it is known that the case will have to be shelved.

Is the Waiting List a Problem?

If the waiting list is inevitable, should an agency devise a new type of intake interview—a less time-consuming one—in which the worker's effort is directed chiefly toward ascertaining simply that the applicant's problem is one for which the agency can offer help and then is focused on the applicant's willingness to wait and his capacity to cope on his own? Experiments of this sort have been reported in the literature.[2] Further thought should be given to

2 See, for example, David Hallowitz and Albert V. Cutter, "Intake and the Waiting List: A Differential Approach," *Social Casework*, Vol. XXXV, No. 10 (1954), pp. 439–45; Albert S. Hotkins, Michael Kriegsfeld, and Rosalind M. Sands, "An interview Group Therapy Program for the Waiting-List Problem," *Social Work*, Vol. III, No. 1 (1958), pp. 29–34; Catherine M. Bitterman, "Serving Applicants When There Is a Waiting List," *Social Casework*, Vol. XXXIX, No. 6 (1958), pp. 356–60; Anita Gilbert, "An Experiment in Brief Treatment of Parents," *Social Work*, Vol. V, No. 4 (1960), pp. 91–97.

developing such intake-and-postponement interviews, in the interests both of saving agency money and time and of more adequately preparing the applicant to wait.

There is some evidence that not all caseworkers view the waiting list as a problem. According to one point of view, an agency's waiting list stands as a reminder to board and community that more people need help than the agency can accommodate and that therefore it needs more money to employ professional staff. Although a waiting list may, in some instances, serve as an opening wedge for getting a larger staff, it cannot be counted on to do so in the face of the great shortage of trained and skilled caseworkers. The conviction and support of an agency board do not always ensure the necessary number of caseworkers.

One may also wonder whether some prestige has become attached to an agency's having a waiting list. Not only is a waiting list a declaration that casework service is in great demand, but it duplicates the usual pattern of private psychiatric or psychoanalytic intake. When a person seeks psychiatric help, he will almost inevitably have to wait until the therapist has an opening in his schedule. Caseworkers who themselves have had the experience of waiting for treatment may come to believe that it is always possible for an applicant to contain the problem for which he has sought help, even to manage to live with it better, because of the hope or promise of help in the future. And what is "possible" may all too readily come to seem "acceptable," perhaps even "desirable."

Those who have drawn an analogy between social casework and the private practice of psychotherapy may have overlooked several considerations. One is that problems differ; some can wait to be solved and some cannot. It may be more accurate to say that problems are likely to be *perceived* and *defined* differently in accordance with the persons who have the problems—the problem-carriers. Another consideration is the differences in individuals; some can bear waiting and some cannot. Yet another is the relation between crisis (or the *experience* of crisis) and the dynamics of change.

Waiting for Psychotherapy

The problem brought to a psychiatrist or psychoanalyst is usually one of intrapersonal malaise. To be sure, it may manifest itself in the person's social relationships, but, as he feels it, it "lives"

196

inside him. Usually the person who owns this problem has felt it for a long time, he has recognized its nature fairly well, and he has managed to live with it by means of various protective and adaptive maneuvers. His decision to seek help with it is not usually an impulsive one but rather is the result of introspection, coping efforts, and thought in relation to the choice of a therapist, the expense, and so on. This behavior reveals something about him as a problem-carrier—that he is able to hold his problem at bay (though it may be anguishing and debilitating), that he is capable of thinking about it (in circles or straight), and that he is able to use the hope of help as a temporary prop or buoy.

Furthermore, the person who tends to locate his problem in himself—"I *am* such and such a person," "I *have* and feel such and such a problem," "I *do* such and such crazy or stupid things"—anticipates that the therapist will attend to *him* and will help *him* to change. Moreover, he believes in the efficacy of the help he will be given. In rough outline he knows something about what will happen between him and his helper. He accepts as a basic premise that talk—"talking out" or "talking over"—has therapeutic value. So conditioned, he actually experiences in his intake-and-wait interview some release of tension and the sustainment of relating to a source of potential help.

Waiting for Social Casework

The person who applies to a social agency may also have the characteristics of containability and staying power, belief in the therapeutic process, and hopefulness. Indeed, the fact that half the persons kept on family agency waiting lists for two months or more *do* return when they are called suggests that some of them have the ability to postpone gratification, to bear tension, and to trust that the agency's helping process will be useful—attributes that are said to be characteristic of middle-class rather than lower-class persons.

For one thing, the middle-class person has more ways of avoiding or cushioning himself against his problems. His everyday world has more escape exits, more opportunities for diversion and sublimation. In general, the middle-class client of the social agency holds the same set of beliefs as the patient of the psychotherapist and as the caseworker himself: belief in the efficacy of counseling for personal and familial problems, in the value of talk as a means

197

of help for one's self and for others; belief in the acceptability—indeed, the inevitability—of waiting for what one wants, especially if what one wants is so valuable that it is in great demand and small supply. The middle-class client is therefore able to wait. Buoyed up by the promise of agency help ahead and by the temporary release he experienced at intake, he "makes do" by using the escape hatches in his environment.

The FSAA study reveals, however, that 72 per cent of the applicants are either lower-class (43 per cent) or lower-middle-class (29 per cent). A number of recent sociological studies on the "culture of poverty" and of marginal groups indicate that certain orientations and expectations are characteristic of people who have long been economically and socially impoverished or who chronically live at the edge of insecurity. Typically, such a person is oriented to the present. He wants what he needs now, at once, because he has had little proof that waiting will yield fulfillment of his needs and wants. Moreover, he has only a narrow margin within which to temporize; his problems push hard. Usually he has had neither education nor experience in the use of words as symbolic substitutes for action, as release valves, or as binding threads between himself and others.

Thus the person of low socioeconomic status (when this is combined with limited education and narrow, hand-to-mouth existence) is not likely to have waiting capacity, hopefulness, or belief in help that he cannot see, smell, or take hold of. He may hunger for, and respond voraciously to, the nurture he experiences in an intake interviewer's warmth and interest. But when this nurture is withdrawn and he is told to hold his needfulness until the agency can find time to help him, the experience becomes just one more frustration.

The FSAA study shows, indeed, that a higher percentage of middle-class than lower-class clients are put on waiting lists—32 per cent of the highest class and only 11 per cent of the lowest. The study notes that the explanation of this finding "probably lies in the relatively high proportion of lower-class cases involving emergency situations where delay cannot be tolerated," and that many more lower-class applicants "are referred immediately to public agencies because of their need for financial assistance." This finding indicates that crises are being recognized and met in family agencies; but it also suggests that ability to wait may be becoming an eligibility criterion for receiving family agency service and that the agency may be gearing its services to the 28 per cent of the applicants who are securely middle-class. In the light of current theory about lower-class psychological orientations, it would be interesting to examine the 11 per cent of the lower-class applicants who are put on waiting lists to compare their rate of return with that of the upper-class group.

The social agency applicant, in contrast to the applicant for psychotherapy, views his problem as a *social* problem—that is to say, as an interpersonal rather than intrapersonal problem. It is usually concerned with the interaction between the applicant and others, or between himself and circumstances. The caseworker, correctly or not, may view the problem as one of personality functioning or character disorder. But the applicant himself sees it as involving other persons or powers that are affecting him. He is likely to say, "The problem I have is that *my wife* is thus-and-so," or "*My child* acts this and that way so as to hurt me," or "I have been hurt by *other persons* and forces." Moreover, one should add, this perception of his problem is frequently a correct one; he is, indeed, involved in a problematic person-to-person or person-to-situation interaction.

When the applicant's problem situation actually does involve others who are in conflictful interaction with him, a waiting period may pose special difficulty. He may be resigned to the necessity of waiting. But how does he manage or deal with the "others" who continue to act in their intolerable ways? Ripple's studies show that in "psychological problems" a major factor in a client's continuance with an agency's services is the support of significant "others" in his life situation.[3] What happens in the applicant's interaction with these others when he has to wait?

Waiting and Prevention

Finally, the problem of the waiting list bears particular scrutiny in the light of recent studies and propositions on crisis and prevention, (many of which appear in this volume). Not all the problems brought to a family agency are actually crises. Many, perhaps most, are long-festering problems that applicants have dealt with un-

[3] Lilian Ripple, with Ernestine Alexander and Bernice Polemis, "Motivation, Capacity, and Opportunity as Related to Casework Services" (prepublication draft, June 1962).

successfully by denial, escape, compromise, or active grappling that has failed to yield surcease. But at the point of calling or walking into an agency the applicant *feels* that his problem is a crisis. He has reached "the limit," and he insists that "something must be done." Even when someone else in his social milieu has sent him, there is the sense of crisis in that he is in a situation that holds potential risk or danger. So it may be assumed that, at the point of application, the person is keyed up about his problem or the need to go to strangers with it. It can also be assumed that his energies are mobilized to cope with his problem or to avoid facing it. His emotional tension is probably heightened if his problem is actually an acute one or has reached an intolerable pitch.

Several recent studies suggest that people are more susceptible to influence during a state of crisis. These studies corroborate what most caseworkers know from experience—that a person's motivation for change and the mobilization of his capacities are at their height when his problem hurts the most. According to Rapoport, "A little help, rationally directed and purposefully focused at a strategic time is more effective than more extensive help given at a period of less emotional accessibility." [5] The "little help" at the "strategic time" is missed when an applicant is assigned to a waiting list.

True, the application interview offers the person some tension release, some binding to the agency, and the promise of help. Actual emergencies are met. But for a large group of applicants what is experienced as urgent and crucial must be held still. Since a static holding state is impossible, what must occur is a process of coping with the self and the others involved in the problem—a process directed toward muting and damping the intensity of affect and the impact of the problem. The concept of "preventive intervention" —intervening to break the vicious cycle of maladaptive problem-solving efforts—is a major contribution of those researchers who have been observing and dealing with people in crisis.

The high malleability or accessibility of the person-problem situation at the point of felt stress or crisis, the possibly greater economy and effectiveness of intervention when the "iron is hot," and the possible prevention of a cycle of maladaptive, problem-entrenching efforts—all suggest the necessity of giving further thought to the waiting list.

[5] Lydia Rapoport, p. 30 of the present volume.

Agencies have already developed many devices for dealing with it: period of closed intake; valiant efforts to recruit and train more students and more staff; ingenious methods to cut down the amount of recording; experiments to trim down supervisory conferences, and other practice experiments. (See footnote 2.) One wonders if yet another, perhaps more radical, approach to dissolving, or at least shrinking, the waiting list might be made. This approach would involve courageous self-questioning and stock-taking of our present ideas about casework goals and means, and of how these ideas affect our receptiveness to new clients.

A New Look at Goals

Is it possible that caseloads are crowded because some cases are carried too long? Is it possible that they are carried too long in some illusion that our goal is to "cure"—to bring our clients to a point where all the problems they, or we, see are "solved"? Instead of setting differentiated goals, realistically based on diagnoses of motivation, capacity, and opportunity for change, are we tending to set goals based on a diagnosis of total needs? Or are we basing our goals on what we wish could happen in a person's or a family's life? Do we almost unwittingly project a vision of so radical a social and personality reorganization that our client will be problem-free? Do we continue to carry the case because this goal is never quite achieved? Are we sufficiently attuned to the idea that helping a person to master one problem or one aspect of his problem may empower him to deal with other problems as they emerge?

These questions about what we are trying to do with the "continuers" in our caseloads bear scrutiny for a number of reasons. One is to make room for new applicants. Another is that, as caseworkers attest, a large percentage of ongoing cases terminate not because caseworker and client have come to an agreement about ending but rather because the client himself stops coming or pulls away. The meaning of these premature endings is surely different in different cases, but their frequency suggests that we hold onto cases longer than the client himself finds useful.

Meanwhile, time is short and waiting lists are long. Many people need and want casework help, and they use it best when they want it most. The problem of the waiting list surely offers us much food for thought, study, and talking together.

201

17. Short-Term Family Therapy*

Mordecai Kaffman

FREUD, IN AN OFTEN QUOTED paper published in 1919,[1] dealt with
the impact of psychoanalysis on the psychiatric needs of society and
stressed the fact that "the therapeutic effects we can achieve are
very inconsiderable in number. . . . Against the vast amount of
neurotic misery which is in the world, and perhaps need not be,
the quantity we can do away with is almost negligible. . . . At
present we can do nothing in the crowded ranks of the people, who
suffer exceedingly from neurosis." Freud raised the possibility that
new simpler forms of psychotherapy based on psychoanalytic principle might be found. Almost half a century later, we still are
searching for new psychotherapeutic tools allowing treatment of
large masses of people.

Present methods of psychotherapy seem to be suitable to a limited
group of people within our society. This is true not only from an
economic standpoint but also in view of their intrinsic content,
which is connected with values and characteristics of the middle and
upper class of our culture.[2] Generally speaking, psychotherapy has
remained an expensive, time consuming, and highly restricted
therapy, out of accord with the pressing needs of the community in
the mental health field. Israel by no means constitutes an exception.
Practical shortcomings determine that only a negligible minority
out of a large number in need of psychotherapy can get the necessary help. This is true, too, of the Israeli Workers Sick Fund, which
maintains an efficient, low-cost, and modern provision of medical
service covering all aspects of curative medicine for 70 per cent of

* Reprinted from *Family Process*, Vol. 2, No. 2 (1963).
[1] Sigmund Freud, "Turnings in the Ways of Psychoanalytic Therapy," *Collected
Papers, Vol. II*, Hogarth Press, London, 1956, pp. 392–402.
[2] A. B. Hollingshead and F. C. Redlich, *Social Class and Mental Illness*, Wiley,
New York, 1958.

the total population. The search for a brief form of psychotherapy continues to be an urgent pragmatic problem, not only because of the scarcity and high cost of the present facilities for prolonged psychotherapy but also because of intrinsic advantages to be found in an available service of short-term psychotherapy.

The simple fact that a large proportion of emotional disturbances, both in children and adults, can be dealt with satisfactorily without resorting to prolonged methods of treatment cannot be denied. This is usually true for the vast majority of reactive emotional disorders and for acute and crisis situations leading to a breakdown of previous apparently "normal" behavior. Opportunely timed assistance can help to restore emotional homeostasis and prevent further impact of disorganizing anxiety that could lead to progressive maladjustment, disintegration, and serious psychopathology. Obviously, the sooner the required help is provided, the better are the expected results. However, clinical experience has shown repeatedly that even long established emotional disturbances may improve following short-term psychotherapy. Not too rarely we witness in children outstanding clinical changes from previous abnormal behavior, or the dramatic disappearance of disturbing pathological symptoms as a result of brief therapeutic intervention destined to alleviate the pressure on a limited but sensitive area of conflict.

On the other hand, it appears [3] that certain shared expectations about the length of treatment as perceived by the therapist and the patient may determine much of the outcome of treatment. Patients of the lower social class in need of psychotherapy would hardly accept the fact already recognized by sophisticated members of the upper and middle class that emotional disturbances, unlike the usual physical complaints, require prolonged and intensive care. The different expectation regarding the length of treatment goes beyond the economic issue and seemingly could not be done away with even if increased psychotherapy services were created. At present, the shared expectation and conditioning of therapists and their patients of the lower class are in the direction of brief forms of psychotherapy. One can assume that an agreement between expectancy and available services may constitute an important ele-

[3] M. T. Orne, "Implications for Psychotherapy Derived from Current Research on the Nature of Hypnosis," *American Journal of Psychiatry*, Vol. 118 (1962), pp. 1097–1103.

ment to assure the continuance of treatment and influence positive outcome. Unindoctrinated patients of the labor class become genuinely surprised when told that more than one single interview is necessary to help solve their problems. They become suspicious and unco-operative if the prospect of long-term psychotherapy is mentioned. From another angle, the sophisticated patient with substantial knowledge about the complexities of mental life and the amount of psychoanalytic treatment necessary for a "definitive cure" would be disappointed, skeptical, and unco-operative, if short-term psychotherapy were offered instead.

We may state, consequently, that short-term psychotherapy is not only an urgent objective need, but also fits into the expectancies of a large mass of people. On these grounds, we consider it valuable to report on our own procedure for short-term family psychotherapy which has been in use throughout the years 1961 and 1962 at two separate clinical settings * devoted to the treatment of emotionally disturbed children. This preliminary report illustrates the rationale of the procedure, methodology, limitations, and initial evaluation of the results of short-term family therapy in 70 consecutive cases referred to the clinics.

Focus on Family Interaction

Although the common reason for referral to the child guidance clinic continues to be some disturbing problem of the child, treatment in all our cases is family-centered. On theoretical and practical grounds the child cannot be seen isolated from the social unit to which his problems are etiopathogenically connected, especially if the dynamic interaction is still actively functioning.[4] Continued osmotic interchange occurs between the intrapsychic and the interpersonal experience. Individual pathology cannot be separated, particularly in the case of a child, from family group psychopathol-

* This program of brief family therapy was initially carried out with Kibbutz children referred to "Oranim" Child Clinic of the Kibbutzim. Since the beginning of 1962, the same plan has been carried over to treat families of urban children at the Child Unit of the Haifa Mental Health Clinic of the Workers Sick Fund. The author serves at the latter Clinic as a Consultant Child Psychiatrist. Mention must be made of the understanding, co-operative attitude and invaluable assistance of the Director of the Haifa Clinic, Dr. S. I. Davidson, and the Psychiatric Social Workers, Mrs. Rosa Yiftah and Marianne Rusell.

[4] Nathan W. Ackerman, *The Psychodynamics of Family Life*, Basic Books, New York, 1958.

ogy. Clinical evidence shows that changes in family dynamics may alleviate individual disturbances even in the absence of systematic individual therapy. On the other hand, skilled and intensive individual psychotherapy of a child may fail to elicit clinical improvement owing to the absence of parallel changes in family psychopathology. Therefore, our clinical approach is neither child-centered nor parent-centered but focused on the integrated family interaction.

As Alpern [5] has rightly pointed out, a clinical approach to brief therapy can be adapted only from the knowledge and experience of long-term clinical psychiatric work with children and their parents. Short-term family psychotherapy requires from the therapist skills and clinical judgment regarding the assessment of the central needs and conflicts of the child and parents' personality. The therapist should be able to reach, on the spot, at the joint sessions with the family members, reliable conclusions on the essential characteristics of the parent-child relationship to enable him to intervene actively in the process of clarification and reorganization of family dynamics. Basically, one cannot conceive a dynamic approach for short-term psychotherapy different from the approach for prolonged psychotherapy.

Goal and Purposes of Brief Family Therapy

It is not within the scope of a short service of family therapy to bring about basic and extensive alterations in character structure of family members. However, sustained changes in family dynamics and improvement of individual pathology can eventually be achieved. The therapist's help to all the members of the family, in obtaining focused insight into the nature of conscious and preconscious conflicts, is likely to lead to a readjusted and healthier family interrelationship, to goal modification, and to full use of potential possibilities.

No feasible resource leading to a healthier family adjustment should be dismissed by the therapist. We are not reluctant to make use of therapeutic counseling to eliminate obvious pathogenic factors, if we believe that this is a necessary step toward improvement and if we consider that the patient is ready to follow the advice. Certainly this is not the most refined therapeutic tool, but there is

[5] Evelyn Alpern, "Short Clinical Services for Children in a Child Guidance Clinic," *American Journal of Orthopsychiatry*, Vol. 26 (1956), pp. 314–325.

no logical reason to delay helpful counseling whenever evident detrimental factors can be quickly removed or reduced.

The aim in this form of therapy is to bring the family to an emotional equilibrium as rapidly as possible with improvement or elimination of symptoms. One may wonder how this goal can be obtained through restricted short-term therapeutic intervention. Clinical experience shows what we call "the snowball phenomenon." The beginning of healthy changes in behavior and attitudes on the part of both the child and the parents induces further mutual shifts in the parent-child relationship with additional positive achievements. Therapy has served to break a vicious circle, and from then on clinical changes do not run parallel to the intensity of therapy.

Any experienced therapist has seen more than once the steadily growing "snowball" of clinical improvement following a short therapeutic intervention. Doubtless a number of operative factors are involved in the therapeutic process and clinical response. But we cannot dismiss the obvious fact that the change is mainly accomplished by direct or indirect intervention in a stressful and pathogenic parent-child interaction. The therapeutic alliance between the therapist and the patient is likely to elicit a prompt symptomatic response. The initial symptomatic improvement may promote further acceptance and understanding of the child on the parental side, while the child's chances to consolidate clinical gains are enhanced by diminished anxiety, increased assertiveness, and higher self-esteem. Moreover, effective alleviation or removal of disorganizing pressure and anxieties may result in an ongoing process of improved child-parent relationship.

Clinical Methodology

Like any other therapeutic procedure, short clinical services for children and parents are not a panacea; they have a specific range of effectiveness and require adequate criteria for selection of patients.

Selection of Cases

First, the nature and severity of family psychopathology—that of the child and significant family members—should be considered. Following an initial period of trial and error, we devised a diagnostic list which was sent to the referral sources, stating which cases should be regarded as inappropriate for short-term family therapy. Among the categories to be excluded, the following ones involving children were mentioned:

1. Long-standing psychosis
2. Sociopathic personality or cases in which institutional care is indicated
3. Established neurological damage and/or mental deficiency as the essential clinical problem
4. Chronic severe psychopathology in which the symptoms are highly structured and have been present and unchanged for several years

On the parental side, we required the presence of a minimal amount of positive family ties and excluded the totally rejected, abandoned child. Complete lack of motivation on the part of both parents to be included in the therapeutic plan was also seen as contraindication for this form of therapy.

Suitable cases embraced all forms of psychopathology in children up to the age of sixteen, provided that the emotional conflict was not totally internalized and the child had enough ego strength and anxiety to feel motivated in establishing a meaningful object-relationship with the therapist.

Clinical experience with the first 70 cases referred for short-term family therapy showed that in a large percentage of instances the above requirements were not met, although the anamnestic data in the referral form appeared to fit the approved criteria of selection. This discordance between reported and actual facts seemed related to a number of factors. Usually, it was due to insufficient knowledge of the case on the part of the referral source, inadequate evaluation of the quality and intensity of the pathology, and last but not least, lack of clinical facilities to refer elsewhere a severe and pressing emotional problem. Therefore, a great many cases referred to us for short-term therapy did not fit our criteria of selection and showed a more disturbed and long-standing psychopathology than we had intended to cope with. On the other hand, several chronic cases which at first glance did not appear to be suitable for short clinical service showed such an evident and positive response to the initial family interview that continuation of treatment seemed imperative. It was decided, therefore, to postpone the final decision about the

207

nature of therapeutic intervention to be offered until direct contact with the family in the course of the first joint interview allowed a proper clinical assessment. Short-term therapy remained the most concrete available therapeutic possibility. Those cases seen as unsuitable for short clinical services were referred to long-term psychotherapy whenever feasible. Otherwise, the therapeutic procedure was restricted to the most practical advice to be given under the circumstances. In these cases, diagnostic work was completed in order to draw practical conclusions on the alternative treatment plan.

History-taking Process

History-taking is a crucial part of the clinical procedure inasmuch as prior knowledge of significant objective data helps the therapist to assume an efficient leading role. The intake interview is conducted by a skilled psychiatric social worker who meets with both parents. The worker is less interested in accumulating a complete and detailed history than in gathering meaningful information on salient points. The interview is so structured as to allow, in the first place, spontaneous elaboration by the parents on the child's present behavior and problems. This is followed by specific questions regarding key developmental features, medical history, possible traumatic events, and factual data on family interaction. Whenever one of the parents in the course of the joint interview requests overtly or tacitly a separate interview to disclose information he finds difficult to bring up in the presence of his marital partner, the demand is fulfilled.

At the end of the intake interview, concrete information is supplied to the parents concerning the steps to be followed in the clinical procedure. An additional purpose of the intake interview is to assist the parents in preparing the child for the first family therapeutic interview. Most of the parents are badly in need of a clear-cut explanation in order to avoid the usual approach of deceiving the child regarding the aim of his visit at the clinic. Of course, the nature of the child's problems, his age, the intelligence level of the parents, and the quality of the parent-child relationship will determine the kind of explanation given regarding the first therapeutic interview. In general terms, children over four years of age require a truthful explanation of the following facts: (1) The parents have sought a "doctor's advice" on the ways to help them and the child resolve their specific obvious difficulties; the problems will be discussed with the doctor at an announced appointment. (2) A simple description of the playroom setting seems helpful in reassuring the young child or preventing an unpleasant reaction of an adolescent youngster to the "kid stuff" equipment.

We find it necessary to stress that the preliminary contact with the family does not include the administration of psychological tests to the child. Clinical experience shows that data gathered from the medical history, the intake process, and the psychiatric interviews with the child and his parents are sufficient for a trustworthy diagnostic and psychodynamic assessment. It appears to us that we avoid confusion on the part of the child and allow for a more intensive focusing of the therapeutic process if the contact of the child with the clinical services starts immediately with the therapeutic interviews, which are, at the same time, of diagnostic nature.

Single Therapist versus Team Work Approach

Traditionally, in most of the child guidance clinics, the interdisciplinary team approach is used, not only for diagnostic purposes but also in the therapeutic procedure. The value and efficiency of the collaborative approach cannot be denied but, when applied to short-term family therapy, the method has obvious limitations and disadvantages. The single therapist approach allows for significant saving in time and effort, a cohesive view of family dynamics and, consequently, a consistent and uniform therapeutic intervention.

Collaborative work in therapy implies the need of additional time and appointments. Furthermore, even in the best staffed clinic and assuming an exceptionally similar theoretical and clinical approach of the members of the team, complete co-ordination is not possible. When time constitutes a crucial factor in therapy, and when immediate confrontation of the members of the family with the findings of the family-therapist interaction is designed to be one of the most important therapeutic elements, a teamwork approach does not seem to be feasible or adequate.

The following two family interviews, briefly summarized, illustrate this particular point of view. They show the effectiveness of a prompt direct intervention performed in a quasi-routine way by a single therapist in family therapy.

209

Case I. A girl, 11 years old, was brought to the clinic because of intense night fears extending over two or three years, disturbing clinical manifestations of separation anxiety, and unrestricted aggressive behavior directed toward her mother. In the course of the first joint interview (with parents, girl, and therapist present), the girl complained about her mother's oversolicitous interfering in all her activities, continuously nagging about small things, and "treating me like a baby." With the help of the therapist, the mother and daughter were able to admit that the excessive contact aroused mutual anger. However, the mother thought that the aggressive responses of the daughter were exaggerated. She brought up examples of the girl's verbal and physical aggressiveness to the point where even death wishes were openly shouted in the course of the rift. The girl showed confusion and obvious guilt feelings.

The therapist pointed out the ambivalent feelings of the child, who felt encouraged to state that she really did not wish for the death of her mother. Then the father interrupted, adding that he had noticed some kind of relation between the quarreling during the day and the intense fears at night. When everyone agreed with this observation and I suggested that sometimes children are afraid that thoughts and words may come true, the girl rushed to her mother, kissed her, and talked about her guilt feelings after the anger explosions.

The long-standing night fears disappeared *after the first therapeutic interview.* During the course of short-term family therapy, which dealt with different pathogenic aspects of the interpersonal relationship, a striking improvement in the family interaction was reached.

Case II. Naomi, a 15-year-old girl, was referred to the clinic because of severe symptoms of emotional disturbance lasting several months. She was the youngest of three children. Her older sister, 19, had an organic brain condition which caused mental retardation, epileptic fits, and progressive blindness. The symptoms of our patient fitted into the picture of adolescent schizophrenia. Naomi had marked persecutory delusions, ideas of reference, and pervasive anxiety. During the weeks preceding the treatment, she felt unable to attend school, did not leave her room, and demanded the constant presence of her mother.

The first joint interview with Noami and both parents yielded significant material regarding the sources of the delusional thoughts. A family pattern of denial of hostility with reaction-formation defensive maneuvers was soon recognized. The chronically sick sister was one of the objects of repressed hostility. Naomi was able to express her feeling of deep guilt and her conviction that people were able to perceive her awful "cruelty." She had started looking around suspiciously to find the confirmation of her fear of being scrutinized by people because of her wrongdoing and soon found that both strangers and her parents looked at her furtively and talked secretively about her. She became convinced that people were plotting to send her to a mental institution. She was full of panic and was unable to leave home and go to school.

Actually, at the joint interview, the parents confirmed that they used to glance furtively at Naomi and talk secretively about her strange behavior. They sought the advice of the family physician who suggested hospitalizing her in a psychiatric setting. All the arrangements were made by the parents to confine the girl without her knowledge.

To my surprise, after one single interview in which sufficient clarification of all these issues was attained, Naomi was able to go back to school and express sound criticism of her former delusional thoughts. Plans were made to institutionalize the sick sister instead of Naomi.

Undoubtedly, the same good clinical results and insight would be obtained with different therapeutic approaches, but the above integrated procedure in the hands of a skilled therapist seems to be less time consuming and at least equally rewarding.

Only in a few cases of extreme marital disharmony and hostility or complete absence of positive ties in the parent-child relationship was a joint therapeutic interview not possible, and the members of the family were seen separately. If we exclude these exceptional cases, no clinical contraindication seems to exist for this integrative family approach. It was necessary, in a few cases, to exert some pressure on the mother to agree to the need for the father's presence at the joint sessions; she thought it was a waste of time in that the father "has nothing to say at home" concerning the upbringing of the children. In most instances, which included a large percentage of patients of the working class, a good deal of co-operation and understanding of the essentials of family therapy was obtained on the part of both parents.

First Therapeutic Interview

The initial joint family interview has paramount importance for the whole treatment process. Usually it is attended by both parents and

211

the child, but sometimes other significant members of the family are also present. This is a prolonged interview, lasting from two to three hours, in which the therapist takes an active leading role that continues throughout the entire therapeutic process.

Free interaction of family members, including verbal communication or play activity with the child, is encouraged by the therapist in his attempt to assess the basic characteristics of family interaction and uncover the central conflict. Often the first emerging issue raised either by the parents or by the therapist is the definition of the problems and difficulties. The verbal interchange that takes place regarding this point provides crucial clues on family dynamics, defense mechanisms, and sensitive areas of conflict. The therapist should help structure this interview in such a way that everyone, including the child, reaches a recognition and clear understanding of the most distressing problems. Therefore, the first step should be to recognize the basic conflict and to avoid going astray with irrelevant issues. One should be sure that sufficient understanding of the problems under discussion has been gained by the child, and that he has formed a clear-cut picture of his own role as well as that of the parents in the treatment plan. Active intervention by the therapist is needed to point out the central problem and overcome a parental approach of either overprotective secretiveness in the presence of the child or moral lectures and accusations. He must dispel any deleterious implications that the therapist is the ally of the parents in stopping or curbing the child's misbehavior.

Once the essential issues have been exposed and defined, and a reasonable dynamic evaluation has been elicited through the joint interaction of the family and therapist, the different members of the family may be seen separately at the time of the initial interview. No fixed formula can be established. Factors like the therapist's clinical assessment, the age of the child and the need to establish a closer individual relationship with him, the necessity for further clarification of marital issues, and so on will all affect the decision about separate interviews.

Individual short meetings with the child contribute to establishing a valuable positive relationship at the child's verbal level on the basis of whatever type of activity is selected by him. The essentials of the insight (but not the factual information) obtained in the separate interview are not kept sealed in the one-to-one relationship but are brought up and discussed in the most convenient way at the next joint family interview. Therefore, in every case, the initial therapeutic interview assembles the whole family at least at the beginning and at the end of the interview process. In some cases, the need for separate interviews is not established, and treatment continues on an indivisible family basis. In most instances, the initial interview embraces four meetings: the whole family interview, the child alone, the parents, and again the entire family. The therapist should not feel under the pressure of time when seeking the necessary clues to reach a sound preliminary dynamic evaluation of family interaction.

The understanding gained by both the therapist and the members of the family throughout the therapeutic interview is immediately utilized. The therapist is now able to help each member of the family make use of the insight gained. Of course, insight alone is worthless in the absence of parallel constructive support in the search for new ways of readjustment. Even if we succeed in uncovering how the self-assumed reasonable behavior is felt and interpreted by other members of the family, nothing will change in the course of the short-term therapy without additional reconstructive measurements encouraged by the therapist.

The search for a better understanding of the characteristics of family relationship and essential areas of conflict may lead to exposing in detail concrete recent incidents, but no planned effort is made to elicit or uncover historical data.

By the end of this initial interview, the therapist summarizes clearly for all members of the family whatever has become evident concerning the basic problems under discussion. He will add specific suggestions and recommendations if they seem necessary and are relevant to the content of this interview. It is assumed that by the close of the first interview, the therapist is already aware of the therapeutic possibilities offered by a short plan of treatment and is capable of setting specific realistic goals, recognizing at the same time the inevitable limitations of the method. The goal of the treatment, including a tentative estimate of the number and frequency of sessions, should be made clear to the members of the family. In certain cases it becomes apparent that short-term therapy is unlikely to dissolve the family pathology; this calls for an early decision to end the clinical contact at the first joint interview and to recommend other methods of treatment.

213

Following Interviews

In subsequent meetings, a flexible schedule continues regarding the length and distribution of the sessions, the number of participants, and the sequence of the separate and integrated talks within the framework of a whole interview. Again the child may be seen alone, or with one or all members of his family, for shorter or longer sessions, more or less frequently, all depending on the judgment of the therapist and the clinical course. The parents may also be seen separately or jointly.

In our view, a structured, fixed framework of treatment curtails the possibilities of a short-term plan of family therapy. Thus, although on the average in our cases a total of ten weekly therapeutic sessions (each one lasting one and a half hours) followed the initial prolonged interview, the distribution of these sessions varied considerably in the different instances. The procedure resembles chess variants to the extent that it is practically impossible to find two cases with the same distribution of therapeutic interviews.

The following example may help to illustrate the point. Two children were referred separately because of seemingly identical complaints consisting of intense night fear, temper tantrums, and aggressive behavior. Both were included in the same diagnostic category (neurotic traits) and by mere coincidence each attended with his respective parents an identical number of therapeutic sessions. Both children showed considerable clinical improvement, with total disappearance of the acute anxiety state. However, a quite different distribution of the allotted time of treatment was scheduled by the therapist. The first child was seen six times together with his parents, once with his father, three times alone, and the parents were seen separately once. The second child was seen only once with his parents, four times with his mother, four times alone; his parents were seen once together, and the mother was seen four times alone.

In most of the cases, the separate interviews with the child, based on play or verbal interchange, helped to build a very positive relationship between the child and the therapist, bringing forth useful elements of imitation and identification. Although Anna Freud does not seem to adhere any longer to her original view regarding the convenience of fostering a positive transference from the child to his therapist in the initial phase of analytic treatment, it seems to us that beyond any doubt the positive nature of the child-therapist connection constitutes an important factor influencing the success of the approach in brief treatment plans.

Usually, after the first interview, children show eagerness to return to the clinic. Parents tell us that their children await the next appointment impatiently and remind them of specific facets of the previous family interview. Young children often call the psychiatrist by all sorts of laudatory names or titles ("the wise dotor," "the good doctor," "my friend, the doctor,") while older children show elements of identification with the psychiatrist. A 7-year-old boy queried his parents on the requirements to become a psychiatrist, including financial questions on the matter, to be sure that he had selected the best choice.

For all the members of the family, each interview usually includes the following components, not necessarily in the same order: redefinition of the problems and summary of what has been established during the preceding session; analysis of recent events to emphasize trends and changes in the family interrelationship; further scrutiny of factors determining failures and accomplishments in the treatment plan; realistic appraisal of the situation and expectations of the treatment; and specific acknowledgment of any gains or improvement.

Termination of Treatment

Since the length of therapy has been planned in advance (to cover a period of three months) and discussed with the whole family as early as the initial interview, one may assume that the close of the treatment does not come as a surprise. In the vast majority of the cases, the closing phase of treatment can be implemented without particular difficulties. Only in a small minority of cases either the children or their parents do not seem to be ready for termination of treatment. The child may not want to give up the secondary gain of extra attention provided by the treatment, while parents may strive to maintain a relationship of further dependency based on continuous advice-seeking rapport.

Usually, termination of treatment comes as a natural and anticipated development. All the cases that are not referred for further long-term psychotherapy, are assured of the possibility of additional isolated contacts if their need is felt by the child, the parents, or the psychiatrist.

215

Criteria and Evaluation of Improvement

A detailed report on the clinical material we dealt with, the type and duration of pathology, case presentations, and results of treatment is beyond the scope of this paper. Although we tried to adhere to our original criteria of selecting disturbed families considered suited for short-term therapy, in practice we felt both forced and entitled to enlarge the frame of our intervention. Thus, some cases of chronically fixated neurotic conflicts, psychotic reactions, obvious parental rejection, broken homes, psychotic unco-operative parents, and so on were accepted for trial treatment.

In our experience, the degree of positive change seems to be significantly related to the following factors:

1. Severity of present psychopathology in the child and family members
2. Presence or absence of positive family ties
3. Presence or absence of adverse environmental circumstances (broken homes, psychotic parents, extreme poverty)
4. Presence or absence of positive motivation for treatment, both on the part of the child and the parents

All these factors should be appraised and weighed as early as the first interview.

Out of 70 families referred to us for short-term family therapy, 41 families were considered unsuitable for this type of treatment, mainly in view of the degree and chronicity of family pathology. In most of the cases, the decision not to attempt short therapy was established in the course of the first exploratory family interview. However, even after a negative conclusion was reached, these families were often seen at two or three subsequent interviews and also referred for psychological evaluation in order to complete the diagnostic study and allow relevant advice on therapeutic alternatives.

The following plan of treatment was proposed to these 41 families:

Guidance with or without Environmental Changes	22
Residential Treatment	10
Prolonged Psychotherapy	7
Diagnostic Evaluation Only	2

Short-term therapy was attempted with the remaining 29 families. The vast majority of the children of these families were 6 to 15 years of age, with similar number of boys and girls. The referral symptoms showed a wide and varied distribution. The following problems were prevalent in the group of 29 children:

Phobic Reactions with Incapacitating Fears	11
Repeated Acute Anxiety Attacks	7
Chronic Night Fears	11
Acute Separation Anxiety	11
Hyperaggressiveness	10
Severe School Discipline Problems	6
School Phobia	2
Stealing	2
Suicidal Threats	2
Long-lasting Enuresis and Encopresis	3
Anorexia Nervosa	1

From a more general diagnostic point of view, the cases were classified as follows:

Primary Behavior Disorders	8
Neurotic Traits	9
Psychoneuroses	11
Schizophrenic Reaction	1

In 20 instances out of the total sample of 29, the symptoms had lasted several years, seemed to be organized and structured, and the chances appeared slim that short-term treatment would be helpful. However, treatment was attempted after the initial clinical contact indicated the possibility of positive influence on the family pathogenic interaction. Actually, in only five cases had the emotional disturbances existed a relatively short time. In all the remaining cases we encountered chronic, well-established symptomatology.

We devised a five-point rating scale as a convenient evaluation method of therapeutic results. The following criteria were used:

1. No objective change in family dynamics. Subjective feeling that problems and symptoms are even worse.
2. No change. No objective evidence of symptomatic relief.
3. Moderate improvement as measured in objective and subjective positive changes. Manifest symptoms diminished in number or became milder.
4. Great improvement seen by the family members and therapist. Obvious better family functioning. Most distressing symptoms and clinical problems disappeared.

217

5. Complete disappearance of referral problems. Complete absence of manifest clinical symptoms. Adequate insight positively used to modify or eradicate sources of former difficulties.

Using this type of rating scale, the results given in Table 1 were obtained at the end of treatment. In most of the cases, a follow-up check six months later confirmed the initial evaluation.

It appears that in three quarters of the cases, a definite high degree of improvement (categories 4 and 5) was obtained as shown by the total disappearance of the central symptoms and referral problems. One may speculate about the significance of this high figure of clin-

TABLE 1. DEGREE OF CLINICAL IMPROVEMENT IN 29 FAMILIES AFTER
SHORT-TERM FAMILY THERAPY

Evaluation	Number
1. Worse	0
2. Unchanged	3
3. Moderate Symptomatic Improvement	4
4. Considerable Improvement	9
5. Considerable Improvement (Still in Treatment)	2
6. Total Symptomatic Improvement	10
7. Unknown—Treatment Discontinued	1

ical cure, especially in those instances of long-standing emotional problems which constitute not the exception but the modal case in our experience. The issue of "deep" versus "short superficial" therapy may be raised on theoretical grounds. But for those families who obtained the necessary help to cope with chronic distressing anxiety states or severe emotional disturbances or interlocked family conflict, the positive outcome of therapy and the stable achievements constitute the most convincing evidence.

Only one case dropped out of treatment in the beginning phase of therapy. In three cases, the need of prolonged psychotherapy for one or more members of the family was recognized at the end of the short-therapy procedure and arrangements were made for this. One additional case was referred for residential treatment.

Summary and Conclusions

1. This paper has discussed the rationale, indications, and techniques of short-term family therapy as practiced by the author at two

different clinical settings (urban and rural areas). It is based on his clinical trial of this therapeutic procedure in 70 families referred to these clinics because of a distressing, child-centered, emotional problem. Instances of chronic severe psychopathology with highly structured and fixed symptomatology were considered out of the scope of a short therapeutic service. However, in view of the fact that in many cases with long-standing internalized conflicts good results were obtained following the initial appraisal interview, it was considered worthwhile to carry out the total plan of short-term treatment.

2. Therapy is centered in the family interaction process. In all the cases the therapist meets several times with the whole family. Additional meetings with separate members of the family are arranged according to a flexible schedule dictated by clinical needs. Duration of treatment is limited in advance to three months. During this period of time, an average of ten family sessions take place. The therapist plays a very active role during both the family and the separate interviews, helping to clarify the nature of conscious and preconscious family conflicts and utilizing any possible approach to a healthier family readjustment. Clinical evidence shows that effective alleviation or removal of a disorganizing stress situation and pervading anxiety may result in a continued process of improvement even in the absence of prolonged psychotherapy.

3. The procedure is based on a single-therapist approach instead of the usual team approach. This permits a cohesive view of family dynamics and allows quick and uniform therapeutic intervention. It should be emphasized that brief family therapy requires skill, clinical judgment, and alertness in evaluation of parental-child needs and conflicts. The required skills can be acquired only through prolonged practice in the traditional methods of dynamic psychotherapy.

4. In 29 families in which the complete plan of short-term family therapy was tried, clinical results were excellent. In more than three quarters of the cases a remarkable improvement was obtained as shown by the total disappearance of the central symptoms and referral problems.

The therapeutic procedure described seems to be particularly suitable and useful in family psychopathology whenever there are still positive family ties, and enough ego strength, anxiety, and motivation to establish a meaningful object relationship between the family and the therapist.

219

18. Children at Risk*

Elizabeth E. Irvine

DR. GERALD CAPLAN has familiarized us, in several publications, with the crisis model of mental health and mental disorder.[1] This draws our attention to certain kinds of sharp discontinuity in development or experience which upset the equilibrium of the individual and expose him to the risk of adopting solutions that are dangerous for his future mental health. Not everyone will emerge from his crisis thus damaged. Some will have responded to the challenge by mobilizing their forces in ways that increase strength and confidence, maturity, and ability to cope with stress. Those who emerge weakened, relying more heavily than before on rigid, brittle, and maladaptive defenses, may well have been predictably more vulnerable at the outset, although Caplan shows reason to believe that the quality of social interaction during the crisis period can often have a decisive effect on the outcome. Young children are particularly vulnerable to separation from their mothers, as Dr. John Bowlby[2] and others have demonstrated, whereas the mother's reliable presence often renders them surprisingly invulnerable to any stress situation that does not upset the mother herself too greatly. It also seems likely that disturbed relationships within the family, especially but not exclusively between the child and his mother, will enhance his vulnerability to most kinds of stress.

Need for Preventive Services

It follows from this reasoning that preventive mental health programs must be especially concerned to identify and support vulnerable

* Reprinted from *Case Conference,* Vol. 10, No. 10 (1964).

[1] *Concepts of Mental Health and Consultation.* U.S. Children's Bureau, Washington, 1959; *A Community Approach to Mental Health,* Tavistock, London, 1961; *Prevention of Mental Disorders in Children,* Tavistock, 1962.

[2] John Bowlby, *Maternal Care and Mental Health,* World Health Organization, 1951; John Bowlby and M. Ainsworth, "The Effects of Mother-Child Separation: A Follow-up Study," *British Journal of Medical Psychology,* 1956.

220

individuals who are exposed to crisis situations. One such group, which as yet has received surprisingly little attention, comprises the children of parents who have recently been admitted to a mental hospital. Such children are likely to be particularly vulnerable on account of previous disturbed relationships within the family, especially if the onset of the illness has been insidious. They are now ex-posed to the sudden loss of a parent, in circumstances that are likely to tinge the natural grief and distress with a heavy coloring of anxiety and guilt. Some of these children may also be vulnerable by heredity. This hypothesis was at one time derived from belief in the tendency of mental illness to run in families, but it now seems likely that much of this tendency could be accounted for by disturbed relationships and the experience of recurrent crisis.

If this reasoning is correct, policy and practice in the treatment and care of the mentally ill should always take the interests of the children explicitly into account in order to harmonize or balance them with those of the patient. There is as yet little evidence that this is systematically done. A very few hospitals are experimentally admitting pre-school children with their mentally ill mothers.[3] This practice is usually advocated on the grounds of benefit to the mother, but it is believed to be of value to the children too, both as avoiding a separation and as affording an opportunity for the child to enjoy skilled support in dealing with the problems with which his mother's illness confronts him. Where no such arrangements exist, the children are automatically separated from the parent who goes into hospital. We should not underestimate the traumatic potential of separation from the father, which will vary according to the age of the child and the degree of attachment to him. Separation from the mother, however, often results in substitute care arrangements which involve separation from the father also, whereas if he is hospitalized the children are likely to remain with the mother. Such arrangements may be formal and official, in which case the Child Care Service takes responsibility and is in a position to help the child deal with his inner crisis; or they may be unofficial, as when relatives open their homes to the child. In this case it is nobody's explicit job to make sure that the child is dealing adequately

---

3 G. Douglas, "Psychotic Mothers," *Lancet*, 1956, pp. 124–125; A. A. Baker, J. A. Game, M. Morrison, and J. G. Thorpe, "Admitting Schizophrenic Mothers with their Babies," *Lancet*, 1961, pp. 237–239; T. Gleser, "A Unit for Mothers and Babies in a Psychiatric Hospital," *Journal of Child Psychology and Psychiatry*, Vol. III, No. 1, (1962), pp. 53–60.

with the crisis, and the lack of public discussion suggests that social workers may be too busy dealing with other urgent problems to investigate whether the relatives are indeed able to give the child the help he needs.

How far can we assume that placement in a kindly family, related or otherwise, provides an adequate solution for the child's emotional needs? Even in the simpler case where the mother goes to the hospital for physical illness, this is expecting a lot. Adults often find it difficult to tolerate a child's grief or his defenses, or to let him express his feelings. If he is sad and listless, unable to respond affectionately, and particularly if he eats poorly and compares the food unfavorably with his mother's cooking, those who are trying so hard to make him happy often feel hurt and personally rejected. This is likely to be all the more so if the mother is insane, and if her behavior and care of the children have been the subject of dissatisfaction and friction for some time, or if there were other tensions between her and the relatives now caring for the children. Other adults can readily sympathize with the child who grieves openly, but may be shocked or antagonized by one who wears a mask of indifference, is unnaturally cheerful, or who expresses hostility to the absent parent.

These reactions may be taken at their face value, and the child perceived as a heartless little wretch, whereas a child who is using these defenses is probably in need of professional understanding and help. Yet other children may express their emotional disturbance by rudeness and rebellion toward anyone who presumes to try to replace the absent parent, or may develop symptoms such as tics, enuresis, or soiling. Many adults find it hard to recognize such behavior as a signal of distress, and their sympathy may be alienated. There is another hazard when the absent parent is mentally ill; these manifestations are apt to be interpreted as the first signs of hereditary mental illness, in which case the child will be treated with anxious over-solicitude, or those in charge may try to protect themselves against this anxiety by nagging or scolding him in the hope that he will stop such behavior, and so prove that he is not ill after all.

When the Parent Is Hospitalized

When a parent goes to the hospital, the mere fact of separation, the pain of missing the absent person, is bound to be complicated more

222

or less by the child's anxiety about the illness and the outcome, and by guilt for past unkindness, demandingness, or thoughtlessness. When these feelings are strong the child will need opportunity to talk them out; this some families or foster-parents can provide, but others may find it too hard to tolerate the expression of such feelings, and may smother it with reassurance or cheerful chatter in a way that relieves themselves more than the child. When the parent is mentally ill, everyone's anxieties are likely to be worse. Physical illness can often be labeled and explained, and the length of absence can often be predicted; this is helpful to all but the youngest children. Mental illness can usually not be named or explained, and questions are apt to evoke uneasy equivocation, which creates an atmosphere of shameful and embarrassing mystery. Older children may suspect madness, and will feel ashamed of this as they would not of a physical complaint. Guilt may well have been stimulated during the period of onset by repeated urging to be good, to keep quiet, for fear of giving mother a headache, because daddy isn't well. They may have been more overtly accused of "getting on Mother's nerves," or of "driving Daddy round the bend." When mother or father eventually "goes round the bend" this will seem to be the fulfillment of a prophecy, the result of all those unheeded warnings.

There may have been scenes of violence, and the children may have not only been very frightened, but also quite confused about who was the victim and who was the aggressor. This is especially so if the child has been attached to a paranoid parent, who may for months or years have been accusing neighbors, relatives, or the other parent of conspiring to "put him (her) away." Now he has been "put away," so he was right all along; or perhaps the child feels he has been sent away as a punishment for difficult behavior. Such children are apt to be both frightened and angry with those who "put away" the missing parent for obscure reasons which they are usually too embarrassed to explain. The children therefore "play up" in ways that set up a new round of anger and anxiety in relatives, since they seem to confirm all the natural fears about heredity.

For all these reasons, the children of parents who have recently entered a mental hospital need help which relatives, friends, or foster-parents *may* be able to give, but on the other hand may not, on account of their own anxieties about grief and loss, and about mental illness in particular. Moreover, these children need help *now*. Within a few weeks they will have resolved the crisis one way or the

223

other. If they adopt pathological defenses and we wait until these have become so crippling or alarming that the children eventually get referred for treatment, it may well take years to undo what could have been prevented by a few timely interviews with the child or the adults about him. This is why an adequate preventive mental health program would require that, in every case where the patient has children, someone should take responsibility, not only for seeing that they are being suitably cared for on the material level, but also that they are being allowed or helped to express their feelings freely, and to overcome unrealistic anxiety and guilt—which are not susceptible to reassurance unless they have been fully expressed to someone who does not secretly or openly share them. Sometimes, as I mentioned in a former paper,[4] a parent or other member of the household may in fact be blaming the child as a way of dealing with his own intolerable guilt, and this may require more extensive casework help.

When the Mother Is at Home

Even where the separation crisis has been dealt with, further crises may arise from the patient's visits home. Moods may vary alarmingly, disappointments may lead to threats of breaking up the home and sending the children away. If the children are in care, there may be jealousy and rows with the foster parents. At all these points help may be needed. The parent's return home will necessitate further readjustments, especially when he or she is still far from well. Fortunately, simple supportive casework, not too time-consuming, can often prove remarkably effective.

Mrs. A, the mother of several children, returned home against advice after a long stay in a mental hospital, following a limited response to one of the new drugs. Her eldest son, who had been living alone with the father meanwhile (the younger children being in care) committed a minor offense soon after his mother's return, and was put on probation. Mrs. A, who was still quite vague and confused, began to demand the return of the other children too, and there were grounds for concern about all these children if she got her way. However, with the support of the probation officer, the mother gradually improved, the younger children came home and settled down, and the eldest boy did not repeat his

[4] Elizabeth E. Irvine, "Psychosis in Parents: Mental Illness as a Problem for the Family," *British Journal of Psychiatric Social Work,* Vol. VI, No. 1 (1962), pp. 21–26.

offense. As the probation officer eventually expressed it: "I think what helped him most was to know that I liked his mother and was not frightened by her in spite of her strangeness."

Not all children are so lucky, especially those with a parent who spends short periods in a mental hospital at frequent intervals. Health visitors are sometimes concerned about young children in this situation.

> Mrs. B's husband sent her back to the hospital whenever her appetite failed, but took her home again as soon as it recovered, even though she was still in terror of enemies whom she felt to be pursuing her with machine-guns from airplanes, and talked about this in a loud and agitated manner to the children and everyone else who would listen. These children were observed to be very strained and withdrawn whenever their mother was at home, and and more happy and spontaneous when she was away. The health visitor arranged for the youngest (aged 20 months) to enter a day nursery, where for some time he was exceptionally difficult and withdrawn. He gradually improved, but was visibly disturbed at each recurrent separation and reunion with his mother. Eventually he became able to enjoy the opportunities for play in the nursery and to respond to the staff, though he was still a solitary child at the age of 4 years. The warm and stable environment provided by the nursery was probably an important factor in this child's gradual improvement.

Reaching Families under Stress

In a recent symposium, entitled *Reluctantly to School,* two authors stress the frequency of ambulant mental illness in the parents of school refusers, particularly in the mothers.[5] Walker describes two examples, of which I shall summarize one.

> An unmarried mother was epileptic, and was periodically admitted to the hospital for severe depression. Her mother looked after the three children at these times, but died when the eldest boy was 10. From this time he felt increasingly responsible for his mother and siblings, especially for reminding his mother to take her medicine, and his school attendance suffered. At age 12 he was charged with non-attendance, and, following a remand in custody, he was enabled to return to school with the help of the probation officer and the mental welfare officer, who was now

[5] A. Walker, "Children Who Refuse to go to School in a Reception Centre" and E. Burgess, "Children Committed to Care for Non-attendance at School," *British Journal of Psychiatric Social Work,* Vol. VII, No. 2 (1963).

225

presumably called in to relieve the boy of the home nursing which he had been doing unaided for two years.

This story illustrates how easily cases can slip through the after-care net, even when the family is in no state to undertake responsibility for the patient, and may be in urgent need of supportive and preventive services itself. It is unclear at the moment how far this is due to the undermanning of services, and how far to lack of liaison between mental hospitals and community services, whether specialized or not. The problem is too big to be solved by specialized services alone, even when the mental hospital really brings itself to trust and use the community services. Child care officers, probation officers, and health visitors all have contact with these families, and the help they offer can be tremendously increased by communication and co-operation with those treating the parent. It is vital that there should be some machinery for ensuring that *somebody* is available and sensitive to the needs of every family exposed to such stress, or at least every family containing children, so that no family in need slips through the net unhelped. We do not know what proportion of these families can manage unaided—not simply to survive intact, but in such a way as to avoid developing a fresh round of mental disturbance. We do know that at present many are left to manage as best they can. We need a study of how families cope with this crisis similar to that reported by Caplan,[6] of families coping with the birth of a premature baby. The other necessity is that all professional people who have contact with such families should be recognized as potential helpers, and that those who do not already have adequate or appropriate training should recognize the need for consultation, and should be generously supported by those with more specialized knowledge, whether of mental illness, or of casework method.

[6] Gerald Caplan, *A Community Approach to Mental Health,* Tavistock, London, 1961.

19. Multiple Impact Therapy: An Experiment*

Agnes Ritchie

THE YOUTH DEVELOPMENT PROJECT, a unit of the Neuropsychiatric Department of the University of Texas Medical Branch at Galveston, came into existence about 1952 to provide a specialized service of therapy and counseling for teen-agers and their families; to offer to medical students, nursing students, residents, and members of related professions an opportunity to study the adolescent and his problems and to learn some techniques of treating them; and—by no means least—to develop and test new ideas, new theories, new techniques of helping. In short, the functions of the Youth Development Project include service, teaching, and research.

Since the Medical Branch serves the entire state of Texas, patients may be referred from any of the 254 counties in the state. The staff and medical consultants of the Youth Development Project faced repeatedly the frustration of having to recommend long-time therapy and counseling for adolescent patients and their families who lived in communities where such treatment was not available within a fifty-mile radius—if they could afford it, which many could not. The wish and need to offer help and hope to some of these troubled

* Reprinted from *Social Work*, Vol. 5, No. 3 (1960). This paper was a preliminary report on a demonstration project done within the Department of Neurology and Psychiatry of the University of Texas Medical Branch. The project was partially supported in its pilot year by a grant from the Hogg Foundation for Mental Health, and subsequently supported in part by a Mental Health Project Grant from the National Institute of Mental Health. Acknowledgment is made for participation in all phases of the project to its directors, Harold A. Goolishian, Ph.D., and Eugene C. McDanald, Jr., M.D., and to the other basic team members, Robert MacGregor, Ph.D., research director, Franklin P. Schuster, M.D., psychiatrist. The final report on the project was published under the title, *Multiple Impact Therapy with Families* by Robert MacGregor, Agnes M. Ritchie, Alberto C. Serrano, and Franklin P. Schuster, under the direction of Eugene C. McDanald, Jr., and Harold A. Goolishian, McGraw-Hill Book Co., New York, 1964.

adolescents and families, many of whom were desperate, was at least as strong a factor as any other in the development of the *multiple impact therapy*.

Multiple impact therapy (referred to familiarly within our agency as "MIT") is a brief, usually two-day, intensive study and treatment of a family in crisis by a guidance clinic team. In our project the team includes a psychiatrist, a clinical psychologist who is also research director, a psychiatric social worker, and a resident clinical psychologist. The multiple impact therapy team has the benefit of regular consultation and supervision of senior staff members of the Department of Neurology and Psychiatry, as well as opportunity for consultation with Medical Branch staff and personnel. The team devotes full time, six or seven hours a day for two (sometimes two and a half) days, to one family. Families come to the clinic frequently from a considerable distance, anywhere from 50 to 450 miles, sometimes viewing the trip to Galveston as their last hope.

The multiple impact therapy plan is based on two assumptions. First, that individuals and families facing a crisis are stimulated to mobilize strength and resources to meet it, and that they are more receptive to interpretations, more likely to be flexible in attitude, than at other times. The second assumption is that in any type of psychotherapy there is likely to be faster and more dramatic change in the early stages of treatment, and that under long-range treatment later change and improvement is more gradual—is a deepening and strengthening of the initial movement, during the first few hours or weeks, toward improved health or adjustment.

The procedures are quite flexible, but consist essentially of an initial family-team conference, followed by a series of individual interviews, joint interviews (two patients with one or more therapists, or two therapists with one or more patients), and overlapping interviews—all these procedures being interrupted by formal and informal team conferences. The family, also, is advised to talk together, to share thoughts, ideas, insights, and feelings, both about themselves and about the clinic experience and the clinic team. Psychological tests are given the adolescent during the first afternoon, and results are shared, in a general way, with the parents and the adolescent, usually early on the second day. The two-day contact terminates with a final family-team conference, sometimes with the adolescent present but sometimes not, and it is in this last conference that "the back-home problem" is discussed in terms of specific recommendations and insights gained during the preceding day and a half are applied to behavior and situations that can be anticipated. This whole project at present is primarily research and demonstration; the family is told of the plan for a follow-up conference six months later, and they understand that this is primarily for the benefit of the research team, to evaluate results of our work with the family, although they are also assured that additional consultation or service from us is available to them, either at the end of six months or earlier if a new crisis arises.

An important feature of multiple impact therapy procedures is the "overlapping interview," in which a team member who has been talking privately with a family member terminates his interview and joins another conference, either alone or accompanied by the person he has been seeing. One or the other of the team gives a brief summary of the conference up to this point. This summary not only informs the newcomer, but gives the patient an opportunity for critique of the therapist on the accuracy and interpretation of what has gone on between them and of the work with the family. Differences of opinion or of interpretation between parents or parent and child are sometimes resolved in the overlapping interviews.

Differences of opinion or interpretation between team members are also brought out and discussed fully in the family's presence. In some families this freedom in the team to disagree—sometimes with heat, but with no decrease in mutual respect or ability to work together effectively and to remain friendly—has tremendous impact on the family; they are exposed to a demonstration rather than an exhortation to express feelings as well as thoughts. Sometimes they are invited to participate in the discussion, which conveys our confidence that they are not so fragile that they cannot bear to disagree with with us or with each other. Frequently differences are not resolved, and we comment, explicitly, that there is frequently room for different interpretations and methods of handling problems, and we express confidence in the individual's or family's ability to find their own answers and solutions. In a few instances, where communication within the family is so poor that no interchange occurs, the team members may present deliberately different versions or interpretations of some material that has been presented, each arguing for the validity of his point of view, with the patients being invited to participate, even to "take sides."

Procedures

The procedures for our multiple impact therapy are generally as follows: the clinical team meets together before the family arrives, and reviews briefly the information already available about the nominal patient, the family, and the situation. This information may have been furnished by the referring person or agency (such as the family doctor, the John Sealy Hospital or outpatient clinic, a school, or a social agency); or the applicants may have been seen previously by our clinic staff for brief screening interviews. In the initial team conference there is usually some speculation about family dynamics and the genesis of the presenting problem, and some tentative plans are made for distribution of labor among the team during the first day, or at least the first morning of the contact.

The family has been advised to arrive at the clinic at nine-thirty in the morning, and at about that time they are invited to meet with the team in a conference room. The initial family-team conference is usually planned to last about an hour, during which time a great deal may happen. There are introductions all around, and the family's attention is called to the tape-recording equipment; in seating arrangement suggestions, both the distance and the position of each person in relation to microphones are considered; and separate chairs are provided for family members (so that they will not sit together on the couch and run the risk of feeling that they are huddled together against an imposing array of "experts").

After a very few moments spent in amenities and in getting settled, the family is invited to explain the problem to us or—since they know we already know why they are there—to bring us up to date on the current situation. Almost invariably one family member will act as spokesman initially, and we encourage participation from the others; all our questions and comments to encourage participation are worded in a way calculated to convey respect for the feelings and opinions of each member of the family, and to convey our recognition, sometimes verbalized, that the behavior of each, whatever it may have been, must have "made sense" at the time if viewed in the light of interpersonal relationships and attitudes, or in terms of the total situation. For example, when parent or parents describe the patient in terms of his difference from another child who is, for example, more obedient or respectful, or more industrious, one of us will usually address a question or comment to the adolescent about sibling relationships: for example, "Your brother seems to know how to get you in bad with your folks. What do you do to get him in bad?" Or to the woman who cashed rubber checks on her husband's bank account, "It looks as if you just had to see if your husband would stand by you!" Or perhaps we would say to her husband at that point, "Mrs. S seems to trust you enough to know that you would protect her!" Interpretation and even speculation by the team are begun very early, usually in the opening conference. For example, when the chief complaint is "school phobia," questions about the problem are couched in terms of the child's "fear to leave home," with verbalized speculation by team members about conscious or unconscious fears the child may have as to what might happen at home in his absence. The theory of the oedipal conflict and its application to the family problem and the crisis usually are presented in simple nontechnical words.

Individual Interviews

Not infrequently there is more communication between family members and more sharing of feelings both positive and negative in the initial conference than has occurred in the family for many years, if ever. However, unaccustomed as most families are to this free communication, considerable tension is built up from things none feel free to say before the others. Usually after about an hour one team member will suggest that we separate into individual sessions, and each team member invites a family member to accompany him to a private office. Although pairing off at this point is extremely flexible, most commonly the psychiatrist will see the adolescent patient after the initial conference, the social worker (who in our team is a woman) interviews the mother, the psychologist interviews the father, and the second psychologist interviews any other participant—who may be another child in the family, or a close relative who lives in or near the home and is an important person in the child's environment, or a referring person (social worker, probation officer, school counselor) who for one reason or another has accompanied the family to the clinic. When only the adolescent and two parents are with us, the fourth team member may participate in one of the individual interviews—may conceivably "visit" from office to office, permitting more use of the overlapping summary

231

technique described—or may withdraw for the balance of the first morning.

The individual interview with the adolescent gives the child an opportunity to receive undivided attention from the doctor, to "present his case" and his side of any argument, and to ventilate his feelings more freely than he could in his parents' presence; at the same time it gives the psychiatrist an opportunity to form a diagnostic impression of the patient. If the matter was not mentioned in the earlier group meeting, the patient is told about psychological tests that will be given him after lunch, and any anxiety or resistance about this can be handled immediately. Individual interviews with adolescents are shorter than with adults, and the staff member who has seen the boy usually calls by telephone for permission to join an interview with one or the other parent.

These initial individual interviews with the parents are frequently used by them to ventilate grievances and present defenses and rationalizations, each for his or her behavior and attitude toward spouse, patient, and community.

Gathering Information

There is very little "history-taking" as such, but relevant family history—developmental history of the adolescent nominal patient, of the other children, and of parents themselves—is usually brought out in these sessions, since this information, in the parent's mind, is pertinent to the problem or offers explanation or defense of his own attitude, behavior, and so on. The therapist soon has an opportunity, either in an overlapping session immediately following the interview or in a later joint session, to review relevant history briefly, integrating it into history or rationalizations presented by other members of the family or condensing or rephrasing information in an interpretive way.

The family members are advised at the end of the morning to share as freely as they can with each other any ideas, insights, or reactions they have had during the morning, and are told that the team, also, will confer during lunch, sharing information and ideas with each other, so that work can be continued together during the afternoon. This same recommendation is made to the family at the end of the day, and some of the most dramatic improvements

232

in communication between family members, and especially between parents, occur away from the office.

During the afternoon of the first day the adolescent is usually given a battery of psychological tests. Parents are seen individually at first in what we call "cross-ventilation interviews"; the team member who has seen the father in the morning now sees the mother, and vice versa. By this time each team member has some fairly clear-cut impression of the strengths and weaknesses of each parent; the one who has seen the mother for an hour or more has some appreciation of what the father "has to put up with." Discrepancies and distortions not uncovered in overlapping sessions during the morning come to light as the team confers during and after lunch, and during subsequent sessions cloudy areas are clarified, not only by the team but also by the patients.

Probably the dominant leitmotif of the team's activity with the family is the emphasis on each member's role in the family: the delineation and spelling out of the appropriate role of father, of mother, of child. In most of the twenty-six families seen during the past twelve months, mothers have been—with a depressing uniformity—preoccupied with motherhood, and the fathers frequently preoccupied with job or with hobby, sometimes to the point of being psychologically excluded from the family; more than one father has seemed and has felt more like a roomer or boarder than a husband and father. Many mothers have defensively protested about their endless efforts to be a "good mother" and have offered (much too readily) to accept full responsibility, even guilt, for the children's difficulties. Both directly and indirectly we have encouraged parents to "rediscover each other," to seek and share adult interests, companionship, and recreation with each other and with their peers. We attempt to build up the father's own confidence, and his wife's, in his ability to function as the head of the house. We point out to the mother and to her husband her feminine attractiveness (actual or potential) and express concern that she is denying herself adult feminine satisfactions in life, giving them up to live in a children's world. The unconscious emotional exploitation of children by parents who are no longer giving and receiving tenderness and emotional satisfaction from each other, and the obstacles this places in the maturation of the children, are frankly presented in simple nontechnical language as a common phenom-

233

enon occurring in many families, and application is made to its operation in this particular family.

The second day is an accelerated version of the previous day, usually starting with a brief team-family conference, followed by individual and joint sessions. The decisions as to "who sees whom" and in what combinations are based on evaluations of relationships established between a family member and a team member or on the team's judgment of the effectiveness of certain special attributes or attitudes of individual team members. Overlapping interviews are more freely used on the second day, and by this time the rewards of freer communication are sufficiently appreciated by the family members that usually no objection is raised to sharing with each other newly discovered insights. This disintegration of the usual confidentiality, with the knowledge and approval of the confider, seems to be evidence of the family's trust in the team and increased trust and confidence in each other.

The final conference, which occurs during the last hour or two of the second day, has been described earlier and is usually devoted to discussion of the "back-home problem," with much more active participation by both parents than in the opening session.

Tentative Evaluation

A wide range of presenting problems and types of crises have been treated by these methods during the past ten months. These have included chronic runaways, delinquent acting-out behavior, school failure and school phobia, homosexual behavior and other sexual deviations, and so on. In fact, the diagnostic categories have included the range from adjustment reactions through the schizophrenias. Six-month follow-up evaluations have been done on all twelve families seen during the pilot study and on seven families of the current series, with quite promising findings. Institutionalization of the adolescent, either in a correctional school, a mental hospital, or some other residential facility, seemed imminent and inevitable in many cases, but has been avoided (or at least postponed) in all but two instances. This is a very gross measure of success, but repeated psychological tests and professional evaluations of change or improvement in various areas of individual and family adjustment indicate that the effectiveness of this type of treatment for the limited number of families seen so far is as great (statistically)

234

as the longer type of conventional therapy. It should be mentioned that as many professional manhours of time are invested in each family we have seen as in six months or more of one-hour-a-week appointments in conventional, individual therapy. A three- or four-member team devoting six or seven hours a day for two days represents between thirty-six and fifty hours of interviewing and conferring, without counting preliminary correspondence or conferring, recording, and the like.

Among the twenty-six cases studied during the past year, two families in which the crisis centered around a preadolescent child were included successfully, and it seems evident that the multiple impact therapy procedures are equally applicable to this kind of family. In six of these twenty-six families the "crisis" situation was the return of the adolescent to the home and community following a period of institutional care in a training school or a psychiatric hospital. These youths had the benefit, of course, of the training and treatment services of the institutions, but prognosis for satisfactory adjustment in the home environment was considered poor in each case; by this is meant that the physicians and agencies who referred these cases to the Youth Development Project expressed the opinion that the adolescent patients would quickly regress to the earlier deviant and antisocial behavior which precipitated their removal from home and community. In the four of these six families in which formal follow-up evaluations have been made, this has not happened. On the other hand, family structure has been strengthened, parents are more supportive, each of the other, and more accepting and more realistically firm with the children. After a period of testing these new strengths and the new limits imposed by parents, the adolescent nominal patients have been able gradually to settle down into reasonably acceptable and appropriate behavior patterns.

Children's institutions and placement agencies have long recognized that planning for discharge is at least as important and in many ways more difficult than initial planning and preparation for placement. Ideally, discharge planning is a part of the work with child and family throughout placement, but frequently this is impractical or sporadic. If an adaptation of multiple impact therapy can be used as part of discharge planning, this will be a valuable tool for many types of institutions.

Much study remains to be done before the possibilities and the limitations of this approach can be clearly understood and described. Originally developed to meet a particular problem in a rather specialized clinic, multiple impact therapy procedures have already proved flexible and adaptable for use in several different settings, and in the treatment of a variety of individual and family problems. Several outpatient clinics have expressed an interest in planning for demonstration or use of multiple impact therapy in their own agencies, and indeed have experimented successfully with these techniques, or with a modification of the procedure adapted to their own agency needs and staff resources. Our experience to date has indicated that this type of procedure will prove a valuable addition to the therapeutic tools of guidance clinics, hospitals, residential treatment centers, and so forth, as well as a teaching device of merit in the training of mental health workers.

20. Assertive Casework in a Short-Term Situation*

Ruth Chaskel

THE FIELD OF SOCIAL WORK, in the last decade, has accepted the validity of reaching-out casework service and of short-term counseling. The manifest success of the majority of the research and demonstration projects that have been undertaken has served to endow both these techniques with a new aura of professional respectability. The profession has recognized that it has the obligation to engage in a continuum of service activities ranging from primary prevention, that is, protection from vulnerability to specific social ills, to rehabilitation and problem-solving. No longer can caseworkers be content always to wait until the individual who is vulnerable or in distress wishes to become a client. No longer are they saying that the individual has the right to make or mar himself. As a group, social workers are now struggling to develop principles of social health to match those of public health, a field from which we have learned a great deal.

Recognizing its responsibility as a public servant—the organized conscience and treatment arm of the community—our profession is increasingly ready to undertake the task of casefinding and caseholding. This is not to say that an authoritative approach must always be used, although there are situations in which it is appropriate and proper, as when the protection of an individual or a family demands such a step. Rather, it is the skillful motivation provided by the caseworker through which the individual is enabled to accept the fact of his momentary helplessness and through which he gains strength and the desire to do something about his trouble-

* Reprinted from *Casework Papers, 1961,* Family Service Association of America, New York, 1961.

237

some problem. The willingness and capacity to furnish this stimulus are the hallmark of the profession's social maturity.

In the area of short-term counseling, also, casework made tremendous strides once it was recognized that this technique could be the preferred method with certain clients and certain problems, rather than being simply a makeshift approach based on the limitations of the agency, the lack of client motivation, or the strictures of time. Short-term counseling has now been incorporated within the conceptual framework of social casework. Thus firmly based, it has gained strength and its practitioners have been given professional security.

Simple Environmental Need

The Travelers Aid program affords an excellent opportunity for combining short-term counseling and assertive casework. This is especially true in those many instances in which the client presents himself as being involved in a crisis, which may or may not be based on reality. Almost all Travelers Aid clients consider the time element to be a crucial factor, and the client's emphasis, therefore, is geared to receiving the service requested with a minimum of so-called "red tape." The problem posed for the caseworker is obvious. He must be able to move quickly enough to evaluate the reality situation "with all deliberate speed" so that a sound plan is expedited and its implementation not endangered. Concurrently, however, he must be alert to the possibility that the client's plan is unrealistic and not in his own or his family's best interest. It takes experience and skill not to allow the agency to become enmeshed in a self-defeating plan and yet be accepting of the applicant and hold his interest.

An example of the client who presents a sound and manageable plan is the man who comes to a new community to begin a job for which he has been employed, only to find that he is without sufficient funds or resources until payday, in spite of what seemed adequate advance planning. In these days of shifting industrial patterns, when workers are forced to relocate or when plants move, this is surely not an isolated instance. Suppose that car repairs en route have absorbed his budgeted money. Clearly, the first step, after listening to the client and assuring him of the agency's interest, is a verification of the facts. In this, the caseworker's activity is äkin to a business operation and is, of course, similar to establishing eligibility for public assistance.

Let us assume that once the facts have been verified, the needed and wanted service, financial assistance, is made available. In this case, the caseworker's holding to the need to verify facts represents an outgoing approach, one to which the client can relate and which he can respect. Above all, the caseworker needs to be perspicacious, skillful in working quickly, and giving, both in attitude and in material assistance. He must have the security to embark on an investigative process and the ability to do so with dispatch, all the while motivating the client to participate in the process.

In this example, the presenting problem was primarily of an environmental nature, treated and recognized as such, and the valid request was speedily met. In general, there should be one or two follow-up interviews with the client involved, in an effort to consolidate his adjustment. Moreover, the agency should be readily available should the newcomer have special difficulties.

Combined Pressures

The vast majority of problems that come to the attention of Travelers Aid are not so clear cut. As a rule, environmental and psychological components are interwoven, with the environmental need precipitating an open crisis. Often the situation is one of individual or family disorder, and the precarious plan presented by the client can only compound the evident distress. Invariably, that precious commodity, time, is about to run out for the client. With the exception of those situations that have a firm base in practical fact, irrational attitudes play an important part in the difficulty and it is imperative that they be analyzed if the worker is to understand the client.

All Travelers Aid clients share in common the fact that they are new or strange to the community or else are contemplating a move away from the familiarity of home. Their very sense of strangeness understandably may lead to anxiety, which is intensified by their awareness that, at best, it takes time to become familiar with resources, especially in the confusing network of a large urban center. Anxiety may breed hostility—hostility that is sometimes created and often confirmed by unfortunate experiences the newcomer has suffered at the hands of the old residents. There may be discrimination in employment or housing and almost certainly so with respect to public health and welfare services. The newcomer generally has two strikes against him from the start and this is the more true the more inadequate and helpless he is.

There is another disturbing element in being a newcomer—the fact that some in-migrants provoke the enmity of local residents by virtue of the economic competition they threaten. People who play it safe and stay at home often have a deep psychological distrust of the person who does take a chance through mobility. Xenophobia is an old phenomenon. In addition, we know that many newcomers from rural settlements to urban areas, from one type of living to another, present serious problems of adjustment which often may be a genuine source of discomfort and embarrassment to the well-established community. Points of friction invariably arise, to the detriment of the newcomers' integration.

The demands made upon the caseworker are great. First of all, he must be able to assess quickly both the emotional and the environmental factors. Not only must he act promptly on the basis of his assessment, but he must also be able to arouse in the client some beginning awareness that he has an internalized problem. Unless he does so, the client has every right to become confused and angry if his initial request is not met. Withdrawal from the worker may be the result. It is true that some of these same elements are present in any intake interview, regardless of setting. A distinctive flavor is given to the Travelers Aid service, however, by the invariable pressure exerted by the client.

A typical example * is the case of Mrs. A, an attractive woman, about 30 years of age, accompanied by her small son, who applied at the Transportation Center desk of an eastern Travelers Aid agency for assistance in locating a family friend with whom she thought they could stay temporarily. In view of the vagueness of the plan, the volunteer did not consult telephone books or the city directory but referred Mrs. A to the caseworker. Mrs. A had run away from an abusive husband in the Midwest. The caseworker assured her that the agency was interested in helping her plan. Because of the lateness of the hour and Mrs. A's evident exhaustion, the worker arranged for Mrs. A and her son to stay overnight in a hotel. Mrs. A still had enough money for this purpose. The next day Mrs. A's friends were found

* The author is grateful to the Travelers Aid Societies of Philadelphia and Pittsburgh for their co-operation in making available this case material.

through the Polish-American Relief Committee and she went to stay with them. By then, however, the caseworker had been able to help her develop insight into the fact that blind running away could not be a permanent solution and that her husband probably was a desperately unhappy man—in short that their problem was a joint one and therefore needed to be worked out by both of them. Mrs. A then welcomed the caseworker's offer of having Mr. A approached by the Travelers Aid agency in their home town.

Since both her husband and Mrs. A were now receiving counseling, and Mr. A had begun to write to his wife in care of the agency, Mrs. A decided to return home. The length of the contact was three weeks which covered seven casework interviews. It is perhaps best evaluated by Mrs. A's parting comment, "I only expected to meet my friend through you and I found this," meaning the possibility, already tested out, of readjusting marriage and life through casework. Both Mr. and Mrs. A were prepared to have further interviews in their home town and followed through on the plan.

The Assertive Approach

In the A case, as in most Travelers Aid situations, the caseworker had to arrive at a quick preliminary diagnostic decision and, therefore, had to be quite affirmative in drawing out the client to give the necessary background information in the first two interviews. This is another important differentiation in the short-term approach, as compared with more traditional long-term counseling in which both the client and the caseworker are much more apt to have a second chance and the caseworker can more readily wait for the client to tell his story piecemeal. Had the focus of the working relationship not been established at intake, the agency might not have been able to reach Mrs. A at all. An initial error in judgment could very well be a final one. Consequently, professional acumen is at a high premium, for the caseworker must always walk a tightrope between being appropriately assertive in eliciting material at the client's pace and avoiding the danger of outdistancing the client, with the result that the interview becomes meaningless or the client leaves in hurt or confusion.

At the same time, of course, the caseworker has the advantage that the crisis situation makes it possible to strike while the iron is hot. Here again he must be able to recognize the occasion when, as it were, he has nothing to lose, that is, when the client would withdraw but for the possibility that the caseworker's persistence may hold him. This concept is illustrated by the D case.

Mrs. D, 35, applied for emergency financial assistance, pending her obtaining a domestic sleep-in job. Since she had had experience in this kind of work, undoubtedly she could secure one, but even the first few minutes of the interview led the caseworker to doubt that this plan would solve Mrs. D's problem. He suggested that he would like to assist Mrs. D in her planning and asked for some background information.

The picture of Mrs. D that emerged was one of great physical and psychological deterioration. Mrs. D vaguely mentioned a marriage and eight children who had been placed for adoption, some through agencies and others through the black market. Gradually she began to talk, in a matter-of-fact way, about her involvements with a number of men. Try as she might, she felt that it had been impossible for her to take root any place. Various social agencies throughout the country had helped her off and on. At this point in the interview, as a reproach to the caseworker, Mrs. D mentioned two Travelers Aid agencies that had "just helped her secure a domestic job and that was that." The caseworker wondered what had caused her to leave these jobs. Mrs. D responded lamely that something had always gone wrong. By degrees a story of alcoholic binges emerged. The caseworker, while impressing upon Mrs. D his desire to help her, nevertheless held to his inability to do so in the way she had told him other agencies had helped her before. Although the worker risked Mrs. D's abrupt termination, actually Mrs. D gained an inkling that all was not well with her way of living and she was motivated to continue with the agency on the strength of the caseworker's interest. True, they began almost entirely on the caseworker's terms, but a little later she reacted quite positively to the caseworker's comment that he would be greatly disappointed if Mrs. D "just left."

Following medical and psychiatric testing, Mrs. D was successfully referred to Alcoholics Anonymous and, after several weeks, was ready for a sleep-in job in a charitable institution. As was to be expected, Mrs. D had several setbacks and needed continuing support. Within two months she had gained sufficient strength to accept the need for continued casework treatment and could make use of it. Had such service been offered to her at the very beginning, it would have been meaningless. The first objective had to be one of holding the client in a productive relationship, and this aim was accomplished.

Pressure of Time

Since the client presents himself at the point of crisis, the psychological pressure exerted by the time element places a tremendous burden on both participants. It makes it hard for the applicant to listen and to relate to the worker, and it can frustrate the worker if he has not yet learned to live with it. The worker's skill lies in not allowing time to become an overbearing and all-powerful robot, but rather in making it subservient to the reality of human need. The obvious pitfall is that he may work with too limited a focus, with the resultant twin dangers of overpermissiveness or overdirection, which really are two sides of the same coin.

Any Travelers Aid agency is familiar with those requests for travel service for children in which the parent comes in at the last minute and presents the caseworker with the *fait accompli* of the child's need to leave instantaneously. The parent's plans for the child may have been made to the last detail, but the agency dare not take professional responsibility unless it can assure itself that the plan is in the child's best interests. By policy, the agency verifies and evaluates the arrangements as expeditiously as possible, but with all due safeguards. This may mean interviews with both parents and child as well as interviews (through the Travelers Aid chain of service) with the person or persons at the destination point, usually relatives. Sometimes collateral data must be secured; for example, evaluation from the school of the child's maturity or of his health status from the health station.

The parent is often completely unprepared for even the slightest delay and reacts with fear, hostility, and frustration. As he sees it, he simply requested that Johnny's trip be safeguarded. Why, then, is the agency intruding on his privacy and questioning his responsibility as a parent? The more inadequate the parent, the more he will feel provoked and the greater the strain will be on the caseworker's professional stamina. Explaining the agency's policy is relatively easy when the client is mature and self-directing and truly has the emotional capacity to have the child's interest at heart. In such cases, evaluation usually can be accomplished quickly, and more often than not the proposed plan is an adequate one. When the parent is immature and emotionally unstable, however, the caseworker's first step must be to help the parent see that, in the

243

long run, haste makes waste. The worker must acquire such diagnostic understanding of the family as is pertinent to the problem at hand. He must also help the parent accept the enabling nature of the agency's regulations.

Mrs. R, at the suggestion of the railroad ticket agent, brought her 9-year-old son, George, who had been born out of wedlock, to the Travelers Aid office with the request that travel service be provided for him to join his alleged father in a southern state. The boy did not know his father, nor did Mrs. R have his address. Her hope was that the father's sister could put them in touch with each other at the point of destination. Mrs. R was certainly an unwilling and captive client. Only the worker's manifest interest in helping her enabled Mrs. R to overcome her resistance sufficiently to talk about being at her wits' end in handling the boy. He was a problem at school and Mrs. R gave the worker permission to consult the school counselor. The counselor confirmed Mrs. R's statements and added that a referral had been made to the juvenile court for evaluation of the need to place George, but the judge had dismissed the case when the alleged father's home was suggested as a solution.

Within two days, Mrs. R had telephoned the caseworker and had canceled her application. She had reached George's father on the telephone and had secured his promise to take care of George. She was now preparing to accompany him herself. The worker immediately consulted with the court probation officer who expressed his strong opinion that so disturbed a boy should be receiving treatment in his home community rather than being exposed to the uncertainties of a new home. He also promised that the court would act if Mrs. R could be persuaded to go to the court herself. Regrettably, the caseworker, who did not want to risk whatever minimal relationship he had established with Mrs. R, did not follow up immediately, but waited to hear from her. He was, of course, fearful of using the professional authority that would have been appropriate for him to exert. When he finally telephoned Mrs. R two weeks later, she had just returned from the South where she had left George. Her mission accomplished, she was cool to the worker's proposal of having the agency in the other city offer casework service. Nevertheless, the worker sent a summary to the agency in the city where George was living. As a result, a home visit was made and continued service was accepted by the father. Mrs. R was genuinely relieved to hear about this. Perhaps this experience has given her a renewed confidence in social agencies. Since she has five children still at home, the chances are that she will need some additional service in the near future.

Need for Relationship

There is an important group of cases in which the worker also has to take firm and direct action in changing or modifying a client's proposed plan. These cases run the gamut from safeguarding children and adolescents to doing protective work with the mentally incapacitated. With the exception of those situations in which the client is in an acute psychotic episode, and therefore quite out of reach, the specific skill required lies in the expeditious establishment of a relationship that is meaningful enough to the client that he will be motivated to begin considering a different approach to his problem.

Thirteen-year-old Paul was approached by the Travelers Aid caseworker at 7:30 A.M. in a large midwestern bus terminal, when the worker observed him hanging around uncertainly. He was on his way to New Mexico, but the ticket clerk, to whom he had given his age as eleven, would not sell him a half-fare ticket without Travelers Aid approval. Paul said that he had just been released from Children's Hospital after a surgical correction of his hand; he had to return to his sick grandmother. When the caseworker invited him to sit down and talk matters over, he suddenly remembered somebody who could give him a ride and he went away—suitcase, fishing pole, and all. The caseworker watched him go.

Since Paul met no one at the door, but wandered aimlessly, the worker followed. It was obvious that he did not want any further dealings with Travelers Aid, but he finally allowed the worker to help him carry his belongings, whereupon they went back to the office. An hour and a half later, a story had emerged of a boy who, following his father's death in an accident, had remained with his grandparents in the Southwest while his mother had remarried, moved to the Midwest with her husband, and had a new family of three children. The previous winter, the grandparents and Paul had joined this household, but Paul did not like the arrangement—he felt like an outsider.

Eventually, Paul's ambivalence resolved itself in favor of allowing the worker to call his parents. He was afraid of punishment, but even more he hoped that "they" would show they really loved him. A telephone call brought both his mother and his stepfather to the Travelers Aid office. They were able to use this episode as a real cathartic experience. They said that the boy had been greatly spoiled by his grandparents when he had been the kingpin in their home. Now Paul could not adjust to being only one part of the show. The parents (the stepfather had adopted Paul) quickly came to the realization that the whole family had to work out a different adjustment and that perhaps inadvertently they had contributed to Paul's feeling of being apart from the rest of the family. They eagerly accepted a referral for continued counseling. Travelers Aid remained in touch with the family long enough to ensure that this was successfully accomplished.

Special Casework Skills

Travelers Aid has an opportunity to affect an individual's life in a meaningful way at short notice in a tremendous range of situations. For example, one young, down-and-out, narcotic addict requested a few dollars to enable him to return to his mother. With the caseworker's help he was able to decide, instead, to commit himself to a mental hospital. A middle-aged migrant man, who had spent many years in a home for mental defectives, was motivated to stay in town longer than just one night so that his home community could be contacted and a long-range plan, including rehabilitation, could be worked out in his place of residence. By definition, Travelers Aid works with a highly mobile group. Fundamental decisions must often be made very rapidly, although, as I have tried to show, this does not necessarily mean rapid physical movement. On the contrary, it may entail slowing down and arresting the client's flight so that he will have time for considered reflection and judgment.

As in all professional activity, the caseworker carries considerable responsibility. Obviously, he cannot allow himself to become trapped into categorizing people as runaways, migrants, newcomers, and so forth, on the assumption that each category can be dealt with in a given fashion. It is only through the casework relationship and an understanding of each individual as a person in his own right that the proper approach can be determined. The Travelers Aid caseworker must have a high degree of flexibility since, by the very nature of his work, a good part of each day is spent in shifting from one emergent situation to the next. The very fact that the client is usually a stranger in the town places an additional burden on the caseworker. When both client and worker are from the same town, they meet on familiar territory, as it were. But when the client is, for example, a Vietnamese student or comes from a section of the United States unfamiliar to the worker, it is much more difficult for the worker to evaluate the cultural milieu and understand the many different factors that are pertinent to the client's life experience. Dr. Ginsburg has said that, "especially in an agency like the Travelers Aid, it is manifestly impossible for any worker conceivably to be familiar with the cultural patterns of all her clients." [1] That is doubtless true, but one can expect that the caseworker will recognize that cultural factors play a role in the client's life, and will strive to become as familiar as possible with the cultural patterns most frequently encountered.

Thus, the caseworker often begins with many unknowns in the client's situation—unknowns that are not only psychological but also environmental. An imaginative and intuitive grasp of the client and his situation, therefore, can be just as important as the sifting out of facts and the use of collateral information. Time is an ever-present and potent factor. If employed wisely, as a servant and not as a master, it becomes an enabling force, in that both client and caseworker must use themselves to the fullest, since literally there is no time for apathy and procrastination.

Conclusion

Travelers Aid, by virtue of its function of serving people who are unsettled both environmentally and psychologically, has a special opportunity to help the client at the point of crisis—a circumstance that often makes him more amenable to counseling. A genuinely helpful service cannot stop with providing environmental aid alone, although it may be an immediate palliative. A long-range approach has to be a problem-solving approach, directed toward a change in the patterns of living. This type of treatment demands that the caseworker have the courage and skill to be appropriately outgoing and assertive. It is not a paradox that such a long-term goal can well be accomplished within the setting of short-term casework. The caseworker here may be forced to take the initiative but, to be truly successful, he must be able to establish quickly a meaningful and productive relationship.

[1] Sol W. Ginsburg, *On Cultural Factors in Casework,* National Travelers Aid Association, New York, 1954, p. 12.

21. The Crisis of Relocation*

H. *Frederick Brown,*
Vera Barad Burditt,
and *Charles W. Liddell*

ON JUNE 28, 1962, under a one-year contract with the Boston Redevelopment Authority, the United South End Settlements (USES)
undertook to provide relocation services to families and individuals
being displaced by urban renewal in Castle Square, a crowded section
of the socially deprived South End area of Boston. An estimated 531
family units to be moved proved to be 644 by actual count.

This report indicates how the interventive efforts of the relocation social worker, the public health nurse, and the welfare worker
can be combined to utilize the crisis of relocation as an opportunity
to help families achieve for themselves a higher level of social functioning.

The work done by the relocation staff assigned to work directly
with families is the front line of any relocation operation. Failure
here means failure throughout the program.[1] The powers of eminent
domain, together with the presence of the crane and the deteriorating conditions in the site area, eventually push all families toward
the inevitable moving date. Since families have to move, the quality
of relocation work depends primarily upon the individual relocation
worker's use of the rehousing crisis to help the family make a good
move. Because the families in Castle Square had had little experi-

* Adapted, by permission, from *Castle Square: Final Report of the Castle
Square Residential Relocation Program,* United South End Settlements, Boston,
Mass., Feb. 1964, pp. 33–55.
[1] For a discussion of the importance of "human renewal" in urban renewal,
see Dorothy S. Montgomery, "Relocation and Its Impact on Families," *Social
Casework,* Vol. XLI, No. 8 (1960), pp. 405–407, and Marc Fried, "Grieving for a
Lost Home," *The Urban Condition,* Leonard Duhl (ed.), Basic Books, New York,
1963, pp. 151–171.

ence with community agencies they were hesitant in accepting the help offered them by the relocation staff.

Program Goals

In addition to undertaking the basic task of rehousing, USES incorporated certain social welfare services into the Castle Square Relocation Program for the purpose of (1) minimizing hardship; (2) minimizing the possibility of destructive impact on neighborhoods due to the influx of unurbanized families; (3) maximizing the opportunity to achieve high levels of living that relocation provides to families; (4) resolving critical social problems that come to issue by virtue of rehousing.[2] In order to ensure the quality of work with families in the rehousing process, and to make available social welfare services, USES filled key positions with professionally trained and experienced social workers possessing skills appropriate to the relocation program. Every effort was made to carry out the relocation responsibility without sacrificing the social workers' basic values and goals which included: (1) recognizing the dignity and worth of every individual and family; (2) achieving relocation through the families' self-determined plans; (3) helping families on an individual basis through consideration of their specific problems, needs, and desires; (4) maintenance of the confidentiality of all work with families; and (5) commitment to an integrated community. Of course, these values are not necessarily exclusive to social work.

Assignment of Workers

In order to maintain consistency of contact with the family, relocation workers were assigned on a geographical "block" basis, and changes in staff assignments were held to a minimum. The workers' principal points of access to residents were those relating to the physical environment; usually they worked with the families in their homes.

The relocation program had a responsibility to reach the total resident population within the boundaries of the Castle Square area. The staff could not restrict itself to doing intensive casework with a few families, but had the responsibility of making a significant effort

[2] Elizabeth Wood, "Special Welfare Services in Relocation," *Memorandum to Relocation and Advisory Committee,* United Community Services of Metropolitan Boston, June 24, 1962, p. 1.

to help the entire caseload in the best possible way. In order to maintain the quality of relocation work with all families, the program established regular staff supervision of all the caseworkers on a weekly basis. Whenever supervision was suspended because of the caseload pressures that developed, it was found that the quality of the casework deteriorated. Sensitive supervision provided the relocation workers with the support they needed in dealing with many difficult situations.

Relocation as a Social Casework Process

From the experience of the Castle Square program seven specific steps have been identified in the relocation process. The relocation worker and the supervisor who understand these steps can ensure careful planning in each situation. Although this dynamic process cannot be blueprinted, its essential stages can be outlined in an admittedly oversimplified way as follows:

1. *Getting to know the family*: Establishing the relocation worker as a helping person—developing trust; learning the neighborhood interrelationships; talking informally with people; getting early but definitive thoughts on relocation.

2. *Helping residents face the reality of relocation*: Watching the advance of the crane; reading newsletters and newspapers; talking about feelings—"You have to move. You don't want to move when you're upset and angry, do you?"

3. *Exploring and handling problems interfering with relocation*: What the neighborhood has meant; loss of friends, of Lincoln House (a local community center), of stores; medical problems; social incapacities; poor housekeeping standards; financial difficulties. "Maybe you need to talk some more about these feelings before you start looking at places."

4. *Agreement about "safe, sanitary, and decent housing"*: Seeing themselves in a nice place; what they can have; what they should have; what they want—"I can help if this is what you want."

5. *Considering alternative choices*: "Have you thought about an area? Where are your friends? Have you ever been to . . . . ? Did you talk with your daughter about moving near her? What rent are you considering? Have you ever known anyone in public housing?

Did you ever consider buying? Why don't we talk it over with our housing specialists?"

6. *Finding the "this-is-it" place*: "Let's go out together and look at something to give you an idea. Why don't you look around in the area you mentioned and let me know? Why don't you look around this neighborhood first? Maybe you need to talk some more about your feelings about leaving Castle Square. It's clear you can't decide when things at home are all upside down. Let me explain the moving claim for you."

7. *Cementing relationships in the new neighborhood*: The relocation worker as "handrail"—"Have you found a new store? There's a place I know like Lincoln House. Have you met the community worker, Mr. X? The new visiting nurse will soon be by. I called your new worker and he'll be over next week."

The traditional social work concepts of study, diagnosis, treatment, and evaluation are fundamental to this entire process. It has been the experience of this relocation program that better use is made of diagnostic skills in the very first steps of relocation, rather than in attempts to diagnose various problems in a caseload prior to the relocation of families.

Relocation Worker as Primary Helper

It is difficult for families undergoing the crisis of relocation to accept a helping relationship from more than one person. Therefore, during this period the relocation worker remained the primary helper. When the family needs the help of other community services, the relocation worker can help the family accept the needed service; for example, a health problem that is interfering with relocation may call for a referral to the Visiting Nurse Association. Prior to and during the move, services other than those of the relocation worker remain ancillary, but nevertheless important. If the relocation experience has been a positive one for families, they will more readily accept help from other community agencies in their new neighborhood.

Case Vignettes

The C family was comprised of a young couple in their late twenties, an 8-year-old girl, and a mother-in-law. Mrs. C, an attractive young woman, came to the site office to ask for referrals to apartments renting at no more than $35 or $40 per month. The relocation worker arranged to show her three such apartments which met minimum standards. While walking through the apartments, Mrs. C began to talk about her family and finally admitted she had to have such a low rent because she and her husband had separated eight months ago. Neither she nor her husband, apparently, was interested in another partner and they did not believe in divorce. Mr. C joined in the apartment hunting and higher rent referrals were requested. With the relocation worker's help, the family was reunited and referred to a $70 per month apartment in a nice neighborhood, close to a school, and convenient to the places of employment of Mr. and Mrs. C. During the follow-up visit, when the relocation worker was invited to supper, the family proudly displayed their apartment and talked about saving to buy their own home.

Mr. and Mrs. S required fewer than ten contacts with the relocation worker. The main problem was the availability of housing to fit their limited finances. After they had contracted for a sub-standard apartment, the relocation worker was able to find them a standard apartment of the same type and size in the same block. They needed considerable support to break their dependence on the slum landlord, but were moved into the standard apartment and expressed much appreciation over having their own bathtub.

Mr. L not only had the problem of low income, but was also alcoholic and suffering from malnutrition. By dint of voluminous correspondence, the relocation worker verified Mr. L's date of birth, and he was enabled to qualify for social security, a veteran's pension, and public welfare. The worker also arranged hospitalization for M. L, and later placement in a nursing home. He is now permanently relocated into a standard lodging house.

The people described were relocated in standard housing with a consequent improvement in their living conditions. In some cases, their income has increased, thus making it possible for them to live with dignity and self-respect. In each case the main technique was supportive casework plus a continuing attempt to make community services available to them. Community resources played a key part in the success of the program. The relocation program sought to provide a channel to existing community agencies through which the Castle Square population could be better served. This objective remained a part of the relocation program throughout its course, although the agencies rendering direct assistance in money and kind continued to be the services most often used.

An Opportunity to Offer Public Health Nursing Services

In their initial contacts, relocation workers became aware of the numerous unattended health problems of Castle Square families. In many instances, these problems interfered with relocation and the services of a public health nurse or medical social worker were needed to facilitate health referrals. The relocation contract of USES did not provide for such services. The Board of Managers of the Visiting Nurse Association, recognizing the need for their agency's services, created a new position of Special Supervisor for Relocation, and assumed the total expense of her employment. The special supervisor began her work in the site office in January 1963, and individual conferences between each worker and the special supervisor were arranged to review the health needs in each caseload. Relocation workers began to make referrals of families in which a public health nurse could be useful, and close teamwork ensued. Extensive use was made of "reaching-out" techniques with the families in the area. The supervisor's intimate knowledge of health resources became very valuable in planning and making referrals to appropriate health agencies.

Extent of Health Problems

In the spring of 1963 a Boston Redevelopment Authority staff member analyzed the remaining caseload of 574 families to determine the incidence of medical problems that related directly to relocation. Four types of medical problems were considered: (1) health problems affecting rehousing, such as the need to live near a medical facility or the inability of family members to climb stairs; (2) health problems affecting or preventing employment, particularly where income was low or erratic; (3) health problems involving continuing expense which markedly affected the family's ability to pay for housing; and (4) health problems, both physical and emotional, which prevented a move until treated.

At that time, 23 per cent (132) of the remaining 574 families were designated as having one or more of these four types of medical

253

problems. Health problems affecting employment and special housing needs accounted for 75 per cent (99) of the families needing
health services. In many cases the difficult problem of low income
was compounded by illness. This prevented increased earnings and
in turn made the housing requirements more restrictive in terms of
rent-paying ability, limited choice of geographical area, and scarcity
of apartments on lower floors or in elevator buildings. Health problems were most prevalent in the elderly single-person families.

Role of the VNA Supervisor

When the VNA special supervisor was assigned to the site office,
only 15 families currently were being visited by a public health
nurse. Within the first six weeks, 27 additional families were referred by the relocation workers and were visited. As of November
1, 1963, 110 households had become an active part of the VNA
caseload in Castle Square. During this same period only 15 cases
were referred by hospitals and doctors who made up the normal
sources of the VNA referrals. There were 60 families that did not
require direct service in Castle Square, but were referred for follow-up by the VNA, because of the ready access of the VNA relocation supervisor in the site office.

Referrals to medical services, such as clinics, hospitals, private
physicians, were made by the VNA supervisor. Some people were
already receiving medical attention, and they responded by keeping
clinic appointments with more regularity and by following doctors'
orders more completely. Others who had not had a medical appraisal for an extended period of time did follow through and receive medical care. Still others did not accept the public health
nurses' suggestions. VNA follow-up visits in new neighborhoods
were often helpful to the families in obtaining needed co-operation
and continuation of medical services. A few residents moved away
from Boston, and they were referred to their local public health
nursing agency. Offering the services of the VNA of Boston during
this crisis has brought these services to many people who would
probably otherwise not have been referred to that agency. A major
reason for the success of the VNA participation in the Castle Square
Relocation program was the good relationship between the public
health nurse and the relocation team.

Case Vignettes

Mrs. P, age 53, with three children at home on AFDC, had consistently refused referrals by the relocation worker for medical evaluation. Immediately upon contact by the VNA relocation supervisor, Mrs. P accepted referral for her needed health services and those of her children. Within a short time she was also able to make realistic relocation plans.

Mr. F, age 70, had a stroke while still living in Castle Square. He made a good recovery with the exception of speech impairment and weakness in one arm. Several months after discharge from a nursing home, he moved to a standard comfortable apartment. Before moving, he was helped by the visiting nurse to secure medical supervision and physical therapy at the out-patient department of a nearby hospital. Since moving, he has joined a group activity, something that he previously would never have considered. He is even wearing his dentures which greatly improve his speech. The visiting nurse had many contacts with Mr. F, and he once remarked that his relocation worker and the visiting nurse were his only two friends.

Mr. C, age 61, had a drinking problem and became quite upset in the process of relocation, which resulted in a binge and the loss of his job which he had held for 15 years. Mrs. C was working part-time in a garment factory. She had recently lost the sight of one eye, and was extremely fearful of going blind and losing her job. She became hysterical during the crisis of relocation. The relocation staff, with the appropriate casework skills, helped handle this family's crisis. Mr. C was reinstated in his job, and Mrs. C was helped to purchase glasses which had been prescribed some time ago. The family was helped to move to a standard apartment close to the oldest son's family. Most of the work with the family was done prior to the VNA relocation supervisor's assignment to the site office. She was able to facilitate follow-up visits by the VNA nurse in the district where the family moved, which resulted in Mrs. C's attendance at the municipal eye clinic and also helped to continue contact with this family.

Role of the Public Welfare Worker

One of the major problems faced by the relocation program was the extremely low incomes of many Castle Square families. There was a high number of elderly householders and unemployed heads of household in Castle Square. In 165 households one or more members of the family received public assistance, and another 60 individual roomers also received it. The total welfare caseload ranged from 180 to 225 active cases during most of the relocation period. The extent of public welfare involvement in Castle Square necessitated the close co-operation of both agencies.

After an initial orientation conference for relocation workers with representatives of the public welfare department, one relocation worker was assigned to serve as liaison to facilitate communications with the social worker assigned by the welfare department. Successful relocation depends a great deal upon the concrete financial help that can be given. Thus, the welfare worker became a necessary and valued member of the relocation team.

The welfare worker has a responsibility for the general welfare of the families receiving public assistance, and this responsibility extends beyond the crisis of relocation. Therefore, the welfare worker and relocation worker jointly planned relocation with the family. In the relocation worker's efforts to raise the level of living through the relocation crisis, a re-examination of welfare budgets was usually indicated. The welfare worker's understanding and support of the goals of the relocation program often resulted in crucial aid to a family which consequently made a good move possible.

Numerous emergency situations came to the relocation worker's attention. Buildings were often flooded from freezing pipes. Sometimes they were vandalized or set afire by derelicts, despite efforts of property maintenance staff and the police. When the special needs arising from these emergencies were brought to the welfare worker's attention, help was given. Conversely, the welfare worker's regular visits to families uncovered situations that needed the attention of the relocation worker. If, as in two cases, families were "burned out," the combined resources of the welfare and relocation workers were utilized to assist the family.

The belongings of some families who had lived in the area for a long time were tattered, worn, and sometimes vermin-infested. As the family moved to a "nice place" it was often good relocation practice to help the family replace necessary household furnishings. In such instances, for welfare recipients, the welfare worker approved purchase of some major items of furniture. The relocation worker utilized other resources to provide smaller items such as bed linen, towels, or clothing.

Assistance came from the welfare worker when families relocated, on their own initiative, to sub-standard housing and were later willing to accept a referral to standard housing. Since the families collected moving expenses from the Boston Redevelopment Authority for their first move, they were ineligible for moving expenses for the second move. In the two instances when this happened, the welfare department paid expenses for the second move. This was a significant contribution to a sound relocation plan for these families.

Relocation workers discovered a number of families or individuals who were living in dire circumstances and receiving no assistance from public welfare. In many cases, these residents (especially the older ones) felt a reluctance about asking for assistance. The relocation worker helped them to understand that society had provided welfare assistance in order for people to have the basic essentials for living, if they were unable to be gainfully employed. Some families came to accept welfare, while others preferred to continue their meager existence. The welfare worker was particularly helpful in determining eligibility and providing emergency relief while applications were being processed. The relocation program also had an impact on the movement of families off public welfare rolls.*

Rental Problems

With an average $31 a month contract rent in Castle Square, the residents were usually faced with a higher rent as they moved to standard housing. The welfare worker's commitment to sound relocation sometimes placed him in conflict with limits imposed by the state's welfare budget allowances. In numerous instances, families receiving public assistance found, on their own or with the relocation worker's assistance, reasonably low-rent standard apartments that were in excess of the rent allowed. Such families had to refuse these housing referrals except when special consideration was granted.

Although there are some variances, public welfare recipients in the Boston area usually pay $47 a month for rent, heat, and utilities

---

* Recently a Boston newspaper portrayed Boston's urban renewal program as a primary cause of increasing welfare costs in the city, particularly in cases of Aid to Families with Dependent Children. As the relocation caseload is examined for its impact on increasing the welfare caseload, a quite different picture emerges. The purported increase in number of welfare cases was exaggerated; and the article did not discuss the families who had obtained employment or had obtained other resources and were consequently removed from welfare rolls.

if the family lives in public housing. To find standard private housing within the cost schedules prescribed by the state is often difficult, if not impossible. This makes it likely that families will move into sub-standard housing. Concentration of families receiving welfare in public housing creates another community problem.

When standard housing was not available at the rents allowed within welfare budget requirements, local welfare officials could sometimes grant increases upon individual case presentation. The welfare department had much more flexibility in cases of Aid to Families with Dependent Children than in other categories of assistance.

The underemployed families were another group with severe economic problems that interfered with relocation. The welfare department was not allowed to render regular assistance to fully employed persons regardless of the level of income. A number of families had a weekly take-home pay ranging from $20 to $40. Especially where children were involved, the family, if no member were employed, could receive more from welfare payments than from gainful employment. These underemployed families were particularly difficult to relocate into standard housing since they had difficulty meeting the minimum public housing rent of $40, even if they were eligible. Unless the relocation worker could help improve the family job situation, the families generally moved into sub-standard housing. The welfare department needs to be flexible in encouraging employment, and yet prevent extreme hardship caused by marginal incomes.

Although communication between the welfare department and the relocation office was excellent, problems sometimes developed for families after they moved. Welfare budget changes made to facilitate a good move were sometimes reviewed by the welfare worker in the new neighborhood and reductions were made. Often these reductions were a matter of interpretation. Intervention by higher level welfare supervisors could usually correct inequities.

Case Vignettes

Mrs. M and Mr. A, ages 63 and 66, brother and sister, lived separately in most deprived conditions, attempting to live on payments from social security and a small insurance policy. The relocation worker helped them make application successfully for public welfare and public housing. They wanted to move together to public housing. When they accepted a vacancy in a South Boston housing project, the relocation worker and the welfare worker mobilized enough funds to buy all reconditioned furniture when they moved.

Mr. M, age 66, lived in the basement of a building without income and was extremely dirty, unhealthy, and alcoholic. After many contacts by the relocation worker, Mr. M was able to accept help. Extensive efforts were extended to establish his birthdate in order that he might receive social security payments. Upon verification of the date, he received over $600 in back payments. The relocation worker had to intervene in behalf of Mr. M when the bank refused him deposit privilege because of his appearance. Mr. M was able to clean up, purchase much needed clothing, and decrease his drinking. When he later became eligible for Old Age Assistance, he was relocated to a standard lodging house. One would not now recognize Mr. M for the man he was before contact by the relocation worker and before the assistance of public welfare.

Summary

In this program, relocation workers with social work training successfully demonstrated their effectiveness in family relocation. They brought the sort of understanding and skills that were needed to help residents with their difficult relocation problems.

The major focus of relocation workers should be upon the rehousing crisis and the problems created by this crisis for each family involved. Some meet the crisis with strength and resourcefulness; others meet it with ineffective, self-defeating, coping efforts. A thorough understanding of the neighborhood environment and the dynamics of family interaction is essential for working with families in relocation programs. We found that the relocation workers sometimes had a tendency to think of people only as individuals and overlooked the effects of the family and neighborhood sociocultural environment.

The seven steps in relocation have been outlined. Understanding these steps is basic to effective relocation work with families. The real problems frequently became clear only when the first steps in the actual relocation of the family were taken. Continuing analysis of the situation was necessary to understand clearly which problems interfered most with the family's ability to move.

Displaced families present a threatening array of feelings even to a trained social worker. He often encounters hostility, suspicion, and fear, and these must be handled skillfully. The need for support of the relocation worker as well as supervisory verification of certain housing and financial matters necessitates a practical kind of social work supervision. With even a limited amount of supervision, a high level of performance can be maintained in a difficult case situation throughout the whole family relocation process.

By undertaking the responsibility for family relocation, United South End Settlements inherited the community failures of the past, the inequities of the present, and the challenge of the future. Building a "New Boston" has meant that much of "Old Boston" must be discarded or changed. But both the "Old" and the "New" Boston are its people; the harsh reality of enforced displacement of families brings this truth into sharp focus. Family relocation is one critical phase in the life cycle of a changing community. Social agencies are not often in the position where the job to be done is so specific, the pressure for results so present, and the failures so public.

With its direct concern for people living in the neighborhood, United South End Settlements attempted to carry out this relocation program in a realistic but imaginative way. The goal was to help the persons being relocated use this opportunity to build a better life for themselves. To the degree that we have achieved this goal, we have been successful. But those families whom, for a variety of reasons, we were unable to help, will continue to remind us of the human impact of urban renewal and the need for improved skills in relocation.

22. Round-the-Clock Emergency Psychiatric Services*

Eleanor Clark

SOCIAL WORK AS A PROFESSION will face many vital questions during the next few years. Among these will be how to use our relatively limited resources to provide for the enormous and varied needs of people in our present complex society. No one answer is acceptable to all of us, and any attempt to solve the problem involves some degree of compromise. Do our values allow us, for example, to devote most of our time and energy to exploration of avenues for primary prevention if this means that in so doing we must neglect the treatable problems from which families and clients currently suffer? Can we afford to direct our limited time toward those problems most treatable in the shortest period, and in so doing neglect those persons with more severe damage who require more of us? Yet the latter group, who consist of shattered, dependent, disorganized families, perpetuate the most severe social dysfunction if their problems are uninterrupted. Certain studies indicate that we serve only small segments of the population and that our practices make us inacessible to large groups of people, particularly the lower classes. Are we satisified? Is this what we want? Or are we prepared to experiment with changes in agency procedures and methods of approach which might widen our area of usefulness?

These questions underlie an experiment currently in progress at the Massachusetts General Hospital. We offer a round-the-clock emergency psychiatric service in which the professional team is asked to give comprehensive evaluation and planning to all patients referred to the service.

Massachusetts General is a busy, private, teaching hospital.

* Reprinted from *Social Work Practice, 1963*, papers from the National Conference on Social Welfare, Columbia University Press, New York and London, 1963.

Within recent years the emergency ward has become informally known as the "front door," and its services are available twenty-four hours a day. Although the majority of patients are diagnosed and treated without admission, a small overnight ward adjacent to the emergency room allows for brief admissions when they are needed. The facilities and specialties of the entire hospital are, of course, on call as required.

The charter, granted 150 years ago, includes in it the cornerstone of present-day philosophy. The visionary men of good will who conceived the idea of the hospital also planned the hospital as a refuge for the sick or injured social outcast or the stranger to the port of Boston. They had in mind specifically destitute merchant seamen and prostitutes. With all of modern medicine's scientific advance, the original commitment remains and is especially in evidence in the emergency ward's activities.[1] As a result, patients come with every degree and type of illness, with or without the ability to pay. Some are brought by relatives, some by agencies, doctors, or the police. On the average, 140 patients are seen during any given twenty-four-hour period in this one facility of the hospital. When the emergency service was instituted it dealt primarily with life-or-death situations. In recent years this is no longer true. Approximately 50 per cent of the admissions are now social or psychiatric problems rather than medical.

For the past thirty years a psychiatrist has been available. In 1952 the psychiatrist saw about 300 patients a year in the emergency ward. This number has risen annually; currently we are seeing that many each month. As psychiatric clinics, private psychiatrists, and social agencies have become more appointment-oriented and waiting lists have grown, people in distress have learned of this open door and use it freely. As the number of patients mounted, additional psychiatric personnel was made available, and by 1959 a psychiatric social worker was on call. This step was taken because patients presented so many social problems intertwined with their psychiatric disorders that the psychiatrist was hard pressed to provide adequate care. For instance, if a young mother required hospitalization the social worker's assistance in planning for the children was often needed.

Since 1956 several studies have been carried out to examine the

[1] Ellsworth Neuman, "The Nature of a Teaching Hospital," unpublished Lowell Lecture, Boston, April, 1963.

results of psychiatric work done in the emergency ward. A study of the patient population by Drs. Chafetz and Mendelson [2] examined the management of one group of patients, those with drinking problems. They learned that although 1,000 individuals with drinking problems were seen annually, and told of the possibility of obtaining treatment in the hospital's alcohol clinic, practically none followed through. Furthermore, a one-month sample of 100 psychiatric patients indicated that of 28 who were referred to the psychiatric clinic, only two kept appointments. Obviously, we had failed to provide an open door, and we began to examine our philosophy, our procedures, and the patient population.

Planning the Research Project

In 1959, with the assistance of an NIMH grant (Mental Health Project Grant O M—218, from the National Institute of Mental Health), we undertook a research project based on the hypothesis that persons with severe alcoholic problems could be motivated for treatment if continuity of care were provided by a staff prepared to meet whatever needs the patient presented. Our procedure involved accepting the first twenty patients arriving in the emergency ward each month who were designated by the senior medical resident as alcoholic. Every alternate patient was designated a control patient and received the routine care of the hospital. Those in the research group were met by a psychiatrist and social worker who instituted a study of the patient and his family and simultaneously offered help with the problems he presented, whether these were requests for help with medical care, food, shelter, employment, marital difficulties, or severe psychiatric disorders. The same team worked with the patient throughout the contact. It is evident that such an approach must rely heavily on the particular skills of the social worker. His duties included participation in the diagnostic appraisal of the patient and his environment; provision of concrete services, with a knowledge and use of community resources; and continuing casework treatment of the patient or his relatives.

Over a two-year period, 150 research patients were seen and an equal number of controls. Our results were substantial.[3] In sum-

[2] J. H. Mendelson and M. E. Chafetz, "Alcoholism as an Emergency Ward Problem," *Quarterly Journal of Studies on Alcohol*, Vol. XX (1959), pp. 270–275.
[3] M. E. Chafetz *et al.*, "Establishing Treatment Relations with Alcoholics," *Journal of Nervous and Mental Disease*, Vol. CXXXIV (1962), pp. 395–409.

mary, 65 per cent of the experimental group versus 5 per cent of the control group made initial contact with the clinic; 58 per cent of the experimental group versus one per cent of the control group continued for five or more appointments in the clinic.

In 1962 the NIMH granted further support to allow us a period for a demonstration project to study the effectiveness of this model when applied not only to alcoholics, but also to the over-all psychiatric population of the emergency ward. In this project we now have social workers on duty from 9 A.M. to 9 P.M., including week ends, and psychiatrists on call twenty-four hours a day. We attempt to provide for all patients referred to psychiatry the continuing, comprehensive care that seemed so effective with alcoholic patients.

Developing a Supportive Relationship

Patients who present themselves to the emergency ward with an immediate problem, such as physical symptoms masking emotional problems, symptoms of alcoholism, and acute social or psychiatric situations, are understood to be indirectly seeking help with an underlying emotional problem. Although the presenting request to the medical team of the emergency ward may concern the physical symptom, the need for a place to stay the night, or pressure to hospitalize an acting-out adolescent, we view the situation as an opportunity to establish a relationship between this patient and a professional worker. This relationship is, in turn, used to assist the troubled person to gain a different perspective of his problem. As trust develops, the anxiety, guilt, or anger mobilized by the internal struggle diminishes, and acceptance of the emotional aspect of the current problem can be gained. Once the patient can trust sufficiently to reveal some of his underlying difficulties, the diagnostic process can begin. The nature of the service requires that we arrive at as full an understanding as possible in a very limited amount of time. We draw first on the patient's own story, which can often be supplemented by relatives or by data collected from collateral sources. In the formulation of a diagnosis and treatment plan our frame of reference is the psychoanalytic understanding of the individual. In what way have the adaptive mechanisms of the ego failed in the present crisis? What has caused the more pathological unconscious forces to overwhelm the healthier aspects of the personality?

264

Simultaneously, we must ask ourselves about the increased pressures from the patient's environment. What critical changes within the family or community structure are responsible for the supportive or destructive elements now converging on the individual's internal resources? Our task in studying the patient is at least threefold. We are presented with a patient, for example, who may view his problem as one of physical pain though the findings of organic studies are entirely negative. First we are challenged to help this individual to accept a different concept of the problem that is threatening his defensive structure. If the pain has arisen as a defense against great anxiety, the patient will inevitably meet the physician's opinion, that it is not organic in nature, with some degree of resistance. He may display anger, fear, and a wish to flee, or perhaps guilt, self-depreciation, and depression. The task of the psychiatric team then lies in understanding these feelings, offering an immediately supportive relationship out of which trust can develop and the threat may diminish. We may need to relinquish our previously held convictions about the degree of motivation or the capacity to look at oneself that is necessary if the patient is to be able to use help. The patient is often unable to communicate verbally in our particular, somewhat sophisticated, manner, and it is up to us to understand his system of communication. One person may need to be fed to learn that we care; another may only respond to careful confrontation with his problem. It is the responsibility of the professional to find a way of offering help that is acceptable to the patient who is not motivated in the traditional sense.

Let me cite a pertinent example.

William, a 28-year-old man, was referred by a surgeon. The patient had been brought to the emergency ward after being hit by a car. He was not badly injured, but the surgeon became concerned when he learned that the man had been involved in a series of "accidents." The patient saw no need to consult a psychiatrist, yet he talked of flirting with death. Once, driving 80 miles an hour, he had been severely injured when his car hit a telephone pole. Despite a spinal fusion resulting from this accident, he skied and swam, and once ventured so far into the harbor that Coast Guard rescue was necessary. Shortly before the earlier admission his marriage had ended in divorce. On the day of admission he had been excluded by his former wife from his older son's birthday party.

In long and careful interviews on the occasion of this admis-

265

sion, the patient was confronted with the self-destructive meaning of his behavior. Although he first stated that he had tried to avoid the car, he finally admitted that he had stepped in front of it. He then showed openly the depressive feelings his behavior had been expressing, and accepted the plan for help offered by the service.

If we have been successful in helping the patient to feel less fearful, to acknowledge the role of his underlying emotional discomfort, and to trust us to help, our first step has been accomplished. We are then faced with the task of understanding the nature of the internal conflict that underlies the symptoms and the predicament in which the patient finds himself. Our first tool is the interview with the patient.

Most crucial in the patient's social environment are his relationships with key persons in his life. Often the meaningful clues, particularly in the diagnostic appraisal of very disturbed persons or young people, are gained from interviews with those closest to them. The involvement of crucial persons at this moment of crisis also has other, often far-reaching implications. Frequently, the future course of treatment hinges in large part upon the modification of attitudes of these key persons. If a spouse requires hospitalization, for example, this step may be the crucial one in the process of alienation, and the period of hospitalization may result in the final breakdown of the family. On the other hand, careful handling at this moment may reduce alien feelings and mobilize the family's capacity to help the patient through this difficult experience without undue disruption. Occasionally, this step can be the beginning of a shift in attitudes leading to greater understanding and healthier relationships in the future.

Finally, the diagnostic appraisal includes the use of information gained from the community, the police, local doctors, hospitals, law-enforcement facilities, and other agencies. The information gathered through these contacts often adds greatly to our understanding of, and capacity to plan for, the patient. More important, however, is the help these persons can offer in providing the support needed to carry out future planning for the patient. Often the involvement of a local doctor, probation officer, or school guidance counselor at this point encourages his continued interest. When they are given guidelines that grow out of their joint appraisal of the patient, and are assured of the future help and interest of the

266

psychiatric team, these professionals frequently continue with less anxiety, more interest, and greater understanding of the meaning of their supportive role.

Meeting Individual Needs

Obviously, the diagnostic period is both the beginning of treatment and a demonstration of its potential helpfulness. We try to offer a program of treatment that is individually tailored to meet the patients' differing needs; for we are clearly aware that only a few of these patients would benefit from the usual type of psychoanalytically oriented psychotherapy or casework.

Our philosophy requires, however, that if a patient does not fit our usual mode of working we will not fall back on a prognosis of "untreatable," "unmotivated," or "hopeless" until we have attempted other approaches—old and new—which may restore previous functioning, or achieve improved adjustment for this particular person.

Many of the patients referred to us suffer from severe psychiatric disorders and complicated social problems. We come to know them in the late stages of their illness and, as is true of many severe chronic physical illnesses, a cure is not possible. Nevertheless, we try to restore that degree of functioning which has been recently lost, or to establish the best level of functioning that is realistically within the patients' capabilities. I believe this point of view is important both for the patient and for the professional person who works with the severely ill. If unrealistic expectations are held but not reached, the patient endures fresh disappointments, and the narcissistic blow to the therapist may create disappointment and anger which endanger the therapeutic relationship.

Let me describe the work on behalf of a severely disabled patient for whom our professional responsibility was essentially that of management.

A 66-year-old Greek woman was brought to us by her daughter, a psychologist. Mrs. L had returned from a visit to Greece five days before. In Greece she felt limp, empty, and depressed. The family history revealed that a previous trip to Greece in 1955 had been occasioned by her sister's suicide, and while she was there her husband had died. The current depression seemed to be a reactivation of these earlier losses. On her visit to the emergency ward she presented a classical picture of depression, including self-accusatory delusions. Her son and daughter would

267

not under any circumstances consider hospitalization although the doctors thought it to be the safest course. Interviews were made more difficult because Mrs. L spoke little English.

Although we were concerned about the severity of the depression, without hospitalization, medication was prescribed, and Mrs. L was placed in a carefully supervised and supportive nursing home within walking distance of her daughter's crowded apartment. Interviews were arranged with the doctor and social worker, and the nursing home was assured that we would help at any time—night or day if need be. Four weeks after she went to the nursing home Mrs. L's depression lifted and she returned to her son's home. She has subsequently had monthly checkups, and her symptoms remain in remission. Careful, intensive efforts with Mrs. L, her son, and her daughter helped this elderly patient through a critical period. Her defenses restored, she now maintains her pre-illness equilibrium.

The "Supper Club"

Another group of severely damaged patients can be helped by continuous treatment if it is fashioned to meet their individual needs. An interesting experiment in group endeavor was tried with a group of homeless, unemployed, isolated men who had long-term histories of chronic alcoholism. They were alienated from their families and usually described as "skid-row" alcoholics. Although initially responsive to the research team's reaching-out efforts, they withdrew and became frightened when a continuing one-to-one relationship was pursued. Their gross early deprivation had left them with a primitive view of life and its interpersonal relationships. We recognized that their needs for human contact and ego-building experiences could not be met by the usual community contacts and decided to structure a specially geared substitute family and small community around them.

We labeled this group therapy endeavor the "supper club." A psychiatrist and a social worker invited the patients to join in a discussion to determine whether a group was wanted and, better yet, what type of group might be indicated. A few wanted to discuss problems, some wanted a more social get-together, and some wanted what they called a "cocktail," or mixture of the two.

They wisely chose the mixture. It was agreed that once a week the doctor and the social worker would meet with the patients in the hospital cafeteria for dinner. Following this, over coffee and dessert, the group would discuss their problems. At first each patient related to the leaders as a child to his parents or a student to his teachers. One would ask a question about physical damage caused by alcohol, and then another would raise a completely unrelated question. Their feelings were not expressed in these discussions. However, intense feelings arose over the kind of doughnuts or cookies to be served, a reflection of their oral pre-occupations. The secretary who provided "oral supplies" was instructed weekly about where to find the best doughnuts. She followed the instructions to the letter. Meanwhile, the leaders gave a great deal of themselves and entered into discussions actively. In addition, if a patient needed medication or hospitalization the leaders took care of it. They held individual interviews between sessions as required. At his first visit each member gave a carefully limited two-minute autobiography and drinking history. The leaders did the same.

Gradually, the patients began to plan the menu, and eventually they took over all the planning. A hospital dietitian became a central figure—giving but limiting. If a last-minute switch was requested, the doughnuts had to be returned and cookies and ice cream substituted. The content of discussion also began to shift. The patients began to reveal their feelings and shared ideas and experiences with each other, not only with the leader. This carried over into friendships on the outside. When a patient demanded hospitalization and the doctor hesitated, the other members waited in the hospital lobby, on a sit-down strike, until the patient was settled. The leaders were consistent in never allowing one member to be made the scapegoat and in avoiding long exploratory confessions. Discussions, in which emotionally charged material was safely displaced, were encouraged.

Gradually, the group members gained pride and self-esteem. One found a civil service job and encouraged the others to try. Now, almost three years later, all of the ten regular members are working, they have addresses, some are reunited with their families, whom they brought to the last Christmas party. The group welcomes new members and visitors, for they feel that they have something to teach about recovery from alcoholism.

Intervention at an Early Stage of Illness

These cases are typical of many that we see, and are examples of patients who need care but are in the late stages of an illness. It is also our aim to reach patients in the early stages of emotional illness and those in danger of becoming ill because of threatening life situations. Our immediate accessibility helps to achieve this goal. The following case is illustrative of this group:

Mrs. S, a 42-year-old mother of seven children, came to the emergency ward one evening a year ago because of a badly cut

269

hand. The surgeon, while stitching her hand, noted her intoxication, inquired a bit into her difficulties, and referred her to our unit.

On arrival Mrs. S was guilty, self-depreciative, and, initially, uninterested in our help. She had come to the hospital about her hand. Gradually, however, she related that her husband had died four months before. She had sold their farm in the West and moved to Boston, hoping that her family would help her in her grief and with the care of her children. She had an aged arthritic mother, two alcoholic siblings, and a brother who ran a liquor store. The family offered alcohol as a solution for her depression, and she accepted it. She had not had a problem with drinking prior to her husband's death.

During these few months she had let the apartment go to pieces, the children were not cared for adequately, and her drinking had been constantly on the increase. The doctor and worker who evaluated the situation decided to offer Mrs. S casework treatment. We hoped to help her to find a healthier way of handling her grief and, simultaneously, to assist with the heavy practical problems of caring for the seven children, the youngest of whom was only two.

Mrs. S was given an appointment to return to see the caseworker but did not keep it. The worker made a home visit and found Mrs. S sober and, though still ashamed of her behavior, beginning to make efforts to pull herself together. She accepted further appointments and began regular casework interviews. To our knowledge she has done no further drinking since the visit to the emergency ward. The casework focus has been on bolstering her self-esteem. The worker has been active in taking care of her through arranging medical appointments and assisting her to deal with the many reality problems in her life. She was helped to manage her finances, and some of the children were sent to summer camps. Interviews have been carefully geared to handle her grief and to help her to function at her best possible level so that her depression will not unduly disrupt the children's development. For the most part, her feelings about her loss have been dealt with indirectly although she has cried and openly grieved to some extent. Much of the work is focused on the oldest boy, now 16, whom his mother identifies with his father. He has acted out some of his discomfort and is also receiving help.

If the referring surgeon had been less perceptive we would probably not have seen this woman until the effects of her drinking and the unresolved grief had intruded enough into the care of the children that the school or an agency like the Society for Prevention of Cruelty to Children would have had to take action. This family has done quite well in a relatively short time. Had many more months gone by, Mrs. S's illness would have been more difficult to treat and the effects on the children more destructive.

Opportunities for Wider Service

Among the 3,000 patients whom we see annually every degree of pathology is represented, and our approach to patients is flexible. Our goal is to attain earlier referral of patients who are in danger of emotional or social breakdown. Our unrestricted intake, immediate availability, and work with the other units of the emergency ward are directed toward this end. As the other services know us better, they begin to look more carefully at the symptoms that mask underlying emotional problems and are more likely to refer patients in the early stages of emotional illness. We are also convinced that, if we are prepared as professional people to introduce greater flexibility of admission procedures and methods of treatment, we can help patients of varied degrees of illness, including those who are quite severely ill. To do so involves giving up many of the traditionally held systems of procedure, measures of treatability, and goals of treatment. Our program offers obvious avenues for tertiary prevention and opens the door for secondary prevention. As we discover more about the early stages of illness and contributory factors we may offer some findings that will be helpful in efforts toward primary prevention. For instance, we are currently planning research aimed at the study and treatment of children of alcoholic parents. We are particularly interested in the effect of a parent's alcoholism on the growth processes of the child. We hope to make some progress in understanding the pathological effects and the development of resistance factors. We also plan a program aimed at the early recognition and treatment of adolescents who show tendencies toward the pathological use of alcohol. Specifically, we shall study teen-agers following their first arrests for an alcohol-related offense.

Many intake practices operate to select those patients whose intelligence, ego strengths, and motivation fit them for psychoanalytically oriented psychotherapy or casework. In our society people need psychological help for problems of all kinds, of greater and less severity. Many different types of treatment are needed, including the more traditional ones, which are effective for a large group of patients. Experimentation and flexibility are required also to benefit the groups who are unable to profit from conventional methods of treatment. Many such experiments are going on in work with delinquents, with multiproblem families, and in new forms of mental hospital treatment. These are purely experimental, however, and many of our present administrative procedures and interviewing methods tend to exclude large groups of people.

In Boston, this past year, the United Community Services undertook a mental health survey.[4] Certain features of this survey replicate others undertaken in various parts of the country. Most interesting here are the findings from a sample of ninety-five cases studied to determine whether or not referral was successful. Two-thirds were unsuccessfully referred from the United Community Services to an appropriate agency of the community. When the high rate of unsuccessful referrals was analyzed, certain features were particularly striking.

Of twelve people with child- or adolescent-centered problems, only one was successfully referred. Of eighteen requests for help with separation or divorce, only two followed through their referrals. Only one of eight illegitimately pregnant girls was successfully referred. Similar to the findings elsewhere across the country, lower-class status correlated highly with unsuccessful referral. It is clear that middle- and upper-class values, educational opportunities, and incomes lead individuals more readily to identify disturbance as an intrapsychic problem. Persons with fewer opportunities are less informed, more of their energies are consumed with "making ends meet," and they are more apt to approach an agency with a definite request. Yet agency practices often require these needful people to travel to the center of a complicated city in order to apply for help. They may have to endure a waiting period, or may be given a definite appointment which they are not able to keep because of the many crises likely to occur in their lives. If they do not keep the appointment and they have no telephone, it is unlikely that the agency will take the initiative to resume the contact. If the client is able to meet all the requirements, all too often he is expected to enter into an examination of the intrapsychic problems that have led him into his predicament before anything is done about the symptomatic request. If the client feels sufficiently misunderstood after all these maneuvers, he is unlikely to return.

---

[4] William Ryan, unpublished report of the Boston Mental Health Survey, 1962.

As agency executives and caseworkers we must examine our policies and beliefs and offer more service at the point of contact with patients, if we want to extend our help. We must be quicker to understand that the presenting problem is the client's felt need and must be taken seriously. We need also to reach below his surface expression of need to find ways to help with the underlying emotional problems. We must make greater use of reaching-out techniques. Specialization of agency function also deserves scrutiny. It is difficult enough for a reasonably well-trained social worker to find the proper resource in a community. How can we expect an anxiety-ridden client to do so?

To draw an analogy from medicine: Each of us endorses wholeheartedly the attempts of the scientists to discover the causes of malignant growths, yet we are not critical of medicine's efforts to treat or to relieve the severe pain of the person suffering from cancer. We also know that if malignancy can be discovered early enough, the disease can be cured or arrested, and this secondary prevention can often offer the patient a full life expectancy. Malignancy, however, has a sneaky way of developing and often does not show itself until the disease process is well advanced.

The medical personnel who give relief from the pain of terminal cancer, who work in early cancer detection, or who strive to find the causes of the disease are all greatly esteemed. Is there not a parallel in social work today? It seems to me that we have a manifold obligation. Our responsibility is to manage, rehabilitate, and treat the ill person with our eye always on his capacity to function in a social world; to intervene as early as possible to prevent the full development of emotional disease and social malfunction, and to examine the social, cultural, family, and intrapsychic processes that are causing emotional and social malfunctioning. Our conceptual framework must embrace all points of view. It is my own philosophy that basic to all our efforts is the understanding of the internal economy of unconscious drives, prohibitions, and defenses with full and increasing appreciation of the adaptive mechanisms of the ego.

23. The Social Worker in a Suicide Prevention Center[*]

S. M. Heilig
and *David J. Klugman*

DR. KARL A. MENNINGER, in the foreword to *Clues to Suicide*, states:

> Once every minute, or even more often, someone in the United States either kills himself or tries to kill himself with conscious intent. Sixty or seventy times every day these attempts succeed. In many instances, they could have been prevented by some of the rest of us.[1]

The U.S. Public Health Service reports that suicide is among the first ten causes of adult deaths in the United States. In certain age groups (15 to 25 years) and in certain occupational groups (college students, peacetime soldiers), it is the third cause of death. It claims victims without discrimination from all social classes and from all socioeconomic levels. Further, a suicide often affects the mental health of many survivors and, thus, the community itself. The magnitude and seriousness of this public health problem led to the foundation, in 1958, of the Suicide Prevention Center (SPC) in Los Angeles—dedicated to saving lives and to furthering basic understanding about the phenomenon of suicide.

The SPC was established within the purview of a five-year (1958–1963) U.S. Public Health Service (National Institute of Mental Health) project grant. In 1962 a seven-year project grant from the U.S. Public Health Service was awarded, and this is the present source of support. The grants have been administered through the University of Southern California.

[*] Reprinted from *Social Work Practice, 1963*, papers from the National Conference on Social Welfare, Columbia University Press, New York and London, 1963.
[1] E. S. Shneidman and N. L. Farberow (eds.), *Clues to Suicide*, McGraw-Hill Book Co., New York, 1957, p. vii.

274

The project is directed by Edwin S. Shneidman and Norman L. Farberow, Co-directors, and Robert E. Litman, M.D., Psychiatrist-Director. The staff consists of two half-time psychiatrists, two psychologists, five psychiatric social workers, one biometrician, one research associate, and consultants in psychiatric nursing and sociology.

Activities and Goals

The activities of the Suicide Prevention Center are directed toward five primary goals:

1. The first and foremost goal is to save lives. Specifically, this means that the SPC is set up to make psychiatric, psychological, and social work evaluations and then to treat or make referrals for persons who are thought to be potentially suicidal. The goal is, not only to save a life at a particular time, but also and equally important, to institute those therapeutic procedures that will reduce the possibility of an individual's attempting or committing suicide at some time in the future.

2. The second goal is to demonstrate that such a center can play a vital role in the health and welfare activities of a large metropolitan community and can establish itself so that the community will eventually wish to maintain and support it; further, that such a center may serve as a pilot project or model for other communities to adapt to their own specific needs.

3. The SPC's purpose is to be a training and educational center in suicide prevention for professional and interested lay personnel, selected from various disciplines and from different geographical areas.

4. By virtue of its very existence, the SPC endeavors to reduce and modify long-standing taboos concerning the study of suicide.

5. It is the SPC's aim to collect and collate heretofore unavailable data regarding suicidal phenomena and to employ this scientific information to develop and test hypotheses concerning suicide. It is hoped that this procedure will lead to more accurate prediction and, ultimately, to lower suicide rates.

The SPC is organized into three closely interrelated sections: (1) the clinical section; (2) training and education; and (3) research and theory. The clinical section functions as an around-the-clock community emergency psychiatric clinic, using the skills of psychiatrists, psychologists, and social workers to study, evaluate, treat, and, often, to refer to community resources persons who are suicidal. Service here is foremost, and this means being easily and readily available to suicidal persons. There are no eligibility requirements, such as age, sex, race, religion, or income, and no geographical restrictions, no fees, and no waiting list. In short, there is nothing to prevent a staff member from seeing immediately anyone who is suicidal and who needs help, at any hour of day or night.

The training and educational section plans, co-ordinates, and carries on a number of programs. A formal training program has been established for university students in psychiatry, psychology, psychiatric social work, and public health psychiatric nursing. Professional graduates and practitioners may receive postdoctoral appointments for periods of one year or less and obtain clinical training and supervision from members of the SPC staff. Arrangements may be made to consult with and train responsible persons who represent other communities that wish to open suicide prevention agencies. Lastly, workshops, lectures, and public presentations to both professional and lay groups, locally and nationally, are held.

The research and theory section attempts to investigate why individuals take their lives, so that suicidal behavior can be more effectively prevented in the future. The data for the numerous ongoing studies within the section consist of suicide notes, case histories, psychological test data, social work data, information from the coroner's office, and sociological data from the community. In addition to its ongoing research functions, there was established in 1962, within the structure of the SPC, the Center for the Scientific Study of Suicide (CSSS). The CSSS is the theoretical research arm of the SPC. Each year it will invite a few outstanding scholars to the CSSS to study as Fellows and to apply their particular wisdom to the manifold problems of suicide prevention.

The goals of the SPC encompass integration with other mental health agencies in the community. With this in mind, liaison has been established with the Los Angeles city and county health departments, the Los Angeles city and county police departments, the Welfare Planning Council, and the California State Department of Mental Hygiene.

276

Our unique relationship with the Los Angeles County Coroner's Office—and especially with the Chief Medical Examiner-Coroner, Theodore J. Curphey, M.D.—merits special mention. SPC staff members have been deputized by the coroner and have been asked to investigate equivocal cases, that is, where the mode of death—whether accident or suicide—is in question. Using procedures that we call the "psychological autopsy" we have learned a great deal about suicide and have at the same time given a valuable service to the chief medical examiner and to the community at large.

We have also been in contact with over fifty health and welfare agencies in Los Angeles County which have telephoned for consultation, or to which we have made direct referrals for extended treatment of some of our patients. At first, social agencies were reluctant to accept even the lowest risk suicidal individuals. However, with referrals that included an evaluation of suicidal potential and the knowledge that consultation by telephone would be readily available, a greater willingness to accept our referrals was noted. Also, the demonstration of our social work staff's work with suicidal persons encouraged social workers in other agencies to do the same. Further, through professional papers, books, and institutes for social work agencies in Los Angeles, the SPC shared its knowledge about suicide and pointed the way for these agencies to use this knowledge in professional contacts with suicidal individuals.

The Role of the Social Worker

At the SPC the social worker performs in a new and exciting role. He works in an area involving life and death and must be receptive to new ideas, for suicide prevention has heretofore been little studied or understood. There is opportunity for creative work in learning more about the nature of suicidal crises and how to deal with them, and he also has the obligation to teach others what he learns.

The social worker accepts an unusually heavy responsibility in working with suicidal crises in that he carries primary responsibility for his cases. He must be able independently to make important clinical judgments, to assess suicidal potential, and to recommend proper action. It is not unusual for him to recommend

277

hospitalization or family separation, and he must be secure enough to trust his own judgment and be able to act quickly in a crisis.

The worker is frequently consulted by members of the other helping professions. These consultations are regarded as just as important as direct requests for help from patients, and their proper handling can be just as effective in lifesaving. Some professionals tend to minimize suicide risk, and this can be especially dangerous; others tend to exaggerate it and need perspective and even reassurance. The role of the consultant is to help his colleagues understand the potential suicide's communication, realistically assess suicide risk, and take appropriate action with the patient.

Most of our casework begins on the telephone. This is a very important instrument in our work, and we use it extensively. We have learned that communication is crucial in prevention of suicide; the telephone provides the lifeline. When communication is indirect or when it breaks down, suicide danger increases.

It is important to understand that people in suicidal crises do call for help. Indeed, we interpret their communications as a "cry for help." Suicidal people are ambivalent about suicide: they wish to die, and they want to be helped. Understanding of this basic fact permits the first step in prevention.

The case of Mrs. A is illustrative:

Mrs. A, age 26, telephoned. She said she had just taken twelve sleeping pills but did not know why. While giving names and phone numbers of her husband, friends, and neighbors, Mrs. A's voice became weak and slurred, and soon she seemed to pass out while on the telephone. The worker notified the police, and emergency medical aid was rushed to her. During the very act of a suicide attempt, Mrs. A demonstrated her ambivalence about death by calling for help.

Our technique for handling calls from a patient is to listen, permitting him to tell his story in his own way, carefully noting pertinent information, particularly the specific request being made. We note names and phone numbers of persons mentioned. If sufficient information is not volunteered, we ask specific questions in a direct, straightforward manner. We need to know identifying data, the current situation, available resources, some aspects of the patient's present psychological status, and his thoughts about suicide.

278

We have learned that our willingness openly to discuss a patient's suicidal thoughts and plans alleviates his anxiety. He is himself frightened by his impulses and is relieved to find someone who is not afraid to discuss this with him and who is ready to help. It is incorrect to think that talking about suicide with a patient may hasten the act. Many professional people avoid talking about suicide when it is indirectly communicated to them for fear of precipitating an attempt. This is a mistake that often leaves both the worker and the patient troubled and anxious.

About 50 per cent of the calls to the Center are from patients. The remainder are from family or friends, physicians, therapists, police, social workers, and other professionals. These calls are usually to ask if someone about whom they are concerned is seriously suicidal and what should be done. Our job on the telephone is to sustain the line of communication, obtain information, evaluate the suicide risk, and recommend a plan of action. In addition, we want to know the nature and the current status of the relationship between the caller and the patient. Family and friends are advised to contact the patient, discuss their concerns about suicide with him, and ask him to call us. They are told that it is important to communicate to the patient that the "cry for help" was heard and help is being obtained.

With professional persons, our aim is to offer a consultation which will help the professional assume responsibility for working with the situation. If he is not in a position to do so, we ask him to have the patient call us.

We always report back to the original caller after we have made contact with the patient. We encourage callers to stay active in the situation and remain available as a resource. We advise that suicide be openly discussed with all persons involved. Suicide is cloaked in secrecy, which often prevents people from responding to suicidal communications and helping promptly. Yet secrecy and delay can cost a life:

> Mrs. B called about her 55-year-old mother. The mother became acutely depressed one month before, talked of being a burden, wished she would die, and made frequent visits to her physician with generalized complaints, including inability to sleep. One week earlier, she changed her will. Mrs. B had been concerned about her mother since the depression began but failed to call the SPC. She was especially concerned on the day of her call,

279

because she had not had a telephone call from her mother, as was customary. She was advised to contact the mother and have her telephone for an appointment. Unfortunately, when she went to her mother's home, it was too late. Her mother had taken an overdose of barbiturates and was dead.

Assessing the Seriousness of the Crisis

Calls to the SPC represent varying degrees of danger, and our task is to get information in order to assess the actual degree. We have learned to do this on the telephone, as well as in the office, based on the following criteria developed from our research and experience:

1. It has long been known that men commit suicide three times more often than women and are therefore higher risks. However, women *attempt* suicide three times more frequently than men, and older persons of both sexes are more serious in their attempt than younger people.

2. If a person has a specific method planned, and the means to carry it through, the situation is more serious than if he merely talks in general terms about various methods.

3. We determine the onset of the crisis. If there has been an acute onset in relation to a specific stress, that usually represents a higher, more immediate danger than would a condition of recurring crises with several prior events similar to the one being described. Although the person who chronically threatens suicide has a poor long-range prognosis, the situation for the immediate crisis is less dangerous. From those earlier experiences he will have devised techniques for getting himself through the crisis.

4. Resources are critical in the suicidal crisis. If a person has family, friends, job, or therapist, the danger is reduced. We have found that people do not commit suicide while they are in communication with other persons.

5. Diagnostic impressions are important. If the patient has exhausted his energy, if his thinking and judgment are badly confused, if he is agitated or psychotic, a higher risk is indicated. Also, certain groups have high rates of suicide: alcoholics, addicts, homosexuals, schizophrenics, and those with impulsive characters.

We do not become alarmed about any single criterion with the possible exception of access to a lethal method. Rather, we look at the total picture. If a person rates high on most of the above items,

280

he is a high risk. If he rates low on most items, that is not so alarming. Mr. M's case illustrates our evaluation process.

The mother-in-law telephoned about a 34-year-old married man, with two children, who drove over a 250-foot cliff one week before. Miraculously, he escaped serious injury and had only cracked ribs. Although he said it was an accident, he had been making veiled remarks about suicide before and after the incident. He had recently lost his business and felt unable to return to a job he had successfully held before. He was described as withdrawn. He felt that people were watching him, he was not eating or sleeping, and had lost fifteen pounds in one month. His wife and mother-in-law were eager to obtain help for him and were his best resources. Here was a young man reacting to a specific stress, with an acute personality change, who had made a lethal attempt. We assessed it as serious on the telephone, and all three were asked to come into the SPC office.

About three out of four suicidal persons who telephone us do not need to be seen in the SPC office. This is because many of the calls either are not about suicide risk *per se,* or are clearly of low lethal potential. We assess the situation and concentrate our efforts on the potentially more serious cases. We are aware, however, that those patients whom we do not see are in search of some kind of help, which we provide on the telephone. Once we are assured that the suicidal risk is low, we help them to focus on the problem that precipitated the call, because we know that suicidal behavior indicates serious psychosocial disturbance. These are usually marital problems, financial problems, job loss, mental and physical illness—problems that are familiar to community agencies and clinics. We refer the patient to appropriate resources and encourage him to continue his search for help. We maintain telephone contact by asking the patient to telephone us at planned intervals, thus offering support until he is started in treatment.

We see the more serious cases in the office, usually on the day of the call. We ask persons close to the patient to come in with him, and we take a position of moving into the situation rather than away from it. In the office we are able to do a more intensive interview assessment. The aim of this interview is to direct attention to the stress that produced the crisis. Usually, the patient's problems have run together in a hopeless, unmanageable way. We help sort out these problems and try to focus on the most immediate ones, helping the patient to start working on these. We also assure him of

281

our willingness and ability to help. We make recommendations while the patient and those close to him still have the momentum of the crisis to move toward hospitalization, out-patient treatment, or other recommendations that we may make.

Suicidal behavior occurs within the context of stressful interperson relationships. Thus, a most important resource in the treatment of suicidal crises is the patient's family or "significant others." In addition, there is the complication of secrecy and lack of communication. There are many reasons for involving family or the "significant others." First, the lines of communication must be opened, so that everyone knows the extent and nature of the situation and the patient is made aware that people are paying attention to his cry for help. Second, the responsibility for seeing the patient through the crisis must be shared with those available to help him. We have learned not to deprive the patient of his most readily available resources but include them in our treatment. Family and friends can stay with a patient during a bad night. They can petition for commitment, provide transporation, and do many things that no one else can do. The case of Mr. M, described above, illustrates this point:

> The telephone evaluation was confirmed in the office with psychiatric and social work consultation and psychological testing. It was made clear to Mr. M and his family that this was a serious situation. Resources were mobilized to help through the crisis. A former employer agreed to have Mr. M return to a less demanding job, and Mrs. M took employment to help with income. Medication was prescribed for Mr. M's depression. Mrs. M was advised to observe her husband, and if he did not respond favorably and regressed, she was to hospitalize him. Daily contact was maintained by telephone, and there were frequent office appointments. During the following week, when Mr. M regressed, his wife had him hospitalized.

Suicide threats and attempts should be understood as communications to "significant others" in the patient's life. The patient is communicating in this way something he is unable to talk about. He may be trying to say, for example, that he cannot tolerate a marital separation, or that he feels helpless and unable to continue his responsibilities and wants someone else to take over. It is necessary always to involve "significant others" and facilitate more direct communication.

Crises are characterized by disorder, helplessness, and a sense of urgency. They are presented in this way by the patient and it is important that the worker not be overwhelmed by these feelings. We have learned that to listen and help sort out the problems, focusing on those with which the patient can begin to deal, will relieve the feeling of helplessness and disorder.

Many professional people shy away from working with suicidal crises. There are many reasons for this. First, it is difficult to make time for emergencies in already overcrowded schedules. Also, there is heavy responsibility for what is really a life-and-death situation, and this creates anxiety in the worker. There is, too, fear of participating in a catastrophe, but in our experience catastrophes are rare. Some patients present frustrating and pessimistic problems that create inordinate anxiety in the worker. We deal with this by consulting with members of our own staff, using all the knowledge and skill available to deal with these cases and also to share the burden of a difficult case with others.

There are some rewarding aspects to working with crises situations. Crises present an opportunity for preventive action, and it is important to use this opportunity to offer professional assistance and help prevent continued suffering and loss of life. Moreover, crises by their very nature are short-lived, and for the worker there is satisfaction in seeing the successful results of his efforts.

For the past five years, the Suicide Prevention Center has demonstrated the value of its lifesaving activities in the Los Angeles area. At the SPC, the social worker occupies a pivotal role and carries major responsibility for cases involving life and death. He makes important clinical judgments independently and takes responsibility to recommend action. To work with this kind of responsibility may well represent a new and expanded role for the social worker.

24. Preventive Casework: Problems and Implications*

Howard J. Parad

MANY YEARS AGO the vigilant eye of Mary Richmond witnessed the tendency to use "prevention" as an empty catchword which disguised all manner of activities:

> Prevention is another one of those words which, as used in proverb and slogan, has been much abused. Who . . . can ever place "prevention" and "cure" in antithesis to each other again? The two processes interplay at every turn, and cure, in and of itself, is a form of prevention, for we learn how to prevent by honestly trying to cure. In other words, prevention is one of the end results of a series of processes which include research, individual treatment, public education, legislation, and then (by retraced steps) back to the administrative adaptations which make the intent of legislation real again in the individual case.
>
> The interplay of these wholesale and retail processes is an indispensable factor in any social progress which is to be permanent.[1]

The recognition of the interdependence between preventive and treatment activities is obvious in Miss Richmond's perceptive and still cogent remarks. Today the need for a clarification of the nature of this connection is repeatedly emphasized in the vast and growing literature struggling with the definition and implementation of the concept of prevention.[2]

* Reprinted from *The Social Welfare Forum, 1961*, papers from the National Conference on Social Welfare, Columbia University Press, New York, 1961.

[1] *The Long View*, Joanna C. Colcord (ed.) Russell Sage Foundation, New York, 1930, p. 587.

[2] See, for example, Bertram M. Beck, *Prevention and Treatment*, National Association of Social Workers, New York, 1959 (mimeographed); Lydia Rapoport, "The Concept of Prevention in Social Work," *Social Work*, Vol. VI, No. 1 (1961), pp. 3–12, and Milton Wittman, "Preventive Social Work: a Goal for Practice and Education," *ibid.*, pp. 19–28; *Preventive Psychiatry in the Armed Forces: with Some Implications for Civilian Use*, Report No. 47, Group for the Advancement of Psychiatry, New York, 1960; *Symposium on Preventive and Social Psychiatry*, Walter Reed Army Institute of Research, U.S. Government Printing

I shall discuss here some problems and techniques involved in an approach to preventive casework, based on my experience in the community mental health program of the Family Guidance Center of the Harvard School of Public Health. This project, a multidiscipline study of how families cope with commonly encountered stress situations (prematurity, cogenital abnormality, and tuberculosis) included a range of selected cases in which I used a family-oriented preventive casework approach while studying the dynamics of family functioning in crisis situations. I believe the techniques of preventive intervention employed in this project have a wider casework relevance to a variety of other settings.

Briefly, my thesis is threefold:

1. A carefully focused "retail" program of short-term, person-to-person casework intervention with families under stress should be systematically and comprehensively included in our total spectrum of social services to implement and bolster the effectiveness of "wholesale" methods of preventing family breakdown.

2. Such an approach, when located in a range of preventive social work activities, may be appropriately labeled "early secondary prevention" since its preventive component outweighs its remedial aspects.

3. More rational organization of family-oriented social services will enable us to identify, reach, and serve a larger number of families in acute stressful situations with an increasingly effective, planned type of preventive intervention which makes more meaningful use of limited professional resources of time and staff.

Types of Prevention

What, then, is preventive casework? If, as we like to believe, it is compounded more of science than of sloganeering, it is incumbent on us to develop a scientific rationale and technique for its implementation. Recent trends in both social work and social psychiatry reveal a heightened interest in the concept of prevention and increasingly offer us hope for a more precise approach.

Office, Washington, D.C., 1957; Ralph H. Ojemann, (ed.), *Four Basic Aspects of Preventive Psychiatry*, State University of Iowa, Iowa City, 1957; Bradley Buell, "Implications for Social Work Education of a Conception of Prevention," in *Education for Social Work*, Council on Social Work Education, New York, 1960, pp. 139–150; Exie E. Welsch, M.D., *et al.*, "Orthopsychiatry and Prevention," *American Journal of Orthopsychiatry*, Vol. XXVII (1957), pp. 223–255.

While there is considerable disagreement about the conceptual boundaries of prevention, treatment, and control, it is generally agreed that any scientific approach to prevention must pay attention to the condition to be prevented or anticipated, the vulnerability and accessibility of the object to be changed, and an evaluation of whether the preventive effort actually fulfilled its purpose.[3]

As the search for clarity in these areas has become intensified we have turned, sometimes with the hope born of desperation, to the field of public health where a wide spread of preventive activities, palpable and testable, await our inspection. Disillusionment, however, often tends to cast a dark cloud over our sanguine efforts as we encounter difficulties in applying quickly the relatively "hard-science" data of public health to the comparatively "soft-science" data of the mental health and social welfare fields.[*] We are told, for example, that with the isolation of the typhoid bacillus, carriers could be identified, sources of mass infection eliminated, vulnerable populations warned, and specific immunization procedures developed for their protection. But, failing to isolate the "psychococcus" or "sociococcus" which would be functionally equivalent to the typhus bacillus as an etiological agent, we immediately confront the problem of applying this public health model to our own field of activities. Since we are constantly dealing with more complicated systems of multiple causation, we are forced to rely on our practice wisdom. We cannot neatly isolate etiological agents, make easy predictions, and quickly locate and immunize our vulnerable clients.

But with the realization that we must make our own theoretical modifications and practical applications, the theory and methods of prevention in the public health field can be enormously useful.[**] Perhaps of most immediate relevance is Leavell's scheme which specifies a range of preventive activities along a continuum of problem severity with five gradients: (1) health promotion; (2) specific protection; (3) early diagnosis and treatment; (4) disability limitation; and (5) rehabilitation.[4]

[3] Bertram M. Beck, "Can Social Work Prevent Social Problems?" *The Social Welfare Forum, 1960*, Columbia University Press, New York, 1960, p. 183.
[*] Editor's Note: For a discussion of the complex problem of etiology in public health, see Gerald Caplan, *Principles of Preventive Psychiatry*, Basic Books, New York, 1964, pp. 28–30.
[**] Editor's Note: See ch. 10 of the present volume.
[4] Hugh R. Leavell and E. Gurney Clark, *Preventive Medicine for the Doctor in His Community*, McGraw-Hill Book Co., New York, 1958, pp. 21–29.

In this continuum primary preventive activities refer to the promotion of an active state of positive health, which obviously involves promoting optimal life conditions at the pre-onset stage of problem or symptom development.[5] They also, ideally, offer specific types of protection against particular stressful agents. Thus we rely, on the one hand, on generalized institutional forms of primary prevention—such as family life education, better hospitals, schools, and recreational services—and, on the other hand, on specific protective devices—such as homemaker service, which is often a safeguard against separation trauma in children—known through empirical wisdom to prevent or forestall various types of subsidiary stress. While both institutional and protective devices have earned an important place in our preventive efforts, they obviously lack the pinpoint precision of certain types of physical approach in the public health field, of which the Salk vaccine is a notable example.

Secondary prevention, encompassing early diagnosis and prompt treatment, is oriented to the earliest incipient signs of problem onset.[6] Much of our traditional family casework and child welfare activity falls in this category; hence the familiar ring of such phrases as "early diagnosis" and "prompt treatment." We must, however, recognize that secondary prevention covers a rather wide, amorphous territory; thus such nagging questions as how soon is "early" and how quick is "prompt" constantly assail the skeptical investigator. The "wisdom research" of social work, based on years of cumulative experience with a most intimate type of participant observation in the lives of our clients, prompts us to beam our preventive efforts to two types of target which are often confused: (1) the earliest identifiable stages of problem onset (clearly attested by our mounting concern over agency waiting lists); and

[5] Sometimes called "presumptive prevention" in contrast to "absolute prevention." See Welsch *et al., op. cit.,* p. 226.

[6] Beck, *Prevention and Treatment,* p. 16. Of course, to the realistic clinician the line that discriminates between certain types of secondary and tertiary prevention is much fuzzier in practice than in this theoretical construct. However, this differentiation is no mere verbal quibble, for it helps to place in perspective the range of casework services in a given program or area. It clarifies, more than any other scheme thus far advanced, the relative preventive ingredients, although the objects to be measured are constantly in flux and our measuring instruments are still rather crude but developing rapidly through social work research. See Martin Wolins, "Measuring the Effect of Social Work Intervention," *Social Work Research,* Norman A. Polansky (ed.), University of Chicago Press, Chicago, 1960, pp. 247–272.

(2) the early stages of the life cycle (seen, for example, in programs aimed at the preschool or young school child and his family).*

Early secondary prevention may be approached by two basic social routes: (1) voluntary application for help at traditional agencies, such as premarital counseling in a family agency where, for example, one can either prevent an unsound marriage from taking place or foster sound attitudes toward a promising marriage relationship; and (2) case-finding or out-reaching preventive efforts experimentally launched in rapidly increasing numbers in prenatal and well-baby clinics, schools, community mental health programs, group service agencies, and a variety of other settings.[7] "Preventive casework intervention," used here to mean a form of early secondary prevention, may be tactically applied to both routes.

This concept has evolved from a theory of crisis developed chiefly by Lindemann and Caplan [8] as well as from related theories of traumatic neurosis and acute situational disorder on which there is a vast literature.[9] Crisis consists of a hazardous circumstance or stress

---

* Tertiary prevention, at the far end of the continuum, covers both disability limitation and rehabilitation. In a relative sense it may more appropriately be called a control measure; however, like other control measures, it has a preventive element. Activities in this category are usually labeled "intensive treatment" or "rehabilitation"; the aim is to control the spread of disability and, while avoiding further deterioration in social functioning, to strengthen the client to make the best use of his available resources. Much of social casework falls in this category, ranging from long-term treatment of persons diagnosed as severely neurotic, borderline, or psychotic, to the sustained work evident in many projects with persons suffering from character disorders. Though my emphasis is on early case finding and prompt treatment, I have no desire to create invidious distinctions which would make these preventive activities heroic and important while other efforts are made to seem puny or hopeless. In this connection a report from the Joint Commission on Mental Illness and Health has again stressed the importance of intensive treatment of the severely ill person who suffers from repeated episodes of breakdown. ("Digest of Action for Mental Health," Final Report of the Joint Commission on Mental Illness and Health, March 24, 1961.) There is an obvious relationship between the use of time-limited secondary prevention, as a form of intervention, and the shortage of mental health and social welfare manpower resources.

[7] See, for example, Elizabeth P. Rice, "Social Work in Public Health," *Social Work*, Vol. 4, No. 1 (1959), pp. 82–88; Cornelia T. Biddle, "Casework Intervention in a School," *Ego Psychology and Dynamic Casework*, Howard J. Parad (ed.), Family Service Association, New York, 1958, pp. 183–99; Beck, "Can Social Work Prevent Social Problems?"; Alastair Macleod and Phyllis Poland, "The Well-Being Clinic," *Social Work*, Vol. VI, No. 1 (1961), pp. 13–18; also chapters 6 and 11 of the present volume. For a controversial example of the use of epidemiological theory in a projected program see also Jessie Bernard, "Neomarital Programs," in *The Social Welfare Forum, 1958*, Columbia University Press, New York, 1958, pp. 239–255.

[8] Chapters 1, 2, and 4 of the present volume.

[9] See, for example, ch. 9 of the present volume; Dexter M. Bullard (ed.), *Psychoanalysis and Psychotherapy*, Selected Papers of Frieda Fromm-Reichmann, University of Chicago Press, Chicago, 1959, pp. 55–61.

which constitutes a threat for individuals and families because (a) the stress jeopardizes important life goals such as health, security, and affectional ties, and (b) the problems posed cannot be immediately solved by the immediate resources of the ego, thereby generating a high level of uncertainty, anxiety, and tension. Obviously, the entire life cycle is full of potential crisis-producing events—for example, the birth of a baby, illness, death, and various types of role transitions, such as entry into school and change of job. In bare outline, this theory postulates that a person, or a family, is in crisis when his internal equilibrium is off balance and his psychological resources overtaxed, thus making him vulnerable to further breakdown. At the same time, however, the person is often challenged to provide a "novel" solution to his present problem as well as to previous problems reactivated by the current stress. The new solution may therefore involve a new use of one's traditional battery of ego-adaptive techniques. As crises typically reactivate unresolved problems from the near and distant past, they provide a fresh opportunity for dealing with old problems. Most significant for our present purposes is the familiar observation that persons in crisis states are usually more ready for, and amenable to, interventive help if it is offered at the right time and at the right place; that is, during the throes of crisis before rigid defenses and related maladaptive solutions have become consolidated by the ego. Therefore, a minimal interventive force, administered by a skilled person with appropriate supporting social services, can produce a maximum result in a relatively short period of time. This concept of crisis is of key importance in any program of preventive intervention, for each stress reaction is affected by earlier modes of resolving stressful situations and will, in turn, affect subsequent efforts to cope with future life stresses.

What are the main diagnostic criteria for this type of short-term preventive intervention? The basic criterion is that the crisis must be a recently developed one involving a sense of "immediacy and urgency," as compared with more or less chronic states of disequilibrium.[10] The focus, then, is on acute situational reactions characterized by temporary but usually intense emotional disequilibrium states which, if unrelieved, would predictably lead to serious per-

[10] Donald C. Klein and Erich Lindemann, "Preventive Intervention in Individual and Family Crisis," *Prevention of Mental Disorders of Children*, Gerald Caplan (ed.), Basic Books, New York, 1961.

sonality disorder, affecting not only the individuals most immediately involved but also a much larger circle of significant others. Thus this theory and its preventive corollaries have important interpersonal dimensions.

In considering the selection of cases, the analogy between brief preventive intervention and traditional short-term casework becomes immediately obvious.[11] It is, however, admittedly difficult to specify rigid, universally applicable criteria as a multitude of questions immediately emerge. When should brief intervention be the treatment of choice? When is it contraindicated? Is the casework method different in brief intervention? How many brief-service case closings are really unplanned terminations—cases apparently closed because the client's major concern with the precipitating stress and the worker's concern with the underlying problem do not come together in a meaningful relationship? To what extent is the closing of a case in ordinary agency practice attributable to exigencies of time and agency function? Clearly, then, a case may be brief- or long-term by choice or by chance.

Despite this morass of variables the brief-intervention approach is appropriate in a variety of acute crisis situations triggered by a significant external threat, where clinical judgment foretells a pathogenic outcome, provided that the intervention is effectively timed to turn to clinical advantage the family's sense of urgency and distress. We must remember in this connection that since nature abhors a vacuum, people are always finding solutions to problems whether or not we are there to help them and whether the outcomes are good, bad, or indifferent. Fortunately, however, there are many new programs designed to fill this vacuum in a planned, thoughtful way.[12]

[11] Gladys E. Townsend, "Short-Term Casework with Clients under Stress," *Social Casework*, Vol. XXXIV (1953), pp. 392–398; Ruth Chaskel, "Short-Term Counseling: a Major Family Agency Service," *Social Work Journal*, Vol. XXXIV (1953), pp. 20–23.

[12] Elise Fell, "Short-Term Treatment in a Child Guidance Clinic," *Journal of Jewish Communal Service*, Vol. XXXVI (1959), pp. 144–149. In her description of an experimental project designed to offer help with parent-child relationship problems through a series of twelve interviews over a period of approximately three months, Fell relies on assumptions similar to ours in that brief intervention is the treatment of choice in such stress situations as acute traumatic experience, death, illness, and birth of a sibling. Fritz Redl in "Strategy and Techniques of the Life Space Interview," *American Journal of Orthopsychiatry*, Vol. XXIX (1959), pp. 1–18, also refers to the complicated problem of case selection. He points up the difference between a "pseudoscientific technical trick-bag, and a more complex, but infinitely more realistic concept of multiple-item conditioned choice of criteria for the selection of strategy as well as of techniques" (p. 18).

Intervention Techniques

We now turn our attention to the techniques of intervention, which, as in any therapeutic endeavor, operate within the context of a relationship. The relationship develops as specific human needs for support and relief from tension are met by an understanding, clinically competent person. While the methods of preventive intervention are basically similar to those used in long-term treatment, a number of technical features deserve brief mention. In a highly summarized form, these are illustrated in the following case vignette:

In accordance with routine practice, the B family was introduced to the Family Guidance Center caseworker by the public health nurse who, in her previous visits, had considered the B's to be an ordinary, stable family. Mrs. B, the shocked mother of premature twins, and her mild-mannered husband, indicated that within a week or two everything would be normal even though they had not known she would deliver twins until a few days before their birth. Overwhelmed with the care of five young children and concerned about persistent economic difficulties due to her husband's marginal income, her defense of denial was excessively strong. Thus the lack of effective recognition of the responsibilities involved in caring for two babies showed signs of becoming a disabling problem. The result, dramatically visible in a matter of days in the family's disrupted daily functioning, was a phobic-like fear that some terrible harm would befall the second twin, whose birth had not been anticipated. Soon Mrs. B's fears threatened to burst into a full-blown panic concerning the welfare of the entire family. Inability to care for the other children, difficulty in feeding the babies, who seemed colicky, bone-weary fatigue, repeated crying episodes, and short tempers reflected the family's helplessness in coping with the stressful situation. Clearly, this was a family in crisis.

Mrs. B compared her feelings of weakness to her feelings of weakness and helplessness at the time of her mother's death when she was 8, as well as her subsequent anger at her father for remarrying. Her previous traumatic experiences flashed through her mind as if they had happened yesterday. On the anniversary of her father's death she poured out with agonized tears her feelings of guilt about not having attended his funeral. In the family's own words (during the third of twelve visits), they had "reached the crisis peak—either the situation will give or we will break!"

Direct confrontation and acceptance of Mrs. B's anger against the second baby soon dissipated her fears of annihilation. Abreaction of her anxiety and guilt concerning the death of her parents, when linked up with her current feelings of anger and her fears of

291

loss, abandonment, and annihilation, produced further relief of tension. In a joint interview Mr. and Mrs. B were helped to understand the meaning of a younger son's wandering away from home in terms of his feelings of displacement in reaction to the arrival of the twins. The father, accurately perceiving the child's needs, not only respected them as worthy of his attention, but immediately satisfied them by taking him on his lap along with the twins, saying, "I have a big lap; there is room for you, too, Johnnie." Simultaneously, a variety of environmental supports —a calm but not too motherly homemaker, referral for temporary economic aid, intelligent use of nursing care, accompaniment to the well-baby clinic for medical advice on the twins' feeding problem—combined to prevent further development of predictable pathological mechanisms. Follow-up visits of the nurse and social worker indicated continued success in the care of the new babies as well as a marked improvement in the family's day-to-day mental health and social functioning.

As seen in the B family, there must be an attempt to help the client develop conscious awareness of the problem, especially in the absence of a formal request for assistance. The lack of awareness usually springs from deep but disguised anxiety, often assuming the superficial guise of "not knowing" or "not caring." The unhealthy use of denial in the initial reaction to a stress must be handled through the medium of a positive controlled transference. In general, the approach is more active than passive, more outreaching than reflective. Although some regression is inevitable, it is discouraged rather than encouraged so that the transference does not follow the stages of planned regression associated with certain casework adaptations of the psychoanalytic model for insight therapy.

To establish an emotionally meaningful relationship the worker must demonstrate actual or potential helpfulness immediately, preferably within the first interview, by meeting the client's specific needs. These needs usually concern the reduction of guilt and some relief of tension. The initial interview must be therapeutic rather than purely exploratory in an information-seeking sense. In this relationship-building the worker must communicate confidence in the client's ability to deal with the problem. In so doing he implicitly offers the positive contagion of hope as a kind of maturational dynamic to counteract feelings of helplessness and hopelessness generally associated with the first stages of stress impact. Thus, the client receives enough ego support to engage in constructive efforts on his own behalf. Here there is a specific preventive component which applies in a more generalized sense to any casework situation. We are preventing or averting pathogenic phenomena such as undue regression, unhealthy suppression and regression, excessive use of denial, and crippling guilt turned against the self. Although some suppression and some denial are not only necessary but healthy, the worker's clinical knowledge must determine how these defenses are being used, what healthy shifts in defensive adaptation are indicated, and when efforts at bringing about change can be most effectively timed.

In steering the family toward ego-adaptive and away from mal-adaptive responses, the worker uses time-honored focused casework techniques of specific emotional support, clarification, and anticipatory guidance. Over a relatively short period of time, usually about four to twelve weeks, the worker must be able to shift the focus, back and forth, between immediate external stressful exigencies ("precipitating stress") and the key, emotionally relevant issues ("underlying problem") which are, often in a dramatic preconscious breakthrough, reactivated by the crisis situation, and hence once again amenable to resolution. Though there is obviously nothing new about these techniques, they do challenge the worker's skill to articulate them precisely on the spot and on the basis of quick and accurate diagnostic assessments. Then, too, the utmost clinical flexibility is necessary in judiciously combining carefully timed family-oriented home visits, single and group office interviews, and appropriate telephone follow-up calls, if the worker is to be genuinely accessible and if the predicted unhealthy outcome is to be actually averted in accordance with the principles of preventive intervention.

In addition, in many cases, a variety of concrete social resources —homemaker, day care, medical and financial aid—must be reasonably available for the reality support needed to bolster the family in its individual and collective coping and integrative efforts. At certain critical stages, and only for sound diagnostic reasons, it may be important to accompany family members in their use of these resources if their problem-solving behavior is to be constructive rather than defeating. Although expensive in time and involving a great deal of adaptation on the part of the worker (in terms of his willingness to leave the sanctity of his office and enter actively into the client's life), techniques of accompaniment were found to be of tremendous value when used in the service of specific preventive objectives. Finally, whatever the techniques used, a twin goal is common to all preventive casework service: to cushion or reduce the force of the stress impact and at the same time to encourage and support family members in mobilizing and using their ego capacities.

Short-Term Casework

Having outlined an approach to the theory and practice of preventive casework, we now address ourselves to our final question: What place should brief, crisis-oriented preventive casework occupy in our total spectrum of services? We should first recognize our tendency to develop a hierarchy of values, locating brief treatment at the bottom and long-term intensive service at the top, instead of seeing the services as part of a continuum, each important in its own right. This problem is perhaps as old as social casework itself. Almost three decades ago Bertha Reynolds undertook a study of short-contact interviewing because of her conviction that short-term casework had an important but neglected place in our network of social services. Her conclusion has been borne out in the experience of many practitioners: ". . . short-contact interviewing is neither a truncated nor a telescoped experience but is of the same essential quality as the so-called intensive case work." [13] Thus, casework involving a limited number of interviews is still to be regarded in terms of the quality of service rendered rather than of the quantity of time expended.

That we are experiencing an upsurge of interest in the many formulations and preventive adaptations of brief treatment in social casework is evident from even a small sampling of current literature.[14] Especially noteworthy is Levinger's finding that the length of treat-

[13] Bertha Capen Reynolds, "An Experiment in Short-Contact Interviewing," *Smith College Studies in Social Work*, Vol. III (1932). In an earlier paper ("Can Case Closing Be Planned as a Part of Treatment?" *The Family*, Vol. XII; No. 4, [1931]), Miss Reynolds linked the use of brief service in casework with the basic growth philosophy of social work as opposed to mechanistic concepts: ". . . we shall both slip in and slip out of case situations more easily, as far as our own need to feel our own personal participation is concerned, but with more humility and with more power." (p. 142)

[14] See, for example, Anita Gilbert, "An Experiment in Brief Treatment of Parents," *Social Work*, Vol. V, No. 4 (1960), pp. 91–97; Wilma Smyth, "Preventive Aspects of Medical Social Work Consultation in a Rural State," Vol. V, No. 3 (1960), pp. 91–96; also ch. 18 of the present volume.

ment per se is not a reliable indicator of successful outcome.[15] According to a number of studies, the important predictors are the nature and management of the client's anxiety as well as the accessibility of the helping person.[16] For example, the level of improvement noted in a recent experiment with a short course of immediate treatment for parent-child relationship problems compared favorably with the results reported by typical child guidance clinics where the hours spent in purely diagnostic study may equal or exceed the number of hours devoted to actual treatment interviews in the experimental project.[17] Of startling significance, too, is the assertion that it was possible to carry out this program with only a 6 per cent attrition rate as compared with a rate of 59 per cent reported for a comparable group of families who were receiving help in traditionally operated child guidance services.[18] These reports refer to a level of secondary prevention in a child guidance clinic approached by the customary route of voluntary referral by the family or by other professional people. Similarities to the approach which I have described are evident in the prompt establishment of a helping relationship, quick appraisal of key issues, and the immediate mobilization of treatment plans as the essential dynamics in helping to further the ego's coping efforts in dealing with the interplay of inner and outer stresses.

Although there are many different possibilities for the timing of casework intervention, the experiments recently reported from a variety of traditional settings all point up the importance of an *immediate* response to the client's initial need for help. In some programs, treatment is concentrated over a short period of time, while in others, after the initial contact is established, flexible spacing of interviews has been experimentally used with apparent success. Willingness to take the risk of early and direct interpretation (with the proviso that if the interpretation is too threatening, the worker can withdraw) is another prominent feature in these efforts. My aim in mentioning this factor obviously is not to give license to "wild therapy" but rather to encourage us to use the time-honored

---

15 George Levinger, "Continuation in Casework and Other Helping Relationships: a Review of Current Research," *Social Work,* Vol. V, No. 3 (1960), pp. 40–41.

16 *Ibid.,* p. 43.

17 Gilbert, *op. cit.,* p. 91.

18 *Ibid.*

295

clinical casework skills we already possess, and to use them with greater confidence, precision, and professional pride.

Although there is obviously great need for continued experimentation with various types of short-term intervention to further efforts in developing an operational definition of prevention at the secondary—or perhaps, in some instances, primary—level, the place of short-term intervention has already been documented by a number of investigators in a wide variety of settings. Woodward, for example, has emphasized the "need for a broad spectrum of services, including very brief services in connection with critical situations." [19] Ideally, brief treatment should be arrived at as a treatment of choice rather than as a treatment of chance. Moreover, the shortage of treatment resources and the chronically persistent shortage of mental health manpower force us to innovate additional refinements of preventive intervention techniques to make services more widely available—and on a more effective basis to more people. Further research in the meaning of crisis as experienced by the consumers of traditional social casework services—including attempts to develop a typology of family structures, crisis problems, reaction mechanisms, and differential treatment approaches—and the establishment of new experimental programs are imperative social needs which should command the best efforts of caseworkers in collaboration with community planners.

Our literature is already replete with a fantastic number of suggestions for preventive agency programing ranging from the immediately practical to the globally utopian.[20] Probably, in the immediate future, we shall have to settle for middle-range efforts that fall short of utopian models. Increased experimentation with multipurpose agencies, especially those that combine afresh the traditional functions of family and child welfare services, holds rich promise for the future. For example, child welfare experience abounds with cases in which the parental request for substitute care is precipitated by a crisis event that is meaningfully linked with a fundamental unresolved problem of family relationships. In responding to the family's request, the agency should make every effort, when diagnostically in-

[19] Luther E. Woodward, "Increasing Social Work Effectiveness in Meeting Mental Health Needs," *Social Work*, Vol. V, No. 3 (1960), p. 65.

[20] See, for example, Buell, *op. cit.*, also Hayden H. Donahue, M.D., and Granville L. Jones, M.D., "A Mental Illness Control Program: Planning a Continuum of Care as It Relates to Health and Welfare Services," *ibid.*, pp. 157–165.

dicated, to avoid separation trauma. This can be done by helping the family cope with the crisis situation adaptively—by dealing with its underlying problem—along the lines here suggested rather than maladaptively through solving its problems at the expense of the child by extruding him from the family unit. The casework process involved in this effort, though often requiring the support of a variety of concrete services such as homemaker, day care, and financial aid, is clinically identical with that used by the family or child guidance agency in its traditional treatment operations.

The purpose, then, of developing an integrated package of agency services—contractable or expandable to meet local community needs—is to make available an appropriate battery of clinical services and social resources to the troubled family as close as possible to the point of crisis impact, thus preventing incipient family breakdown in specific predictable terms.[21] At the same time, structural and administrative reorganization to facilitate new and more creative alignments of public and private services would deal with a number of evils that now plague our professional souls—such as purely study-oriented intake and the related problem of time-consuming disposition conferences, debilitating interagency communication, and referral and re-referral from one waiting list to another. The controlling question that should guide us in planning new directions in social agency services should be: Are our contemporary organization and distribution of family-oriented social services consistent with socially accountable professional behavior?

Mine is not a plea for superficiality. I am not suggesting that we spread the jam thin. Rather my plea is for more imaginative, socially responsible community planning, involving a fresh look at certain dysfunctional institutionalized agency rituals which easily become endemic to modern forms of social organization. The axiom that there be no diagnosis without treatment,[22] the crucial importance of avoiding administrative delays in intake procedures, stereotyped attitudes against reaching out to crisis-ridden families, promiscuous referral for often unused psychological tests, the tendency to overcentralize certain family services so that they become inaccessible to those who need them most—these and other problems can be

21 Robert H. MacRae, "New Knowledge—Consequences for People," *Social Welfare Forum, 1959*, Columbia University Press, New York, 1959, pp. 7–10.
22 *Social Casework, Generic and Specific*, American Association of Social Workers, New York, 1929, p. 64.

297

profitably scrutinized because of the barriers they create to rendering the kind of service that families in crisis need.

I shall resist the customary temptation to conclude with an exhortation for more research, because the kind of agency climate that would make it possible to render more truly preventive services does *not* require further research. We already know more than "we do." According to Norman Cousins: "We know virtually everything except what to do with what we know. We are being hurt or threatened not by what we don't know but by what we do know that we can't put to good use." [23] The path, then, to truly effective preventive programing points to the application of what we already know from the best of social work practice.

[23] Norman Cousins, "The Human Commonwealth," *Problems and Perspectives*, The Nation's Children, Eli Ginzberg (ed.), Vol. III, Columbia University Press, New York, 1960, p. 219.

Part IV
The Measurement
of Crisis Phenomena

ANY BOOK ON CRISIS BEHAVIOR must include some observations on the research that needs to be done. In the introductory note to Part I, the contribution of exploratory research in opening pathways for constructive inquiry was stressed. But one cannot ignore the pressing need for *rigorous* research to test and refine the propositions of crisis theory. The papers in this section are focused on efforts at making increasingly precise measurements of various aspects of the crisis sequence, including the impact of a stressful event, the perception of that event as a meaningful threat, the response to the stress, and the coping mechanisms related to crisis resolution.

Research concerned with the scientific measurement of crisis phenomena is still in a state of infancy. The opportunity and, indeed, the responsibility confronting the advocates of various models of crisis intervention is to formulate and test typologies of the stress-response-resolution configuration. Ideally these typologies should then promote the development of specific propositions regarding the behavior of individuals and families and other groups in crisis which should, in turn, lead to propositions about interventive strategies to be validated by rigorous experimental designs.

An array of unanswered—and at the moment perhaps unanswerable—questions may be raised. Among them are these: (1) How high a rate of agreement can we expect in assessing "crisis" as compared with "noncrisis" case situations? (2) If there is a crisis state operative in a given situation, how can we identify those individuals and families who will recover on their own or with the help of significant others in their social orbit as compared with those who, in all probability, will be fated for a mentally unhealthy outcome without some sort of focused intervention? In other words, how can we develop reliable criteria to select those who should be the primary targets for our interventive efforts? (3) If clinical and research judgments suggest that these persons have shown improvement in the direction of a mentally healthy adaptation to a crisis situation, can we be certain that the observed improvement is attributable to our intervention rather than to some other source of help, whether planned or fortuitous?

To raise these questions is not to suggest that we should stand idly by until the millennium when definitive research is available and then lay out a master course of action in the light of proven verities. Rather we should assign priority consideration to the incorporation of sophisticated research designs at the outset of new crisis intervention programs. In other words, research should not replace practice but should accompany practice.[1]

Bernard L. Bloom's paper is addressed to the first question raised: How do we differentiate a crisis state from a noncrisis state, that is, from ordinary day-to-day problem-solving behavior? If, as was indicated earlier, the timing of focused intervention is of controlling importance, it then follows that, in Bloom's words, "relevant life events must be unambiguously sortable as either crisis or not crisis." Thus, a precondition for studying the effectiveness of intervention techniques is a clear-cut assessment of the existence of a crisis state.

Everett D. Dyer's paper is focused on the fundamental question posed by Bloom, but his nonprofessional independent judges seem to have much greater success than Bloom's mental health workers in arriving at "crisis scores" or "ratings of the crisis state." Using Hill's recovery-reorganization equilibrium model (see chapter 3), Dyer

[1] An example of such a practice-oriented research approach may be found in the conjugal bereavement project currently projected at the Harvard Laboratory of Community Psychiatry. (See Lenin Baler and Peggy Golde, "Conjugal Bereavement: A Strategic Area of Research in Preventive Psychiatry," in *Working Papers in Community Mental Health*, Vol. 2 1964, No. 1, Harvard School of Public Health, pp. 1–18.) Using an experimental design, the project investigators candidly take the position that the postulates of crisis theory must be regarded, not as axioms, but as hypotheses to be tested in the field. Three specific hypotheses will be tested: (1) that the widowed, in comparison with the married, experience a significantly higher risk of mental disorder and psychosomatic illness; (2) that there is a significant association between mental and physical health outcome and patterns of coping behavior in response to the intrapsychic and external reality tasks imposed by the loss of one's spouse; and (3) that the anticipated greater risk of mental disorder and psychosomatic illness among the widowed can be significantly modified through the use of preventive intervention techniques that are specifically oriented toward modifying coping behavior.

reports a partial replication of LeMasters' study of the crisis of parenthood (see chapter 8). We recall that the accession of a new member of the family is viewed by Hill as a transitional stress that often leads to a crisis situation. Although LeMasters found a higher prevalence of severe crisis reactions than did Dyer, we are cautioned not to make unjustified comparisons between the two samples. Both LeMasters' and Dyer's studies suffer from a common shortcoming: they are retrospective rather than current. We know from experience that the longer the time that elapses between crisis onset and post-crisis equilibrium, the greater the likelihood that the subjects will distort the events of the crisis sequence.* Still, evidence from both studies suggests that the birth of the first child in middle-class urban families is a significant "crisis of accession."

It is important to note that Dyer's methodology differs significantly from LeMasters' because of its apparent greater degree of objectivity. Dyer used independent judges, whereas LeMasters arrived at a crisis rating during the interviews with the couples whom he studied. Also worth mentioning is that future researchers will have to confront the tough problems of establishing the reliability and validity of the measures used, a criticism that Dyer makes of his own study.

Although bereavement phenomena have been rather extensively investigated, scant attention has been paid to the study of children who are confronted with imminent death. James R. Morrissey assesses the types of anxiety reaction to fatal illness in a group of children. His inquiry supports the hypothesis that the type of anxiety reaction is associated with the child's age. It also suggests the importance of therapeutic work with the child as he faces the greatest of all life crises, death.[2]

While the previous papers deal with precipitating events that are often perceived as crisis states, the paper by Jacob I. Hurwitz and his colleagues is oriented to another aspect of the crisis configuration—the coping efforts utilized during the resolution stage. This report describes the development of an instrument for measuring parental mechanisms for coping with the crisis of a court-deter-

---

* Editor's Note: For a different point of view on this problem, see Rhona Rapoport, ch. 5 of the present volume, p. 78.

[2] A recent study by Maurice B. Hamovitch, *The Parent and the Fatally Ill Child*, Duarte, California, 1964, Delmar Publishing Company, Los Angeles, pp. 112–113, of which this investigation is a part, also emphasizes the importance of therapeutic intervention with the parents of these fatally ill children.

mined delinquent act. Although this paper does not focus on treatment processes, there are still important implications for crisis intervention. Obviously, those families who are found to lack appropriate coping patterns are the ones who should receive priority attention.

The precipitating stress study of the Langley Porter Neuropsychiatric Institute of San Francisco has produced a series of investigations on the crisis configuration, one of which is included in this section. Conducted in the context of a psychoanalytic approach to crisis behavior, this inquiry tests the agreement of clinical judges concerning the complex nature of the precipitating stress and the behaviors related to it. Among other findings, this paper reports a high agreement on assessments of precipitating events. It also indicates that research techniques can be devised for the effective use of narrative clinical material to help answer some of the pressing study questions previously mentioned.

25. Definitional Aspects of the Crisis Concept*

Bernard L. Bloom

AMONG PSYCHOLOGICALLY STRESSFUL experiences, those particular events referred to as crises are receiving increasing attention by mental health workers. Interest in the crisis has arisen partly because it is felt that the consequences of the management of such periods of stress often include significant and long-lasting changes in level of adequacy of mental functioning. Many workers who apply public health concepts to the field of mental health believe that good mental health is in large measure the result of a life history of successful crisis resolutions; and, therefore, by providing therapeutic intervention to people while they are in crisis, the incidence of subsequent mental disorder in these persons may be significantly reduced.

Clinical studies of crises precipitated by specific events have appeared in recent years. Bereavement has been studied by Lindemann; [1] reactions to surgery have been studied by Janis; [2] and reactions to the birth of a premature child have been studied by Caplan [3] and by Kaplan and Mason.[4] These studies are related to earlier investigations of combat reactions and responses to natural disasters, although it is only within the past several years that the concept of crisis has been given focal importance.

During the exploratory phase of the investigation of many new concepts, there is a danger that definitions can be too limiting. The boundary between what is included and what is not included in a

---

* Reprinted from the *Journal of Consulting Psychology,* Vol. 27, No. 6 (1963).
[1] See ch. 1 of the present volume.
[2] I. L. Janis, *Psychological Stress,* Wiley & Sons, New York, 1958.
[3] Gerald Caplan, "Patterns of Mental Disorders in Children," *Psychiatry,* Vol. XXIII (1960), pp. 365–374.
[4] See ch. 9 of the present volume.

particular concept might appropriately be kept fluid and deliberately vague so as not to restrict unduly the span of inquiry. Precise definitions of concepts are required, however, as one advances beyond initial exploration toward the testing of hypotheses which have been advanced involving the concepts. This phase appears to have been reached regarding the concept of crisis. Caplan has suggested, for example, that "during the period of upset of a crisis, a person is more susceptible to being influenced by others than at times of relative psychological equilibrium." [5] Referring to this increased susceptibility, Caplan suggests that "from a preventive psychiatric point of view, this is a matter of supreme importance; because by deploying helping services to deal with individuals in crisis, a small amount of effort leads to a maximum amount of lasting response." [6]

Whatever else may be required to test this provocative hypothesis, relevant life events must be unambiguously sortable as either crises or not crises. The success of studies of attempts to intervene and influence the outcome of such life experiences will be partially dependent on the adequacy of this fundamental definition. The present investigation has been designed to explore the nature of agreement with respect to the crisis concept among clinicians, highly skilled in both crisis theory and community mental health practice.

Method

In the normal noncrisis state the existing repertoire of responses available to an individual is adequate to meet and solve problems as they occur. A crisis occurs when an individual finds himself unable to deal effectively with an emerging problem. Crises vary in severity, with mild crises shading into the usual ups and downs of problem-solving behavior which characterize the ordinary functioning of an individual. Review of the relevant literature suggests that the crucial elements in the identification of the crisis state appear to be (a) a stressful precipitating event of which the individual is aware; (b) significant subsequent rapid cognitive and affective disruption unusual for that particular individual; and

[5] Gerald Caplan, *Prevention of Mental Disorders in Children*, Basic Books, New York, 1961, p. 13.
[6] Gerald Caplan, *Manual for Psychiatrists Participating in the Peace Corps Program*, Medical Program Division, Peace Corps, Washington, D.C., 1962, p. 82.

(c) duration of the disruption of at least several days. With regard to these elements a number of questions may be raised concerning the behavior of clinicians in judging the presence or absence of a crisis. Is a reaction sequence viewed as a crisis if there is no awareness of a precipitating event either by the individual himself or by significant persons in his environment? How rapid must behavioral changes be in order to suspect that a crisis is present? Does a person need to have some awareness of inner discomfort or tension in order to be judged to be in crisis? Is a person considered to be in crisis if there are no external manifestations of disequilibrium? Does the rapidity of the resolution of the stressful experience have any bearing on whether the experience is judged to be a crisis?

The test instrument utilized in this investigation consisted of 14 brief case histories (averaging approximately 175 words each). These fictional histories each described a single stressful event in which the central character was named Mr. Jones. Each case history was constructed to appear as realistic as possible, yet each contained information bearing on (a) the awareness or lack of awareness of a precipitating event; (b) the rapidity of the onset of the disruption; (c) presence or absence of internal discomfort; (d) external evidence of behavioral disruption on the part of the presumed victim of the crisis; and (e) rapidity of resolution of the conflict. Starting by dichotomizing each of these five components, 13 of the stories were so constructed that the five variables under study appeared in more or less random conjunction with each other. Thus, for example, Story B was composed in which a known precipitating event was followed by sudden onset of both internal discomfort and external manifestations of disequilibrium following which there was slow resolution of the conflict. Story M was composed in which there was gradual onset of externally visible disorganization, no awareness of internal tension, no known precipitating event, and rapid resolution. The fourteenth story (Story N) involved a known precipitating event followed by no symptoms of any kind, neither internal discomfort nor behavioral disorganization. A group of professionally trained mental health workers served as judges during the construction of these stories, and a story was included in the final test instrument if there was 80 per cent agreement by the judges as to the presence or absence of all five of the components intended to characterize each story. As examples of the fourteen stories, Stories B, M, and N are herewith presented.

Story B

Mr. Jones slammed on the brakes but not in time to avoid hitting the boy who had dashed out in the street in front of his car. Before he could even open the door of the car, he felt nauseated and very frightened. He managed, almost blindly, to reach the front of the car but found himself unable to do anything to assist the moaning teen-ager who was badly cut and bleeding. When help arrived, Mr. Jones was in a dazed condition, unable to talk coherently about the accident but aware that he was tremendously disturbed. Fortunately, the boy's injuries seemed much more severe than they actually were, and he recovered with no permanent injuries. Although Mr. Jones was found not to be legally responsible for the accident—and the boy whom he hit fully admitted that it was not Mr. Jones' fault—it was months before Mr. Jones was able to talk about the accident and drive his car comfortably.

Story M

Mr. Jones' peculiar behavior had begun very gradually. At first he seemed to become forgetful, then simply "off on another planet" most of the time. When Mrs. Jones would try to call it to his attention, she found him completely unaware of his actions. Then one day he just disappeared. There was simply no trace of him for nearly a week, when he was found by a United States Customs officer returning to New York on a flight from Europe. He was arguing with the officer about paying duty on a guitar he had bought in Spain, and he had attracted quite a crowd. He was very belligerent and the officer, suspecting he was not well, called the police—who in turn called an ambulance. In the ambulance Mr. Jones suddenly seemed to realize who and where he was and, after satisfying the medical authorities that he was well, was released. He was home again the next day, virtually back to normal.

Story N

The day after Mrs. Jones was killed in a plane accident, Mr. Jones reported for work on time just as he had done more or less regularly for the past several years. The office staff were rather surprised to see him, particularly since Mrs. Jones' death had been so tragic—and they had been so much in love. The staff remarked to each other how well he was reacting to the tragedy and how no one could ever have guessed that so terrible a thing had happened so recently. Mr. Jones' boss was particularly understanding and tried to induce him to take time off, but Mr. Jones seemed willing to work and was as friendly and relaxed as ever.

306

Weeks later Mr. Jones remarked that his wife's death had been a blow to him, but life had to go on. He said that he had never felt any serious discomfort or any real difficulty in carrying on his normal activities.

Enumeration of the components of the 14 test stories is presented in Table 1. As will be seen, there are considerably more stories in

TABLE 1

ENUMERATION OF THE COMPONENTS OF THE TEST STORIES

Story	Precipitating event		Onset of symptoms		Internal tension		Behavioral disorganization		Resolution of conflict	
	Known	Un-known	Sud-den	Grad-ual	Recog-nized	Not recog-nized	Visi-ble	Not visi-ble	Rapid	Slow
A	X		X		X		X		X	
B	X		X		X		X			X
C	X		X		X			X	X	
D	X		X		X			X		X
E	X		X			X	X		X	
F	X		X			X	X			X
G	X			X	X		X			X
H	X			X	X			X	X	
I	X			X		X	X		X	
J	X			X		X	X			X
K		X	X		X		X			X
L		X		X	X			X	X	
M		X		X		X	X		X	
N	X		None			X		X	Not relevant	

which a precipitating event is present than in which no precipitating event is known. Except for this variable, the stories distribute themselves nearly equally with regard to each of the components under study.

The test instrument was individually administered to eight experts in the field of crisis theory, all members of the staff of the Community Mental Health Program at the Harvard School of Public Health. Each story appeared on a separate sheet followed by the same two questions. The first asked, "On the basis of your understanding of the concept of 'crisis,' did this event constitute a crisis for Mr. Jones?" The judge was asked to check one of the three choices, namely, "yes," "no," or "do not know." The second question was, "In a sentence or two, why did you check this alternative?"

Results

The measure employed to determine the extent to which each event was judged to constitute a crisis was to divide the total number of "yes" judgments by the sum of the "yes" and "no" judgments on each story. This measure treats the "don't know" judgments as qualitatively different from both "yes" and "no," and a separate estimate of uncertainty was made by calculating the proportion of all judgments to each story which were in the "don't know" category. In only 5 of the 14 stories were the crisis judgments unanimous. In the case of the remaining 9 stories, "yes" percentages ranged from 20 to 86. In 4 of the stories, the "yes" percentages were between 40 and 63. "Don't know" per cents ranged from 0 to 50. In only 5 stories were there no "don't know" judgments. The judges were thus clearly not unanimous in their judgments.

In the analysis of the judgments of crisis as a function of the five components under study, the set of 14 stories was repeatedly subdivided so that judgments to all stories containing each particular component could be contrasted with judgments to all stories not containing that same component. Analysis of the relationship of these components to judgments of crisis is presented in Table 2. Of the five variables, the crisis judgment seems related to two. The judgment of crisis is made significantly more often when there is a known precipitating event than when the precipitating event is unknown—and is made significantly more often when there is slow resolution as contrasted with rapid resolution. Judgments of crisis are made with particular difficulty when the precipitating event is unknown. Under this circumstance there is a high level of uncertainty on the part of the judges. With respect to knowledge of the precipitating event, it should be pointed out that the six individuals who made a crisis judgment to Story N are unanimous in considering it a crisis—although in this story no reactions follow the event. Crisis judgments appear to be unrelated to variations in the other three variables.

A rapid resolution was defined as one which took place within

TABLE 2

CRISIS JUDGMENTS AS A FUNCTION OF THE EXPERIMENTAL VARIABLES

Experimental variable		No. of stories	Judgments					
			N	Yes	No	Dk	Yes%	Dk%
Precipitating event	Known	11	88	65	16	7	80	8
	Unknown	3	24	3	11	10	21	42
	Difference						59	34
	S.E. Diff.						11.7	10.5
	C.R.						5.0*	3.2*
Rapidity of onset	Sudden	7	56	36	13	7	73	13
	Gradual	6	48	26	14	8	65	17
	Difference						8	4
	S.E. Diff.						9.8	7.0
	C.R.						ns	ns
Internal tension	Recognized	8	64	36	18	10	67	16
	Not recognized	6	48	32	9	7	78	15
	Difference						11	1
	S.E. Diff.						9.1	6.9
	C.R.						ns	ns
Behavioral disorganization	Visible	9	72	43	18	11	70	15
	Not visible	5	40	25	9	6	74	15
	Difference						4	0
	S.E. Diff.						9.5	7.0
	C.R.						ns	ns
Speed of resolution	Rapid	7	56	27	20	9	57	16
	Slow	6	48	35	7	6	83	13
	Difference						26	3
	S.E. Diff.						9.3	6.9
	C.R.						2.8*	ns

* $p < 0.01$.

a week; a slow resolution was one which required between one and two months. In the case of this variable, episodes in which there is slow resolution are judged significantly more often to be crises than episodes in which the resolution is rapid. In view of the fact that episodes with known precipitating events tend to be judged as crises and episodes with rapid resolution tend not to be judged as crises, it might be anticipated that histories characterized by *both* known precipitating events *and* rapid resolution would be particularly ambiguous to the judges. Five stories share these two attributes, and "yes" per cents to these particular stories range between 57 and 72, indicating extensive disagreement among the judges.

The results of the analysis would seem to indicate that, in practice, a crisis is defined primarily in terms of knowledge of a precipitating event and secondarily in terms of a slow resolution. Known precipitating events are generally judged to lead to crises if (a) there is no reaction or if (b) there is a reaction of any kind and resolution requires a month or more. The judges' comments suggest that situations in which the resolution is rapid are commonly viewed as episodes illustrating appropriate responses to reality situations. Reactions of any kind which appear when there is no known precipitating event are likely to be considered psychiatric disorders rather than crises. Since in practice intervention ordinarily takes place after the identification of some precipitating event which might lead to crisis but before resolution of any resultant stress, the data were reanalyzed in order to determine whether, within the group of 11 episodes in which a precipitating event was known, crisis judgments were related to the nature of subsequent reactions. Crisis judgments in the case of the histories in which there was a known precipitating event and sudden onset were contrasted with crisis judgments in which there was a known precipitating event and gradual onset. Similarly, comparison was made between judgments in instances of known precipitating events and recognized internal tension and judgments in instances of known precipitating events and unrecognized internal tension. The final analysis contrasted crisis judgments in cases of known precipitating events and visible behavioral disorganization with judgments in cases of known precipitating events and no visible behavioral disorganization. In no case was a significant difference found.

Discussion

In order to test the efficacy of intervention at times of crisis, a sample of people in crisis must be identified. Following this identification, one could contrast outcome in a subgroup who had been exposed to intervention procedures with another subgroup who had not been exposed to such procedures. Outcome in both subgroups could be compared with that in a noncrisis group. But whether or not a controlled study of this kind is undertaken, the identification of the crisis subgroup should be sufficiently unambiguous so that it is the *intervention* which is clearly the subject of study. Failure of intervention procedures should not be attributable to misdiagnosis of the crisis state. The single most contributory variable involved in the crisis judgment in the present sample appears to be the existence of a precipitating event.

On this basis, one could simply define the crisis state as inevitably following certain specified events. This is an appealing operational solution to the task of definition, but judges do not maintain that crises inevitably follow certain events. If one does not define crisis solely by the existence of some event in the life of the person, actual practice would dictate that within a group in which some specific event occurs, one should be able to distinguish between those people for whom the event results in a crisis state and those people who seem not to be in crisis as a consequence of the event. The present findings suggest that this kind of discrimination may not now be possible. Until further refinement of the crisis concept is undertaken, assessment of the effectiveness of intervention efforts will be difficult.

26. Parenthood as Crisis: A Re-Study[*]

Everett D. Dyer

OVER THE PAST thirty or more years family sociologists have devoted considerable attention to the study of various kinds of family crises. Many investigators have concerned themselves with crises of extra-family origin, such as war, depression, or unemployment.[1] Others have studied crises whose sources were essentially intrafamily in origin. Crises of this kind could be divided into two subtypes: [2] (1) those due to "dismemberment," or loss of some family member (for example, by divorce, desertion, or death); and (2) those due to "accession," or the addition of an unprepared-for member (for example, re-marriage of widow or widower, return of deserter, or birth of an unprepared-for child). Most of the studies here have dealt mainly with the effects of dismemberment rather than accession.[3]

One of the very few studies devoted entirely to accession was recently made by E. E. LeMasters, who investigated the various effects of the addition of the first child to the family.[4]

[*] Reprinted from *Marriage and Family Living*, Vol. XXV, No. 2 (1963).

[1] See, for example, Robert C. Angell, *The Family Encounters the Depression,* Charles Scribner's Sons, New York, 1936; Ruth Cavan and Katherine Ranck, *The Family and the Depression,* University of Chicago Press, Chicago, 1938; E. L. Koos, *Families in Trouble,* King's Crown Press, New York, 1946; Mirra Komarovsky, *The Unemployed Man and His Family,* Dryden Press, New York, 1940.

[2] Reuben Hill, *Families Under Stress,* Harper and Brothers, New York, 1949, pp. 9–10.

[3] See, for example, Thomas D. Eliot, "Bereavement: Inevitable But Not Insurmountable," *Family, Marriage, and Parenthood,* Howard Becker and Reuben Hill (eds.), Heath and Co., Boston, Second Edition, 1955; Willard Waller, *The Old Love and the New,* Liveright, New York, 1930; William J. Goode, *After Divorce,* The Free Press of Glencoe, 1956. Hill, *op. cit.* Hill's study is one of the few concerned with both dismemberment and accession.

[4] Chapter 8 of the present volume.

Purpose

The research reported on here was prompted by the LeMasters study, and the dearth of studies of intra-family crises of the accession type. Although not a true replication of the LeMasters study, the present one concerns itself with the same basic problems: What effects does the arrival of the first child have upon the family roles and relationships? Is is true, as LeMasters suggests, that the arrival of the first child constitutes a "crisis" or "critical event"? Does the addition of this new member to the family system constitute a structural change which will force a drastic reorganization of statuses, roles, and relationships in order to re-establish an equilibrium in the family system? How does the crisis (if there be such) manifest itself? How may it be related to various social and demographic variables (such as age, number of years married, marriage-preparation courses in school, planned parenthood, etc.)? How does the family cope with the crisis, and go about establishing a new equilibrium?

Patterned along the lines suggested by Hill,[5] and followed by LeMasters in general, the present study seeks to investigate (1) the state or level of the family organization up to the time of the crisis, (2) the impact of the crisis upon the family, and (3) recovery and the subsequent level of family reorganization.

Method

Sample. To seek answers to some of these questions, a group of young first-time parents were given questionnaires. Husbands and wives each had separate questionnaires, administered separately.

In an effort to obtain a homogeneous sample (and one quite similar to that obtained by LeMasters in his study), each couple had to meet the following qualifications: (1) unbroken marriage; (2) urban or suburban residence (all were living in Houston); (3) ages, 35 or under; (4) college education for husband and/or wife; (5) husband's occupation middle class; (6) wife not employed after birth of child; (7) must have had their first child within two years of the time studied.

Applying the above criteria, a final sample of 32 couples was obtained by asking people in the community to supply names of young first-time parents. Each couple was then asked to fill out the

5 Hill, *op. cit.*, ch. 2.

questionnaires. Of those contacted, 74 per cent met the qualifications and agreed to participate in the study (that is, the final 32 couples). It is recognized that this sample has its limitations both as to representativeness of the urban middle class and as to size. The data were obtained from the couples in 1959.

Definition of Crisis. "Crisis" may be defined in various ways. For the purposes at hand, Reuben Hill's definition should suffice. In his study of *Families Under Stress*, Hill defines crisis as "any sharp or decisive change for which old patterns are inadequate. . . . A crisis is a situation in which the usual behavior patterns are found to be unrewarding and new ones are called for immediately." [6]

Method of Measuring Crisis. A Likert-type scale was devised for the purpose of measuring the extent to which the arrival of the first child represented a crisis to each couple. While LeMasters arrived at a "crisis rating" for each couple jointly with the couple during the interview, the writer sought an objective way of identifying and measuring crisis. Items for the scale were drawn from areas of marriage and family life upon which the advent of the first child was felt most likely to have disruptive effects, according to previous studies and professional opinion.[7] Item analysis was employed in selecting those items which would yield an internally consistent scale.[8] The crisis score for each couple was based upon responses

[6] Hill, *op. cit.*, p. 51. The present study is concerned primarily with the exploration of the crisis experience itself, and is not designed to explore the new behavior patterns that are worked out by the family following recovery from the crisis period.

[7] Areas of family life from which the items were drawn: (1) husband-wife division of labor; (2) husband-wife division of authority; (3) husband-wife companionship patterns; (4) family income and finances; (5) home-making and housework; (6) social life and recreational patterns; (7) husband and wife mobility and freedom of action; (8) child care and rearing (i.e., anxieties, difficulties, burdens, etc.); (9) health of husband, wife, and child; and (10) extra-family interests and activities. See LeMasters, *op. cit.*, pp. 111–117; Robert O. Blood, *Marriage*, The Free Press of Glencoe, 1962, pp. 415–25; Robert O. Blood and Donald M. Wolfe, *Husbands and Wives*, The Free Press of Glencoe, 1960, pp. 138–145; Ruth Cavan, *The American Family*, Crowell Co., New York, 1953, pp. 504–517; Evelyn M. Duvall, *Family Development*, Lippincott Co., New York 1957, pp. 187–227; Willard Waller, *The Family*, Dryden Press, New York, 1938, pp. 375–393; Harvey J. Locke, *Predicting Adjustment in Marriage*, Henry Holt and Co., New York, 1951, pp. 158–170.

[8] The discriminative power of each item was calculated, and a final scale of 16 items, each having a discriminative power of 0.50 or higher, was obtained. Of 26 original items, 10 failed to show a discriminative power of 0.50 or higher and were dropped. Each item represented a 5-point continuum with values assigned from 0 to 4, with the largest value indicating the greatest degree of crisis. See William J. Goode and Paul K. Hatt, *Methods in Social Research*, McGraw-Hill, New York, 1952, pp. 274–281.

to the items in this scale. (i.e., the crisis score for the couple was the average of the summed item scored for both husband and wife.)

The scores were then used to indicate the position of the family on a 5-point continuum similar to that employed by LeMasters: (1) no crisis, (2) slight crisis, (3) moderate crisis, (4) extensive crisis, and (5) severe crisis. The score ranges were: (1) no crisis: 0; (2) slight crisis: 1–16; (3) moderate crisis: 17–32; (4) extreme crisis: 33–48; (5) severe crisis: 49–64.

The reliability of the scale was tested by the split-half method.[9] Correlating the odd-even responses yielded a coefficient of .84, which, when corrected by the Spearman-Brown formula, gave a reliability coefficient of .94.   Insofar as reliability can be based upon this single method, the scale would appear to be reliable.

An effort was made to assess the validity of the scale by the "jury opinion" method.[10]   Confirmation of the logical validity of the measure was sought from a jury of six young married couples each having one or more small children.   The sole qualification of these couples as experts lies in their experiences as parents of young children.   All agreed that the scale should yield a valid measure of the extent of crisis experienced by new first-time parents.   It is recognized that this is a relatively limited kind of evidence for validity and that the measure has need to be validated against external criteria.

Findings

The State of the Organization of the Family up to the Time of the Birth of the First Child.   Studies of family crisis have shown that the impact of the crisis will depend not only upon the nature of the crisis event but also upon the state of the organization of the family at the time the crisis occurs, and the resources the family has to draw upon to help meet the crisis event.   Accordingly, a series of questions were asked to determine the strength of the marriage up to the time of the child's arrival.   On the basis of these questions each couple was rated on a four-point scale ranging from "excellent" to "poor."   The 32 couples were distributed as follows: Excellent–40.5 per cent; Good–50 per cent; Fair–9.5 per cent; Poor–none.   This suggests that

[9] Goode and Hatt, *op. cit.,* p. 236.
[10] *Ibid.*, pp. 237–8.   This method seeks a confirmation of the logical or face validity of the scale through the judgment of "experts" in the field where the scale applies.

the state of the marriage and the family organization was average or above for the large majority of these couples, up to the advent of their first child. The couple's family organization score was based upon: (1) a self-rating of the couple's marital adjustment up to the birth of the child; (2) the degree of confidence expressed by the husband and wife in their ability to perform their respective roles as husband and wife; and (3) the couple's evaluation of their economic and financial adequacy. It should be noted that the method used in assessing the state of the family organization has yet to be tested as to reliability and validity.

A comparison of these family organization scores and the crisis scores (to be discussed below) shows a direct correlation between the two. This suggests that those couples whose marriage is stronger and who have more resources to draw on tend to experience less crisis when their first child is born.

Impact of the First Child on the Family. To what extent did the arrival of the first child represent a crisis to these couples? In what ways did the crisis manifest itself?

1. Distribution of Families According to Crisis Scores. As indicated above, each family was given a crisis rating or score. The 32 families were distributed as follows: (1) No crisis–none; (2) Slight crisis–9 per cent; (3) Moderate crisis–38 per cent; (4) Extensive crisis–28 per cent; (5) Severe crisis–25 per cent. By comparison, LeMasters found only 17 per cent of his families in the first categories, and the remaining 83 per cent in the Extensive and Severe crisis categories.

It is recognized that caution must be exercised in making the above comparisons. Although the effort was made to draw a sample from a population defined so that it would be similar to that of Le-Masters, the samples were somewhat different. In the LeMasters study, all of the husbands had graduated from college, and each couple must have had its first child within five years of the date interviewed; while in the present study 59 per cent of the husbands had graduated from college, and each couple must have had its first child within two years of the time interviewed. Other unknown sample differences which might bias the findings could have been present. Also, the "crisis" distribution in the two samples was probably affected by differences in defining and classifying crisis, and by the above-described differences in measuring crisis.

For the present sample, as for that of LeMasters, the evidence tends to support the hypothesis that adding the first child to the urban, middle-class married couple does constitute a crisis event to a considerable degree.

2. How Did the Crisis Manifest Itself?

A. Experiences, problems, and reactions reported *by the new mothers* in adjusting to the first child, starting with items most frequently mentioned: (1) tiredness and exhaustion (87 per cent); (2) loss of sleep, especially during the first 6-8 weeks (87 per cent); (3) feelings of neglecting husband, to some degree (67 per cent); (4) feelings of inadequacy and uncertainty of being able to fill the mother role (58 per cent); (5) inability to keep up with the housework (35 per cent); (6) difficulty in adjusting to being tied down at home; curtailing outside activities and interests (35 per cent). Here are some typical expressions by the mothers: "There is not enough time to be housekeeper, wife, and mother." "I had very little prior realization of the vast amount of time and attention the baby requires." "We were unable to foresee the number and drasticness of the changes in our lives the child would bring." "I'm not able to go out with my husband anymore."

B. Experiences, problems, and reactions reported *by the new fathers* in adjusting to the first child: The fathers repeated many of the above-mentioned reactions of their wives, but felt more strongly about certain things and less so about others. They also added a few items of their own. Following are the items, starting with those most frequently mentioned: (1) loss of sleep, up to six weeks (50 per cent); (2) adjusting to new responsibilities and routines (50 per cent); (3) upset schedules and daily routines (37 per cent), one father ruefully exclaiming, "I expected not too much change in daily routine—Ha!"; (4) ignorance of the great amount of time and work the baby would require; (5) financial worries and adjustments for the majority of the families, involving adjustment to one income with the added expenses of the child, from two incomes before the child came. (Sixty-two per cent of the wives had been employed before having the child.)

Some of the fathers expressed their feelings in these words: "You must get used to subjugating your feelings and desires to those of the child." "Getting used to being tied down was our big problem." "Wife has less time for me."

C. Most Severe Problems: Each husband and wife was asked to indicate which of the problems encountered was considered the most severe. Eighty-seven per cent of the wives admitted to one or more severe problems. Among those mentioned: (1) adjusting to being tied down or being restricted to the home was most frequently indicated; (2) "getting accustomed to being up at all hours"; (3) "inability to keep up with the housework . . . everything piled above my head!"; (4) "the feeling of anti-climax, or let down, after the birth of the child. It is a black feeling while it lasts."

Eighty per cent of the husbands admitted to one or more severe problems. Among those mentioned: (1) "adjusting to one income after my wife quit her job and the baby came"; (2) "adjusting to the new demands of parenthood"; (3) "getting used to the new routines"; (4) "sharing with grandparents and other relatives."

Relationship Between Crisis and Other Social and Demographic Variables. It was hypothesized that some middle-class couples would be better equipped and prepared than others for the advent of the first child, and thus experience a lesser degree of crisis. The rationale was that those couples would probably be better able to meet the demands of parenthood who were better educated, who had studied about and planned for parenthood, who were not too young and had not started their families too quickly after marriage, where the husband and wife were quite close in both age and education, and where the wife had not become too attached to a work role outside the home. It was also felt that those couples whose marital adjustment was very good would likely experience less crisis on becoming new parents. Accordingly, correlations were made between the crisis scores and variables selected on the basis of the above-mentioned considerations. Chi-square tests were used to determine the presence or absence of a significant relationship. (It should be noted that the relative homogeneity of the sample tended to rule out much range on certain variables, such as education and age.)

Significant relationships were found between "crisis" and the following variables: (a) marital adjustment rating of the couple after the birth of the child,[11] those rating their marriage as excellent having experienced significantly less crisis; (b) preparation for marriage courses in high school or college, those taking the courses

[11] The marital adjustment rating for each couple was based upon a self-rating scale similar to that used by Judson Landis, "The Length of Time Required to Achieve Adjustment in Marriage," *American Sociological Review,* Vol. 11 (1946), pp. 666–676. See p. 674. Each husband and wife was asked to rate his marriage on a 5-point scale: very happy, happy, average, unhappy, or very unhappy. The separate ratings of the husband and wife were then combined and averaged to give the marital adjustment rating for the couple.

TABLE 1. CRISIS BY MARITAL ADJUSTMENT, PREPARATION FOR MARRIAGE COURSES, YEARS MARRIED, HUSBAND'S EDUCATION, PLANNED PARENTHOOD, AND AGE OF FIRST CHILD, IN 32 FAMILIES *

	Slight and Moderate	Extensive and Severe
Marital Adjustment		
Excellent	12	3
Good, and Fair	3	14
Preparation for Marriage Courses		
None	4	12
Husband and/or Wife	11	5
Years Married		
Under 3 Years	0	10
3 Years and over	15	7
Husband's Education		
High School and Some College	2	11
College Graduate	13	6
Planned Parenthood		
Followed Plan	14	5
Failed to Follow Plan, and No Plan	1	12
Age of First Child		
Under 6 Months	1	10
6 Months and Over	14	7

* Differences in each of the above analyses are statistically significant at the 0.5 level.

having experienced less crisis; (c) number of years married, those married three years or more having experienced less crisis; (d) education of husband but not wife, couples where the husband was not a college graduate having experienced greater crisis; (e) "planned parenthood," crisis being less among those who had "planned" their parenthood and followed their plan, and greater among those who had no plan or had failed to follow their plan; (f) age of the child, couples whose child was under six months were still experiencing more crisis problems than those whose child was six months or over.

No significant relationships were found between "crisis" and the following variables: (a) employment of the wife before the child arrived; (b) ages of husband or wife; (c) number of years between marriage and birth of the child; (d) husband and wife differences in preparation for parenthood; (e) educational differences between husband and wife; (f) age differences between husband and wife; (g) education of the wife. It may be that higher education for the wife has some dysfunctional aspects relative to her adjustment to her mother role. Her needs and expectations may become so oriented to extra-family values and other roles that it is harder for her to stay home as a new mother. LeMasters found that the mothers with professional work experience suffered extensive or severe crisis in every case.

What Was the Subsequent Level of Family Reorganization? Each couple was given a "recovery and reorganization score" based upon (1) the duration of the crisis problems specified, and (2) the couple's success in solving their problems up to the time of the study. A four-point rating scale was used: (1) excellent recovery and reorganization; (2) good recovery and reorganization; (3) fair recovery and reorganization; (4) poor recovery and reorganization. Neither the reliability nor the validity of this measure has been established; accordingly, not too much weight can be given to the findings based upon its use here. The sample was distributed as follows: (1) excellent recovery and reorganization: 19 per cent; (2) good to fair recovery and reorganization: 65.5 per cent; (3) poor recovery and reorganization: 15.5 per cent.

A large majority (80 per cent) of both husbands and wives admitted that things were not as they expected them to be after the child was born. Forty per cent of the couples indicated they were still experiencing problems at the time the study was made, which was on the average 12 months after the birth of the child. Only 24 per cent of the mothers and 38 per cent of the fathers felt they had largely overcome the "crisis" at the time of the study. Those couples manifesting the greatest crisis were experiencing the most difficulty in recovering, quite understandably.

Discussion and Interpretation. The findings will be discussed as they relate to various questions and hypotheses that have been raised about parenthood as crisis. Some comparisons will be made with LeMasters' findings and interpretations.

1. It has been suggested that many American parents—especially middle-class parents—experience some incompatability between their parental roles and certain other roles.[12] It would seem that, if true, such incompatability would be acutely felt with the arrival of

[12] Arnold W. Green, "The Middle-class Male Child and Neurosis," *American Sociological Review*, Vol. 11 (February 1946), pp. 31–41.

the first child. LeMasters found this to be true in his study. Although the scope of the present study was not sufficient for a thorough testing of this hypothesis, the findings do appear to support it to some degree. Both husbands and wives expressed feelings of loss at being tied down with the baby and thus being less free to do other customary things together. However, although 62 per cent of the wives had been employed before their child was born, only 12 per cent expressed feelings of loss since quitting, and not one wife said she wanted to return to her job!

2. Is there a significant lack of preparation or "training" for parenthood among middle-class couples? And, if so, is this lack related to the crisis?

LeMasters' findings on these questions were in the affirmative. His interpretations: "One can see that these couples were not trained for parenthood, that practically nothing in school, or out of school, got them ready to be fathers and mothers—*husbands* and *wives*, yes, but not *parents*."

In the present study 38 per cent of the mothers and 65 per cent of the fathers admitted to no formal or informal preparation for parenthood. Only 35 per cent of the wives and 12 per cent of the husbands had taken any courses in high school or college involving preparation for parenthood (generally as part of a preparation for marriage course); 25 per cent of the couples had had a Red Cross course, and 50 per cent of the wives and 12 per cent of the husbands mentioned such informal preparation as care of younger brothers and sisters, Girl Scout activities, and "some reading."

While a majority said they had thought they were adequately prepared before their child arrived, still a large majority (80 per cent) admitted that things were not what they had expected after the child was born. In offering advice to other parents-to-be a frequently expressed item was a heart-felt "Be prepared!"

As noted above, a correlation was found between "crisis" and formal courses taken in high school or college, those having had such courses experiencing less crisis. This lends support to LeMasters' contention that more formal education in preparation for parenthood is needed by middle-class parents-to-be.

3. Is the change from the pre-parenthood husband-wife pair relationship to the husband-wife-child triad relationship a difficult adjustment for the middle-class husband and wife to make?

The husband-wife courtship and pre-parenthood marriage relationship has become routinized and satisfying to the couple over the years, and then the intrusion of a third member (non-socialized and all-demanding) calls inevitably for substantial readjustments in the husband-wife interaction patterns. Will the child's claim of priority on the mother make the husband feel he is the third party in the trio, a semi-isolate perhaps, as LeMasters suggests? Or, in some instances, does the wife come to feel that her husband is more interested in the child than in her now?

The present findings supported this hypothesis in some degree. While 37 per cent of the husbands felt their wives never neglected them for the baby, 50 per cent felt she sometimes did, and another 12 per cent said she often did. Recall that among the more frequently mentioned "crisis" problems of the wives were such items as "husband grew tired of being second," and "less time to give to my husband," etc. Only 12 per cent of the wives felt their husbands sometimes neglected them for the child, however.

4. LeMasters suggests "that parenthood (not marriage) marks the final transition to maturity and adult responsibility in our culture. Thus the arrival of the first child forces the young married couples to take the last painful step into the adult world," jarring them out of the honeymoon stage of marriage, as it were.

In the present study 50 per cent of the husbands and 87 per cent of the wives felt that parenthood had indeed been a maturing experience.

Indication of the maturing function of parenthood, and increased awareness of adult responsibilities, may be seen in the comments and advice they offer to other young couples expecting their first child: (1) "Realize your life will be different because of addition of the baby, but it will be a better and more complete life." (2) "If the husband and wife want the child and will share the responsibilities, I think they will be happier, and the child will deepen their love for each other. It is a new but very rewarding experience." There were many other similar expressions. All of the husbands and all but two of the wives said they now felt much better prepared for any subsequent children they might have.

Conclusions

1. The findings tend to support the main hypothesis that the addition of the first child would consitute a crisis event for these middle-

class couples to a considerable degree, forcing each couple to re-organize many of their roles and relationships. A majority of couples experienced extensive or severe crisis.

2. The degree to which the advent of the first child represents a crisis event appears to be related to: (a) the state of the marriage and family organization at the birth of the child; (b) the couple's preparation for marriage and parenthood; (c) the couple's marital adjustment after the birth of the child; and (d) certain social background and situational variables such as the number of years married, "planned parenthood," and the age of the child.

3. The large majority of the couples appear to have made a quite satisfactory recovery from the crisis, although this often followed a difficult period of several months. Eighty-one per cent made "fair to good" or "excellent" on their recovery scores. As would be expected, those couples experiencing the severest crisis were having the hardest time recovering.

4. More study is needed of the characteristics and backgrounds of the families experiencing the greater and the lesser crises. In addition to social and demographic background and situational variables, certain personality variables may be important, not only with respect to the parents, but also the child. Many of us who have been blessed with a "fast-excitable" type of infant who never seems to need much sleep and who demands constant attention, would be willing to wager that our parenthood crisis traumas would have been greatly diminished had we been blessed with a child of the "easy-going-passive" type—the kind with which our friends generally seem to be blessed.

5. The findings in the present study lead the writer to concur with LeMasters that by emphasizing preparation for parenthood, family life educators can probably make an important contribution to young married couples who are contemplating parenthood.

27. Death Anxiety in Children with a Fatal Illness[*]

James R. Morrissey

IN OUR SOCIETY, denial and ritual are employed to distort death as a meaningful fact. Even psychiatrists, with a few noteworthy exceptions,[1] have been reluctant to face and examine the dying patient and the meaning of death. Alexander and Alderstein's coverage of studies regarding death indicates that such inquiries are comparatively rare.[2] In more recent years there appears a greater tendency to examine questions in this area.[3] With respect to children who are dying, the literature is quite barren. Very few studies based on empirical data and reasonable premises have been made.[4]

Lourie notes that little has been written regarding the handling of problems regarding death in children. He cites Lauretta Bender's viewpoint that "the younger child does not see death as permanent

[*] Published originally in the *American Journal of Psychotherapy*, Vol. XVIII No. 4 (1964), and reprinted here with additional formulations.

[1] K. R. Eissler, *The Psychiatrist and the Dying Patient*. International Universities Press, New York, 1955; L. J. Saul, "Reactions of a Man to Natural Death," *Psychoanalytic Quarterly*, Vol. 28 (1959), p. 383; H. Feidel (ed.), *The Meaning of Death*, McGraw-Hill, New York, 1959.

[2] I. E. Alexander and A. M. Alderstein, "Studies in the Psychology of Death." *Perspectives in Personality Research*, Henry P. David and J. C. Brengelmann (eds.), Springer Publishing Co., New York, 1960.

[3] D. Cappon, "The Dying," *Psychiatric Quarterly*, Vol. 33 (1959), p. 466; D. G. Langsley, "Psychology of a Doomed Family," *American Journal of Psychotherapy*, Vol. 15 (1961), p. 531; H. MacLaurin, "In the Hour of Their Going Forth," *Social Casework*, Vol. XL (1959), p. 136.

[4] J. M. Natterson and A. G. Knudson, "Observations Concerning Fear of Death in Fatally Ill Children and Their Mothers," *Psychosomatic Medicine*, Vol. 22 (1960), p. 456.

but as associated with violence and punishment." [5] Bender's observations, however, were of emotionally disturbed children, and are not suitable for comparison with children actually facing imminent death. Solnit and Green's article suggests guides for helping the family of the fatally stricken child. They make an interesting comment: "Because each child has his own fearful concepts about the nature of death, an attempt should be made to individualize the approach to informing him of his sibling's death." [6] While one would not inform a fatally ill child of his diagnosis or prognosis, the stricken child also has his own fearful concepts regarding the nature of death, and may have numerous clues that something strange and terrible is happening to him.

The study of Friedman, et al., which focused on parents of children with neoplastic disease and not the children per se, contains a pertinent observation relative to the children: "Our impression is that some acknowledgment of the illness is often helpful, especially in the older child, in preventing the child from feeling isolated, believing that others are not aware of what he is experiencing, or feeling that his disease is 'too awful' to talk about." [7]

Although there have been several studies on how to help the parents of children with catastrophic illness, the writer is not aware of any programs or studies of direct services for the emotional problems assumed to be associated with the fatally ill child. This writer would like to stress that an awareness of death (that is, a biologic concept), may extend to some younger children, particularly in death-threatening circumstances. A small and limited pilot study of children hospitalized with catastrophic illness suggests that a child's verbalizations and behavior tended to correlate with his prognosis. [8] The research supporting this article also suggests that death anxiety in hospitalized leukemic children is not a rare event. [9]

[5] R. S. Lourie, "The Pediatrician and the Handling of Terminal Illness," *Pediatrics*, Vol. 32 (1963), p. 477.

[6] A. J. Solnit and M. Green, "Psychological Considerations in the Management of Deaths on Pediatric Hospital Services." *Pediatrics*, Vol. 24 (1959) p. 106.

[7] S. B. Friedman, *et al.*, "Behavioral Observations on Parents Anticipating the Death of a Child," *Pediatrics*, Vol. 32 (1963), p. 610.

[8] J. R. Morrissey, "A Note on Interviews with Children Facing Imminent Death," *Social Casework*, Vol. XLIV (1963) p. 343.

[9] J. R. Morrissey, "Children's Adaptation to Fatal Illness." *Social Work*, Vol. 8 (1963) p. 81.

As part of a dissertation study,* an effort was made to ascertain death anxiety in children hospitalized because of leukemia.[10] This paper, based on that study, is concerned with different types of death anxiety in children hospitalized with a fatal illness. It poses the following questions: (1) At what age are children capable of experiencing death anxiety? (2) How is death anxiety expressed and handled by the child? (3) What are the implications for service (management and treatment) when a child is aware of his impending death?

Method and Procedure

The data composing this study are based on a sample of 50 children who were admitted to the pediatric ward of the City of Hope Medical Center, Duarte, California with a diagnosis of leukemia or cancer between February 1960 and April 1962—a period of 27 months. Nine of the 50 children who had cancer were included on the grounds that the emotional problems, pattern of hospitalization, and parent participation are quite similar to those of children with leukemia. Children with non-fatal diagnoses were excluded from the study.

The central aim of the dissertation was to *identify* and *evaluate* the nature and extent of the emotional problems of these children, with a view to providing additional services to the children if warranted. The focus was on the child's over-all adaptation to his illness and hospitalization; anxiety was seen as a focal point in making such an assessment. The study concerned itself not only with anxiety per se, but also the type of anxiety, how the child was handling his anxiety, his defense mechanisms, relationships, use of hospital resources—in short, his general adaptation to a very stressful situation. The following suppositions formulated the guiding framework for the research:

1. Hospitalization of a child is a traumatic experience of varying degree. Anxiety, in excessive degree, is considered a disorganizing and destructive agent for healthy adaptation.

---

* This dissertation is related to a larger research project conducted by Maurice B. Hamovitch, "Parent Participation in a Hospital Pediatrics Program," a demonstration project supported by the National Institute of Mental Health, Grant #OM419.

[10] J. R. Morrissey, "Children's Adaptation to Fatal Illness in a Family Oriented Hospital Program." Unpublished dissertation, School of Social Work, University of Southern California, Los Angeles, June, 1963.

2. Anxiety, of varying types (separation, castration, and death),* is believed to be inherent in the milieu of the hospital.

3. Three primary variables are thought to influence strongly the child's over-all adjustment in this setting: (a) the child's character structure; (b) the child-parent relationship; ** and (c) the actual medical circumstances of the child.

The various types of anxiety were defined as follows: *Separation anxiety:* anxious responses judged to relate to the child's reaction to removal from his familial surroundings, for example, family, peers, neighborhood. *Castration anxiety:* anxious responses connected with medical procedures such as blood transfusions, bone marrow aspirations, and the like. *Death anxiety:* apprehensive responses related to the child's concerns with his existence, his identity, *as he perceives it.*

The sample of 50 children, largely Caucasian, included an equal number of boys and girls. Twenty-nine children (58 per cent) were under 6 at the time of their death, 16 children (32 per cent) were 10 or older, and a few children were between 6 and 9. The majority (62 per cent) resided in California prior to admission to the Medical Center. Religious affiliation appeared representative of the larger universe with respect to Protestant and Catholic faiths, as reflected by the parent's acknowledged religious affiliation. It was estimated that all but two of these children were average or above in intelligence. Twenty-nine (58 per cent) were diagnosed as having acute lymphocytic leukemia. Forty-one children had leukemia, and nine children had other forms of cancer.

The data of the study came from three primary sources: (1) the medical charts, with physicians and nurses the primary authors; (2) data related to the child's family background and parents, the primary informant being the hospital social worker who had frequent contacts with the parents for social service purposes as well as for research purposes concerning another study; and (3) weekly tape-recorded interviews conducted by the author with a variety of staff

---

* Clear and consistent differentiation between separation anxiety and death anxiety is vague; these concepts are closely related, and often equated. Death anxiety is also separation anxiety, the *final* separation; however, it is treated separately for the purposes of this study.

** A primary factor is thought to be the cultural aspects, which are reflected by the child's parents, and thus, treated within the child-parent relationship in this study.

personnel—physicians, nurses (all three shifts), school teacher, and occupational therapist.

The criteria for making an assessment of the presence of anxiety was based on the collective evidence from all sources. The data were then independently rated by four judges (a psychiatrist, a research social worker, a medical social worker, and the author—a psychiatric social worker). The four judges read summaries of the patient's condition plus abstracts of observational data systematically obtained from hospital personnel. Two types of evidence were considered: (a) direct evidence—patient's verbalizations, questions, and comments, for example, "I'm going to die soon"; and (b) indirect evidence—physiologic symptoms, the patient's behavior, and symbolic references.

A child in this situation may have physiologic manifestations of anxiety related to pain, discomfort, or medications. It is recognized that the effects of medication (for example, steroids) can create personality changes and induce physiologic indices of anxiety which may be mistaken for functional indices of anxiety. The observations of this study were concerned with functional anxiety; care was exerted in noting anxious responses when the child was receiving medication or when he was in pain. Also, some children discuss their illness with other children, and this exchange of information regarding their experiences can lead to awareness of their reality situation and breed anxiety.

Four categories were used to obtain judgments relevant to whether a child was aware of his prognosis: Awareness, Suspicion, Nonawareness, and Undetermined. Whether a child displayed separation anxiety, castration anxiety, or death anxiety was rated separately from the item regarding awareness of prognosis.

The method for the study was a systematic collection of data on each consecutive admission or readmission of a patient with leukemia or any other form of cancer. A schedule was used for the weekly interviews with staff members; these interviews were tape-recorded. The primary technique, however, was open-ended research oriented interviews. The study approach was largely statistical, with case study examples to illustrate criteria used and points under discussion.

One of the hypotheses of the research study is pertinent to this paper. According to the hypothesis, the focal point of anxiety in these children was believed to be associated with their ages. The hypothesis has been advanced by others that in children up to the age of five, separation anxiety would be dominant or primary during their hospitalization; children from six to nine would display mostly castration (or mutilation) anxiety; and children over nine would show the greatest anxiety in relation to death itself.[11]

Results and Discussion

It is difficult to delineate the source or type of anxiety, and this problem is more complex in a setting such as this study of children who receive medications which may produce personality changes, who undergo numerous medical procedures which may be painful, who may have severe organic pain, and who are confronted with other factors that may breed anxiety, for example, parental anxiety conveyed to the child. With awareness of these difficulties, an attempt was made to evaluate and make a judgment on the most prominent type of anxiety in these children during their over-all hospitalization. These ratings of death anxiety are bound to be value judgments which are dependent on the adequacy of the definitions employed, the accuracy of the observations, and the validity and depth of the interpretations. (See Tables 1, 2, and 3 on following pages.)

A child may show anxiety in all three areas cited (separation, castration, and death anxiety), but one type might stand out as more prominent. In 42 of the 50 patients, the ratings pertaining to the type of anxiety permitted consensus classification, that is, agreement on the type of anxiety by at least three of the four judges. Table 1 shows that of the 42 patients in whom a prominent type of anxiety was judged, fear of death was rated in 13 cases (31 per cent) as the primary type of anxiety. No direct evidence of death anxiety was observed in younger children where it is obviously more difficult to detect. Some older children who were thought to have been aware or suspicious of their prognosis acted out their anxiety. A number of older girls were noted to have been depressed.

The relatively low frequency of ratings of castration anxiety may have been related to reassurance and support from the children's parents who were frequently present, as this hospital has a unique parent participation program.[12] Or, it may have been due to bias introduced into the ratings.

11 Natterson and Knudson, *op. cit.*
12 A. G. Knudson and J. M. Natterson, "Practice of Pediatrics: Participation of Parents in the Hospital Care of Fatally Ill Children," *Pediatrics*, Vol. 26 (1960), p. 482.

TABLE 1

TYPE OF ANXIETY

Type of Anxiety	Cumulative No. of Times Cited	Final Rating
Separation	136	25
Castration	76	4
Death	62	13
Total No. of Cases		42

The prominent type of anxiety judged to be present in these children as related to age is presented in Table 2. It is readily seen from this table that death anxiety is present largely when the children are older. Since the theoretical frequencies were too small for chi-square analysis of castration anxiety, the categories were condensed to permit an analysis of the relationship of death anxiety and age level. Table 3 contains a summary of the condensed data. Chi-square for Table 3 was 22.30, and with one degree of freedom was significant beyond the .001 level. Differences observed in Table 3 could not logically be attributed to sample variation or chance. The relationship between age and death anxiety appears strongly related.

These data suggest that while it is possible to have death anxiety at an early age (approximately three and a half in this study) the vast majority of children judged to have been afraid of death were ten or older. However, at least two of the four judges rated death anxiety to be present in 17 children: of these, one patient was 3 years and 7 months old, and five children were between the ages of 6 and 9. Thus six children under the age of 10 were rated to have death anxiety by at least two of the four judges, although in the

TABLE 2

AGE AND TYPE OF ANXIETY

Age Category	Prominent Type of Anxiety			Total No. of Cases
	Separation	Castration	Death	
Up to 5	22	1	1	24
6 to 9	2	1	1	4
10 to 14	1	2	11	14
Total	25	4	13	42

TABLE 3

AGE AND DEATH ANXIETY

Age Category	Prominent Type of Anxiety		Total No. of Cases
	Separation or Castration	Death	
Up to 9	26	2	28
10 to 14	3	11	14
Total	29	13	42

final composite ratings only two children under 10 were judged to have death anxiety as the prominent type of anxiety.

Although it is very difficult to make an assessment of the presence of death anxiety, the data of this study lend themselves to the belief that children often experience emotions without verbalizing or conceptualizing the feelings involved. Children are prone to use symbolization. The child does not adequately convey his subjective meaning by speech; he is prone to use drawing, painting, play, and symbols in handling anxiety. One may speculate that in this situation (children hospitalized with leukemia) death anxiety is largely dealt with via symbolization.

Although the material was not systematically organized or analyzed, the author observed hundreds of drawings of these children and was impressed by the symbols of death, and the frequency of the use of dark colors, namely, blacks and browns. The importance and use of symbolism has been noted by many authors.[13]

In view of the data in this study it appears reasonable to assume that death anxiety *may* be present in children, at least those hospitalized with castastrophic illnesses, much more frequently than some authors believe. Nagy's data, for example, were largely a reflection of socioeconomic conditions and dealt with children not faced with threat or crisis.[14] Natterson's observations, although acknowledging death fears in younger children, tend to support the hypothesis of age and type of anxiety experienced.[15] It seems more accurate to

[13] J. Piaget, *Play, Dreams and Imitation in Childhood.* W. W. Norton, New York, 1951; R. Griffiths, *A Study of Imagination in Early Childhood.* Kegan Paul, London, 1955; S. K. Langer, *Philosophy in a New Key: A Study in the Symbolism of Reason, Rite, and Art.* Penguin Books, New York, 1958.

[14] M. Nagy, "The Child's Theories Concerning Death," *Journal of Genetic Psychology,* Vol. 73, No. 3 (1948).

[15] See footnote 4.

331

state that the younger child expresses and handles death anxiety in a more subtle and symbolic manner. The traditional argument regarding young children not being able to experience death anxiety is that one cannot fear what one cannot conceive of—and nothingness is difficult to conceive. But one can form an idea of, and fear, death.[16]

In the final composite judgments, only two children under 10 years were judged to have death anxiety as the prominent type of anxiety. One was an 8½-year-old boy, and the other was a girl approximately 3½ years of age. The case of the girl is here presented in highly condensed form.

At the time of her first and only admission to the Medical Center, the patient was 3 years and 3 months old. A Caucasian from a Protestant family, she was the youngest of three siblings with brothers two and three years older. The patient had been previously hospitalized in her own community for a period of 19 days. The history states that patient was well until July, 1959, when she had a series of recurrent fevers. Gradually other symptoms appeared, such as decreased appetite, listlessness, and lethargy. In September, 1959, the patient skinned her knee. The lesion would not heal even after it was sutured; she had a lump in the sole of her foot and a kernel in her groin.

Interestingly, the mother feared a diagnosis of leukemia, and in October, 1959, insisted on a blood count. The patient was found to be anemic and treatment was begun. Later, leukemia was suspected, and this diagnosis was confirmed at the Medical Center as acute lymphocytic leukemia. The patient was apparently in no severe pain during the course of her illness. She was treated largely on an outpatient basis and was in the hospital for a period of only two days.

The patient was described by her parents as an active youngster, who tended to be very inquisitive. She had asked many questions related to death and dying around the time, and perhaps before, her illness was diagnosed. She made remarks such as these: Jesus was coming down from Heaven to take her there. She wondered if Jesus had toys in Heaven. She seemed very worried and upset about dying and said she did not want to go to Heaven; she wanted to stay here and be with her mother. Previously her grandfather had died. The patient had asked her grandmother what had happened to the grandfather and was told that he had gone to Heaven. The mother reported that on

[16] M. Klein, P. Heinmann and R. E. Money-Kyrle (eds.), *New Directions in Psycho-Analysis: The Significance of Infant Conflicts in the Patterns of Adult Behavior.* Basic Books, New York, 1955.

one occasion, when the child was being prepared for sleep, she had asked, "Am I going to die?" and added, "You know, God is going to come down from Heaven and take me back with Him."

Possible explanations for this patient's remarks and questions vary. In the first place, the mother could not be sure whether the child's preoccupation with death occurred after she became ill or before. The father thought that it might have been the result of something said by neighbors, or by children in the neighborhood since apparently all the family's friends and neighbors knew of the child's condition. The fact that someone in the family has died—in this case it was the patient's grandfather who had died just before she became ill—is a factor that normally is conducive to curiosity, and sometimes anxiety, in children. The mother was described as a serious person with a lot of emotional concern for the patient. Then, too, the nature of the onset of the symptoms and the unfortunate difficulty in confirming the diagnosis at the first hospital in which the patient was treated may have contributed to the mother's anxiety and frustrated perplexity; these feelings may have unwittingly been communicated to the child who became anxious and asked numerous questions.

In rating this case it is unfortunate that there were few observational data except those reported by the parents, as the patient was only in the hospital for two days. No other type of anxiety was noted in the patient's medical chart; on outpatient visits, the patient was described as asymptomatic and doing well. The four judges all rated this patient as having experienced death anxiety.

Study Findings

Data from this study suggest that in a death-threatening situation children may experience death anxiety at a very young age. Many children with leukemia are hospitalized for a relatively long period of time, undergo many medical procedures, and receive medications. They endure the "role playing" of their parents and staff and the experience is characterized by a stoic kind of "make the best of it but let's not talk about it" atmosphere. The child, however, empathically perceives parental anxiety and embarrassment regarding death.

These research data concerning death anxiety in fatally ill hospitalized children support the following conclusions:

333

1. Sixteen out of 50 patients were judged to have been aware or suspicious of the significance of their illness. This leads one to think that many children in similar situations might also speculate on the significance of their illness, and that this creates death anxiety.

2. Although death anxiety is generally associated with the older child, aged 10 or older, younger children are thought to be capable of experiencing it also; one child in this study, approximately $3\frac{1}{2}$ years of age, was judged to have experienced such death anxiety. A relevant question is whether it is possible that children in such a desperate situation perceive much more of the factual reality than is sometimes believed.

3. Children handle death anxiety in several ways: (a) younger children probably express it symbolically and physiologically; (b) older boys tend to act out; and (c) older girls are prone to become depressed.

Treatment Implications

Although the above findings are based on the study of children with leukemia or cancer, the implications for treatment may well apply to children with any form of catastrophic illness—that is, children who are facing imminent death or the possibility of death. When a child is experiencing death anxiety, it seems imperative that he be helped by a trained psychotherapist or by qualified caretaking personnel who have access to professional mental health consultation. The purpose of such intervention is to provide emotional support through recognition and acknowledgment of the underlying anxiety, thus helping the patient to alleviate or endure his anxiety so that he can function more effectively and with dignity—even while he is dying.

On the basis of the writer's work with the children involved in this study, several treatment principles emerge as guides to intervention activities.

1. Rather than utilizing a shotgun approach that is aimed at the alleviation of anxiety through massive reassurance and generalized support, treatment is more effective if based on the specific type of anxiety—separation, castration, or death—which is pre-eminent for that child. Here, understanding the child's coping and defensive

mechanisms, as well as the dynamics of his family's relationships are, of course, essential.

2. In alleviating the child's anxiety, the social worker is caught in a bind, for he must guard against unwarranted or false reassurance. Medical knowledge about the illness, its symptoms, characteristic course, and prognostic implications serve as a reality gauge. While the patient's feelings of hope, however limited they may be, must be respected, the therapist can only work within realistic medical possibilities.

3. The patient's perspectives on time—past, present, and future —are of particular importance in focusing the content of the therapeutic interview. The concept of time becomes a focal point in mobilizing or supporting the patient's energies, interests, and activities—and his dreams and hopes when they are judged appropriate. Within the realistic framework of time, the child can be helped to utilize his own resources and those available in the hospital setting to promote maximum adaptation.

To any individual a serious physical illness is a stressful situation, but to the child with a catastrophic illness the impact of the stress can be an overpowering crisis. The objective degree of stress increases with the immediacy of the death threat. Brief excerpts from four cases illustrate the relationship between the intensity of the stress and the treatment principles we have just cited.

For Mary the period of acute crisis was past; her prognosis was excellent.

> Mary, a 10-year-old, was seen during a postoperative checkup. Open-heart surgery had successfully repaired a cardiac defect. Her anxiety about the return visit was mainly expressed through mildly defiant behavior regarding parental controls; she appeared to be testing the limits in an effort to obtain reassuring information about her illness and what she could and could not do.
>
> During the interviews she appeared to be relatively at ease in discussing the past, present, or future—with more interest in the latter. Medical knowledge allowed the interviewer to offer a simple, direct statement that the surgeons and others were very pleased with the results of her operation. The patient had displayed some behavior indicating sibling rivalry toward a younger sister. The therapist wondered if Mary had thoughts about what her illness meant to her and her whole family—whether she would again ride her bike and run. Patient mused about this and seemed attentive when worker informed her that the doctors

335

thought she could resume *all* her activities in the near future. The focus continued on the present-future perspective. Mary was quite elated about how lucky she had been, expressed appreciation for the hospital's care and treatment, and discussed her anticipated return to school.

In the above case, knowledge of the child's medical and family situation guided direct activity in clarifying the child's anxiety; realistic reassurance was given, with a major focus on early return to normal routines, such as school. However, for most children with catastrophic illness, the crisis peak is not in the past but in the immediate future—as in the case of Sam.

Sam, age 11, was interviewed the day before he was to have open-heart surgery. He came from a large family where several members had cardiac illness, including a younger sibling who had died during open-heart surgery. The patient, in an acute anxiety state, was trembling, had a worried, tense expression, and was quite withdrawn. He seemed to welcome the interview, although he had little to say. He displayed interest in some ship models in the office and this led to some discussion about building models. The worker acknowledged Sam's forthcoming surgery and said that most everyone felt funny and scared before surgery. This broke the dam and he uttered: "I'm scared to *death!*" He went on to say that he kept wondering if he would wake up following surgery. He was not afraid that it would hurt—it wouldn't—but, how could he know whether he would ever wake up again. The worker acknowledged that he did have a serious illness. However, the medical center was one of the best in the world. The worker indicated the doctor's opinion that Sam's heart problem could be repaired and that his operation would be successful. He made an appointment to see Sam after his operation, as soon as visitors were allowed. The patient responded to this gesture of support and symbol of hope and much less anxiety was noticed. The rest of the interview focused on the past, particularly the patient's interests and past achievements.

The interview here was directed to helping the patient manage his anxiety during the waiting hours and mobilizing his hope as a coping mechanism to deal with an acute crisis situation. Sam did "wake up"; he survived the dreaded surgery but died of a postoperative infection.

Catherine, a 7½-year-old, ill a long time with leukemia, had been overindulged by well-meaning parents. She displayed a great deal of separation anxiety and demanded her mother's

336

presence almost constantly. As her illness progressed, she displayed much regression.

During one interview she showed tremendous anxiety about her future and volunteered that she had many "bad" dreams about it. Although she did not reveal any direct clues about her awareness of her prognosis, she tended to be vague and guarded about the future, agitated about the present, and tenaciously preoccupied with the past. Content of the interviews was focused on the past to a large extent and, to some degree, on what she was doing or could do at the present time.

In the above situation the worker attempted to help the patient manage day-by-day hospital activities a bit more effectively by accepting her regression, reliving past gratifications, and offering support by acknowledging his awareness of Catherine's restrictions and the pain related to her illness. The thin margin of hope was delimited to statements that, as she felt better, she could better enjoy some of her interests in and around the hospital.

Saul, age 8, had a diagnosis of leukemia, chronic type. This was his third hospitalization, and he appeared to be aware of his fatal prognosis. He came from a close knit, supportive family. Saul, a very bright child, had a tremendous capacity for relationships with both peers and adults. He was sensitive, perceptive, spontaneous, thoughtful, and had a good sense of humor. He was seen about twice a week for a period of three months just prior to his death.

Ill for two years, he handled his anxieties quite well by a variety of activities (school, hobbies, games, outings, and the like), and by not pushing questions at his mother or the staff about his illness. He had good defenses and utilized supportive resources well, for example, mother, staff, peer relationships, and the hospital facilities in general.

The interviews were conducted over a chess game at the patient's request. Gradually Saul revealed his concerns about his illness and his future. He liked to get people mad at him so he could get mad too—perhaps an index of his inner frustration. He talked in an animated fashion about the past and was matter of fact about the present, but volunteered little about his future. The interviewer gauged his comments to the patient's medical condition. As the months passed, the time focus of the interviews narrowed.

On several occasions Saul requested interviews which he used for emotional support, and, to some extent, to act out symbolically his fears, and pent-up aggression. He made several statements about killing in reference to winning chess pieces and would

337

laugh in an anxious manner. For example, during one chess game he commented: "I killed your mother," (the queen). This behavior appeared to be an outlet for his anxiety about dying.

By providing support and an opportunity for emotional expression, these interviews helped Saul maintain his good adjustment to a prolonged crisis situation.

Therapeutic efforts with children in these kinds of crises are still in an exploratory state. There are unsolved moral or ethical considerations in any such endeavors. Beyond these considerations, this limited experience suggests that children can be helped to manage their anxieties in the desperate situations described. Paradoxically, treatment efforts should entail a special kind of *hope* in what is commonly a hopeless situation. The approach should be based on reason, not fear. Knowledge of the actual medical circumstances, the child's resources, and the family's dynamics provides guides. The perspectives of time are useful in providing support, clarification, and guidance toward the goal of maximizing functioning to cope with the dimensions of the crisis.

28. Designing an Instrument to Assess Parental Coping Mechanisms*

Jacob I. Hurwitz,
David M. Kaplan,
and Elizabeth Kaiser

AMONG THE PROPOSED approaches for curbing delinquent behavior in children is the modification of disruptive parent-child relationship patterns. Before such patterns can be modified, however, effective methods of assessing them must be devised. To be fully adequate, these methods must distinguish between constructive and disruptive parent-child relationship patterns in a manner that will provide clear blueprints for remedial action.

This article describes an attempt to devise a measurement tool to make such an assessment of parental coping mechanisms.[1] Made within the context of an extensive multidisciplinary delinquency research project, the endeavor, carried out at the South Shore Guidance Center, combined clinical social work methods with quantitative research techniques.

The theory underlying this part of the over-all study is based largely on the concepts of Erich Lindemann and Gerald Caplan concerning crisis situations and David M. Kaplan's related concept of acute situational disorders.[2] According to their formulations, when

* Reprinted from *Social Casework*, Vol. XLIII, No. 10 (1962).
[1] The over-all delinquency research project has been co-directed by the senior author and supported principally by the U.S. Public Health Service under the National Institute of Mental Health Special Grant 3M-9149 (C3). For a description of the goals and methods of this project, see Jacob I. Hurwitz, B. R. Hutcheson, and Saul Cooper, "Problems in Refining the Psychiatric Assessment of Juvenile Delinquents." *Journal of Health and Human Behavior*, Vol. II, Winter 1961, pp. 276–283.
[2] For a discussion of these concepts, see Erich Lindemann, chapter 1 of the present volume; Gerald Caplan, "An Approach to the Study of Family Mental Health," *Public Health Reports*, Vol. LXXI, October 1956, pp. 1027–1030; David M. Kaplan, "A Concept of Acute Situational Disorders," *Social Work*, Vol. VII, April 1962, pp. 15–23.

an acute, stress-producing situation, or crisis, occurs in a family—for example, the death of a family member—the manner in which the family members respond to the situation and cope with it is a matter of considerable theoretical and practical importance. They postulate that for each major type of acute situational disorder there is a specific set of psychological tasks—for example, "grief work"—that must be accomplished if the situational problem is to be successfully resolved. If these tasks are not accomplished, the acute situational disorder can generate chronic intrapsychic or social maladjustment.

In the study reported here, this conceptual framework was applied to the problem of juvenile delinquency, and an effort was made to specify some of the psychological tasks that parents of court delinquents must accomplish if the acute disorder is not to become chronic—that is to say, if recidivism is to be prevented. The view was taken that each family of a court delinquent goes through a crisis created by the court summons and that this experience is a painful and upsetting one to most families, although in different degrees and perhaps for different reasons. The results of a pilot study had suggested that there is only a limited number of ways in which parents generally respond to this crisis and handle it with each other, with the delinquent boy, and with the court. It was recognized, of course, that the family's functioning at such a time may differ somewhat from its usual behavior, but it was believed that parental responses to the crisis situation should provide clues to the family's basic structure, its strengths, and its weaknesses. The initial plan had been to make a conventional assessment of family structure. This was impossible, however, because members of the social work team were limited to a single interview in which to gather data for the project psychiatrist on the juvenile offender's social-developmental history and the context of the offense. It was decided, therefore, to focus on current parental mechanisms as being of equal theoretical relevance, a more feasible approach practically, and more useful for control purposes.

The project staff postulated that it should be possible, by focusing on how the parents responded to the delinquent act, to make a family diagnosis that would lead directly to a constructive treatment plan for the family. Such an outcome could be expected because the factors to be assessed are those that bear directly on *current* parent-child relations, about which something can be done.

For example, if the kind of plan the parents make for the boy as a result of the court experience is deemed ineffectual in preventing further delinquent behavior, or actually likely to encourage it, it is open to modification.

Most families who are sent by the court to the South Shore Guidance Center are not highly motivated to accept clinical treatment, and many are inaccessible. The project staff believed, however, that the family diagnosis resulting from the clinic's study and evaluation would make it possible to spot trouble areas and that a quite direct approach to the parents, frequently on a short-term basis, might help them to modify some of their coping patterns. A joint treatment plan, a kind of milieu therapy, was thus envisaged, in which direct social work intervention with the family would supplement some type of intervention with the boy. Such a plan is not appropriate for all families. It works best with those parents who fall within the upper range of emotional health. These are the parents who are likely to make progress on their own after a brief series of interviews. This same approach may be used in a more limited way with certain more disturbed families; they can be pulled through the crisis and encouraged to return to the clinic for further clinical intervention.

Strategy of Interdisciplinary Collaboration

To facilitate making a family diagnosis, a rating schedule was devised by a team of four experienced psychiatric social workers operating under the technical direction of the senior author, a research specialist. The reason for this approach to the task of devising the schedule was to avoid imposing upon the social work raters an alien, custom-made measurement model—to make maximum use of the professional judgment and clinical competence of the social work team in devising the instrument, not merely in using it. The basic strategy was to make the tool-building process a joint, collaborative effort in which the knowledge and skills of social practice and of social research could be productively integrated.

This strategy was implemented in several ways. First, the social work team decided, as was explained earlier, to focus on current parental responses to the delinquent act, rather than on prior family structure, for the purpose of getting a measure of family coping

341

mechanisms. The team then analyzed records of court cases interviewed during the previous year to isolate the nature and range of parental responses to the delinquency crisis. After a series of modal responses had been selected and refined, several measurement models were tested until an appropriate one was found. The major criteria applied in assessing appropriateness were ease in rating and in interpretation, reliability and validity of ratings, and quantifiability of clinical interview material to permit its statistical manipulation.

Structure of the Schedule

The rating schedule focuses not on the personality structure of the parents or the child, but on some interpersonal factors perceived as potential determinants of the delinquent child's future behavior —which are therefore promising targets in a delinquency control program.

After a considerable amount of trial-and-error experimentation,* five general areas of parental coping were selected for empirical study: (1) parent-to-child communication, (2) parent-to-parent communication, (3) parent-to-court communication, (4) parental assessment of the problem, and (5) the parental remedial action plan.

The specific behaviors tapped by the schedule are these: (1) the nature and quality of parent-child and parent-parent communications in relation to the crisis situation, (2) the parents' views on what particular problems are responsible for the delinquent act, (3) their choice of problem areas on which to focus their respective action plans, (4) the nature of the action plan directed toward the child, and (5) the kind of help they want from the court.

The schedule is structured in terms of a rough sequence of parental behaviors considered necessary—though not by themselves sufficient—to deter further delinquency. *Its function is to permit an assessment of the degree to which, and the areas within which, parental coping mechanisms in this situation are adaptive or maladaptive in delinquency control.*

---

* Research design in all its phases is rarely the neat, orderly, and sure-footed process that it appears to be from a reading of most research reports. When social practitioners and social researchers attempt to combine creatively their respective bodies of knowledge and skill to carry out a piece of research, the process necessarily entails even more floundering than usual. Thus, for example, a high level of frustration tolerance is probably as essential in *studying* delinquent behavior as in *curbing* it.

Adaptive coping on the part of parents is conceptualized as the parents' seeing the child's need for help, showing a capacity for self-involvement, formulating and carrying out a constructive action plan, communicating effectively with the child and with each other, and using the court constructively. The following abbreviated summary is an illustration of typical parental adaptive coping mechanisms.

> Mrs. K talked seriously to Walter about what he had done. Walter told his mother that he resented the many restrictions put on him because of his poor school work and felt he could not achieve the standard his parents set.
>
> Mrs. K does feel that some blame should be placed on Walter for his attitude. On the other hand, she feels that the neighborhood environment makes it hard for a boy to be interested in academic achievement and that she has not taken time to listen to and understand her son. Mrs. K plans to get him some tutorial help if he can use it. She has also talked with her husband, and they have agreed that they will both try to de-emphasize school performance.
>
> Mrs. K thinks that the court hearing served a useful purpose. Though she thinks she can manage without further help, she sees the probation officer as someone who could help her if the need arose.
>
> Mr. K also talked with his son. Since he already knew from Mrs. K how Walter felt, he raised the issues that concerned Walter and offered to try to see the boy's side of the problem and to make some changes.
>
> Mr. K agrees with what his wife said about Walter and the neighborhood. He also recognizes that education is important to him and that he is angry with his son for not doing well in school.
>
> Mr. K and his wife discussed the problem, and Mr. K agreed to support Mrs. K's plan.
>
> The communication between the parents was strengthened by this crisis. For a few years Mr. K had been so engrossed in his business that he had taken little time to talk to his wife. They now realized how much they missed their earlier discussions.

Maladaptive coping is defined as the parents' denying the delinquent act, despite official verification; projecting responsibility onto the child, onto bad environmental influences, or onto the other parent; or seeing the court appearance as an unwarranted intrusion into their lives. An illustration of typical maladaptive coping mechanisms follows.

343

Mrs. T tried to confront Bert with the delinquent act, but in a very half-hearted and cursory fashion, since she has no relationship with him. As a result, no serious discussion between mother and child took place.

She blames Bert and his friends for his getting into trouble and does not consider herself in any way responsible for the act.

Mrs. T thinks it is useless to do anything about the boy's delinquent act because she feels she cannot carry out a plan. She thinks anything she tries to do will be futile.

Mrs. T wants the court to take over and not involve her. It is all right with her if they wish to place Bert.

Mr. T did not come for the interview. Mrs. T thinks he feels much as she does about the boy. However, she cannot talk to her husband and therefore is not sure.

Data-Gathering, Rating, and Assessment

The parents of each court delinquent were scheduled for an interview of about an hour and a half, first together and then individually. The joint session was held to observe their interaction patterns and to get basic data on parental coping mechanisms. The individual sessions were used to supplement and validate these data in a somewhat freer atmosphere. The interview with the mother was also used to elicit the social-developmental data required by the psychiatrist.

Each set of parents was rated by the examining social worker immediately after the interview. A statistical clerk computed assessment scores for the mother and for the father in each of the five specific areas of parental coping listed above. These scores ranged from *very constructive* to *constructive* to *destructive* to *very destructive*. Thus, for example, an earnest and serious two-way discussion of the delinquent act between a parent and the child was assessed as *very constructive* parent-child communication; a one-way discussion, earnest and serious on the parent's part but with little participation by the boy, was assessed as *constructive* communication; a token parental confrontation of the boy was assessed as *destructive;* and no discussion at all as *very destructive*. Over-all paternal and maternal coping scores were derived by summating the five area assessments, assigning a weight of 3 to the type of action plan envisaged, since it was considered the most crucial factor in deterring further delinquency. Over-all family coping scores were then derived by combining the father's and mother's over-all coping scores with a measure of their congruence.

Figure 1. Formula for Deriving Over-all Family Coping Scores.

Parental Coping Score							Over-all Family Coping Score
Father	++	++	+				
		or	or			=	++
Mother	++	+	++				
Father	+	++	−				
		or	or			=	+
Mother	+	−	++				
Father	+	−	−	++	−−		
		or	or	or	or	=	−
Mother	−	+	−	−−	++		
Father	+	−−	−	−−	−−		
		or	or	or	or	=	−−
Mother	−−	+	−−	−	−−		

Code: ++ = very constructive
 + = constructive
 − = destructive
 −− = very destructive

The formula was evolved as a result of the repeated difficulties encountered in trying to achieve satisfactory inter-rater reliability on high-level inferences. It was decided to modify conventional practice by using highly experienced psychiatric social workers to rate factual items and low-level inferences but not to rate the crucial high-level inferences. The problem of avoiding the rating of high-level inferences was solved by getting a consensus on the criteria for deriving these inferences from the descriptive ratings.

Utility of the Instrument

When thoroughly mastered, the instrument can produce a rating in less than ten minutes. As new workers were trained by the same process that had been used in testing for reliability, the use of the instrument was found to be easy to teach. It can be readily used by nonclinical personnel, such as probation officers, with the help of a good operational manual. This is true because, as stated earlier, the high-level inferences are made with the help of formulae that can be applied with nothing more than good clerical skill.

Increasing Reliability

Since the focus of this schedule is on current behavioral data, reliability was easier to achieve than for schedules whose items require the rating of clinical inferences. Items were operationally defined in a rating manual where necessary, but many items were defined on the rating schedule itself.

The schedule went through three major revisions. Before each revision, a pretest was conducted on ten to twelve cases, each rated by three or four raters. The final schedule was tested for reliability on twenty cases. During this formal reliability test the social workers interviewed in rotation and were observed by two or three other social workers through a one-way screen. The schedule was rated by both interviewer and observer. Reliability conferences were held after each interview (as they had been on previous pretests), and ambiguous items were operationally defined. Items that remained unreliable were either revised or deleted. Good reliability * was achieved on most items.

The first draft of the schedule was structured mainly in the form of dichotomous items calling for statements about the presence or absence of various attitudes or behavior. Owing to the difficulties encountered in trying to rate these items reliably, many of them were opened up into seven-point scales requiring rather sophisticated clinical inferences. The team soon discovered, however, that the interview did not provide an adequate observational basis for rating some of these items with any degree of subjective confidence or objective reliability. At this point it was decided to eliminate unratable inferential items from the schedule, to replace them by essentially factual dichotomous items or three- to four-point ordinal scales, and to derive the basic clinical assessment items objectively by predetermined formulae from the pattern of responses to the factual items.**

---

* Good reliability is here defined as agreement at the .05 level of significance as determined by chi-square test.

** For example, an unratable inferential item, such as "How adequate was the mother's (father's) diagnosis?" structured as a seven-point ordinal scale ranging from *highly adequate* to *highly inadequate*, was converted into a series of dichotomous factual ratings, such as: In discussing the causes of the delinquent act, where does the mother (father) locate the problem(s):

(a) Outside the family?   Yes   No
(b) In the child?   Yes   No
(c) In the self?   Yes   No

Validity of the Schedule

Since the thirty-seven ratings called for by the schedule are all descriptive rather than inferential in nature, item reliability levels were, of course, quite high. For the same reason considerable confidence can be placed in the accuracy of the behavioral data yielded by the instrument. Since, however, the crucial assessments of parental handling were derived from predetermined formulae based on clinical judgment, their validity requires empirical verification.

The factors differentiating delinquents coming from families who coped constructively with the court crisis from those who coped destructively with it were examined for evidence relating to the validity of assessing parental coping patterns as a major factor in delinquency. The latter cases more often showed evidences of social maladjustment and emotional disturbance than did the former. This was manifested by such characteristics among the delinquents as a history of developmental difficulties, recent major failure experiences, overtly aggressive delinquent acts, an absence of feelings of guilt, a disruptive attitude toward the diagnostic group, and the high level of psychopathology of the offenders and their mothers. All these factors differentiated constructive from destructive parental coping mechanisms more sharply than they did high- from low-delinquency areas of residence. These factors, therefore, cannot be attributed solely (or perhaps even primarily) to sociocultural influences.

The findings suggest that the assessment of parental coping mechanisms is a valid diagnostic procedure. They further suggest that current parental coping mechanisms may reflect earlier child-rearing patterns, and so reflect stable and persisting aspects of family structure.

Summary

This article has described an attempt made, in the context of a wider study, to devise a tool for assessing parent-child relationship patterns in a manner that will provide clear blueprints for remedial action. The related concepts of *crisis situation* and *acute situational disorder* were applied to the delinquency situation, and an effort was made to specify some of the coping mechanisms parents of court

347

delinquents must use in order to help prevent the acute disorder brought on by the court experience from becoming chronic. It was postulated that, by focusing on how the parents responded to the delinquent act, it should be possible to make a family diagnosis that could lead directly to a constructive, and frequently short-term, treatment plan for the family.

The tool-building process was set up as a collaborative effort between researcher and practitioners to exploit to the full the clinical knowledge of the social work team in devising the measurement instrument, not merely in using it. The instrument that was devised is designed to tap the parents' assessment of the court crisis and their actions to prevent recurrences. Its function is to assess, within selected areas, the degree to which parental coping mechanisms are adaptive or maladaptive for purposes of delinquency control. Adaptive and maladaptive coping mechanisms were conceptually and operationally defined.

In this presentation, the data-gathering, rating, and assessment processes have been described in some detail, the formula for deriving assessments of family coping patterns has been presented, and the ratability of the instrument and its use by personnel not clinically trained have been discussed. The methodological procedures utilized to refine and standardize the instrument have been reviewed, and evidence concerning its reliability and validity has been presented. In conclusion, it has been asserted that parental coping mechanisms in this crisis situation appear, in general, to reflect stable and persisting aspects of family structure.

29. Assessing Patient Characteristics from Psychotherapy Interviews[*]

Edith H. Freeman,
Betty L. Kalis,
and M. Robert Harris

A PREVIOUS REPORT FROM the precipitating stress study described a variety of findings about the kinds of personal disruption which bring people to the point of requesting psychotherapeutic help.[1] Other papers described the refinements of therapeutic concepts and techniques which led to the emergence of such data within the context of brief psychotherapy.[2] This paper will describe some methods employed in arriving at these findings, methods developed to deal quantitatively with interview material and to impose objectivity upon judgments made by clinical raters.

Assessment of complex, highly organized aspects of behavior from relatively unstructured clinical material has received increasing attention in recent years. In particular, the tape recording of interviews has led to a number of studies of the interaction processes in

* Reprinted from the *Journal of Projective Techniques and Personality Assessment*, Vol. 28, No. 4 (1964). The study on which the paper was based was supported in part through a grant (No. 55–1–8 "A Study of the Meaning and Correlates of the Concept of Precipitating Stress in Mental Illness") from the State of California, Department of Mental Hygiene. Marian C. Chay served as interviewer and rater and Julia Bloomfield was independent rater for ten selected cases.

1 Betty L. Kalis, M. Robert Harris, A. R. Prestwood, and Edith H. Freeman, "Precipitating Stress as a Focus in Psychotherapy," *Archives of General Psychiatry*, Vol. V (1961), pp. 219–226.
2 M. Robert Harris, Betty L. Kalis, and Edith H. Freeman, "Precipitating Stress: An Approach to Brief Therapy," *American Journal of Psychotherapy*, Vol. III (1963), pp. 465–471; Betty L. Kalis, Edith H. Freeman, and M. Robert Harris, "Influences of Previous Help-Seeking Experiences on Applications for Psychotherapy," *Mental Hygiene*, Vol. II (1964), pp. 267–272.

psychotherapy.[3] These studies differ in the degree of objectivity and the complexity of the questions asked. They all, however, have encountered problems in bringing some order and objectivity to conclusions drawn from material involving the many variables in a fifty-minute interchange between patient and therapist. Most studies using psychotherapy interviews as basic data focus on interaction and process variables or study therapist behavior. The precipitating stress project used therapy interviews as the basis for investigating a variety of *patient* characteristics. The primary focus was on what information the interviews could yield about the personality and current behavior of the patient, as opposed to studies dealing with interaction or therapist variables. A second major area of difference between this and other studies is that the entire interview series for each patient was included in the analyses rather than restricting information-gathering to one or a limited number of interviews or predetermined segments from them.

The concentration in this study was on description of those aspects of personality, behavior, and past history which were predicted to relate to the major research question—why a person requested professional help at a particular time. The aim of the research was an investigation into and identification of those stresses precipitating the request for help. The material came from a brief series of individual interviews with 43 unselected applicants to a psychiatric outpatient clinic. The focus of the interviews, aside from the research questions, was a psychotherapeutic one, and the emphasis was on the disruptive elements in the patient's current life circumstances. The study proceeded from broadly psychoanalytic assumptions.[4] In this view, an individual's previous adaptation is interrupted by events or external occurrences which, by associative processes, bring closer to awareness derivatives of genetically important conflicts. The events may appear to the outside observer, and to the patient himself, to be of minor importance, but because of their reactivation of conflict they occasion considerable anxiety, render a previously attained adjustment inadequate, and lead the individual to seek some kind of external aid. The postulate of this

[3] J. B. Rotter, "Psychotherapy," *Annual Review of Psychology*, Vol. XI (1960), pp. 381–414; *Research in Psychotherapy: Proceedings of a Conference*, Hans H. Strupp, and Lester Luborsky (eds.), Conference on Research in Psychotherapy, Chapel Hill, N.C., 1961.

[4] Harris *et al.*, 1963, see footnote 2.

project was that *all* patients who apply for psychotherapeutic help do so out of such a disruption. The aim was to identify specific correlates of such disruptions in each case by means of focused therapeutic interviews, and to achieve some resolution of the crisis. Such a focus meant that the interviewer directed efforts toward the exploration of the patient's current life situation and the events which might have disturbed a previously maintained equilibrium.

Because of the empirical nature of the study, patient characteristics were not controlled and structured interviews were not employed; instead, controls were imposed during the phase of data analysis. There were two basic means of imposing objectivity: the first was the development of rating scales which were subject to qualification; the second was investigating the reliability with which personality characteristics and other variables in question could be identified and assessed by two independent raters of differing professional affiliation. It was only with the demonstration of some interrater agreement on precipitating events and evoked conflicts that hypotheses could be formulated for further study. These areas of data analysis will be a primary consideration of this paper.

Since the interest of the investigators was in what could be learned about patients' help-seeking behavior from their verbal productions in psychotherapy, clarification and refinement of relevant therapeutic techniques were extremely important. Activity of the therapist contributes in a major way to the kinds of material the patient discusses, and intensive staff conferences throughout the project were aimed at development of ways to sharpen the therapeutic focus on current life circumstances and conflicts. It was assumed that, while this general orientation on the part of the therapist would be responded to differently by individual patients, in general the response would be in the direction of increased information about the present. These modifications of technique mean that information about precipitating stress was probably more available from these interviews than would have been the case with less active therapeutic focusing. This restriction on the generalizability of results would be a meaningful area for further research.

Procedures

A. *The Sample.* Forty-three adults who applied to a psychiatric out-patient clinic were selected for this study at the point of their initial phone call. The phone calls were selected only on the basis of randomizing time of day and day of week, with the exception of excluding calls regarding ongoing cases. The rationale for randomizing the time and day of the accepted phone calls was to avoid a possible source of bias in the kinds of stresses that lead to requests for help since, for example, there may be differences between patients who ask for help at 4:55 P.M. Friday vs. those who do so at 8:30 A.M. Monday. Applicants walking into the clinic without phoning were included when their arrival coincided with the time sampling. Patients completed personal information forms including identifying data, living situation, and treatment history. This material, shown in Table I, indicated that the sample was comparable in personal characteristics to the population of the outpatient clinic from which it was drawn.

All callers were offered an appointment within 24 hours of their call and were seen intensively (two to three times weekly) thereafter. The interviewers were both women, one a psychiatric social worker, and the other a clinical psychologist. The aim of the interviews was to achieve some resolution of the presenting difficulty within the brief therapy context described above. Although the adequacy of such resolutions appeared to vary widely, 38 of the 43 patients (88 per cent) were seen for seven or fewer interviews. Thirteen of the

TABLE I. SAMPLE CHARACTERISTICS (N-43)

Age		Sex		Nationality-Race	
16–20	1	Male	25	White American	36
21–25	10	Female	18	Negro American	2
26–30	17			Indian American	1
31–35	7	Marital Status		British	2
36–40	1	Single	20	European	1
41–45	1	Married	12	South American	1
46–50	3	Separated	8		
51–55	0	Divorced	2	Education	
56–60	0	Widowed	1	5–8 years	2
61–65	1			9–11 years	7
66–70	1			H. S. graduate	13
71–75	1	Religion		13–14 years	12
		Protestant	17	15–16 years	7
Range	18–71 years	Catholic	13	16+	2
Mean	31.4	None declared	13	Range	5–19 years
				Mean	12.56

patients (30 per cent) entered long-term treatment after this interview series; three (7 per cent) returned for a second brief series of
contacts within several months, and one (2 per cent) required
hospitalization after four interviews. The remaining 26 patients
(61 per cent) expressed no wish for additional treatment at the point
of terminating this series. (See Table II.)

TABLE II. TREATMENT HISTORY, REFERRAL, DISPOSITION

Previous Psychiatric Treatment	Patients	Referral Source	Patients
None	21	Self	22
1 Consultation	6	Private psychiatrist	4
2–6 Interviews	5	Other physician	3
7+ OP Interviews	7*	Social agency	1
Hospitalization	6*	Psychiatric clinic	9
*2 had both inpatient and		Psychiatric hospital	2
outpatient treatment		Court	1
		Mental Health Assoc.	1

Number of Interviews	Patients	Disposition	Patients
1	3	Termination	25
2	6	Further treatment at clinic	12
3	4	Private psychiatrist	1
4	8	Hospitalization	1
5	4	Returned to previous agency	4
6	8		
7	5		
8	1		
9	1		
10	0		
11	1		
12	1		
13	1		
Range	1–13		
Mean	5		

B. *Description of instruments.* Material for data analysis was
provided by the complete series of tape recordings of interviews and
a written summary of each. (Each patient had also completed the
Minnesota Multiphasic Personality Inventory after the first interview, but conventional scoring of the inventory did not correlate
with the variables under investigation.) One rater listened to the
entire taped series of interviews; from these and from the interview
summaries, she compiled two sets of information on each patient:
1. The Social History, and 2. The Life Experiences Check List.

1. The Social History was a detailed inquiry into many areas of the patients' background and current life. Individual items in the 9-page questionnaire were subsumed under the broad categories of Social, Family, Marital, Educational, Occupational, and Military History; Societal Conflicts; Marital-Sexual Relations; Current Living Situation; Financial Situation; Attitudes toward family of origin; and Current attitudes toward expressions of anger, dependence, and anxiety. The rater's task was to complete this questionnaire as fully as possible from information which emerged in the interviews. Because the interviews did not follow a history-taking format, in some cases a few areas of information were absent, but for the most part relevant historical material did emerge in the context of discussing current life stresses.

2. The Life Experiences Check List adapted from Sargent,[5] involved the ratings of changes occurring in a patient's life circumstances. Included in the check list were eight major areas of functioning; Background, Interpersonal Relations, Marital Sexual Relations, Living Situation, Occupation, Community and Leisure Time, Physical Condition, and Previous Help-Seeking Experience. Under each broad area, many sub-sections were provided. The rater was asked to judge for each patient: a) whether any changes had occurred in any part of these areas; b) whether the change was current, in the recent past, or in the remote past; c) when specifically in time the change occurred; and d) whether the patient was the passive recipient or an active agent in producing the event or change. (This latter dimension was not used in the data analysis, since measurement of inter-rater agreement would have required a major amendment to the design of the study.) Finally, the rater was asked to judge which of the changes in life circumstances were precipitating to the present application and which other ones contributed significantly. The Life Circumstances Check List yielded, therefore, a kind of inventory of all the changes in each patient's current life and a judgment by the rater as to which of all these events were relevant to the request for help.

3. Ratings of Personality Variables. A major phase of this project involved the development of techniques which would permit raters

[5] H. D. Sargent, "The Psychotherapy Research Project of the Menninger Foundation: Second Report. III. Situational Variables." *Bulletin of the Menninger Clinic*, Vol. 22 (1958) pp. 148–166.

to make judgments about relevant personality variables in a quanti-
fiable form. The following variables were rated after a review of
all taped interviews for each patient: areas of personal conflict,
mode of conflict expression, defenses, and symptoms. Variables
were chosen for measurement because of their predicted relationship to precipitating stress. A description of the techniques used
in rating each dimension follows:

a. The Assessment of Conflict Form was especially developed for
this study. The form was divided into two broad sections, first a
list of 25 conflict areas and secondly, a continuum of mode of expression for each area. The 25 conflict areas were selected through
pretesting to represent as broad a spectrum as possible of the basic
and derivative conflictual concerns commonly observed in clinical
practice. It was assumed that each area of concern existed to some
degree and could therefore be characterized as minimally to maximally conflictual for each applicant. Moreover, it was recognized
that correlation existed among the conflict areas, but the direction
and extent of correlation for any pair or constellation of areas was
unknown.

The rater was asked to order the 25 areas for each applicant in
a fixed distribution. That is, a modified Q sort was employed. A
rating of 5 was to be assigned to the three areas judged most conflictual; a rating of 4 to the five most conflictual areas in the remaining pool; a rating of 1 to the three least conflictual areas, and so on.
The total distribution was as follows:

	Most Conflictual				Least Conflictual	
	5	4	3		2	1
f	3	5	9		5	3

b. Ratings of mode of conflict expression were made independently of the areas of conflict judged most salient. That is, an extreme rating on one dimension did not require an extreme rating on
the other. While a 5-point continuum was utilized here also, the
rater was not confined to a fixed distribution. On the contrary,
bi-modal expression could be denoted by double ratings, provided
that a principal mode was designated. One continuum was used
for each conflict area with the exception of Sexuality, where four
ratings of behavioral mode were required: Identity, Object Choice,
Degree of Expression, and Form of Expression. Anchoring terms
were provided for each extreme of the continuum for all variables,

and additional anchoring terms, where appropriate, for some. A rating at some point on the continuum was required for each behavioral mode.

c. A check list of current salient defenses was also included. The items on this checklist were compiled largely from *The Ego and the Mechanisms of Defense* [6] with additional references from other major psychoanalytic sources.[7] To insure common definitions by the raters, a glossary of these defenses was provided. The glossary represented a distillation of opinion from theoretical writings about each defense—a description of behavioral manifestations, mode of operation, relation to conflict, and level of psychosexual development. The rater was asked to double-check the four most characteristic current defenses and was permitted, when it seemed appropriate, to single-check an additional four items out of the total of twenty-one.

d. A similar procedure was used for ratings of symptoms; that is, each rater double-checked the four most characteristic current symptoms and was permitted to include a maximum of four additional ones when relevant. Twenty-seven items were included on this list.

4. *Narrative Summaries.* Each rater also prepared a narrative impression of each case. The major function of this summary was to describe fully the precipitating stress. This task involved identifying the critical events in the patient's life and indicating what special factors made them critical; that is, specifying the unique ways in which events and constellations of personal conflicts interacted for each patient. The nature of the disruption itself was described, and some attempt was made to indicate the patient's level of adaptation prior to this disruption. The purpose of these narrative impressions was to make available for each case a relatively thorough formulation which would tie together all of the separate ratings that had been made by each rater.

C. *Raters.* Four women, two clinical psychologists and two psychiatric social workers, served as raters. One rater, a psychologist (R1), listened to the entire interview series and completed all forms

[6] Anna Freud, Hogarth Press, London, 1937.
[7] Otto Fenichel, *The Psychoanalytic Theory of Neurosis*, Norton, New York, 1945; Erik H. Erikson, *Childhood and Society*, Norton, New York, 1950; L. E. Hinsie and Jacob Shatzky, *Psychiatric Dictionary*, Oxford University Press, New York, 1940.

and a narrative impression on each case. A psychiatric social worker (R2), who was not otherwise connected with the study, listened to the interviews with ten randomly selected cases and completed the following: (a) Assessment of Conflict Areas; (b) Behavioral Mode of Conflict Expression; (c) Defenses; (d) Symptoms; and (e) Narrative Impression. Ten cases (See Table III for the characteristics of this sub-sample) were thereby made available for more intensive

TABLE III. CHARACTERISTICS OF THE SUB-SAMPLE OF TEN CASES

Age		Sex		Nationality-Race	
21–25	2	Male	6	White American	8
26–30	5	Female	4	Indian American	1
31–35	3			British	1
		Marital Status			
Range	22–23	Single	6	*Education*	
Mean	27.9	Married	1	5–8 years	0
		Separated	3	9–11 years	1
				High School grad.	4
				13–14 years	3
Occupational Status		*Religion*		15–16 years	2
Employed	6	Protestant	2		
Unemployed	3	Catholic	3	*Range*	10–16 years
Housewife	1	None Declared	5	*Mean*	13.1 years

Previous Psychiatric				Referral Source	
Treatment		*Patients*		Self	5
None		6		Psychiatric Clinic	2
1 Consultation		1		Other Physician	1
2–6 Interviews		1		Private Psychiatrist	1
7+ Interviews		2		Mental Health Assoc.	1

Number of Interviews		Patients	Disposition	
1		0	Termination	5
2		0	Further treatment	
3		1	in clinic	5
4		0		
5		0		
6		3		
7		3		
8		0		
9		1		
10		1		
11		0		
12		1		
13		0		
Range	3–12			
Mean	7.3			

study. It was not within the scope of the project to have two raters listen to all of the cases. Reports of inter-rater agreement, therefore, are primarily based on these ten cases. Additionally, the interviewers (R3 and R4) had completed a summary of each patient they saw for clinic records. It was possible in almost all cases to compare these summaries with the narrative impressions of the two independent raters who had not interviewed these patients. Thus, a third set of ratings of precipitating stress was obtained.

Results

A. Agreement Between Raters.

Percentage of agreement between raters was, for several reasons, chosen as the method of data presentation. First, agreement between raters has been a question of the extent of agreement or disagreement on *each case* individually, rather than across the sample as a whole. Second, use of a Q sort, as in the Assessment of Conflict, makes it impossible to work with the usual methods for determining degrees of freedom. On the one hand, each single rating decreases the degrees of freedom for each subsequent rating; on the other hand, the areas being rated are intercorrelated to an unknown degree. Lastly, most requirements of parametric techniques obviously cannot be met with this kind of rated data, and conversion to standard scores seems a dubious procedure when it is unknown how much the obtained differences are due to rater biases and how much to differences within the sample itself. For all these reasons, the most straightforward approach to this kind of data would seem to be the presentation of an admittedly approximate index of agreement.

1. *Identification of Precipitating Stress.* The basic methodological question was: Could the nature of stress precipitating the treatment application, including the conflicts evoked, be identified from the taped interview material? A special problem had to do with establishing whether there was agreement in the identification of precipitating stress as described in each rater's written narrative impressions. Each rater's task in listening to the tapes was to select out of the patient's account of his recent experiences those events that seemed to be critical in leading to the request for help. It required choosing from all the material a patient presented from his recent life just those particular events that seemed to be espe-

cially stressful or disruptive in light of the nature of his salient personal conflicts, his behavior around the events, and his relevant past history.

A useful means of comparing the raters' judgments about precipitating stress was a summary comparison of events they considered important or critical and events they considered unimportant for the treatment application. If there had been five events of some consequence in a patient's life for the previous six months, the raters would be compared on whether they had agreed on which of these were important, as well as which were unimportant, and their total agreement would be the sum of the two.

Specifically, the method involved two steps: 1. Extracting from each narrative impression a capsule statement of the rater's formulation of precipitating stress; 2. Relating the critical events selected and described by each rater to the total pool of recent events checked for each patient on the Life Experiences Check List. An example of such capsule statements from the narrative impressions on one case will illustrate the method.

Statement from R1's narrative impression:

"I believe it is the likelihood of living with her mother again—and her currently doing so during the mother's visits—that disrupts her very tenuous adjustment and leads her to seek treatment now."

Statement from R2's narrative impression:

"Perhaps most important was the fact that patient was told some time before that her mother might be discharged from the nursing home soon. During this period the mother had come home on visits. Patient found herself getting very angry with her mother to the point of hitting her."

These two events mentioned by both raters were the mother's anticipated discharge from the nursing home and her current visits with the patient. Four other recent events were listed on the Life Experiences Check List for this patient. These were: recent loss of a job; diagnosis of a condition requiring minor surgery; her sister's developing a romantic attachment and the patient's fear that the sister might marry; her decision to return to school. The raters also agreed that these four events were not an important aspect of the precipitating stress. Out of six recent events, then, the two raters agreed on two events they considered precipitating and on four others they did not consider to be crucial in the request

359

for psychiatric treatment. This would be considered a case of perfect agreement.

Agreement between the two raters was measured by adding the number of agreements on precipitating events across cases plus the agreement on non-precipitating events vs. the number of disagreements. In the case described above, six agreements were counted. Agreement for these two raters on ten cases was 89.4 per cent. On 40 of the 43 cases, it was also possible to extract such a capsule statement from the therapist's case summary; agreement on these 40 cases between the therapist's and R1's statements was 88.2 per cent.

The reliability with which such capsule statements could be extracted from the narrative was studied by having two psychologists make excerpts from the therapist's summaries and R1's impressions on ten cases. Each rater extracted what he considered to be the most relevant statements about precipitating stress from the two sets of narrative impressions. The extent to which the two agreed in what they extracted from the impressions was measured by comparing the events extracted from each narrative or case summary. Here, it was appropriate to consider agreement only on the events listed as relevant to stress by these two raters. The degree of agreement between the events listed in the various capsule statements was 88 per cent.

2. *Assessment of Conflict.* As indicated earlier, the Assessment of Conflict involved sorting 25 conflict areas on a 5-point scale in terms of how characteristic each item was for the individual being rated. The rater was asked to Q sort the items on the basis of current conflicts only. Agreement between R1 and R2 on the ten cases was 74.8 per cent. There was a high degree of commonality in the areas selected by the two raters as most conflictual across the sample. The five areas R1 most often gave a high rating to were Sexuality, Dependency, Hostility, Guilt, and Identification. For R2, the top-ranking five conflict areas were Hostility, Guilt, Superego Values, Dependency, and Identification. Disagreement appeared to be greatest around conflict areas that were used rather sparingly, such as Self-Expression, Interpersonal Distance, Activity, and Mobility. (The exception was Superego Values, which was an important area in the ratings of R2 but less so for R1.) For both raters there may have been a lack of clarity about definition for the in-

frequently used conflict areas, partially explaining both the disagreement and their typical placement at the lower end of the scale.

3. *Behavioral Mode.* In addition to the assessment of the degree of conflict in each of the 25 listed areas, each rater was asked to characterize on a 5-point scale the direction of the behavior relevant to each conflict area. On the ten cases, the agreement between the two raters was 82.5 per cent. Highest agreement occurred in the behavioral modes associated with the conflict areas of Sexuality, Interpersonal Distance, Identification, Dependency, and Dominance. Low agreement on behavioral mode occurred in the areas of Conformity, Awareness, Ambition, Trust, and Affect Sharing. A major source of disagreement had to do with one rater's preferences for mid-point ratings and the other rater's tendency to favor more extreme characterizations. It seemed likely that use of a fixed distribution for behavioral mode similar to the one used for degree of conflict would have avoided this particular difficulty.

4. *Defenses.* Each rater double-checked the four most characteristic current defenses and was permitted to single-check a maximum of four additional items out of the total of 21 listed defenses. In spite of attempts to define the defense mechanisms explicitly by means of the glossary, agreement between raters for the ten cases was 71.9 per cent, a lower percentage than for any of the other rating tasks. Item analysis of high and low agreement items showed that repression, regression, denial, and rationalization were agreed upon frequently, while projection, turning upon the self, and intellectualization were the items of highest disagreement.

5. *Symptoms.* On the checklist of symptoms the raters were similarly asked to indicate the four chief current symptoms and were permitted to include a maximum of four additional ones out of the list of 27. Agreement between the raters on ten cases on the four salient symptoms was 76.7 per cent. The symptoms most frequently agreed upon were: physical symptoms, inhibition of affect, marital difficulties, and other interpersonal difficulties. Disagreements occurred most often around items that might be considered more inferential; depression, demanding dependency, rumination, and irritability. (Disagreement on irritability seemed to be partially due to alternative use of other items, such as poorly controlled hostility and agitation.)

361

B. Interrelationships Between Variables.

Theoretical interest in the interrelationships of variables led to the comparison of some of the measures and rating scales with each other. Of particular interest was the question of whether certain types of stressful events might be associated with some conflicts more often than with others. The various events described by the raters for each patient had been roughly grouped into five categories on the basis of the assumed meaning of these events to the patient (Kalis, *et al.,* 1961). This grouping was done after the data were collected, as a means of ordering some of the information and trying to find commonalities between patients. These categories were: (1) Object Loss (N-8), includes not only actual loss but threat of loss and opportunities to restore a lost object. (2) Bind with previous therapist or source of help (N-10) refers to some difficulty or impasse with a previous therapist or agency leading to the present application. (3) Identification with another (N-7) produces a call for help when the person identified with becomes involved in a situation similar to one in the patient's own past, thereby reactivating an important conflict. (4) Surge of unmanageable impulses (N-9) is a more internally focused category and includes cases for whom the stimuli giving rise to the impulses can be identified and others for whom they cannot. (5) Threat to current adjustment (N-9) occurs when the patient is confronted with a new, attractive, but threatening choice which would involve leaving the present psychic equilibrium for a new commitment.

Comparison of the three most highly rated conflicts for the patients grouped in each category did not suggest any significant patterning. Rather, the most frequently rated conflicts for the sample as a whole (Dependency, Sexuality, Hostility, Identification, and Guilt) tended to be the most frequent within each stress category also. Such a finding is congruent with the theoretical view that certain types or classes of events might be stressful to a number of patients, but that the subjective meaning of these events—the nature of the conflict such events would evoke—would be unique to each patient.

The extent to which frequently rated conflicts might be associated with frequently rated defenses was also investigated. Repression, projection, and acting out were highly characteristic defenses in patients for whom sexuality was one of the three most conflictual

362

areas. Hostility as a conflict and projection as a defense were associated with some frequency; dependency was often associated with acting out and projection. In a matrix of 25 conflicts by 21 defenses, this was a small and insignificant number of pairings. The frequent association of projection with sexuality and hostility, and repression with sexuality, is congruent with psychoanalytic theory; it is possible, however, that rater bias or chance contributed to these pairings. A similar matrix was prepared for symptoms and defenses, but here, too, there were no tendencies for any defenses and symptoms to be associated by the raters.

Discussion

The findings concerning inter-rater agreement on precipitating stress were some of the most interesting in the study. The results indicate that narrative material of an impressionistic nature can be handled in ways that are suitable for answering research questions. First, two judges in this study were quite successful in independently lifting out of a narrative context the same kinds of descriptive statements. When judges understood precisely what they were looking for in a lengthy narrative, they tended with high frequency to choose the same statements. Second, two raters independently assessed ten randomly selected cases out of the total sample of 43, and in these ten cases there were no instances of marked disagreement between the two about stress. Thus, the hypothesis was confirmed that clinicians listening independently to taped psychotherapy interviews could agree in their assessments of precipitating stress. The disagreements that did occur between the two raters involved one rater's assigning importance to more events than did the other; R2 in a formulation about precipitating stress might assign importance to two recent events in a patient's life whereas R1 might mention only one of these.

When the forty cases for whom there were usable narrative impressions by the therapist were compared with R1's ratings, there were only three cases of marked disagreement. In these three there was little commonality between the events chosen by these two raters, and there were similar disagreements in statements about the kinds of conflicts evoked. It appeared that for these few cases disagreement was quite pervasive.

In general, inter-rater agreement appeared to be a function of

363

two factors: (1) the level of abstraction of any particular judgment, and (2) its closeness or relatedness to the specific focus of the study. Agreement on precipitating events and on the mode of conflict expression were quite high, while defenses, conflicts, and symptoms attained more moderate agreement. In listening to the interviews, the raters' focus of attention was on the interplay of forces leading a person to seek psychiatric treatment; as a consequence, and perhaps also as a result of the clarity achieved through continuing staff discussion of theoretical views about precipitating stress, agreement was quite high. Behavioral mode of conflict expression was a relatively non-inferential characterization of behavior patterns, and the inter-rater agreement there, consequently, was also high. Defenses and conflicts were considerably more inferential and probably not so actively attended to by the listeners. Even though a manual was developed in which mechanisms of defense were carefully described and defined, agreement was relatively low.

Agreement about symptoms was the lowest of all areas, although this difference is not a significant one. That it did rank fairly low, however, suggests that there is less professional agreement about these "surface characteristics" than is ordinarily assumed. There may be several reasons for this. In the development of forms and rating scales, symptoms received the least attention, so that the list given the raters may have been inadequate. Second, all the other ratings required a kind of process orientation on the listener's part, rather than the static and more traditional approach that rating symptoms requires. Additionally, it is interesting to speculate that social workers and psychologists as therapists do not elicit symptomatic descriptions from patients to the extent a psychiatrist would, both because of the nature of their training and because of the patient's expectations.

A possible conclusion from these results is that only moderate inter-rater agreement can be attained when the rating task involves many complex judgments. Attention to precipitating stress was a very complicated task in itself; the results suggest that the raters devoted proportionately more time and concentration to this variable than the others and were therefore able to agree at a very high level. It is very likely that, as a result, some other variables received considerably less attention during the actual listening process and that judgments may have been formulated largely at the time of rating. These discrepancies suggest the need for future research into the effects of varying levels of complexity on reliability of judgments and the precise effects of increasing the number of simultaneous judgments.

It is possible that the fairly high degree of over-all inter-rater agreement may have been due to the raters being accurate perceivers of the interviewers' hypotheses about precipitating stress. In that case the raters' task would have been one of simply listening for what the interviewer seemed to consider important and labeling this precipitating stress. The fact that the raters agreed highly in areas other than precipitating stress, such as behavioral mode of conflict expression, and at least moderately in all other judgments mitigates against such a view.

Systematic exploration of the effect of the interviewers' bias on raters' judgments, however, is needed. It would be important in future studies, for instance, to use a number of interviewers; this would permit some assessing of the effects of interviewer techniques on level of agreement between raters and would also make it possible to judge whether the kinds of stresses considered to be precipitants vary with the interviewer.

Finally, it should be noted that the raters and the therapists were all women; although discipline varied (psychologists and social workers), certainly one major basis for disagreement was eliminated. This too would need modification in future, more expanded studies.

During the course of the study there was continuous evolution of ideas about precipitating stress through frequent discussions and presentation of cases. Many theoretical formulations were evolved since hypothesis-finding rather than hypothesis-testing was the approach. Methodology was developed to suit such an investigation; it was intended to be flexible rather than rigorous, to permit answering previous questions and to raise new ones. The approach to the analysis of qualitative data described here was useful for these purposes and stimulated suggestions for many avenues of further research.

Index

A

Accession of new family member, 37–38, 112–113, 300–301, 312–313, 323

Acute situational disorder, 118–119, 339–340, 347–348

Angell, Robert C, 41, 47, 111

Anticipatory guidance, 94–95, 139

Anxiety: castration, 179, 327; death fears in children, 324–338; and prematurity, 123–124; ratings of, 328–334; related to hospitalization, 150–151, 327; response to crisis, 25; types of, 327

B

Baler, Lenin, 4, 300

Bereavement, see Grief

Blos, Peter, 167–168

Boston Lying-in Hospital, 89

Bowlby, John, 27, 74, 220

C

Caplan, Gerald, 4, 23, 27, 76, 220, 288, 303, 339

Castle Square Relocation Program, 248–260

Cavan, Ruth S., 41–42, 47, 111

Chicago Institute for Psychoanalysis, 167

Child placement, 222, 235

City of Hope Medical Center, 326

Clark, E. Gurney, 129, 286

Cognitive mastery, 138

Community Mental Health and Social Psychiatry: A Reference Guide, 3

Community planning, 30, 49–52, 273, 294, 296–297

Coping behavior: 23, 28–29, 79–84, 130, 339–348; in adolescence, 159–161; and prematurity, 124–126; ratings of, 342–347

Crisis: adjustment to, 48–49; definition of, 24, 55–56, 113, 304, 314; dimensions of, 66–67, 111–112; duration of, 26, 113, 242–243; maturational, 73, 76, 158; measurement of, 299–300, 315–318, 355–357; phases of, 26–28, 147; ratings of, 304–311; reactions to, 47–48, 114; signs of, 26–29, 317–318; situational, 74

366

Crisis intervention

Crisis intervention: definition of, 2; policy and practice implications, 29, 51–52, 72, 214, 293; role of social worker, 29–30, 51, 107, 109–110, 132, 277–280; techniques of, 291–294

D

Defenses: avoidance, 122–123; denial, 108, 120, 126, 127–128, 152–153

Depletion: in aging, 181–182

Depression, 16–17, 25, 126

Diagnostic assessment, 191, 266

E

Ego reactions: in aging, 176–177

Environment: modification of, 94; problems of, 238–239; supports in, 132; resources, 297

Equilibrium, 24, 56, 71, 76, 320

Erikson, Erik, 22, 73, 74, 157–158

F

Family: communication network, 65–66; diagnosis, 340–341; life-style, 57–58; psychopathology, 206–207; as a small group, 33–34, 59, 115–116; as a transactional system, 77, 111–112, 204–205, 230; treatment of, 204–219, 228–229, 282, 285

Family Service Association of America, 193

Freud, Sigmund, 20, 73, 202

G

Galveston Youth Development Project, 227

Golde, Peggy, 4, 300

Grief: 7–21; anticipatory grief, 19–20, 126

Group: activity programs, 150–151; discussion, 148; treatment, 141–143, 268–269

H

Harvard School of Public Health: 6; Community Mental Health Program, 76; Family Guidance Center, 27, 54, 119, 129, 285; Family Health Clinic, 89